Praise for the First Edition

The definitive how-to manual for unit testing Java EE components. Pick up one of the other books if you're looking for something more motivational, but when you're ready to sit down and bang out some code, you'll want this book at your side.

—JavaRanch.com

I would definitely recommend JUnit in Action *for anyone interested in testing their code.... It is a book that flows nicely, and offers a great mix of technology theory and how to put it all into practice.*

—TheServerSide.com

An essential guide for intermediate level Java programmers who want to learn how to build Java EE applications properly...clear, simple and fun...the best I have seen thus far.... The book actually goes into detail about using mock objects and stubs, further expanding your understanding of basic software design.... I highly recommend it.

—Killersites.com

Not a JUnit tutorial, it covers JUnit in depth. It also explains the importance of JUnit in the context of software development process. This well-edited book is highly recommended both for the beginner and advanced users of JUnit.

—Denver JUG

With a number of Manning books I can see myself start to think differently about problems and so I end up being a better developer; JUnit in Action *was like that for me. At first it bothered me that I was changing my code in order to test it, but then I started seeing that the changes made the code better overall. Now my code is littered with factory methods and similar patterns. You guys are doing good stuff.*

—Joshua Smith, a reader

The examples are clear and real-world. The authors address the complex issues of unit testing EJBs and web apps head-on. They don't shy away from the real issues that come with testing these kinds of applications.

—Wade Matveyenko, a reader

JUnit in Action

Second Edition

PETAR TAHCHIEV
FELIPE LEME
VINCENT MASSOL
GARY GREGORY

MANNING
Greenwich
(74° w. long.)

Manning Publications Co.
180 Broad St.
Suite 1323
Stamford, CT 06901

Development Editor: Sebastian Stirling
Copyeditor: Linda Recktenwald
Proofreader: Katie Tennant
Typesetters: Dennis Dalinnik
Cover designer: Marija Tudor

ISBN 9781935182023
Printed in the United States of America
1 2 3 4 5 6 7 8 9 10 – MAL – 16 15 14 13 12 11 10

brief contents

contents

preface

As an award-winning mathematician, I don't tolerate mediocrity. That's what mathematics taught me—never stop until you get it done, and not just in a good way but in the best way.

When I started writing software, I found that the same principles apply. I knew some colleagues who were neglectful of their work, and I saw how their results suffered from that. They were impatient to finish their tasks, not worrying about the quality of the software they produced, let alone searching for the best possible solution. For those guys, reusing the same code meant simply copying and pasting it everywhere they needed it. I saw how being impatient to finish the task as quickly as possible led to that same task being reopened again and again, because of bugs and problems with the code as written.

Thankfully, those colleagues have been few and far between. Most of my friends were people that I could learn from. I had the opportunity to work for Hewlett Packard, not only with the technical team, but also with the project managers on every level, and from them I learned the secret of delivering a quality software product. Later, I became involved with the Apache Software Foundation (ASF), where I had the chance to work with some of the best software developers on the planet. I studied their best practices and habits of writing code, writing test cases and sharing information among ourselves, and I was able to apply the things I learned to projects for some of the biggest clients of HP.

Gradually I got interested in the question of ensuring the sustainable quality of a software product. Then I met Vincent Massol and Felipe Leme in the spring of 2008. I had worked with both of them on the Cactus framework at the ASF. Vince proposed that I write an up-to-date revision of the bestselling book he authored five years ago. The plan was clear, but I needed some soul mates to help me achieve it. That's when I contacted Felipe Leme and Gary Gregory. They both agreed to help with some of the chapters.

Things moved faster after that, and we spent a year and a half writing with the primary goal of revising Vince's work. If someone had told me in the beginning how hard it would be, I wouldn't have believed him. And that is why I feel that I need I to express my sincere gratitude to the Manning team—they made the whole journey a lot easier.

Now that the book is finished and you hold it in your hands, I hope you enjoy it. It has been a rough journey to get it done, but here it is. I know you'll learn a lot of new things from our book, the way I'm sure you'll improve the quality of your software—you've already taken the first step.

PETAR TAHCHIEV

preface to the first edition

To date tests are still the best solution mankind has found to deliver working software. This book is the sum of four years of research and practice in the testing field. The practice comes from my IT consulting background, first at Octo Technology and then at Pivolis; the research comes from my involvement with open source development at night and on weekends.

Since my early programming days in 1982, I've been interested in writing tools to help developers write better code and develop more quickly. This interest has led me into domains such as software mentoring and quality improvement. These days, I'm setting up continuous-build platforms and working on development best practices, both of which require strong suites of tests. The closer these tests are to the coding activity, the faster you get feedback on your code—hence my interest in unit testing, which is so close to coding that it's now as much a part of development as the code that's being written.

This background led to my involvement in open source projects related to software quality:

- Cactus for unit-testing J2EE components (http://jakarta.apache.org/cactus/)
- Mock objects for unit-testing any code (http://www.mockobjects.com/)
- Gump for continuous builds (http://jakarta.apache.org/gump/)
- Maven for builds and continuous builds (http://maven.apache.org/)
- The Pattern Testing proof of concept for using Aspect-Oriented Programming (AOP) to check architecture and design rules (http://patterntesting.sf.net/)

JUnit in Action is the logical conclusion to this involvement.

Nobody wants to write sloppy code. We all want to write code that works—code that we can be proud of. But we're often distracted from our good intentions. How often have you heard this: "We wanted to write tests, but we were under pressure and didn't have enough time to do it"; or, "We started writing unit tests, but after two weeks our momentum dropped, and over time we stopped writing them."

This book will give you the tools and techniques you need to write quality code. It demonstrates hands-on how to use the tools in an effective way, avoiding common pitfalls. It will empower you to write code that works. It will help you introduce unit testing in your day-to-day development activity and develop a rhythm for writing robust code.

Most of all, this book will show you how to control the entropy of your software instead of being controlled by it. I'm reminded of some verses from the Latin writer Lucretius, who, in 94 –55 BC wrote in his *On the Nature of Things* (I'll spare you the original Latin text):

> *It is lovely to gaze out at the churning sea from the safety of the shore when someone else is out there fighting the waves, not because you're enjoying their troubles, but because you yourself are being spared.*

This is exactly the feeling you'll experience when you know you're armed with a good suite of tests. You'll see others struggling, and you'll be thankful that you have tests to prevent anyone (including yourself) from wreaking havoc in your application.

VINCENT MASSOL

acknowledgments

We'd like to acknowledge all of the people who played important roles in the creation of this book. First of all, the project wouldn't have started if not for Michael Stephens and Marjan Bace of Manning. After that, any coherence the book exhibits is largely due to our developmental editor, Sebastian Stirling. We'd also like to thank Megan Yockey, Steven Hong, Mary Piergies, Karen Tegtmeyer, Katie Tennant, Linda Recktenwald, and any other folks at Manning whose efforts we're less aware of than we should be. Special thanks to Ivan Ivanov who did the final technical proofread of the book shortly before it went to press.

We'd also like to thank all the developers who spent time reading this manuscript during its development and pointing out the problems. The following reviewers proved invaluable in the evolution of this book from a manuscript to a book that's worth a reader's investment of time and money: Robert Wenner, Paul Holser, Andy Dingley, Lasse Koskela, Greg Bridges, Pratic Patel, Martijn Dashorst, Leonardo Galvao, Amos Bannister, Jason Kolter, Steffen Müller, Marion Sturtevant, Deepak Vohra, Eric Raymond, Andrew Rhine, Robert Hanson, Tyson S. Maxwell, Doug Warren, David Strong, John Griffin, and Clint Howarth.

Finally, we'd like to extend a sincere thank-you to the people who participated in the Manning Early Access Program; those who left feedback in the Author Online forum had a strong impact on the quality of the final printed product.

Thanks to all!

Petar Tahchiev

I'd like to begin by thanking my family—a big thank-you for always believing in me. A special thank-you goes to my sister, who showed me the real meaning of the word *courage*. Another big thank-you goes to my cousin Ivan Ivanov, who made me start this crazy computer journey in my life. I'm also grateful for all of the English teachers I've had in my life—thank you. This book wouldn't be here if it weren't for the hard work of Vincent Massol—thank you for making this possible. Finally, I'd like to thank both Felipe Leme and Gary Gregory for being such great coworkers. I hope to meet you in person one day.

Felipe Leme

First of all, I'd like to thank those who directly contributed to my career development and hence made my participation in this book possible: my parents, who always understood the importance of education; my middle school teachers (particularly Mr. Ivo), who taught me the fundamentals of good writing and sparked my interest in science; and Leonardo Galvão, whose tough reviews of my *Java Magazine* articles made me a better author. Then special thanks go to Petar, not only for inviting me to be a coauthor but also for his vision and effort that made this project a reality. Finally, I'd like to thank my wife and children for their support and inspiration.

Vincent Massol

Back in 2003, *JUnit in Action* was the first book I ever wrote. I had no idea how long the writing process would take. It took me 18 months to give birth to it (twice as long as for a natural baby!). The great thing about long-running tasks is that when they're done you reap the benefits for a long time, enjoying it even more. It's always with the same initial trepidation that I follow *JUnit in Action* sales and I'm delighted that seven years later the first edition is still selling. However, it was time for an update. Although a good portion of the book is still valid, most of the examples and frameworks have evolved and new ones have surfaced. It was a real pleasure for me that Petar agreed to write this second edition, giving the book a second life. You'll see that Petar, Felipe, and Gary have done a wonderful job of updating the book with a lot of exciting new topics. Well done, guys!

Gary Gregory

I'd like to thank my parents for getting me started on my journey, providing me the opportunity for a great education, and giving me the freedom to choose my path. I'm eternally grateful to my wife, Lori, and my son, Alexander, for giving me the time to pursue a project like this one. Along the way, I've studied and worked with truly exceptional individuals too numerous to name. Finally, I thank my coauthors and all of the people at Manning for their support, professionalism, and great feedback.

about this book

Welcome to the second edition of *JUnit in Action*! If you've picked up this book, we suspect you're a Java developer who cares about the quality of software you produce. Perhaps you've worked with the previous versions of the JUnit framework in the past, perhaps you've worked with other testing frameworks, or perhaps this is your first step into the testing world. Whichever path has led you here, you're probably interested in improving your software process and the quality of the software you write. The goal of this book is to give the basic foundation you need—and much more. The world of software testing consists of many projects that solve specific tasks, of testing different components and layers of your application. The central player in this world is the JUnit framework. Written by Erich Gamma and Kent Beck about a decade ago, this framework has become the de facto standard in Java testing. The latest 4.x versions of the JUnit framework are much more than a revision of the old 3.x JUnit framework. If you haven't heard anything about the JUnit framework yet, you might expect, based on the name, to find a new release of that old proven framework. But this is not the case. Unlike the old version of JUnit, the 4.x versions introduce a new approach and rewrite of the whole framework. Hence the need for an up-to-date copy of the first edition.

In this second edition of the book, we introduce the core concepts you need to know in order to start testing your projects with the JUnit framework. But that's not the whole picture! This book will not only teach you how to write your test cases with the JUnit framework; it will also guide you through the process of writing your code, giving you suggestions of how to make it more testable. This book will also teach you about fundamental software development principles like test-driven development

(TDD). It will also guide you step by step through the process of testing each and every layer of a typical Java EE application: the front layer, with external tools like Selenium and JSFUnit; the business layer, with tools like Cactus, mock objects, and stubs; and finally the database and JPA layer, with tools like DBUnit.

The book is organized into several parts, the goal being to walk you through JUnit in a sequence of increasing complexity. The first part contains the preliminary chapters that introduce the technological context of the framework, give a high-level overview of the architecture, and present a bare-bones HelloWorld sample application to get your environment up and running. After this brief introduction, we set off into a series of chapters that cover the core concepts and components of the framework one by one. We take time to explain the functionality of each component in depth.

The second part of the book deals with the different techniques of testing: the mock approach and the in-container approach. It introduces some new tools to create the fake objects we need. The third and fourth parts of the book look into detailed explanations of third-party tools/JUnit extensions that we use to test the different layers of our applications. In addition, the book has several appendixes that will help you to switch easily to the latest version of JUnit and integrate easily with your favorite IDE.

Roadmap

Chapter 1 gets you started right away. The gentle introduction defines what testing is, how to perform it efficiently, and how to write your first test cases. This chapter is a must to give you the confidence to realize that testing is something natural that should always happen during development.

Chapter 2 dives into the architecture of JUnit and shows how it's organized. We introduce most of the common features of JUnit in this chapter.

In chapter 3 we start to build a sample real-life application. You get to know several design patterns and use them to build our application. Later in the chapter, we demonstrate how to test the application efficiently using the JUnit features introduced in chapter 2.

Chapter 4 looks at several important aspects: the need for unit testing, the various flavors of software tests that exist, and the difference between those kinds of tests. We also give handy advice on how to set up different development and testing environments.

In chapter 5 we discuss the quality of tests. We go on to answer several key questions, such as how to improve your tests, how to improve your test coverage, and how to design your application architecture in such a way that your application will be easily testable. The last point is a brief introduction to the test-driven development (TDD) approach.

Chapter 6 takes a closer look at stubbing as a technique for faking system resources that normally aren't available. We use an example of stubbing a servlet container by using the Jetty embedded servlet container.

Chapter 7 demonstrates another technique for incorporating fake objects in your tests: mock objects. This technique is useful when you program against a closed API and you can't modify or instantiate the available resources. In this chapter, we give an example of mocking a servlet and testing it by using two of the most popular frameworks, EasyMock and JMock.

Chapter 8 briefly introduces the final technique that we can use when we're missing important system objects: in-container testing. We provide this introduction so that in chapters 14, 15, and 16 we can expand on it and discuss real-world examples of in-container testing. Chapter 8 also serves as a summary chapter for this part of the book, so it compares the previously discussed approaches: stubs, mocks, and in-container testing.

Chapter 9 is the opening chapter for the third part of the book. In this part, we focus on the integration of JUnit with various build frameworks; specifically in this chapter, we introduce the Ant build framework. We show you how to execute your tests automatically and how to produce efficient, great-looking reports with the results of the execution. We run some of the examples from the previous chapter using the Ant framework.

Chapter 10 continues the approach of introducing build frameworks and integrating JUnit with them. This time we take a closer look at Maven.

Chapter 11 is dedicated to the theory of continuous integration (CI)—building our project and executing our tests in a continuous manner in order to make sure none of our changes break the project. We take a closer look at two of the most popular software projects for practicing continuous integration: CruiseControl and Hudson. We also take the opportunity to import some of our previous examples into both of the tools, set them up, and execute them.

Chapter 12 opens the last part of the book. This part deals with various JUnit extensions, which enhance the testing framework to do specific tasks that normally aren't possible. Also in this last part of the book, we walk through all the layers of a typical application and explain how to test those layers. Chapter 12 deals with the presentation layer of a web application. We introduce the HtmlUnit and Selenium tools and show exactly how to use them.

Chapter 13 continues with the presentation layer of a web application, but this time we focus on one of the hardest parts: Ajax. We detail what Ajax is and why it's difficult to test, and we also describe various testing scenarios. Finally, we introduce the JsUnit project and give some special hints on testing a Google Web Toolkit (GWT) application.

Chapter 14 explores testing your presentation layer with a different approach: the in-container testing we introduced in chapter 8. For this purpose, we introduce the first in-container testing framework ever made: the Apache Cactus project.

Chapter 15 reveals techniques that are specifically applicable for testing JSF applications. This chapter explains how to use another recent tool called JSFUnit—a new, in-container testing framework that builds on Apache Cactus and is specifically designed to test JSF applications.

Chapter 16 is for those of you who are interested in OSGi applications. It starts with a brief introduction of what OSGi means. Then we introduce the JUnit4OSGi extension of JUnit and show several techniques for testing OSGi applications, using both mocking and in-container testing.

Chapter 17 is the first of the last three chapters, which deal with database testing. Here we tell you everything you need to know about a project called DBUnit. We demonstrate several techniques for testing your database, regardless of the persistence technology that you use.

Chapter 18 reveals all the secrets of JPA testing: testing multilayered applications and JPA persistence-layer applications.

Chapter 19 is the final chapter. Here we demonstrate techniques for making your tests more efficient. We introduce a new project that will help you to test your Spring applications: Unitils.

Code conventions

The following typographical conventions are used throughout the book:

- Courier typeface is used in all code listings.
- Courier typeface is used within text for certain code words.
- *Italics* are used for emphasis and to introduce new terms.
- Annotations are used in place of inline comments in the code. These highlight important concepts or areas of the code. Annotations appear with numbered bullets like this ❶ that are referenced later in the text.

In addition, in the code listings you might occasionally find

- **bold** code—We use this for two purposes: to highlight some of the Java keywords (for your convenience) or to highlight the differences between two or more code listings.

Code downloads

You can download the sample code for this book via a link found on the book's home page on the Manning website, www.manning.com/JUnitinActionSecondEdition, or www.manning.com/tahchiev. This page contains a folder structure of all the submodules for the different chapters. Each of the subfolders contains a build script to compile and package, and you can execute the tests associated with it. Instructions on how to install the application are contained in a README file in that download.

We should make a couple of points about the source code. Initially we wanted to have a large-scale application demonstrating the various testing approaches in the application layers. Later, we realized the difficulties of having such a large-scale application, and instead we followed the folder-structure notation; each chapter has a source code example associated with it. Those are split into subfolders, clearly labeled with the name of the chapter. All of them contain a Maven build script, and some of them contain an Ant build script as well. In order to run the examples in the book, you will need to have Maven2 installed on your computer.

Author Online

The purchase of *JUnit in Action, Second Edition*, includes free access to a private forum run by Manning Publications where you can make comments about the book, ask technical questions, and receive help from the authors and other users. You can access and subscribe to the forum at www.manning.com/JUnitinActionSecondEdition. This page provides information on getting on the forum once you're registered, what kind of help is available, and the rules of conduct in the forum.

Manning's commitment to our readers is to provide a venue where a meaningful dialogue among individual readers and between readers and authors can take place. It's not a commitment to any specific amount of participation on the part of the authors, whose contribution to the book's forum remains voluntary (and unpaid). We suggest you try asking the authors some challenging questions, lest their interest stray!

The Author Online forum and the archives of previous discussions will be accessible from the publisher's website as long as the book is in print.

About the title

By combining introductions, overviews, and how-to examples, the *In Action* books are designed to help with learning and remembering. According to research in cognitive science, the things people remember are things they discover during self-motivated exploration.

Although no one at Manning is a cognitive scientist, we're convinced that for learning to become permanent, it must pass through stages of exploration, play, and, interestingly, retelling of what is being learned. People understand and remember new things, which is to say they master them, only after actively exploring them. Humans learn *in action*. An essential part of an *In Action* book is that it is example driven. It encourages the reader to try things out, to play with new code, and to explore new ideas.

There is another, more mundane reason for the title of this book: our readers are busy. They use books to do a job or solve a problem. They need books that allow them to jump in and jump out easily and learn just what they want just when they want it.

They need books that aid them *in action*. The books in this series are designed for such readers.

about the authors

PETAR TAHCHIEV is a software engineer who serves as a Jakarta PMC member with the Apache Software Foundation. For many years he has been the Jakarta Cactus lead developer and part of the Apache Maven development team. In addition, he is also a member of the JCP, leader of the Bulgarian Java User Group (BGJUG), and a frequent speaker at OpenFest, ApacheCON, CommunityONE, and many other conferences. Born and raised in Bulgaria, Petar graduated with honors in mathematics from Sofia University. He spent many years working in Germany and the Netherlands for companies like Unic and Hewlett Packard. Now he is back in lovely Sofia, working predominantly with Phamola, his own company, which assists and advises clients on how to excel through technology. Petar authored chapters 1–11 and 14–16, and appendixes A–D.

FELIPE LEME is a software engineer who is very passionate about TDD (test-driven development), Java, and computers in general. He got his first computer at age 11, learned Java in 1996, and wrote his first JUnit test case in 2000. Since he earned a Bachelor degree in Computer Engineering at the State University of Campinas (Unicamp) in 1997, he has worked almost exclusively with Java, and has contributed back to the community in many ways: as a committer for open source projects such as DbUnit, as a speaker in conferences such as JavaOne, as an individual member of the JCP, and as a blogger and writer at java.net. Felipe authored chapters 17–19. After living alternately in São Paulo, Brazil, and California, U.S., he finally settled down in the San Francisco Bay Area, where he lives with his wife, kids, and hermit crabs.

VINCENT MASSOL, after spending several night-years creating Jakarta Cactus and Codehaus Cargo and participating to the Apache Maven open source projects, is now enjoying full-time development of XWiki, an open source project offering a state-of-the-art enterprise wiki. Vincent is also the CTO of XWiki SAS, a company offering services around the XWiki open source project. He was the lead author of the first edition. Vincent lives in Paris, France, and can be found online at www.massol.net.

GARY GREGORY has more than 20 years of experience in object-oriented languages including Smalltalk, Java, and the whole soup of XML and database technologies. Gary has held positions at Ashton-Tate, ParcPlace-Digitalk, and several other software companies, including Seagull Software, where he currently develops application servers for legacy integration. He is an active member of the Apache Software Foundation and the Apache Jakarta Project Management Committee, and contributes regularly to various Apache Commons projects. Born and raised in Paris, France, Gary received a B.A. in linguistics and computer science from the University of California at Los Angeles. Gary authored chapters 12–13 and appendix E. He lives in Los Angeles with his wife, their son, golf clubs, and assorted surfboards. He can be reached at http://www.garygregory.com.

about the cover illustration

The figure on the cover of *JUnit in Action, Second Edition* is captioned "Burco de Alpeo," taken from a Spanish compendium of regional dress customs first published in Madrid in 1799. The same figure appeared on the cover of the first edition of the book, and we have not been successful in the intervening years in finding an accurate translation of the figure caption, in spite of having asked our first edition readers to help out. Please post any new suggestions in the Author Online forum for the second edition.

The title page of the compendium states thus:

> *Coleccion general de los Trages que usan actualmente todas las Nacionas del Mundo desubierto, dibujados y grabados con la mayor exactitud por R.M.V.A.R. Obra muy util y en special para los que tienen la del viajero universal*

which we translate, as literally as possible, thus:

> *General collection of costumes currently used in the nations of the known world, designed and printed with great exactitude by R.M.V.A.R. This work is very useful especially for those who hold themselves to be universal travelers*

Although nothing is known of the designers, engravers, and workers who colored this illustration by hand, the "exactitude" of their execution is evident in this drawing, which is just one of many in this colorful collection. Their diversity speaks vividly of the uniqueness and individuality of the world's towns and regions just 200 years ago.

This was a time when the dress codes of two regions separated by a few dozen miles identified people uniquely as belonging to one or the other.

The collection brings to life a sense of isolation and distance of that period—and of every other historical period except our own hyperkinetic present. Dress codes have changed since then and the diversity by region, so rich at the time, has faded away. It is now often hard to tell the inhabitant of one continent from another. Perhaps, trying to view it optimistically, we have traded a cultural and visual diversity for a more varied personal life. Or a more varied and interesting intellectual and technical life.

We at Manning celebrate the inventiveness, the initiative, and, yes, the fun of the computer business with book covers based on the rich diversity of regional life of two centuries ago, brought back to life by the pictures from this collection.

Part 1

JUnit essentials

Welcome to *JUnit in Action, Second Edition.* JUnit is a framework that was started by Kent Beck and Erich Gamma in late 1995. Ever since then, the popularity of the framework has been growing, and it's now the de facto standard for unit testing Java applications.

This book is a second edition. The first edition was a best seller, written by Vincent Massol and Ted Husted in 2003, and was dedicated to version 3.x of JUnit.

We cover the newest version of JUnit, 4.6, and we talk about many features that were included after the first edition of the book. At the same time, we focus on some other interesting techniques in testing your code: mock objects, JUnit extensions, testing different layers of your application, and many more.

This part starts by exploring JUnit itself. We focus on the other tools and techniques later in the book.

The first chapter gives you a quick introduction to the concepts of testing. You need this information to get started. You'll jump straight to the code and see how to write a simple test, execute it, and see the results.

The second chapter introduces JUnit at its best. We build a bigger project and walk through the code. We not only explain the JUnit concepts, widgets, and guts, but we also show you the best practices in writing a test case and demonstrate them with the project we build.

The third chapter is dedicated to tests as a whole. We describe different kinds of tests and the scenarios to which they apply. We also explore the various platforms (development, production, and so on) and show you which tests and which scenarios are best to execute there.

The last chapter in this part of the book is dedicated to improving your testing skills. We show you how to measure your test coverage and how to improve it. We also explain how to produce testable code before you write your tests as well as how to write the tests before you write a single line of code.

JUnit jump-start

Never in the field of software development was so much owed by so many to so few lines of code.

—Martin Fowler

This chapter covers

- Exploring JUnit
- Installing JUnit
- Writing our first test
- Running tests

All code is tested.

During development, the first thing we do is run our own programmer's "acceptance test." We code, compile, and run. When we run, we test. The *test* may just be clicking a button to see if it brings up the expected menu. Nevertheless, every day, we code, we compile, we run, and *we test*.

When we test, we often find issues—especially on the first run. Therefore, we code, compile, run, and test again.

Most of us quickly develop a pattern for our informal tests: we add a record, view a record, edit a record, and delete a record. Running a little test suite like this by hand is easy enough to do, so we do it—*over and over again.*

Some programmers like this type of repetitive testing. It can be a pleasant break from deep thought and hardcoding. When our little click-through tests finally succeed, there's a feeling of accomplishment: *Eureka! I found it!*

Other programmers dislike this type of repetitive work. Rather than run the test by hand, they prefer to create a small program that runs the test automatically. Play-testing code is one thing; running automated tests is another.

If you're a play-test developer, this book is for you. We'll show you how creating automated tests can be easy, effective, and even fun.

If you're already "test-infected,"[1] this book is also for you. We cover the basics in part 1 and then move on to the tough, real-life problems in parts 2, 3, and 4.

1.1   Proving it works

Some developers feel that automated tests are an essential part of the development process: you can't *prove* a component works until it passes a comprehensive series of tests. Two developers felt that this type of unit testing was so important that it deserved its own framework. In 1997, Erich Gamma and Kent Beck created a simple but effective unit testing *framework* for Java, called JUnit. Their work followed the design of an earlier framework Kent Beck had created for Smalltalk, called SUnit.

> **DEFINITION**   A *framework* is a semi-complete application.[2] A framework provides a reusable, common structure to share among applications. Developers incorporate the framework into their own application and extend it to meet their specific needs. Frameworks differ from toolkits by providing a coherent structure, rather than a simple set of utility classes.

If you recognize those names, it's for good reason. Erich Gamma is one of the Gang of Four who gave us the now-classic *Design Patterns* book.[3] We know Kent Beck equally well for his groundbreaking work in the software discipline known as Extreme Programming (http://www.extremeprogramming.org).

JUnit (http://www.junit.org) is open source software, released under IBM's Common Public License Version 1.0 and hosted on SourceForge. The Common Public License is business friendly: people can distribute JUnit with commercial products without a lot of red tape or restrictions.

JUnit quickly became the de facto standard framework for developing unit tests in Java. The underlying testing model, known as xUnit, is on its way to becoming the standard framework for any language. There are xUnit frameworks available for ASP, C++, C#, Eiffel, Delphi, Perl, PHP, Python, REBOL, Smalltalk, and Visual Basic—to name a few!

---

[1] *Test-infected* is a term coined by Gamma/Beck, "Test-Infected: Programmers Love Writing Tests," *Java Report*, 3, 7, 37–50: 1998.

[2] Ralph E. Johnson and Brian Foote, "Designing Reusable Classes," *Journal of Object-Oriented Programming 1.5* (June/July 1988): 22–35; http://www.laputan.org/drc/drc.html.

[3] Erich Gamma et al., *Design Patterns* (Reading, MA: Addison-Wesley, 1995).

The JUnit team did not invent software testing or even the unit test. Originally, the term *unit test* described a test that examined the behavior of a single *unit of work*.

Over time, usage of the term *unit test* broadened. For example, IEEE has defined unit testing as "Testing of individual hardware or software units *or groups of related units*" (emphasis added).[4]

In this book, we use the term *unit test* in the narrower sense of a test that examines a single unit in isolation from other units. We focus on the type of small, incremental tests that programmers apply to their own code. Sometimes we call these *programmer tests* to differentiate them from quality assurance tests or customer tests (http://c2.com/cgi/wiki?ProgrammerTest).

Here's a generic description of a typical unit test from our perspective: "Confirm that the method accepts the expected range of input and that the method returns the expected value for each input."

This description asks us to test the behavior of a method through its interface. If we give it value *x*, will it return value *y*? If we give it value *z* instead, will it throw the proper exception?

> **DEFINITION**   A *unit test* examines the behavior of a distinct *unit of work*. Within a Java application, the "distinct unit of work" is often (but not always) a single method. By contrast, *integration tests* and *acceptance tests* examine how various components interact. A *unit of work* is a task that isn't directly dependent on the completion of any other task.

Unit tests often focus on testing whether a method follows the terms of its *API contract*. Like a written contract by people who agree to exchange certain goods or services under specific conditions, an API contract is a formal agreement made by the signature of a method. A method requires its callers to provide specific object references or primitive values and returns an object reference or primitive value. If the method can't fulfill the contract, the test should throw an exception, and we say that the method has broken its contract.

In this chapter, we walk through creating a unit test for a simple class from scratch. We start by writing a test and its minimal runtime framework, so you can see how we used to do things. Then we roll out JUnit to show you how the right tools can make life much simpler.

> **DEFINITION**   An *API contract* is a view of an application programming interface (API) as a formal agreement between the caller and the callee. Often the unit tests help define the API contract by demonstrating the expected behavior. The notion of an API contract stems from the practice of, popularized by the Eiffel programming language (http://archive.eiffel.com/doc/manuals/technology/contract).

---

[4]   *EEE Standard Computer Dictionary: A Compilation of IEEE Standard Computer Glossaries* (New York, IEEE, 1990).

1.2   *Starting from scratch*

For our first example, we create a simple calculator class that adds two numbers. Our calculator provides an API to clients and doesn't contain a user interface; it's shown in listing 1.1.

> **Listing 1.1   The test calculator class**

```
public class Calculator {
    public double add(double number1, double number2) {
        return number1 + number2;
    }
}
```

Although the documentation isn't shown, the intended purpose of the `Calculator`'s `add(double, double)` method is to take two doubles and return the sum as a double. The compiler can tell us that it compiles, but we should also make sure it works at runtime. A core tenet of unit testing is, "Any program feature without an automated test doesn't exist."[5] The `add` method represents a core feature of the calculator. We have some code that allegedly implements the feature. What's missing is an automated test that proves our implementation works.

> **Isn't the `add` method too simple to break?**
>
> The current implementation of the `add` method is too simple to break. If `add` were a minor utility method, then we might not test it directly. In that case, if `add` did fail, then tests of the methods that used `add` would fail. The `add` method would be tested indirectly, but tested nonetheless. In the context of the calculator program, `add` isn't just a method; it's a *program feature*. In order to have confidence in the program, most developers would expect there to be an automated test for the add feature, no matter how simple the implementation appears. In some cases, we can prove program features through automatic functional tests or automatic acceptance tests. For more about software tests in general, see chapter 3.

Testing anything at this point seems problematic. We don't even have a user interface with which to enter a pair of `doubles`. We could write a small command-line program that waited for us to type in two `double` values and then displayed the result. Then we'd also be testing our own ability to type numbers and add the result ourselves. This is much more than what we want to do. We want to know if this unit of work will add two `doubles` and return the correct sum. We don't want to test whether programmers can type numbers!

Meanwhile, if we're going to go to the effort of testing our work, we should also try to preserve that effort. It's good to know that the `add(double,double)` method worked when we wrote it. But what we really want to know is whether the method will

---

[5] Kent Beck, *Extreme Programming Explained: Embrace Change* (Reading, MA: Addison-Wesley, 1999).

work when we ship the rest of the application or whenever we make a subsequent modification. If we put these requirements together, we come up with the idea of writing a simple test program for the add method.

The test program could pass known values to the method and see if the result matches our expectations. We could also run the program again later to be sure the method continues to work as the application grows. What's the simplest possible test program we could write? What about the CalculatorTest program shown in listing 1.2?

Listing 1.2 A simple test calculator program

```java
public class CalculatorTest {
    public static void main(String[] args) {
        Calculator calculator = new Calculator();
        double result = calculator.add(10,50);
        if (result != 60) {
            System.out.println("Bad result: " + result);
        }
    }
}
```

The first CalculatorTest is simple indeed. It creates an instance of Calculator, passes it two numbers, and checks the result. If the result doesn't meet our expectations, we print a message on standard output.

If we compile and run this program now, the test will quietly pass, and all will seem well. But what happens if we change the code so that it fails? We'll have to watch the screen carefully for the error message. We may not have to supply the input, but we're still testing our own ability to monitor the program's output. We want to test the code, not ourselves!

The conventional way to signal error conditions in Java is to throw an exception. Let's throw an exception instead to indicate a test failure.

Meanwhile, we may also want to run tests for other Calculator methods that we haven't written yet, like subtract or multiply. Moving to a modular design would make it easier to catch and handle exceptions as well as extend the test program later. Listing 1.3 shows a slightly better CalculatorTest program.

Listing 1.3 A (slightly) better test calculator program

```java
public class CalculatorTest {

    private int nbErrors = 0;

    public void testAdd() {
        Calculator calculator = new Calculator();
        double result = calculator.add(10, 50);
        if (result != 60) {                                              ❶
            throw new IllegalStateException("Bad result: " + result);
        }
    }
```

```
public static void main(String[] args) {
    CalculatorTest test = new CalculatorTest();
    try {
        test.testAdd();
    }
    catch (Throwable e) {
        test.nbErrors++;
        e.printStackTrace();
    }
    if (test.nbErrors > 0) {
        throw new IllegalStateException("There were " + test.nbErrors
            + " error(s)");
    }
}
}
```

Working from listing 1.3, at ❶ we move the test into its own testAdd method. It's now easier to focus on what the test does. We can also add more methods with more unit tests later, without making the main method harder to maintain. At ❷, we change the main method to print a stack trace when an error occurs and then, if there are any errors, end by throwing a summary exception.

Now that you've seen a simple application and its tests, you can see that even this small class and its tests can benefit from the bit of scaffolding code we've created to run and manage test results. As an application gets more complicated and tests more involved, continuing to build and maintain our own custom testing framework becomes a burden.

Next, we take a step back and look at the general case for a unit testing framework.

1.3   *Understanding unit testing frameworks*

Unit testing frameworks should follow several best practices. These seemingly minor improvements in the CalculatorTest program highlight three rules that (in our experience) all unit testing frameworks should follow:

- Each unit test should run independently of all other unit tests.
- The framework should detect and report errors test by test.
- It should be easy to define which unit tests will run.

The "slightly better" test program comes close to following these rules but still falls short. For example, in order for each unit test to be truly independent, each should run in a different class instance and ideally in a different class loader instance.

We can now add new unit tests by adding a new method and then adding a corresponding try/catch block to main. This is a step up, but it's still short of what we'd want in a real unit test suite. Our experience tells us that large try/catch blocks cause maintenance problems. We could easily leave out a unit test and never know it!

It would be nice if we could add new test methods and continue working. But how would the program know which methods to run? Well, we could have a simple registration procedure. A registration method would at least inventory which tests are running.

Another approach would be to use Java's reflection and introspection capabilities. A program could look at itself and decide to run whatever methods follow a certain naming convention—like those that begin with `test`, for example.

Making it easy to add tests (the third rule in our earlier list) sounds like another good rule for a unit testing framework. The support code to realize this rule (via registration or introspection) wouldn't be trivial, but it would be worthwhile. There'd be a lot of work up front, but that effort would pay off each time we added a new test.

Happily, the JUnit team has saved us the trouble. The JUnit framework already supports introspecting methods. It also supports using a different class instance and class loader instance for each test and reports all errors on a test-by-test basis.

Now that you have a better idea of why you need a unit testing framework, let's look specifically at JUnit.

1.4   JUnit design goals

The JUnit team has defined three discrete goals for the framework:

- The framework must help us write useful tests.
- The framework must help us create tests that retain their value over time.
- The framework must help us lower the cost of writing tests by reusing code.

We return to these goals in chapter 2.

Next, before we get into the action, we'll show you how to set up JUnit.

1.5   Setting up JUnit

In order to use JUnit to write your application tests, you need to add the JUnit JAR file to your project's compilation classpath and to your execution classpath. Follow these steps:

Download the JUnit distribution (junit-4.6 or newer) from http://www.junit.org. JUnit contains several test samples that you'll run to get familiar with executing JUnit tests.

Unzip the distribution zip file to a directory on your computer system (for example, C:\ on Windows or /opt/ on UNIX).

In this directory, unzipping will create a subdirectory for the JUnit distribution you downloaded (for example, C:\junit4.6 on Windows or /opt/junit4.6 on UNIX).

You're now ready to run the tests provided with the JUnit distribution. JUnit comes complete with Java programs that you can use to view the result of a test, including a text-based test runner with console output (figure 1.2).

To run the text test runner, open a shell in C:\junit4.6 on Windows or in /opt/ junit4.6 UNIX, and type the appropriate command for your operating system:

```
C:\WINDOWS\system32\cmd.exe                                    _ □ x

C:\junit4.6>java -cp junit-4.6.jar;. junit.samples.AllTests
.................................................
.................................................
.....
Time: 0.375

OK (129 tests)

C:\junit4.6>_
```

Figure 1.1   Execution of the JUnit distribution sample tests using the text test runner

Windows

```
java -cp junit-4.6.jar;. junit.samples.AllTests
```

UNIX

```
java -cp junit-4.6.jar:. junit.samples.AllTests
```

The `AllTests` class contains a `main` method to execute the sample tests:

```
public static void main (String[] args) {
    junit.textui.TestRunner.run(suite());
}
```

Figure 1.1 shows the result of the test execution.

Notice that the JUnit text test runner displays passing tests with a dot. Had there been errors, they would have displayed with an *E* instead of a dot.

In part 3 of the book, we look at running tests using the Ant build tool and also the Maven build tool.

1.6   *Testing with JUnit*

JUnit has many features that make it easy to write and run tests. You'll see these features at work throughout this book:

- Separate test class instances and class loaders for each unit test to avoid side effects
- JUnit annotations to provide resource initialization and reclamation methods: `@Before`, `@BeforeClass`, `@After`, and `@AfterClass`
- A variety of assert methods to make it easy to check the results of your tests
- Integration with popular tools like Ant and Maven, and popular IDEs like Eclipse, NetBeans, IntelliJ, and JBuilder

Without further ado, let's turn to listing 1.4 and see what the simple `Calculator` test looks like when written with JUnit.

Listing 1.4   The JUnit `CalculatorTest` program

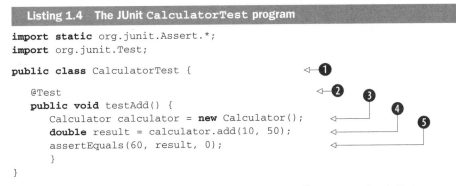

```
import static org.junit.Assert.*;
import org.junit.Test;

public class CalculatorTest {

    @Test
    public void testAdd() {
        Calculator calculator = new Calculator();
        double result = calculator.add(10, 50);
        assertEquals(60, result, 0);
    }
}
```

This is a much simpler test; let's walk through it. At ❶, we start by defining a test class. The only restriction is that the class must be public; we can name it whatever we like. It's common practice to end the class name with *Test*. Notice also that in contrast to JUnit 3 where we needed to extend the `TestCase` class, this requirement has been removed in JUnit 4.

At ❷, we mark the method as a unit test method by adding the `@Test` annotation.[6] A best practice is to name test methods following the test*XXX* pattern. JUnit doesn't have method name restrictions. You can name your methods as you like; as long as they have the `@Test` annotation, JUnit will execute them.

At ❸, we start the test by creating an instance of the `Calculator` class (the "object under test"), and at ❹, as before, we execute the test by calling the method to test, passing it two known values.

At ❺, the JUnit framework begins to shine! To check the result of the test, we call an `assertEquals` method, which we imported with a static import on the first line of the class. The Javadoc for the `assertEquals` method is as follows:

```
/**
 * Asserts that two doubles or floats are equal to within a positive delta.
 * If the expected value is infinity then the delta value is ignored.
 */
static public void assertEquals(
    double expected, double actual, double delta)
```

In listing 1.4, we passed `assertEquals` these parameters:

```
expected = 60
actual = result
delta = 0
```

Because we passed the calculator the values 10 and 50, we tell `assertEquals` to expect the sum to be 60. (We pass 0 as the delta because we're adding integers.) When we called the `calculator` object, we tucked the return value into a local double named `result`. Therefore, we pass that variable to `assertEquals` to compare against the expected value of 60.

---

[6] Annotations were first introduced in JDK 1.5, so in order to use them you need to have version 1.5 or later of the JDK.

If the actual value isn't equal to the expected value, JUnit throws an unchecked exception, which causes the test to fail.

Most often, the `delta` parameter can be zero, and we can safely ignore it. It comes into play with calculations that aren't always precise, which includes many floating-point calculations. The `delta` provides a range factor. If the actual value is within the range `expected - delta` and `expected + delta`, the test will pass. You may find it useful when doing mathematical computations with rounding or truncating errors or when asserting a condition about the modification date of a file, because the precision of these dates depends on the operating system.

Let's assume that we've entered the code from listings 1.1 and 1.4 in the C:\junit-book\ch01-jumpstart directory (/opt/junitbook/ch01-jumpstart on UNIX). Let's first compile the code by opening a command shell in that directory and typing the following (we'll assume we have the javac executable on our PATH):

Windows

```
javac -cp \junit4.6\junit-4.6.jar *.java
```

UNIX

```
javac -cp /opt/junit4.6/junit-4.6.jar *.java
```

We're now ready to start the console test runner, by typing the following:

Windows

```
java -cp .;\junit4.6\junit-4.6.jar
    org.junit.runner.JUnitCore CalculatorTest
```

UNIX

```
java -cp .:/opt/junit4.6/junit-4.6.jar
    org.junit.runner.JUnitCore CalculatorTest
```

Figure 1.2 shows the test result.

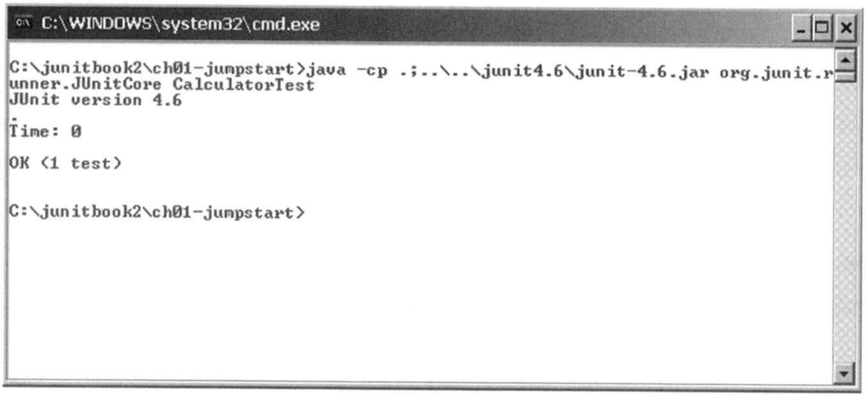

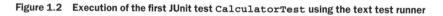

Figure 1.2   Execution of the first JUnit test `CalculatorTest` using the text test runner

The remarkable thing about the JUnit `CalculatorTest` class in listing 1.4 is that the code is easier to write than the first `CalculatorTest` program in listing 1.2. In addition, we can run the test automatically through the JUnit framework.

When we run the test from the command line (figure 1.2), we see the amount of time it took and the number of tests that passed. There are many other ways to run tests, from IDEs like Eclipse to build tools like Ant. This simple example gives you a taste of the power of JUnit and unit testing.

1.7   *Summary*

Every developer should perform some type of test to see if code works. Developers who use automatic unit tests can repeat these tests on demand to ensure that *new* code works *and doesn't break existing tests.*

Simple unit tests aren't difficult to create without JUnit, but as tests are added and become more complex, writing and maintaining tests becomes more difficult. JUnit is a unit testing framework that makes it easier to create, run, and revise unit tests.

In this chapter, we scratched the surface of JUnit by stepping through a simple test. JUnit has much more to offer.

In chapter 2 we take a closer look at the JUnit framework classes (different annotations and assertion mechanisms) and how they work together to make unit testing efficient and effective. We also walk through the differences between the old-style JUnit 3 and the new features in JUnit 4.

Exploring core JUnit

2

Mistakes are the portals of discovery.
—James Joyce

This chapter covers

- Using the core JUnit classes
- Understanding JUnit mechanisms
- Understanding the JUnit lifecycle

In chapter 1, we decided that we need a reliable and repeatable way to test our program. Our solution is to write or reuse a framework to drive test code that exercises our program's API. As our program grows with new classes and new methods to existing classes, we need to grow our test code as well. Experience has taught us that sometimes classes interact in unexpected ways; we need to make sure that we can run all of our tests at any time, no matter what code changes took place. The question becomes, how do we run multiple test classes? And how do we find out which tests passed and which ones failed?

In this chapter, we look at how JUnit provides the functionality to answer those questions. We begin with an overview of the core JUnit concepts—the test class, test suite, and test runner. We take a close look at the core test runners and the test suite before we revisit our old friend the test class. We also examine how the core classes work together.

Then, in the next chapter, we use an example application to show you how to use these core JUnit concepts. We demonstrate best practices for writing and organizing test code.

2.1 Exploring core JUnit

The `CalculatorTest` program from chapter 1, shown in listing 2.1, defines a test class with a single test method `testAdd`.

The requirements to define a test class are that the class must be public and contain a zero-argument constructor. In our example, because we don't define any other constructors, we don't need to define the zero-argument constructor; Java creates it for us implicitly.

The requirements to create a test method are that it must be annotated with `@Test`, be public, take no arguments, and return `void`.

Listing 2.1 The `CalculatorTest` test case

```
import static org.junit.Assert.assertEquals;
import org.junit.Test;

public class CalculatorTest {

    @Test
    public void testAdd() {
        Calculator calculator = new Calculator();
        double result = calculator.add(1, 1);
        assertEquals(2, result, 0);
    }
}
```

JUnit creates a new instance of the test class before invoking each `@Test` method. This helps provide independence between test methods and avoids unintentional side effects in the test code. Because each test method runs on a new test class instance, we can't reuse instance variable values across test methods.

To perform test validation, we use the `assert` methods provided by the JUnit `Assert` class. As you can see from the previous example, we statically import these methods in our test class. Alternatively, we can import the JUnit `Assert` class itself, depending on our taste for static imports. Table 2.1 lists some of the most popular assert methods.

`Assert` methods with two value parameters follow a pattern worth memorizing: the first parameter (`A` in the table) is the expected value, and the second parameter (`B` in the table) is the actual value.

JUnit provides many other methods, such as `assertArrayNotEquals`, `assertNotSame`, `assertNotTrue`, and so on. It also provides the same methods with a different signature—without the `message` parameter. It's a best practice to provide an error message for all your assert method calls. Recall Murphy's Law and apply it here; when an assertion fails, describe what went wrong in a human-readable message.

Table 2.1   JUnit `assert` method sample

assert*XXX* method	What it's used for
`assertArrayEquals("message", A, B)`	Asserts the equality of the A and B arrays.
`assertEquals("message", A, B)`	Asserts the equality of objects A and B. This `assert` invokes the `equals()` method on the first object against the second.
`assertSame("message", A, B)`	Asserts that the A and B objects are the same object. Whereas the previous `assert` method checks to see that A and B have the same value (using the `equals` method), the `assertSame` method checks to see if the A and B objects are one and the same object (using the `==` operator).
`assertTrue("message", A)`	Asserts that the A condition is true.
`assertNotNull("message", A)`	Asserts that the A object isn't null.

When you need to run several test classes at once, you create another object called a test suite (or `Suite`.) Your test suite is a special test runner (or `Runner`), so you can run it as you would a test class. Once you understand how a test class, `Suite`, and `Runner` work, you'll be able to write whatever tests you need. These three objects form the backbone of the JUnit framework.

On a daily basis, you need only write test classes and test suites. The other classes work behind the scenes to bring your tests to life.

> **DEFINITIONS**   *Test class (or TestCase or test case)*—A class that contains one or more tests represented by methods annotated with `@Test`. Use a test class to group together tests that exercise common behaviors. In the remainder of this book, when we mention a *test*, we mean a method annotated with `@Test`; when we mention a test case (or test class), we mean a class that holds these test methods—a set of tests. There's usually a one-to-one mapping between a production class and a test class.
>
> *Suite (or test suite)*—A group of tests. A test suite is a convenient way to group together tests that are related. For example, if you don't define a test suite for a test class, JUnit automatically provides a test suite that includes all tests found in the test class (more on that later). A suite usually groups test classes from the same package.
>
> *Runner (or test runner)*—A runner of test suites. JUnit provides various runners to execute your tests. We cover these runners later in this chapter and show you how to write your own test runners.

Table 2.2 JUnit core objects

JUnit concept	Responsibilities	Introduced in
Assert	Lets you define the conditions that you want to test. An assert method is silent when its proposition succeeds but throws an exception if the proposition fails.	Section 2.1
Test	A method with a @Test annotation defines a test. To run this method JUnit constructs a new instance of the containing class and then invokes the annotated method.	Section 2.1
Test class	A test class is the container for @Test methods.	Section 2.1
Suite	The Suite allows you to group test classes together.	Section 2.3
Runner	The Runner class runs tests. JUnit 4 is backward compatible and will run JUnit 3 tests.	Section 2.2

Let's take a closer look at the responsibilities of each of the core objects that make up JUnit; see table 2.2.

We can move on to explaining in detail the objects from this table that we've not seen yet: the test Runner and test Suite objects.

To run a basic test class, you needn't do anything special; JUnit uses a *test runner* on your behalf to manage the lifecycle of your test class, including creating the class, invoking tests, and gathering results. The next sections address situations that may require you to set up your test to run in a special manner. One of these situations alleviates a common problem when creating tests: invoking tests with different inputs. We discuss this specific scenario with an example in the next section before looking at the remaining test runners provided by JUnit.

2.2 *Running parameterized tests*

The Parameterized test runner allows you to run a test many times with different sets of parameters. Listing 2.2 demonstrates the Parameterized runner in action (you can find this test in the source code samples for chapter 1).

Listing 2.2 Parameterized tests

```
[...]
@RunWith(value=Parameterized.class)          ◁─❶
public class ParameterizedTest {

    private double expected;                   ❷
    private double valueOne;
    private double valueTwo;                              ❸

    @Parameters                                        ◁─┘
    public static Collection<Integer[]> getTestParameters() {
      return Arrays.asList(new Integer[][] {
```

```
            {2, 1, 1},   //expected, valueOne, valueTwo
            {3, 2, 1},   //expected, valueOne, valueTwo
            {4, 3, 1},   //expected, valueOne, valueTwo
        });
    }

    public ParameterizedTest(double expected,          ➍
        double valueOne, double valueTwo) {
        this.expected = expected;
        this.valueOne = valueOne;
        this.valueTwo = valueTwo;
    }

    @Test                                          ➎
    public void sum() {
        Calculator calc = new Calculator();                      ➏   ➐
        assertEquals(expected, calc.add(valueOne, valueTwo), 0);
    }
}
```

To run a test class with the Parameterized test runner, you must meet the following requirements. The test class must carry the @RunWith annotation with the Parameterized class as its argument ➊. You must declare instance variables used in the tests ➋ and provide a method annotated with @Parameters ➌, here called getTest-Parameters. The signature of this method must be @Parameters public static java.util.Collection, without parameters. The Collection elements must be arrays of identical length. This array length must match the number of arguments of the only public constructor. In our case, each array contains three elements because the public constructor has three arguments. Our example uses this method to provide the input and expected output values for the tests. Because we want to test the add method of our Calculator program, we provide three parameters: expected value and two values that we add together. At ➍ we specify the required constructor for the test. Note that this time our test case doesn't have a no-argument constructor but instead has a constructor that accepts parameters for the test. At ➎ we finally implement the sum @Test method, which instantiates the Calculator program ➏, and assert calls for the parameters we've provided ➐.

Running this test will loop exactly as many times as the size of the collection returned by the @Parameters method. The execution of this single test case has the same result as the execution of the following test cases with different parameters:

```
sum: assertEquals(2, calculator.add(1, 1), 0);
sum: assertEquals(3, calculator.add(2, 1), 0);
sum: assertEquals(4, calculator.add(3, 1), 0);
```

It's worth stepping through the JUnit runtime to understand this powerful feature: JUnit calls the static method getTestParameters ➌. Next, JUnit loops for each array in the getTestParameters collection ➌. JUnit then calls the only public constructor ➍. If there is more than one public constructor, JUnit throws an assertion error. JUnit then calls the constructor ➍ with an argument list built from the array elements. In our case, JUnit calls the three-argument constructor ❹ with the first element in the array, itself an array: {2, 1, 1}. JUnit then calls each @Test method ❺ as usual. JUnit repeats the process for the next array in the getTestParameters collection ❸.

When you compare the test results with the previous example, you see that instead of running one test, the parameterized JUnit test runner ran the same method three times, once for each value in our @Parameters collection.

The JUnit class Parameterized is one of JUnit's many *test runners*. A test runner allows you to tell JUnit how a test should be run. Next, we look at the other JUnit test runners.

2.3 JUnit test runners

When you're first writing tests, you want them to run as quickly and easily as possible. You should be able to make testing part of the development cycle: *code-run-test-code* (or *test-code run-test* if you're test-first inclined). There are IDEs and compilers for quickly building and running applications; JUnit lets you build and run tests.

2.3.1 Test runner overview

JUnit 4 is built with backward compatibility with version 3.8.x. Because the 4.x version of JUnit is completely different from the 3.x versions, it should be possible to execute not only JUnit 4 tests but also 3.x-style tests. That's why in its latest versions JUnit provides different runners (listed in table 2.3) for running JUnit 3.x tests, JUnit 4 tests, and different sets of tests.

Table 2.3 JUnit 4 test runners

Runner	Purpose
org.junit.internal.runners.JUnit38ClassRunner	This runner is included in the current release of JUnit only for backward compatibility. It will start the test case as a JUnit 3.8 test case.
org.junit.runners.JUnit4	This runner will start the test case as a JUnit 4 test case.
org.junit.runners.Parameterized	A Parameterized test runner runs same sets of tests with different parameters.
org.junit.runners.Suite	The Suite is a container that can hold different tests. The Suite is also a runner that executes all the @Test annotated methods in a test class.

JUnit will use a default test runner if none is provided based on the test class. If you want JUnit to use a specific test runner, specify the test runner class using the `@Run-With` annotation, as demonstrated in the following code:

```
@RunWith(value=org.junit.internal.runners.JUnit38ClassRunner.class)
public class TestWithJUnit38 extends junit.framework.TestCase {
    [...]
}
```

Now that we've seen an overview of the different test runners and how to direct JUnit to use them, we look at various test runners in more detail.

2.3.2 The JUnitCore façade

To make running tests as quick and easy as possible, JUnit provides a façade (`org.junit.runner.JUnitCore`), which operates with any of the test runners. JUnit designed this façade to execute your tests and gather results and statistics. You can see the `JUnitCore` class in action in figure 1.3 in the previous chapter.

> ### Design patterns in action: façade
> A *façade*[1] is a design pattern that provides a unified interface to a set of interfaces in a subsystem. Façade defines a higher-level interface that makes the subsystem easier to use. You can use a façade to simplify a number of complicated object interactions into a single interface.

The JUnit façade determines which runner to use for running your tests. It supports running JUnit 3.8 tests, JUnit 4 tests, and a mixture of both.

Before JUnit 4, JUnit included Swing and AWT test runners; these are no longer included. Those graphical test runners had a progress indicator running across the screen, known as the famous JUnit green bar. JUnit testers tend to refer to passing tests as *green bar* and failing tests as *red bar*. "Keep the bar green to keep the code clean" is the JUnit motto.

Figure 2.1 shows the Eclipse JUnit view after a green-bar test run.

These days, all major IDEs support integration with JUnit.

2.3.3 Custom test runners

Unlike other elements of the JUnit framework, there is no `Runner` interface. Instead, the various test runners bundled with JUnit all extend the `org.junit.runner.Runner` class. To create your own test runner, you'll need to extend the `Runner` class. Please refer to appendix B, where we cover this topic in detail.

---

[1] The definition is taken from the Portland Pattern Repository: http://c2.com/cgi/wiki?FacadePattern.

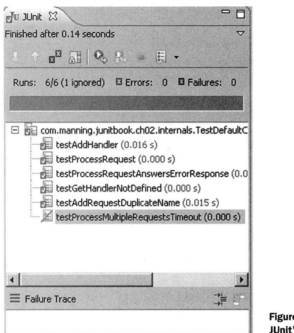

Figure 2.1
JUnit's green bar, shown in Eclipse

2.4 Composing tests with a suite

For a simple test, you can compile the simple calculator test program from listing 2.1 and hand it to the console façade runner, like this:

```
>java org.junit.runner.JUnitCore CalculatorTest
```

The test should run fine assuming the classpath is configured properly. This is simple enough—at least as far as running a single test case is concerned.

2.4.1 Composing a suite of test classes

The next step is to run more than one test class. To facilitate this task JUnit provides the *test* Suite. The Suite is a container used to gather tests for the purpose of grouping and invocation.

JUnit designed the Suite to run one or more test cases. The test runner launches the Suite; which test case to run is up to the Suite.

You might wonder how you managed to run the example at the end of chapter 1, when you didn't define a Suite. To keep simple things simple, the test runner automatically creates a Suite if you don't provide one of your own.

The default Suite scans your test class for any methods that you annotated with @Test. Internally, the default Suite creates an instance of your test class for each @Test method. JUnit then executes every @Test method independently from the others to avoid potential side effects.

If you add another test to the CalculatorTest class, like testSubtract, and you annotate it with the @Test, the default Suite would automatically include it.

The Suite object is a Runner that executes all of the @Test annotated methods in the test class. Listing 2.3 shows how to compose multiple test classes in a single test suite.

Listing 2.3   Composing a Suite from test classes

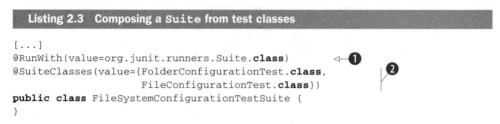

```
[...]
@RunWith(value=org.junit.runners.Suite.class)
@SuiteClasses(value={FolderConfigurationTest.class,
                     FileConfigurationTest.class})
public class FileSystemConfigurationTestSuite {
}
```

In listing 2.3, we specify the appropriate runner with the @RunWith annotation ❶ and list the tests we want to include in this test by specifying the test classes in the @Suite-Classes annotation ❷. All the @Test methods from these classes will be included in the Suite.

For the CalculatorTest in listing 2.1, you can represent the default Suite like this:

```
@RunWith(value=Suite.class)
@SuiteClasses(value={CalculatorTest.class})
public class AllTests {
}
```

2.4.2   *Composing a suite of suites*

Because of the clever way JUnit is constructed, it's possible to create a suite of test suites. For example, listing 2.4 concatenates various files to show how test cases make up suites, which in turn make up a master suite.

Listing 2.4   Suite of suites

```
[...]
public class TestCaseA {
    @Test
    public void testA1() {
        // omitted
    }
}

[...]
public class TestCaseB {
    @Test
    public void testB1() {
        // omitted
    }
}

[...]
@RunWith(value=Suite.class)
@SuiteClasses(value = {TestCaseA.class})
```

```
public class TestSuiteA {
}

[...]
@RunWith(value=Suite.class)
@SuiteClasses(value = {TestCaseB.class})
public class TestSuiteB {
}

[...]
@RunWith(value = Suite.class)
@SuiteClasses(value = {TestSuiteA.class, TestSuiteB.class})
public class MasterTestSuite{
}
```

Our simple test suites `TestSuiteA` and `TestSuiteB` have only one test case each, a simplification to abbreviate this example. A real suite would contain more than one test class, like our master suite.

You can run any of the classes in this listing as a JUnit test, one of the two test classes, one of the two test suites, or the master test suite. Figure 2.2 displays the result of running the master suite in Eclipse.

Test suites provide a powerful way to organize your tests. The convenience isn't unique to JUnit, as you'll see in the next section, which will make us reconsider creating any JUnit suites at all.

2.4.3   *Suites, IDEs, Ant, and Maven*

Ant and Maven also provide ways to run groups of test classes and suites by allowing you to specify, with a type of regular expression, the names of test classes and suites to run. In addition, IDEs like Eclipse allow you to run all test classes and `Suites` in a selected package or source directory. This is enough to make us reconsider whether it's worth creating JUnit `Suites` in the first place.

JUnit `Suites` are useful if you want to organize your tests in Java, independent of the capability of your build system, because it's common for someone or a group other than the developers to maintain builds. Similarly, you may wish to provide independence from any given IDE and its JUnit integration capabilities.

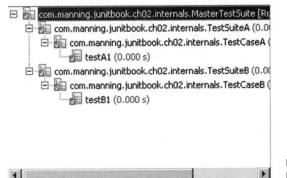

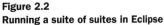

Figure 2.2
Running a suite of suites in Eclipse

2.5   *Summary*

In this chapter, we introduced the core JUnit concepts and classes. We showed you how to fuse a test class, a `Suite`, and a `Runner`.

Use a test class to test one domain object where each test method focuses on one domain method or a specific set of methods. JUnit 4 makes extensive uses of annotations to define and manage tests. JUnit 4 has made obsolete the JUnit 3 requirement of making a test class a `TestCase` subclass.

You use a test suite to group related test classes together, allowing you to invoke them as a group. You can even group suites together in higher-level suites.

You use a `Runner` to invoke unit tests and test suites.

In the next chapter, we introduce the Controller design pattern and build a sample Controller component application that we test with JUnit. This way, we not only show you how to use the JUnit components we've been discussing so far, but we also introduce many JUnit best practices.

Mastering JUnit

Tests are the Programmer's Stone,
transmuting fear into boredom.

—Kent Beck,
Test First Development

This chapter covers

- Implementing a sample application
- Testing the sample application with JUnit
- Following JUnit best practices

So far, we've made a JUnit survey and shown how to use it (chapter 1). We also looked at JUnit internals, what the core classes and methods are, and how they interact with each other (chapter 2).

We now dive deeper by introducing a real-life component and testing it. In this chapter, we implement a small application using the Controller design pattern. We then test every part of the application using JUnit. We also look at JUnit best practices when writing and organizing your tests.

3.1   Introducing the controller component

Core Java EE Patterns describes a *controller* as a component that "interacts with a client, controlling and managing the handling of each request," and tells us that it's used in both presentation-tier and business-tier patterns.[1]

In general, a controller does the following:

- Accepts requests
- Performs any common computations on the request
- Selects an appropriate request handler
- Routes the request so that the handler can execute the relevant business logic
- May provide a top-level handler for errors and exceptions

You'll find controllers to be handy in a variety of applications. For example, in a presentation-tier pattern, a web controller accepts HTTP requests and extracts HTTP parameters, cookies, and HTTP headers, perhaps making the HTTP elements easily accessible to the rest of the application. A web controller determines the appropriate business logic component to call based on elements in the request, perhaps with the help of persistent data in the HTTP session, a database, or some other resource. The Apache Struts framework is an example of a web controller.

Another common use for a controller is to handle applications in a business-tier pattern. Many business applications support several presentation layers. HTTP clients may handle web applications. Swing clients may handle desktop applications. Behind these presentation tiers, there's often an application controller, or state machine. Programmers implement many Enterprise JavaBean (EJB) applications this way. The EJB tier has its own controller, which connects to different presentation tiers through a business façade or delegate.

Given the many uses for a controller, it's no surprise that controllers crop up in a number of enterprise architecture patterns, including Page Controller, Front Controller, and Application Controller.[2] The controller you'll design here could be the first step in implementing any of these classic patterns. Let's work through the code for the simple controller, to see how it works, and then try a few tests. If you'd like to follow along and run the tests as you go, all the source code for this chapter is available at SourceForge (http://junitbook.sf.net). See appendix A for more about setting up the source code.

3.1.1   Designing the interfaces

Looking over the description of a controller, four objects pop out: the `Request`, the `Response`, the `RequestHandler`, and the `Controller`. The `Controller` accepts

---

[1] Deepak Alur, John Crupi, and Dan Malks, *Core Java EE Patterns: Best Practices and Design Strategies* (Upper Saddle River, NJ: Prentice Hall, 2001).

[2] Martin Fowler, *Patterns of Enterprise Application Architecture* (Boston: Addison-Wesley, 2003).

a Request, dispatches a RequestHandler, and returns a Response object. With a description in hand, you can code some simple starter interfaces, like those shown in listing 3.1.

Listing 3.1 Request, Response, RequestHandler, and Controller interfaces

```
public interface Request
{
    String getName();                                              ◄─❶
}
public interface Response                                          ◄─❷
{
}
public interface RequestHandler
{
    Response process(Request request) throws Exception;            ◄─❸
}
public interface Controller
{                                                                         ❹
    Response processRequest(Request request);                      ◄─┐   ❺
    void addHandler(Request request, RequestHandler requestHandler); ◄─┘
}
```

First, define a Request interface with a single getName method that returns the request's unique name ❶, so you can differentiate one request from another. As you develop the component, you'll need other methods, but you can add those as you go along.

Next, specify an empty interface ❷. To begin coding, you need only return a Response object. What the Response encloses is something you can deal with later. For now, you need a Response type you can plug into a signature.

The next step is to define a RequestHandler that can process a Request and return your Response ❸. RequestHandler is a helper component designed to do most of the dirty work. It may call on classes that throw any type of exception. Exception is what you have the process method throw.

Define a top-level method for processing an incoming request ❹. After accepting the request, the controller dispatches it to the appropriate RequestHandler. Notice that processRequest doesn't declare any exceptions. This method is at the top of the control stack and should catch and cope with all errors internally. If it did throw an exception, the error would usually go up to the Java Virtual Machine (JVM) or servlet container. The JVM or container would then present the user with one of those nasty white pages. It's better that you code for it yourself.

Finally, ❺ is an important design element. The addHandler method allows you to extend the Controller without modifying the Java source.

> **Design patterns in action: Inversion of Control**
> Registering a handler with the controller is an example of Inversion of Control. You may know this pattern as the *Hollywood Principle*, or "Don't call us, we'll call you." Objects register as handlers for an event. When the event occurs, a hook method on the registered object is invoked. Inversion of Control lets frameworks manage the event lifecycle while allowing developers to plug in custom handlers for framework events.[3]

3.1.2   *Implementing the base class*

Following up on the interfaces in listing 3.1, listing 3.2 shows a first draft of the simple controller class.

Listing 3.2   The generic controller

```
[...]
import java.util.HashMap;
import java.util.Map;

public class DefaultController implements Controller
{
    private Map requestHandlers = new HashMap();                          ← 1

    protected RequestHandler getHandler(Request request)                 ← 2
    {
        if (!this.requestHandlers.containsKey(request.getName()))
        {
            String message = "Cannot find handler for request name "
                                    + "[" + request.getName() + "]";
            throw new RuntimeException(message);                          ← 3
        }
        return (RequestHandler)
                    this.requestHandlers.get(request.getName());         ← 4
    }

    public Response processRequest(Request request)                      ← 5
    {
        Response response;
        try
        {
            response = getHandler(request).process(request);
        }
        catch (Exception exception)
        {
            response = new ErrorResponse(request, exception);
        }
        return response;
    }
```

---

[3]   4 http://c2.com/cgi/wiki?HollywoodPrinciple

```
public void addHandler(Request request, RequestHandler requestHandler)
{
    if (this.requestHandlers.containsKey(request.getName()))
    {
        throw new RuntimeException("A request handler has "
            + "already been registered for request name "
            + "[" + request.getName() + "]");
    }
    else
    {
            this.requestHandlers.put(request.getName(), requestHandler);
    }
}
}
```

⑥

First, declare a HashMap (java.util.HashMap) to act as the registry for your request handlers **①**. Next, add a protected method, getHandler, to fetch the Request-Handler for a given request **②**. If a RequestHandler has not been registered, you throw a RuntimeException (java.lang.RuntimeException) **③**, because this happenstance represents a programming mistake rather than an issue raised by a user or external system. Java doesn't require you to declare the RuntimeException in the method's signature, but you can still catch it as an exception. An improvement would be to add a specific exception to the controller framework (NoSuitableRequest-HandlerException, for example).

Your utility method then returns the appropriate handler to its caller **④**.

The processRequest method **⑤** is the core of the Controller class. This method dispatches the appropriate handler for the request and passes back the handler's Response. If an exception bubbles up, it's caught in the ErrorResponse class, shown in listing 3.3.

Finally, check to see whether the name for the handler has been registered **⑥**, and throw an exception if it has. Looking at the implementation, note that the signature passes the request object, but you use only its name. This sort of thing often occurs when an interface is defined *before* the code is written. One way to avoid overdesigning an interface is to practice test-driven development (see chapter 5).

Listing 3.3   Special response class signaling an error

```
[...]
public class ErrorResponse implements Response
{
    private Request originalRequest;
    private Exception originalException;
    public ErrorResponse(Request request, Exception exception)
    {
        this.originalRequest = request;
        this.originalException = exception;
        }
    public Request getOriginalRequest()
    {
```

```
      return this.originalRequest;
   }
   public Exception getOriginalException()
   {
      return this.originalException;
   }
}
```

At this point, you have a crude but effective skeleton for the controller. Table 3.1 shows how the requirements at the top of this section relate to the source code.

Table 3.1   Resolving the base requirements for the component

Requirement	Resolution
Accept requests	`public Response processRequest(Request request)`
Select handler	`this.requestHandlers.get(request.getName())`
Route requests	`response = getRequestHandler(request).process(request);`
Error handling	`Subclass ErrorResponse`

The next step for many developers would be to cobble up a stub application to go with the skeleton controller. As test-infected developers, we can write a test suite for the controller without fussing with a stub application. That's the beauty of unit testing. We can write a package and verify that it works, all outside a conventional Java application.

3.2   *Let's test it!*

A fit of inspiration has led us to code the four interfaces shown in listing 3.1 and the two starter classes shown in listings 3.2 and 3.3. If we don't write an automatic test now, the Bureau of Extreme Programming will be asking for our membership cards back!

Listings 3.2 and 3.3 began with the simplest implementations possible. Let's do the same with the new set of unit tests. What's the simplest-possible test case we can explore?

3.2.1   *Testing the DefaultController*

How about a test case that instantiates the `DefaultController` class? The first step in doing anything useful with the controller is to construct it, so let's start there. Listing 3.4 shows the bootstrap test code. It constructs the `DefaultController` object and sets up a framework for writing tests.

Listing 3.4   `TestDefaultController`—a bootstrap iteration

```
[...]
import org.junit.core.Test;
import static org.junit.Assert.*;
```

```java
public class TestDefaultController                        ←①
{
    private DefaultController controller;

    @Before
    public void instantiate() throws Exception            ←②
    {
        controller = new DefaultController();
    }
    @Test
    public void testMethod()                              ←③
    {
        throw new RuntimeException("implement me");        ←④
    }
}
```

Start the name of the test case class with the prefix *Test* ①. The naming convention isn't required, but by doing so, we mark the class as a test case so that we can easily recognize test classes and possibly filter them in build scripts. Alternatively, and depending on your native language, you may prefer to postfix class names with *Test*.

Next, use the @Before annotated method to instantiate DefaultController ②. This is a built-in extension point that the JUnit framework calls between test methods. At ③ you insert a dummy test method, so you have something to run. As soon as you're sure the test infrastructure is working, you can begin adding real test methods. Although this test runs, it also fails. The next step is to fix the test!

Use a best practice by throwing an exception for test code that you haven't implemented yet ④. This prevents the test from passing and reminds you that you must implement this code.

Now that you have a bootstrap test, the next step is to decide what to test first.

JUnit's details

The @Before and @After annotated methods are executed right before/after the execution of each one of your @Test methods and regardless of whether the test failed or not. This helps you to extract all of your common logic, like instantiating your domain objects and setting them up in some known state. You can have as many of these methods as you want, but beware that if you have more than one of the @Before/@After methods, the order of their execution is not defined.

JUnit also provides the @BeforeClass and @AfterClass annotations to annotate your methods in that class. The methods that you annotate will get executed, only once, before/after all of your @Test methods. Again, as with the @Before and @After annotations, you can have as many of these methods as you want, and again the order of the execution is unspecified.

You need to remember that both the @Before/@After and @BeforeClass/@AfterClass annotated methods must be public. The @BeforeClass/@AfterClass annotated methods must be public and static.

3.2.2 *Adding a handler*

Now that you have a bootstrap test, the next step is to decide what to test first. We started the test case with the `DefaultController` object, because that's the point of this exercise: to create a controller. You wrote some code and made sure it compiled. But how can you test to see if it works?

The purpose of the controller is to process a request and return a response. But before you process a request, the design calls for adding a `RequestHandler` to do the processing. So, first things first: you should test whether you can add a `RequestHandler`.

The tests you ran in chapter 1 returned a known result. To see if a test succeeded, you compared the result you expected with whatever result the object you were testing returned. The signature for `addHandler` is

```
void addHandler(Request request, RequestHandler requestHandler)
```

To add a `RequestHandler`, you need a `Request` with a known name. To check to see if adding it worked, you can use the `getHandler` method from `DefaultController`, which uses this signature:

```
RequestHandler getHandler(Request request)
```

This is possible because the `getHandler` method is protected, and the test classes are located in the same package as the classes they're testing. This is one reason to define the tests under the same package.

For the first test, it looks like you can do the following:

- Add a `RequestHandler`, referencing a `Request`.
- Get a `RequestHandler` and pass the same `Request`.
- Check to see if you get the same `RequestHandler` back.

WHERE DO TESTS COME FROM?

Now you know what objects you need. The next question is, "Where do these objects come from?" Should you go ahead and write some of the objects you'll use in the application, such as a logon request?

The point of unit testing is to test one object at a time. In an object-oriented environment like Java, you design objects to interact with other objects. To create a unit test, it follows that you need two flavors of objects: the *domain object* you're testing and *test objects* to interact with the object under test.

> **DEFINITION**   *Domain object*—In the context of unit testing, the term *domain object* is used to contrast and compare the objects you use *in* your application with the objects that you use to *test* your application (*test objects*). Any object under test is considered a domain object.

If you used another domain object, like a logon request, and a test failed, it would be hard to identify the culprit. You might not be able to tell whether the problem was with the controller or the request. So, in the first series of tests, the only class you'll use in production is `DefaultController`. Everything else should be a special test class.

> ## JUnit best practices: unit test one object at a time
>
> A vital aspect of unit tests is that they're finely grained. A unit test independently examines each object you create, so that you can isolate problems as soon as they occur. If you put more than one object under test, you can't predict how the objects will interact when changes occur to one or the other. When an object interacts with other complex objects, you can surround the object under test with predictable test objects. Another form of software test, integration testing, examines how working objects interact with each other. See chapter 4 for more about other types of tests.

WHERE DO TEST CLASSES LIVE?

Where do you put the test classes? Java provides several alternatives. For starters, you could do one of the following:

- Make them public classes in your package.
- Make them inner classes within your test-case class.

If the classes are simple and likely to stay that way, then it's easiest to code them as inner classes. The classes in this example are simple. Listing 3.5 shows the inner classes you can add to the TestDefaultController class.

Listing 3.5 Test classes as inner classes

```java
public class TestDefaultController
{
[...]
   private class SampleRequest implements Request          <--1
   {
      public String getName()
      {
         return "Test";
      }
   }
   private class SampleHandler implements RequestHandler    <--2
   {
      public Response process(Request request) throws Exception
      {
         return new SampleResponse();
      }
   }
   private class SampleResponse implements Response         <--3
   {
      // empty
   }
[...]
```

First, set up a request object ❶ that returns a known name (Test). Next, implement a SampleHandler ❷. The interface calls for a process method, so you have to code that too. You're not testing the process method right now, so you have it return a SampleResponse object to satisfy the signature. Go ahead and define an empty SampleResponse ❸ so you have something to instantiate.

With the scaffolding from listing 3.5 in place, let's look at listing 3.6, which shows the test for adding a RequestHandler.

Listing 3.6   TestDefaultController.testAddHandler

```
[...]
import static org.junit.Assert.*;

public class TestDefaultController
{
[...]
    @Test
    public void testAddHandler()                              ←❶
    {
        Request request = new SampleRequest();                   ❷
        RequestHandler handler = new SampleHandler();            ❸
        controller.addHandler(request, handler);        ←
        RequestHandler handler2 = controller.getHandler(request);   ←❹
        assertSame("Handler we set in controller should be the
                        same handler we get", handler2, handler);   ←❺
    }
}
```

Pick an obvious name for the test method, and annotate your test method with the @Test annotation ❶. Remember to instantiate your test objects ❷. This code gets to the point of the test: controller (the object under test) adds the test handler ❸. Note that the DefaultController object is instantiated by the @Before annotated method (see listing 3.4).

Read back the handler under a new variable name ❹, and check to see if you get back the same object you put in ❺.

JUnit best practices: choose meaningful test method names

You can see that a method is a test method by the @Test annotation. You also must be able to understand what a method is testing by reading the name. Although JUnit doesn't require any special rules for naming your test methods, a good rule is to start with the test*XXX* naming scheme, where *XXX* is the name of the domain method to test. As you add other tests against the same method, move to the test*XXXYYY* scheme, where *YYY* describes how the tests differ. Don't be afraid that the names of your tests are getting long or verbose. As you'll see by the end of the chapter, it's sometimes not so obvious what a method is testing by looking at its assert methods. Name your test methods in a descriptive fashion, and add comments where necessary.

Although it's simple, this unit test confirms the key premise that the mechanism for storing and retrieving RequestHandler is alive and well. If addHandler or getRequest fails in the future, the test will quickly detect the problem.

As you create more tests like this, you'll notice that you follow a pattern:

1 Set up the test by placing the environment in a known state (create objects, acquire resources). The pretest state is referred to as the *test fixture*.

2 Invoke the method under test.

3 Confirm the result, usually by calling one or more assert methods.

3.2.3 *Processing a request*

Let's look at testing the core purpose of the controller, processing a request. Because you know the routine, we present the test in listing 3.7 and review it.

Listing 3.7 `testProcessRequest` method

```java
import static org.junit.Assert.*;

public class TestDefaultController
{
[...]
    @Test
    public void testProcessRequest()                               ←①
    {
        Request request = new SampleRequest();
        RequestHandler handler = new SampleHandler();              ②
        controller.addHandler(request, handler);
        Response response = controller.processRequest(request);    ←③  ④
        assertNotNull("Must not return a null response", response); ←
        assertEquals("Response should be of type SampleResponse",
                SampleResponse.class, response.getClass());        ←⑤

    }
}
```

First, annotate the test with the @Test annotation and give the test a simple, uniform name ①. Set up the test objects and add the test handler ②.

At ③ the code diverges from listing 3.6 and calls the processRequest method. You verify that the returned Response object isn't null ④. This is important because you call the getClass method on the Response object. It will fail with a dreaded Null-PointerException if the Response object is null. You use the assertNotNull(String, Object) signature so that if the test fails, the error displayed is meaningful and easy to understand. If you'd used the assertNotNull(Object) signature, the JUnit runner would have displayed a stack trace showing a java.lang.AssertionError exception with no message, which would be more difficult to diagnose.

Once again, compare the result of the test against the expected SampleResponse class ⑤.

JUnit best practices: explain the failure reason in assert calls

Whenever you use any of the JUnit `assert*` methods, make sure you use the signature that takes a `String` as the first parameter. This parameter lets you provide a meaningful description that's displayed in the JUnit test runner if the assert fails. Not using this parameter makes it difficult to understand the reason for a failure when it happens.

FACTORIZING SETUP LOGIC

Because both tests do the same type of setup, you can try moving that code into a `@Before` annotated method. At the same time, you don't want to move it into a new `@Before` method because you aren't sure which method will be executed first, and you may get an exception. Instead, you can move it into the same `@Before` method.

As you add more test methods, you may need to adjust what you do in the `@Before` methods. For now, eliminating duplicate code as soon as possible helps you write more tests more quickly. Listing 3.8 shows the new and improved `TestDefault-Controller` class (changes are shown in bold).

Listing 3.8   `TestDefaultController` after some refactoring

```
[...]
public class TestDefaultController
{
   private DefaultController controller;
   private Request request;
   private RequestHandler handler;

   @Before
   public void initialize() throws Exception      {
      controller = new DefaultController();
      request = new SampleRequest();                          ❶
      handler = new SampleHandler();

      controller.addHandler(request, handler);
   }
   private class SampleRequest implements Request
   {
      // Same as in listing 3.1
   }
   private class SampleHandler implements RequestHandler
   {
      // Same as in listing 3.1
   }
   private class SampleResponse implements Response
   {
      // Same as in listing 3.1
   }
   @Test
   public void testAddHandler()                             ❷
   {
```

```
        RequestHandler handler2 = controller.getHandler(request);
        assertSame(handler2, handler);
    }
    @Test
    public void testProcessRequest()                                    ⟵ ❸
    {
        Response response = controller.processRequest(request);
        assertNotNull("Must not return a null response", response);
        assertEquals("Response should be of type SampleResponse",
                     SampleResponse.class, response.getClass());
    }
}
```

We move the instantiation of the test `Request` and `RequestHandler` objects to initialize ❶. This saves us from repeating the same code in `testAddHandler` ❷ and
`testProcessRequest` ❸. Also, we make a new `@Before` annotated method for adding
the handler to the controller. Because `@Before` methods are executed before every single `@Test` method, we make sure we have a fully set up `DefaultController` object.

> **DEFINITION** *Refactor*—To improve the design of existing code. For more
> about refactoring, see Martin Fowler's already-classic book, *Refactoring: Improv-
> ing the Design of Existing Code.*[4]

Note that you don't try to share the setup code by testing more than one operation in
a test method, as shown in listing 3.9 (an anti-example).

Listing 3.9   Anti-example: *don't* combine test methods

```
public class TestDefaultController
{
[...]
    @Test
    public void testAddAndProcess()
    {
        Request request = new SampleRequest();
        RequestHandler handler = new SampleHandler();
        controller.addHandler(request, handler);
        RequestHandler handler2 = controller.getHandler(request);
        assertEquals(handler2,handler);

        // DO NOT COMBINE TEST METHODS THIS WAY
        Response response = controller.processRequest(request);
        assertNotNull("Must not return a null response", response);
        assertEquals(SampleResponse.class, response.getClass());
    }
}
```

---

[4] Martin Fowler, *Refactoring: Improving the Design of Existing Code* (Reading, MA: Addison-Wesley, 1999).

JUnit best practices: one unit test equals one @Test method

Don't try to cram several tests into one method. The result will be more complex test methods, which will become increasingly difficult to read and understand. Worse, the more logic you write in your test methods, the more risk there is that they won't work and will need debugging. This slippery slope can end with writing tests to test your tests!

Unit tests give you confidence in a program by alerting you when something that had worked now fails. If you put more than one unit test in a method, it becomes more difficult to zoom in on exactly what went wrong. When tests share the same method, a failing test may leave the fixture in an unpredictable state. Other tests embedded in the method may not run or may not run properly. Your picture of the test results will often be incomplete or even misleading.

Because all the test methods in a test class share the same fixture, and JUnit can now generate an automatic test suite, it's just as easy to place each unit test in its own method. If you need to use the same block of code in more than one test, extract it into a utility method that each test method can call. Better yet, if all methods can share the code, put it into the fixture.

Another common pitfall is to write test methods that don't contain any assert statements. When you execute those tests, you see JUnit flag them as successful, but this is an illusion of successful tests. Always use assert calls. The only time when not using assert calls may be acceptable is when an exception is thrown to indicate an error condition.

For best results, your test methods should be as concise and focused as your domain methods.

Each test method must be as clear and focused as possible. This is why JUnit provides you with the `@Before`, `@After`, `@BeforeClass`, and `@AfterClass` annotations: so you can share fixtures between tests without combining test methods.

3.2.4   *Improving testProcessRequest*

When we wrote the `testProcessRequest` method in listing 3.7, we wanted to confirm that the response returned is the expected response. The implementation confirms that the object returned is the object that we expected. But what we'd like to know is whether the response returned equals the expected response. The response could be a different class. What's important is whether the class identifies itself as the correct response.

The `assertSame` method confirms that both references are to the same object. The `assertEquals` method utilizes the `equals` method, inherited from the base `Object` class. To see if two different objects have the same identity, you need to provide your own definition of identity. For an object like a response, you can assign each response its own command token (or name).

The empty implementation of `SampleResponse` didn't have a name property you could test. To get the test you want, you have to implement a little more of the `Response` class first. Listing 3.10 shows the enhanced `SampleResponse` class.

Listing 3.10   A refactored `SampleResponse`

```
public class TestDefaultController
{
[...]
   private class SampleResponse implements Response
   {
      private static final String NAME = "Test";
      public String getName()
      {
         return NAME;
      }
      public boolean equals(Object object)
      {
         boolean result = false;
         if (object instanceof SampleResponse)
         {
            result = ((SampleResponse) object).getName().equals(getName());
         }
         return result;
      }
      public int hashCode()
      {
         return NAME.hashCode();
      }
   }
[...]
```

Now that `SampleResponse` has an identity (represented by `getName()`) and its own `equals` method, you can amend the test method:

```
@Test
public void testProcessRequest()
{
   Response response = controller.processRequest(request);
   assertNotNull("Must not return a null response", response);
   assertEquals(new SampleResponse(), response);
}
```

We've introduced the concept of identity in the `SampleResponse` class for the purpose of the test. But the tests are telling you that this should have existed in the proper `Response` class. You need to modify the `Response` interface as follows:

```
public interface Response
{
   String getName();
}
```

As you see, tests can sometimes "talk" and guide you to a better design of your application. But this isn't the real purpose of the tests. Don't forget that the tests are used to protect us from introducing errors in our code. To do this we need to test every condition under which our application might be executed. We start investigating the exceptional conditions in the next chapter.

3.3   *Testing exception handling*

So far, your tests have followed the main path of execution. If the behavior of one of your objects under test changes in an unexpected way, this type of test points to the root of the problem. In essence, you've been writing *diagnostic tests* that monitor the application's health.

But sometimes bad things happen to good programs. Say an application needs to connect to a database. Your diagnostics may test whether you're following the database's API. If you open a connection but don't close it, a diagnostic can note that you've failed to meet the expectation that all connections must be closed after use.

But what if a connection isn't available? Maybe the connection pool is empty. Or perhaps the database server is down. If the database server is configured properly and you have all the resources you need, this may never happen.

All resources are finite, and someday, instead of a connection, you may be handed an exception. "Anything that can go wrong will."

If you're testing an application by hand, one way to test for this sort of thing is to turn off the database while the application is running. Forcing error conditions is an excellent way to test your disaster-recovery capability. Creating error conditions is also time consuming. Most of us can't afford to do this several times a day—or even once a day. In addition, many other error conditions aren't easy to create by hand.

Testing the main path of execution is a good thing—and a requirement. Testing exception handling is just as important and should also be included as a requirement. If the main path doesn't work, your application won't work either (a condition you're likely to notice.)

> ### JUnit best practices: test anything that could possibly fail
>
> Unit tests help ensure that your methods are keeping their API contracts with other methods. If the contract is based solely on other components' keeping their contracts, then there *may* not be any useful behavior for you to test. But if the method changes the parameter's or field's value in any way, then you're providing unique behavior that you should test. The method is no longer a simple go-between—it's a method with its own behavior that future changes could conceivably break. If a method is changed such that it isn't simple anymore, then you should add a test *when that change takes place* but not before.
>
> As the JUnit FAQ puts it, "The general philosophy is this: if it can't break *on its own*, it's too simple to break." This is also in keeping with the Extreme Programming rule: "No functionality is added early."

> **(continued)**
> What about things like JavaBean getters and setters? Well, that depends. If you're coding them by hand in a text editor, then yes, you might want to test them. It's surprisingly easy to miscode a setter in a way that the compiler won't catch. But if you're using an IDE that watches for such things, then your team might decide not to test simple JavaBean properties.

We're all human, and often we tend to be sloppy when it comes to exception cases. Even textbooks scrimp on error handling so as to simplify the examples. As a result, many otherwise great programs aren't error proofed before they go into production. If properly tested, an application should not expose a screen of death but should trap, log, and explain all errors gracefully.

3.3.1 *Simulating exceptional conditions*

The exceptional test case is where unit tests shine. Unit tests can simulate exceptional conditions as easily as normal conditions. Other types of tests, like functional and acceptance tests, work at the production level. Whether these tests encounter systemic errors is often a matter of happenstance. A unit test can produce exceptional conditions on demand.

During our original fit of inspired coding, we had the foresight to code an error handler into the base classes. As you saw back in listing 3.2, the `processRequest` method traps all exceptions and passes back a special error response instead:

```
try
{
    response = getHandler(request).process(request);
}
catch (Exception exception)
{
    response = new ErrorResponse(request, exception);
}
```

How do you simulate an exception to test whether your error handler works? To test handling a normal request, you created a `SampleRequestHandler` that returned a `SampleRequest` (see listing 3.5). To test the handling of error conditions, you can create a `SampleExceptionHandler` that throws an exception instead, as shown in listing 3.11.

Listing 3.11   Request handler for exception cases

```
public class TestDefaultController
{
[...]
    private class SampleExceptionHandler implements RequestHandler
    {
```

```
    public Response process(Request request) throws Exception
    {
        throw new Exception("error processing request");
    }
  }
}
```

This leaves creating a test method that registers the handler and tries processing a request—for example, like the one shown in listing 3.12.

Listing 3.12   `testProcessRequestAnswersErrorResponse`, first iteration

```
public class TestDefaultController
{                                                             Create request
[...]                                                          and handler
  @Test                                                           objects
  public void testProcessRequestAnswersErrorResponse()
  {
    SampleRequest request = new SampleRequest();
    SampleExceptionHandler handler = new SampleExceptionHandler();
    controller.addHandler(request, handler);          ◁─── Reuse controller
    Response response = controller.processRequest(request);    object from
                                                               listing 3.8
    assertNotNull("Must not return a null response", response);
    assertEquals(ErrorResponse.class, response.getClass());
  }                                                           Test the
}                                                             outcome
```

If you ran this test through JUnit, it would fail! A quick look at the message tells you two things. First, you need to use a different name for the test request, because there's already a request named `Test` in the fixture. Second, you may need to add more exception handling to the class so that a `RuntimeException` isn't thrown in production.

As to the first item, you can try using the request object in the fixture instead of your own, but that fails with the same error. (Moral: Once you have a test, use it to explore alternative coding strategies.) You could consider changing the fixture. If you remove from the fixture the code that registers a default `SampleRequest` and `Sample-Handler`, you introduce duplication into the other test methods—not good. Better to fix the `SampleRequest` so it can be instantiated under different names. Listing 3.13 is the refactored result (changes from listings 3.11 and 3.12 are in bold).

Listing 3.13   `testProcessRequestExceptionHandler`, fixed and refactored

```
public class TestDefaultController
{
[...]
  private class SampleRequest implements Request
  {
    private static final String DEFAULT_NAME = "Test";        ❶
    private String name;
```

```
      public SampleRequest(String name)
      {                                                              ❷
          this.name = name;
      }

      public SampleRequest()
      {                                                              ❸
          this(DEFAULT_NAME);
      }
      public String getName()
      {
          return this.name;
      }
  }
[...]
  @Test
  public void testProcessRequestAnswersErrorResponse()
  {
      SampleRequest request = new SampleRequest("testError");           ◁—❹
      SampleExceptionHandler handler = new SampleExceptionHandler();
      controller.addHandler(request, handler);
      Response response = controller.processRequest(request);

      assertNotNull("Must not return a null response", response);
      assertEquals(ErrorResponse.class, response.getClass());
  }
}
```

Introduce a member field to hold the request's name and set it to the previous version's default ❶. Next, introduce a new constructor that lets you pass a name to the request ❷, to override the default. At ❸ you introduce an empty constructor, so existing calls will continue to work. Finally, call the new constructor instead ❹, so the exceptional request object doesn't conflict with the fixture.

If you added another test method that also used the exception handler, you might move its instantiation to the @Before fixture, to eliminate duplication.

JUnit best practices: let the test improve the code

Writing unit tests often helps you write better code. The reason is simple: a test case is a user of your code. It's only when using code that you find its shortcomings. Don't hesitate to listen to your tests and refactor your code so that it's easier to use. The practice of test-driven development relies on this principle. By writing the tests first, you develop your classes from the point of view of a user of your code. See chapter 5 for more about TDD.

Because the duplication hasn't happened yet, let's resist the urge to anticipate change and let the code stand (Extreme Programming's "No functionality is added early" rule).

3.3.2 *Testing for exceptions*

During testing, you found that addHandler throws an undocumented Runtime-Exception if you try to register a request with a duplicate name. (By *undocumented*, we mean that it doesn't appear in the signature.) Looking at the code, you see that get-Handler throws a RuntimeException if the request has not been registered.

Whether you *should* throw undocumented RuntimeException exceptions is a larger design issue. (You can make that a to-do for later study.) For now, let's write some tests that prove the methods will behave as designed.

Listing 3.14 shows two test methods that prove addHandler and getHandler will throw runtime exceptions when expected.

Listing 3.14   Testing methods that throw an exception

```
public class TestDefaultController
{
[...]
   @Test(expected=RuntimeException.class)                            ◀━①
   public void testGetHandlerNotDefined()                            ◀━②
   {
       SampleRequest request = new SampleRequest("testNotDefined");  ◀━③

       //The following line is supposed to throw a RuntimeException
       controller.getHandler(request);                               ◀━④
   }

   @Test(expected=RuntimeException.class)
   public void testAddRequestDuplicateName()
   {
       SampleRequest request = new SampleRequest();
       SampleHandler handler = new SampleHandler();                  ⑤

       // The following line is supposed to throw a RuntimeException
       controller.addHandler(request, handler);
   }
}
```

Annotate your method with the @Test annotation to denote that it's a test method ①. Because we're going to test an exceptional condition and we expect that the test method will produce an exception of some kind, we need also to specify what kind of an exception we expect to be raised. We do this by specifying the expected parameter of the @Test annotation. Give the test an obvious name ②. Because this test represents an exceptional case, append NotDefined to the standard testGetHandler prefix. Doing so keeps all the getHandler tests together and documents the purpose of each derivation.

At ③, you create the request object for the test, also giving it an obvious name. Pass the (unregistered) request to the default getHandler method ④. Because this request has no handler attached, a RuntimeException should be raised.

You follow the same pattern ❺ as the first method:

1 Insert a statement that should throw an exception.

2 Add the `expected` parameter to the `@Test` annotation to denote what kind of an exception you expect.

3 Proceed normally.

JUnit best practices: make exception tests easy to read

Normally the `expected` parameter in the `@Test` annotation clearly tells the developers that an exception of that type should be raised. But you can go even further. Besides naming your test methods in an obvious fashion to denote that this method is testing an exceptional condition, you can also place some comments to highlight the line of the code that produces the `expected` exception.

The controller class is by no means finished, but you have a respectable first iteration and a test suite proving that it works. Now you can commit the controller package, along with its tests, to the project's code repository and move on to the next task on your list.

JUnit best practices: let the test improve the code

An easy way to identify exceptional paths is to examine the different branches in the code you're testing. By *branches*, we mean the outcome of `if` clauses, `switch` statements, and `try-catch` blocks. When you start following these branches, sometimes you may find that testing each alternative is painful. If code is difficult to test, it's usually just as difficult to use. When testing indicates a poor design (called a *code smell*, http://c2.com/cgi/wiki?CodeSmell), you should stop and refactor the domain code. In the case of too many branches, the solution is usually to split a larger method into several smaller methods.[5] Alternatively, you may need to modify the class hierarchy to better represent the problem domain.[6] Other situations would call for different refactorings.

A test is your code's first "customer," and as the maxim goes, "the customer is always right."

The next task on our list is timeout testing.

3.4   *Timeout testing*

So far, we've tested our application for proper functionality—when supplied with the right data, not only does it behave in the expected manner, but it also produces

---

[5] Fowler, *Refactoring*, "Extract Method."
[6] More about writing testable code can be found in chapter 4.

the expected result. Now we want to look at another aspect of testing our application: scalability. How scalable is our `DefaultController` class?

We're going to write some tests and expect that they run below a given time barrier. To do this, JUnit provides us with another parameter to the `@Test` annotation called `timeout`. In this parameter, you can specify your time barrier in terms of milliseconds, and if the test takes more time to execute, JUnit will mark the test as failed. For example, let's look at the code in listing 3.15.

Listing 3.15   Timeout tests

```
[...]
public class TestDefaultController
{
[...]
    @Test(timeout=130)                                            ◀─❶
    public void testProcessMultipleRequestsTimeout()
    {
        Request request;
        Response response = new SampleResponse();                    ❷
        RequestHandler handler = new SampleHandler();             ◀─┐
                                                                   │
        for(int i=0; i< 99999; i++)                               ◀─┤
        {                                                          │ ❸
            request = new SampleRequest(String.valueOf(i));        │
            controller.addHandler(request, handler);              ◀─┘
            response = controller.processRequest();
            assertNotNull(response);                                 ❹
            assertNotSame(ErrorResponse.class, response.getClass());
        }
    }
}
```

We start by specifying the `timeout` parameter in milliseconds, which we expect to be our time barrier ❶. Then ❷ we declare the `Request`, `Response`, and `RequestHandler` objects we're going to use in the test. At ❸ we start a `for` loop to create 99,999 `SampleRequest` objects and add them along with a handler to the controller. After that, we invoke the `processRequest()` method of the controller and assert ❹ that we get a non-null `Response` object and also that the `Response` we get isn't an `ErrorResponse`.

You might consider the 130 milliseconds time barrier to be optimistic, and you're right. This time barrier was the lowest possible on my machine. But the execution time depends on the hardware it runs on (processor speed, memory available, and so on) and also on the software it runs on (mainly the operating system, but also the Java version, and so on). For different developers this test would fail or pass. Further, when adding more functionality in the `processRequest()` method, the time barrier we've chosen will become insufficient for our needs.

We get to the point where a few timeout tests might fail the whole build for some developers. Sometimes it's good to skip some of the tests. In JUnit 3.x we had to change the name of the test method (to not start with the `test` prefix). In version 4.x of JUnit, however, we have a nice way to skip a test. The only thing we need to do is annotate the @Test method with an @Ignore annotation. Look at the code in listing 3.16.

Listing 3.16   Ignoring a test method in JUnit 4.x

```
[...]
@Test(timeout=130)
@Ignore(value="Ignore for now until we decide a decent time-limit")
public void testProcessMultipleRequestTimeout()
{
    [...]
}
```
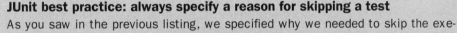

As you can see, the only thing we've added is the @Ignore annotation ❶ to the method. This annotation accepts the value parameter, which lets us insert a message as to why we skip the test.

> **JUnit best practice: always specify a reason for skipping a test**
>
> As you saw in the previous listing, we specified why we needed to skip the execution of the test. It's a good practice to do that. First, you notify your fellow developers why you want to skip the execution of the test, and second, you prove to yourself that you know what the test does, and you don't ignore it just because it fails.

As we mentioned, in JUnit 3 the only way to skip the execution of a test method was to rename it or comment it out. This gives you no information whatsoever as to how many tests were skipped. In JUnit 4, when you annotate methods with @Ignore, you get statistics that include how many tests JUnit skipped in addition to how many tests passed and failed.

3.5   *Introducing Hamcrest matchers*

The statistics show that people are easily infected with the unit testing philosophy. Once you get accustomed to writing tests and see how good it feels to have someone protecting you from possible mistakes, you'll wonder how it was possible to live without unit testing before.

As you write more and more unit tests and assertions, you'll inevitably encounter the problem that some of the assertions are big and hard to read. For example, consider the code in listing 3.17.

Listing 3.17   Cumbersome JUnit `assert` method

```
[...]
public class HamcrestTest {
    private List<String> values;
```

```
@Before                                          ←  ❶
   public void setUpList() {
            values = new ArrayList<String>();
       values.add("x");
       values.add("y");
       values.add("z");
   }

@Test                                            ←  ❷
public void testWithoutHamcrest() {
   assertTrue(values.contains("one")
            || values.contains("two")           ❸
            || values.contains("three"));
   }
}
```

What we do in this example is construct a simple JUnit test, exactly like the ones we've been constructing so far. We have a @Before fixture ❶, which will initialize some data for our test, and then we have a single test method ❷. In this test method you can see that we make a long and hard-to-read assertion ❸ (maybe it's not that hard to read, but it's definitely not obvious what it does at first glance). Our goal is to simplify the assertion we make in the test method.

To solve this problem we're going to present a library of matchers for building test expressions. Hamcrest (http://code.google.com/p/hamcrest/) is a library that contains a lot of helpful matcher objects (known also as constraints or predicates), ported in several languages (Java, C++, Objective-C, Python, and PHP). Note that Hamcrest isn't a testing framework itself, but rather it helps you declaratively specify simple matching rules. These matching rules can be used in many different situations, but they're particularly helpful for unit testing.

Listing 3.18 is the same test method, this time written using the Hamcrest library.

Listing 3.18 Hamcrest library to simplify our assert declarations

```
[...]
import static org.junit.Assert.assertThat;
import static org.hamcrest.CoreMatchers.anyOf;           ❶
import static org.hamcrest.CoreMatchers.equalTo;
import static org.junit.JUnitMatchers.hasItem;
[...]

   @Test
   public void testWithHamcrest() {
      assertThat(values, hasItem(anyOf(equalTo("one"), equalTo("two"),   ←  ❷
                  equalTo("three"))));
   }
[...]
```

Here we reuse listing 3.17 and add another test method to it. This time we import the needed matchers and the assertThat method ❶, and after that we construct a test method. In the test method we use one of the most powerful features of the matchers—they can nest within each other ❷. Whether you prefer assertion code

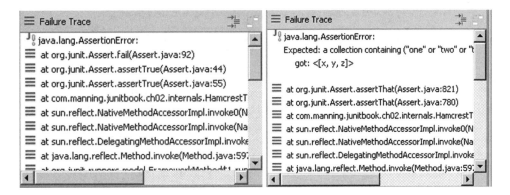

Figure 3.1 The screen on the left shows the stack trace from the execution of the test without using Hamcrest, and the one on the right shows the same thing using Hamcrest.

with or without Hamcrest matchers is a personal preference. What Hamcrest gives you that standard assertions don't provide is a human-readable description of an assertion failure.

If you followed the examples in the two previous listings, you've probably noticed that in both the cases we construct a List with the "x", "y", and "z" as elements in it. After that we assert the presence of either "one", "two", or "three", which means that the test, as written, will fail. Let's execute that test. The result from the execution is shown in figure 3.1.

As you can see from the two screens, the one on the right gives a lot more details, doesn't it? Table 3.2 lists some of the most commonly used Hamcrest matchers.

Table 3.2 Some of the most commonly used Hamcrest matchers

Core	Logical
anything	Matches absolutely anything. Useful in some cases where you want to make the assert statement more readable.
is	Is used only to improve the readability of your statements.
allOf	Checks to see if all contained matchers match (just like the && operator).
anyOf	Checks to see if any of the contained matchers match (like the || operator).
not	Traverses the meaning of the contained matchers (just like the ! operator in Java).
instanceOf, isCompatibleType	Match whether objects are of compatible type (are instances of one another).

Table 3.2   Some of the most commonly used Hamcrest matchers *(continued)*

Core	Logical
sameInstance	Tests object identity.
notNullValue, nullValue	Tests for null values (or non-null values).
hasProperty	Tests whether a JavaBean has a certain property.
hasEntry, hasKey, hasValue	Tests whether a given Map has a given entry, key, or value.
hasItem, hasItems	Tests a given collection for the presence of an item or items.
closeTo, greaterThan, greaterThanOrEqual, lessThan, lessThanOrEqual	Test whether given numbers are close to, greater than, greater than or equal to, less than, or less than or equal to a given value.
equalToIgnoringCase	Tests whether a given string equals another one, ignoring the case.
equalToIgnoringWhiteSpace	Tests whether a given string equals another one, by ignoring the white spaces.
containsString, endsWith, startWith	Test whether the given string contains, starts with, or ends with a certain string.

All of them seem straightforward to read and use, and remember that you can combine them with each other.

Finally, Hamcrest is extremely extensible. It's easy to write your own matchers that check a certain condition. The only thing you need to do is implement the Matcher interface and an appropriately named factory method. You can find more on how to write custom matchers in appendix D of this book, where we provide a complete overview of how to write your own matchers.

3.6   *Setting up a project for testing*

Because this chapter covers testing a realistic component, let's finish up by looking at how you set up the controller package as part of a larger project. In chapter 1, you kept all the Java domain code and test code in the same folder.

They were introductory tests on an example class, so this approach seemed simplest for everyone. In this chapter, you've begun to build real classes with real tests, as you would for one of your own projects. Accordingly, you've set up the source code repository as you would for a real project.

So far, you have only one test case. Mixing this in with the domain classes would not have been a big deal. But experience tells us that soon you'll have at least as many test classes as you have domain classes. Placing all of them in the same directory will begin to create file-management issues. It will become difficult to find the class you want to edit next.

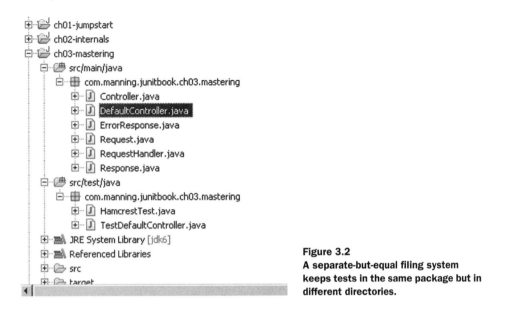

Figure 3.2
A separate-but-equal filing system keeps tests in the same package but in different directories.

Meanwhile, you want the test classes to be able to unit test protected methods, so you want to keep everything in the same Java package. The solution is to have one package in two folders. Figure 3.2 shows a snapshot of how the directory structure looks in a popular integrated development environment (IDE).

This is the code for the third chapter, so we used ch03-mastering for the top-level project directory name (see appendix C). Under the root directory, we created separate src/main/java and src/main/test folders. Under each of these, the package structure begins.

In this case, all of the code falls under the com.manning.junitbook.ch03.mastering package. The working interfaces and classes go under src/main/java; the classes we write for testing only go under the src/main/test directory.

Beyond eliminating clutter, a separate-but-equal directory structure yields several other benefits. Right now, the only test class has the convenient Test prefix. Later you may need other helper classes to create more sophisticated tests. These might include stubs, mock objects, and other helpers. It may not be convenient to prefix all of these classes with Test, and it becomes harder to tell the domain classes from the test classes.

Using a separate test folder also makes it easy to deliver a runtime JAR with only the domain classes. And it simplifies running all the tests automatically.

JUnit best practices: same package, separate directories

Put test classes in the same package as the class they test but in a parallel directory structure. You need tests in the same package to allow access to protected methods. You want tests in a separate directory to simplify file management and to clearly delineate test and domain classes.

3.7   *Summary*

As you saw in chapter 1, it isn't hard to jump in and begin writing JUnit tests for your applications. In this chapter, we created a test case for a simple but complete application controller. Rather than test a single component, the test case examined how several components worked together. We started with a bootstrap test case that could be used with any class. Then we added new tests to the test case one by one until all of the original components were under test. Because the assertions were getting more and more complicated, we found a way to simplify them by means of the Hamcrest matchers. We expect this package to grow, so we created a second source code directory for the test classes. Because the test and domain source directories are part of the same package, we can still test protected and package default members.

In the next chapter, we put unit testing in perspective with other types of tests that you need to perform on your applications. We also talk about how unit testing fits in the development lifecycle.

Software testing principles

A crash is when your competitor's program dies. When your program dies, it is an "idiosyncrasy." Frequently, crashes are followed with a message like "ID 02." "ID" is an abbreviation for idiosyncrasy and the number that follows indicates how many more months of testing the product should have had.

—Guy Kawasaki

This chapter covers

- The need for software tests
- Types of software tests
- Types of unit tests

Earlier chapters in this book took a pragmatic approach to designing and deploying unit tests. This chapter steps back and looks at the various types of software tests and the roles they play in the application's lifecycle.

Why would you need to know all this? Because unit testing isn't something you do out of the blue. In order to become a well-rounded developer, you need to understand unit tests compared to functional, integration, and other types of tests. Once you understand why unit tests are necessary, then you need to know how far to take your tests. Testing in and of itself isn't the goal.

4.1   *The need for unit tests*

The main goal of unit testing is to verify that your application works as expected and to catch bugs early. Although functional testing accomplishes the same goal, unit tests are extremely powerful and versatile and offer much more than verifying that the application works. Unit tests

- Allow greater test coverage than functional tests
- Increase team productivity
- Detect regressions and limit the need for debugging
- Give us the confidence to refactor and, in general, make changes
- Improve implementation
- Document expected behavior
- Enable code coverage and other metrics

4.1.1   *Allowing greater test coverage*

Unit tests are the first type of test any application should have. If you had to choose between writing unit tests and writing functional tests, you should choose the latter. In our experience, functional tests are able to cover about 70 percent of the application code. If you wish to go further and provide more test coverage, then you need to write unit tests.

Unit tests can easily simulate error conditions, which is extremely difficult to do with functional tests (it's impossible in some instances). Unit tests provide much more than just testing, as explained in the following sections.

4.1.2   *Increasing team productivity*

Imagine you're on a team working on a large application. Unit tests allow you to deliver quality code (tested code) without having to wait for all the other components to be ready. On the other hand, functional tests are more coarse grained and need the full application (or a good part of it) to be ready before you can test it.

4.1.3   *Detecting regressions and limiting debugging*

A passing unit test suite confirms your code works and gives you the confidence to modify your existing code, either for refactoring or to add and modify new features. As a developer, you'll get no better feeling than knowing that someone is watching your back and will warn you if you break something.

A suite of unit tests reduces the need to debug an application to find out why something is failing. Whereas a functional test tells you that a bug exists somewhere in the implementation of a use case, a unit test tells you that a specific method is failing for a specific reason. You no longer need to spend hours trying to find the problem.

4.1.4   *Refactoring with confidence*

Without unit tests, it's difficult to justify refactoring, because there's always a relatively high risk that you may break something. Why would you chance spending hours of debugging time (and putting the delivery at risk) only to improve the implementation or change a method name? Unit tests provide the safety net that gives you the confidence to refactor.

Let's move on with our implementation and try to improve it further.

JUnit best practice: refactor

Throughout the history of computer science, many great teachers have advocated iterative development. Niklaus Wirth, for example, who gave us the now-ancient languages Algol and Pascal, championed techniques like *stepwise refinement*.

For a time, these techniques seemed difficult to apply to larger, layered applications. Small changes can reverberate throughout a system. Project managers looked to up-front planning as a way to minimize change, but productivity remained low.

The rise of the xUnit framework has fueled the popularity of *agile methodologies* that once again advocate iterative development. Agile methodologists favor writing code in vertical slices to produce a working use case, as opposed to writing code in horizontal slices to provide services layer by layer.

When you design and write code for a single use case or functional chain, your design may be adequate for this feature, but it may not be adequate for the next feature. To retain a design across features, agile methodologies encourage *refactoring* to adapt the code base as needed.

But how do you ensure that refactoring, or improving the design of existing code, doesn't *break* the existing code? This answer is that unit tests tell you when and where code breaks. In short, unit tests give you the confidence to refactor.

The agile methodologies try to lower project risks by providing the ability to cope with change. They allow and embrace change by standardizing on quick iterations and applying principles like *YAGNI* (You Ain't Gonna Need It) and *The Simplest Thing That Could Possibly Work*. But the foundation on which all these principles rest is a solid bed of unit tests.

4.1.5   *Improving implementation*

Unit tests are a first-rate client of the code they test. They force the API under test to be flexible and to be unit testable in isolation. You usually have to refactor your code under test to make it unit testable (or use the TDD approach, which by definition spawns code that can be unit tested; see the next chapter).

It's important to monitor your unit tests as you create and modify them. If a unit test is too long and unwieldy, it usually means the code under test has a design smell and you should refactor it. You may also be testing too many features in one test method. If a test can't verify a feature in isolation, it usually means the code isn't flexible enough and you should refactor it. Modifying code to test it is normal.

4.1.6 *Documenting expected behavior*

Imagine you need to learn a new API. On one side is a 300-page document describing the API, and on the other are some examples showing how to use it. Which would you choose?

The power of examples is well known. Unit tests are exactly this: examples that show how to use the API. As such, they make excellent developer documentation. Because unit tests match the production code, they *must* always be up to date, unlike other forms of documentation,

Listing 4.1 illustrates how unit tests help provide documentation. The test-TransferWithoutEnoughFunds() method shows that an AccountInsufficientFunds-Exception is thrown when an account transfer is performed without enough funds.

> **Listing 4.1 Unit tests as automatic documentation**

```
import org.junit.Test;
public class TestAccount {
    [...]
    @Test(expected=AccountInsufficientFundsException.class)       ◄─❶
    public void tranferWithoutEnoughFunds() {
        long balance = 1000;                                       ◄─┐
        long amountToTransfer = 2000;                              ◄─┤ ❷
        Account credit = new Account(balance);                     ◄─┘
        Account debit = new Account();                             ❸
        credit.transfer(debit, amountToTransfer);                  ◄─❹
    }
}
```

At ❶ we declare the method as a test method by annotating it with @Test and declare that it must throw the AccountInsufficientFundsException (with the expected parameter). Next, we create a new account with a balance of 1000 ❷ and the amount to transfer ❸. Then we request a transfer of 2000 ❹. As expected, the transfer method throws an AccountInsufficientFundsException. If it didn't, JUnit would fail the test.

4.1.7 *Enabling code coverage and other metrics*

Unit tests tell you, at the push of a button, if everything still works. Furthermore, unit tests enable you to gather code-coverage metrics (see the next chapter) showing, statement by statement, what code the tests caused to execute and what code the tests did not touch. You can also use tools to track the progress of passing versus failing tests from one build to the next. You can also monitor performance and cause a test to fail if its performance has degraded compared to a previous build.

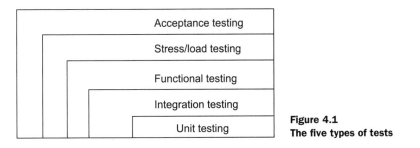

Figure 4.1
The five types of tests

4.2 *Test types*

Figure 4.1 outlines our five categories of software tests. There are other ways of categorizing software tests, but we find these most useful for the purposes of this book. Please note that this section is discussing *software tests in general*, not just the automated unit tests covered elsewhere in the book.

In figure 4.1, the outermost tests are broadest in scope. The innermost tests are narrowest in scope. As you move from the inner boxes to the outer boxes, the software tests get more functional and require that more of the application be present.

Next, we take a look at the general test types. Then, we focus on the types of unit tests.

4.2.1 *The four types of software tests*

We've mentioned that unit tests each focus on a distinct unit of work. What about testing different units of work combined into a workflow? Will the result of the workflow do what you expect? How well will the application work when many people are using it at once? Different kinds of tests answer these questions; we categorize them into four varieties:

- Integration tests
- Functional tests
- Stress and load tests
- Acceptance tests

Let's look at each of the test types, starting with the innermost after unit testing and working our way out.

INTEGRATION SOFTWARE TESTING

Individual unit tests are essential to quality control, but what happens when different units of work are combined into a workflow? Once you have the tests for a class up and running, the next step is to hook up the class with other methods and services. Examining the interaction between components, possibly running in their target environment, is the job of integration testing. Table 4.1 describes the various cases under which components interact.

Just as more traffic collisions occur at intersections, the points where objects interact are major contributors of bugs. Ideally, you should define integration tests before

Table 4.1   Testing how objects, services, and subsystems interact

Interaction	Test description
Objects	The test instantiates objects and calls methods on these objects.
Services	The test runs while a servlet or EJB container hosts the application, which may connect to a database or attach to any other external resource or device.
Subsystems	A layered application may have a front end to handle the presentation and a back end to execute the business logic. Tests can verify that a request passes through the front end and returns an appropriate response from the back end.

you write application code. Being able to code to the test dramatically increases a programmer's ability to write well-behaved objects.

FUNCTIONAL SOFTWARE TESTING

Functional tests examine the code at the boundary of its public API. In general, this corresponds to testing application use cases.

Developers often combine functional tests with integration tests. For example, a web application contains a secure web page that only authorized clients can access. If the client doesn't log in, then trying to access the page should result in a redirect to the login page. A functional unit test can examine this case by sending an HTTP request to the page to verify that a redirect (HTTP status code 302) response code comes back.

Depending on the application, you can use several types of functional tests, as shown in table 4.2.

Table 4.2   Testing frameworks, GUIs, and subsystems

Application type	Functional test description
The application uses a framework.	Functional testing within a framework focuses on testing the framework API (from the point of view of end users or service providers).
The application has a GUI.	Functional testing of a GUI verifies that all features can be accessed and provide expected results. The tests access the GUI directly, which may in turn call several other components or a back end.
The application is made up of subsystems.	A layered system tries to separate systems by roles. There may be a presentation subsystem, a business logic subsystem, and a data subsystem. Layering provides flexibility and the ability to access the back end with several different front ends. Each layer defines an API for other layers to use. Functional tests verify that the API contract is enforced.

STRESS TESTING

How well will the application perform when many people are using it at once? Most stress tests examine whether the application can process a large number of requests within a given period. Usually, you implement this with software like JMeter,[1] which automatically sends preprogrammed requests and tracks how quickly the application responds. These tests usually don't verify the validity of responses, which is why we have the other tests. Figure 4.2 shows a JMeter throughput graph.

You normally perform stress tests in a separate environment, typically more controlled than a development environment. The stress test environment should be as close as possible to the production environment; if not, the results won't be useful.

Let's prefix our quick look at performance testing with the often-quoted number-one rule of optimization: "Don't do it." The point is that before you spend valuable time optimizing code, you must have a specific problem that needs addressing. That said, let's proceed to performance testing.

Aside from stress tests, you can perform other types of performance tests within the development environment. A profiler can look for bottlenecks in an application, which the developer can try to optimize. You must be able to prove that a specific bottleneck exists and then prove that your changes remove the bottleneck.

Unit tests can also help you profile an application as a natural part of development. With JUnit, you can create a performance test to match your unit test. You

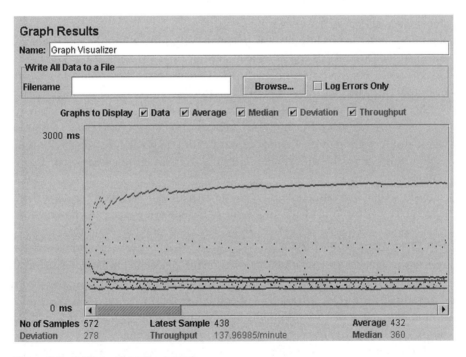

Figure 4.2   A JMeter throughput graph

---

[1] http://jakarta.apache.org/jmeter

might want to assert that a critical method never takes too long to execute. Listing 4.2 shows a timed test.

Listing 4.2   Enforcing a timeout on a method with JUnit

```
package com.manning.junitbook2;
import org.junit.Test;

public class ExampleTimedTest {

    @Test(timeout=5000)                    ◁━❶
    public void someVeryLongTest() {
        [...]
    }
}
```

The example uses the timeout parameter ❶ on the @Test annotation to set a timeout in milliseconds on the method. If this method takes more than 5,000 milliseconds to run, the test will fail.

An issue with this kind of test is that you may need to update the timeout value when the underlying hardware changes, the OS changes, or the test environment changes to or from running under virtualization.

ACCEPTANCE SOFTWARE TESTING

It's important that an application perform well, but the application must also meet the customer's needs. Acceptance tests are our final level of testing. The customer or a proxy usually conducts acceptance tests to ensure that the application has met whatever goals the customer or stakeholder defined.

Acceptance tests are a superset of all other tests. Usually they start as functional and performance tests, but they may include subjective criteria like "ease of use" and "look and feel." Sometimes, the acceptance suite may include a subset of the tests run by the developers, the difference being that this time the customer or QA team runs the tests.

For more about using acceptance tests with an agile software methodology, visit the wiki site regarding Ward Cunningham's *fit* framework (http://fit.c2.com/).

4.2.2 *The three types of unit tests*

Writing unit tests and production code takes place in tandem, ensuring that your application is under test from the beginning. We encourage this process and urge programmers to use their knowledge of implementation details to create and maintain unit tests that can be run automatically in builds. Using your knowledge of implementation details to write tests is also known as *white box testing*.

Your application should undergo other forms of testing, starting with unit tests and finishing with acceptance tests, as described in the previous section.

As a developer, you want to ensure that each of your subsystems works correctly. As you write code, your first tests will probably be logic unit tests. As you write more tests and more code, you'll add integration and functional unit tests. At any one time, you

Table 4.3   Three flavors of unit tests: logic, integration, and functional

Test type	Description
Logic unit test	A test that exercises code by focusing on a single method. You can control the boundaries of a given test method using mock objects or stubs (see part 2 of the book).
Integration unit test	A test that focuses on the interaction between components in their real environment (or part of the real environment). For example, code that accesses a database has tests that effectively call the database (see chapters 16 and 17).
Functional unit test	A test that extends the boundaries of integration unit testing to confirm a stimulus response. For example, a web application contains a secure web page that only authorized clients can access. If the client doesn't log in, then trying to access the page should result in a redirect to the login page. A functional unit test can examine this case by sending an HTTP request to the page to verify that a redirect (HTTP status code 302) response code comes back.

may be working on a logic unit test, an integration unit test, or a functional unit test. Table 4.3 summarizes these unit test types.

Figure 4.3 illustrates how these three flavors of unit tests interact.

The sliders define the boundaries between the types of unit tests. You need all three types of tests to ensure your code works. Using this type of testing will increase your test code coverage, which will increase your confidence in making changes to the existing code base while minimizing the risk of introducing regression bugs.

Strictly speaking, functional unit tests aren't pure unit tests, but neither are they pure functional tests. They're more dependent on an external environment than pure unit tests are, but they don't test a complete workflow, as expected by pure

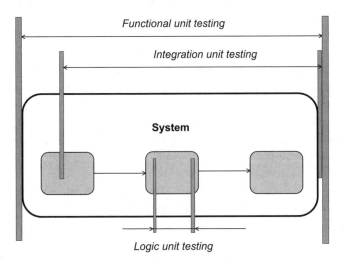

**Figure 4.3
Interaction among the three
unit test types: functional,
integration, and logic**

functional tests. We put functional unit tests in our scope because they're often useful as part of the battery of tests run in development.

A typical example is the `StrutsTestCase` framework (http://strutstestcase.source-forge.net/), which provides functional unit testing of the runtime Struts configuration. These tests tell a developer that the controller is invoking the appropriate software action and forwarding to the expected presentation page, but they don't confirm that the page is present and renders correctly.

Having examined the various types of unit tests, we now have a complete picture of application testing. We develop with confidence because we're creating tests as we go, and we're running existing tests as we go to find regression bugs. When a test fails, we know exactly what failed and where, and we can then focus on fixing each problem directly.

4.3 *Black box versus white box testing*

Before we close this chapter, we focus on one other categorization of software tests: black box and white box testing. This categorization is intuitive and easy to grasp, but developers often forget about it. We start by exploring black box testing, with a definition.

> **DEFINITION**   *Black box test*—A black box test has no knowledge of the internal state or behavior of the system. The test relies solely on the external system interface to verify its correctness.

As the name of this methodology suggests, we treat the system as a black box; imagine it with buttons and LEDs. We don't know what's inside or how the system operates. All we know is that by providing correct input, the system produces the desired output. All we need to know in order to test the system properly is the system's *functional specification*. The early stages of a project typically produce this kind of specification, which means we can start testing early. Anyone can take part in testing the system—a QA engineer, a developer, or even a customer.

The simplest form of black box testing would try to mimic manually actions on the user interface. Another, more sophisticated approach would be to use a tool for this task, such as HTTPUnit, HTMLUnit, or Selenium. We discuss most of these tools in the last part of the book.

At the other end of the spectrum is white box testing, sometimes called glass box testing. In contrast to black box testing, we use detailed knowledge of the implementation to create tests and drive the testing process. Not only is knowledge of a component's implementation required, but also of how it interacts with other components. For these reasons, the implementers are the best candidates to create white box tests.

Which one of the two approaches should you use? Unfortunately, there's no correct answer, and we suggest that you use both approaches. In some situations, you'll need user-centric tests, and in others, you'll need to test the implementation details of the system. Next, we present pros and cons for both approaches.

USER-CENTRIC APPROACH

We know that there is tremendous value in customer feedback, and one of our goals from Extreme Programming is to "release early and release often." But we're unlikely to get useful feedback if we just tell the customer, "Here it is. Let me know what you think." It's far better to get the customer involved by providing a manual test script to run through. By making the customer think about the application, they can also clarify what the system should do.

TESTING DIFFICULTIES

Black box tests are more difficult to write and run[2] because they usually deal with a graphical front end, whether a web browser or desktop application. Another issue is that a valid result on the screen doesn't always mean the application is correct. White box tests are usually easier to write and run, but the developers must implement them.

TEST COVERAGE

White box testing provides better test coverage than black box testing. On the other hand, black box tests can bring more value than white box tests. We focus on test coverage in the next chapter.

Although these test distinctions can seem academic, recall that divide and conquer doesn't have to apply only to writing production software; it can also apply to testing. We encourage you to use these different types of tests to provide the best code coverage possible, thereby giving you the confidence to refactor and evolve your applications.

4.4   Summary

The pace of change is increasing. Product release cycles are getting shorter, and we need to react to change quickly. In addition, the development process is shifting—development as the art of writing code isn't enough. Development must be the art of writing complete and *tested* solutions.

To accommodate rapid change, we must break with the waterfall model where testing follows development. Late-stage testing doesn't scale when change and swiftness are paramount.

When it comes to unit testing an application, you can use several types of unit tests: logic, integration, and functional unit tests. All are useful during development and complement each other. They also complement the other software tests that are performed by quality assurance personnel and by the customer.

In the next chapter, we continue to explore the world of testing. We present best practices, like measuring test coverage, writing testable code, and practicing test-driven development (TDD).

---

[2] Black box testing is getting easier with tools like Selenium and HtmlUnit, which we describe in chapter 12.

Part 2

Different testing strategies

This part of the book reveals the various strategies and techniques used in testing. Here we take a more scientific and theoretical approach to explain the differences. We describe incorporating mock objects, or stubs, and dive into the details of in-container testing.

The first chapter of this part describes different techniques for improving the quality of your tests—measuring test coverage, practicing test-driven development, and writing testable code.

The sixth chapter of the book is dedicated to stubs. We look into another solution to isolate the environment and make our tests seamless.

The seventh chapter starts by explaining what mock objects are. We give a thorough overview of how to construct and use mock objects. We also give a real-world example showing not only where mock objects fit best but also how to benefit by integrating them with JUnit tests.

The last chapter describes a totally different technique: executing tests inside a container. This solution is different from the previous ones, and just like them it has its pros and cons. We start by presenting an overview of what *in-container* means and how it's achieved, and at the end of the chapter we compare the mocks/stubs approach to the in-container approach. Along with the theoretical benefits, this chapter serves as a good starting point to understanding chapters 13 and 16.

Test coverage and development 5

I don't think anybody tests enough of anything.

—James Gosling

This chapter covers
- Measuring test coverage
- Writing testable code
- Practicing test-driven development

In the previous chapters, we introduced testing software and started exploring testing with JUnit. We also presented various test methodologies.

Now that we're writing test cases, it's time to measure how good these tests are by using a *test coverage* tool to report what code is exercised by the tests and what code is not. We also discuss how to write code that's easy to test. We finish by looking at test-driven development (TDD).

5.1 Measuring test coverage

Writing unit tests gives you the confidence to change and refactor an application. As you make changes, you run tests, which gives you immediate feedback on new features under test and whether your changes break existing tests. The issue is that these changes may still break existing untested functionality.

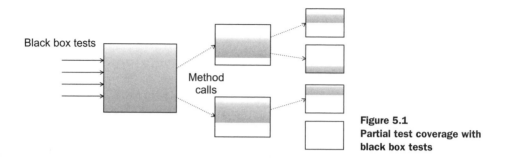

Figure 5.1
Partial test coverage with black box tests

In order to resolve this issue, we need to know precisely what code runs when you or the build invokes tests. Ideally, our tests should cover 100 percent of our application code. Let's look in more detail at what benefits test coverage provides.

5.1.1   Introduction to test coverage

Using black box testing, we can create tests that cover the public API of an application. Because we're using documentation as our guide and not knowledge of the implementation, we don't create tests, for example, that use special parameter values to exercise special conditions in the code.

One metric of test coverage would be to track which methods the tests call. This doesn't tell you whether the tests are complete, but it does tell you if you have a test for a method. Figure 5.1 shows the partial test coverage typically achieved using only black box testing.

You *can* write a unit test with intimate knowledge of a method's implementation. If a method contains a conditional branch, you can write two unit tests, one for each branch. Because you need to see into the method to create such a test, this falls under white box testing. Figure 5.2 shows 100 percent test coverage using white box testing.

You can achieve higher test coverage using white box unit tests because you have access to more methods and because you can control both the inputs to each method and the behavior of secondary objects (using stubs or mock objects, as you'll see in later chapters). Because you can write white box unit tests against protected, package-private, and public methods, you get more code coverage.

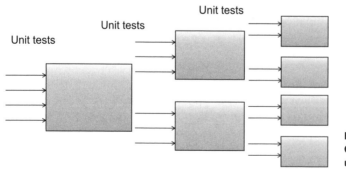

Figure 5.2
Complete test coverage using white box tests

5.1.2 *Introduction to Cobertura*

Cobertura is a code coverage tool that integrates with JUnit. Cobertura provides the following features:

- Is free and open source
- Integrates with Ant and Maven; also callable from a command line
- Generates reports in HTML or XML
- Sorts the HTML results by various criteria
- Computes the percentage of code lines and code branches covered for each class, package, and the entire project

In order to measure test coverage, Cobertura creates *instrumented* copies of class files you specify. This process, called byte-code instrumentation, adds byte codes to *existing* compiled code to enable logging of what executed byte codes. Instead of, or in addition to, running the normally compiled unit tests, you run the compiled and instrumented tests. Let's now get started with Cobertura.

Download Cobertura from http://cobertura.sourceforge.net/ and extract the archive. Define a COBERTURA_HOME environment variable and add it to the execution PATH environment variable. The COBERTURA_HOME folder contains several command-line scripts we use in this section. Although our examples drive Cobertura from the command line, note that the program also provides Ant tasks.

We start by compiling our test cases with the following command:

```
>javac -cp junit-4.6.jar -d uninstrumented src\*.java
```

We instrument our classes with the following command:

```
>cobertura-instrument --destination instrumented
    uninstrumented\Calculator.class
```

The --destination parameter specifies where to place the instrumented classes. The application argument specifies the path to the precompiled classes, in our case, uninstrumented\Calculator.class.

Next, we run the unit tests against the instrumented code. Cobertura integrates with JUnit and Ant, but it's also tool agnostic and can work with any other testing framework. To run your tests, you need to place two resources on your CLASSPATH:

- Cobertura.jar
- The directory containing the instrumented classes before the directory containing the uninstrumented classes. You can run the tests from the command line or Ant, with identical results. For example, the following runs tests from the command line:

```
>java -cp junit-4.6.jar;$COBERTURA_HOME\
    ➥cobertura.jar;instrumented;uninstrumented;
        -Dnet.sourceforge.cobertura.datafile=
        cobertura.ser org.junit.runner.JUnitCore TestCalculator
```

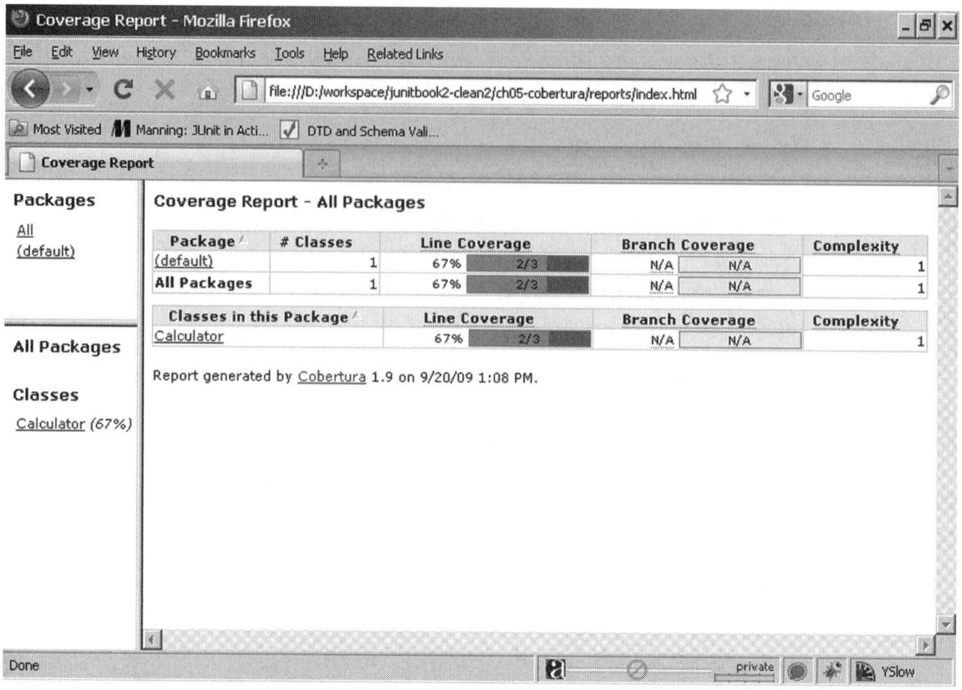

Figure 5.3   A Cobertura code-coverage report

The `net.sourceforge.cobertura.datafile` property points to a file where Cobertura will store the code coverage results. If you don't specify this property, Cobertura will create a file called cobertura.ser in the current directory.

5.1.3   Generating test coverage reports

After you run these scripts, you'll get your instrumented classes in the instrumented folder and a code coverage file for a given test run. To produce an HTML report, use the `cobertura-report` script.

```
>cobertura-report --format html --datafile cobertura.ser
    --destination reports src
```

The `destination` parameter specifies the output directory for the report. The reports folder contains the HTML report shown in figure 5.3.

Cobertura shows code coverage not only by package but also by class. You can select any of the classes in the report to see the extent to which that particular class was tested. Figure 5.4 shows the report for one class.

The report shows good test coverage of the `squareRoot` method in the `Calculator` class. The numbers next to the line number show that the tests called the method 10 times, covering all lines in the method (there's only one line in this case.) On the other hand, we have zero executions of the `sum` method. Overall, we have 67 percent code coverage of the `Calculator` class, indicating that developers need to create more tests.

Depending on how you compose your application, it might not be possible to reach all code in the test environment. You may consider refactoring your code to allow for better coverage in combination with the use of mock objects or stubs.[1] Whether you choose this approach to reach 100 percent code coverage is a policy decision your team can review through the development cycle.

5.1.4 *Combining black box and white box testing*

If we can achieve higher test coverage with white box unit tests, and we can generate reports to prove it, do we need to bother with black box tests?

If you think about the differences between figure 5.1 and figure 5.2, there's more going on than how many methods the tests execute. The black box tests in figure 5.1 are verifying interactions between objects. The white box unit tests in figure 5.2, by definition, don't test object interactions. If a white box test does interact with another object, that object is usually a stub or a mock object designed to produce specific test behavior (see chapters 6 and 7).

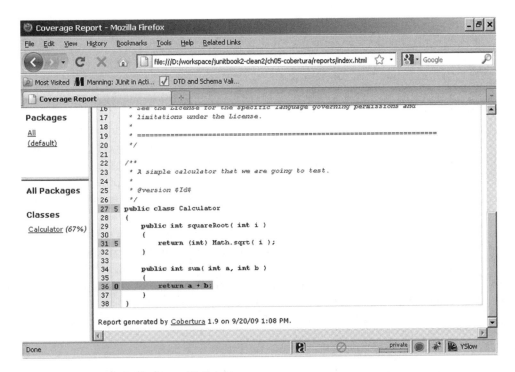

Figure 5.4   Class code coverage with Cobertura

---

[1] You'll learn about stubs in the next chapter and about mocks in chapter 7.

If you want to thoroughly test your application, including how runtime objects interact with each other, you need to use black box integration tests as well as white box tests.

We've completed our overview of code coverage and Cobertura to see precisely which parts of an application unit tests exercise. Let's now move on to how different implementation techniques affect how to write tests for an application.

5.2 Writing testable code

This chapter is dedicated to best practices in software testing. We introduced JUnit (in chapters 1, 2, and 3) and discussed different types of tests (in chapter 4). We're now ready to get to the next level: writing code that's easy to test. Sometimes writing a single test case is easy, and sometimes it isn't. It all depends on the level of complexity of the application. A best practice avoids complexity as much as possible; code should be readable and testable. In this section, we discuss some best practices to improve your architecture and code. Remember that it's always easier to write easily testable code than it is to refactor existing code to make it easily testable.

5.2.1 Public APIs are contracts

One of the principles in providing backward-compatible software states says that you "never change the signature of a public method." An application code review will show that most calls are made to public APIs. If you change the signature of a public method, then you need to change every call site in the application and unit tests. Even with refactoring wizards in tools like Eclipse, you must always perform this task with care.

In the open source world, and for any API made public by a commercial product, life can get even more complicated—many people use your code, and you should be careful of the changes you make to stay backward compatible.

Public methods become the articulation points of an application among components, open source projects, and commercial products that usually don't even know of one another's existence.

Imagine a public method that takes a *distance* as a `double` parameter and a black box test to verify a computation. At some point, the meaning of the parameter changes from *miles* to *kilometers*. Your code still compiles, but the runtime breaks. Without a unit test to fail and tell you what's wrong, you may spend a lot of time debugging and talking to angry customers. This example illustrates that you must test all public methods. For nonpublic methods, you need to go to a deeper level and use white box tests.

5.2.2 Reduce dependencies

Remember that unit tests verify your code in isolation. Your unit tests should instantiate the class you want to test, use it, and assert its correctness. Your test cases should be simple. What happens when your class instantiates, directly or indirectly, a new set of objects? Your class now depends on these classes. In order to write testable code, you should reduce dependencies as much as possible. If your classes depend on many other classes that need to be instantiated and set up with some state, then your tests will be complicated—you may need to use some complicated mock-objects solution (see chapter 6 for mock objects).

A solution to reducing dependencies is to separate your code between methods that instantiate new objects (factories) and methods that provide your application logic. Consider listing 5.1.

Listing 5.1 Reduce dependencies

```
class Vehicle {

    Driver d = new Driver();
    boolean hasDriver = true;

    private void setHasDriver(boolean hasDriver) {
        this.hasDriver = hasDriver;
    }
}
```

Every time we instantiate the Vehicle object, we also instantiate the Driver object. We've mixed the concepts. The solution would be to have the Driver *interface* passed to the Vehicle class, as in listing 5.2.

Listing 5.2 Pass the `Driver` to the `Vehicle`

```
class Vehicle {

    Driver d;
    boolean hasDriver = true;

    Vehicle(Driver d) {
        this.d = d;
    }

    private void setHasDriver(boolean hasDriver) {
        this.hasDriver = hasDriver;
    }
}
```

This allows us to produce a *mock* Driver object (see chapter 6) and pass it to the Vehicle class on instantiation. Furthermore, we can *mock* any other type of Driver implementation—JuniorDriver, SeniorDriver, and so on—and pass it to the Vehicle class.

5.2.3 *Create simple constructors*

By striving for better test coverage, we add more and more test cases. In each of these test cases, we do the following:

- Instantiate the class to test
- Set the class into a particular state
- Assert the final state of the class

By doing work in the constructor (other than populating instance variables), we mix the first and second points in our list. It's a bad practice not only from architectural point of view (we'll do the same work every time we instantiate our class) but also because we always get our class in a predefined state. This code is hard to maintain and test.

5.2.4 *Follow the Principle of Least Knowledge*

The Law of Demeter, or Principle of Least Knowledge, is a design guideline that states that one class should know only as much as it needs to know. For example, consider listing 5.3:

Listing 5.3 Law of Demeter violation

```
class Car {
    private Driver driver;

    Car(Context context) {
        this.driver = context.getDriver();
    }
}
```

In this example, we pass to the `Car` constructor a `Context` object. This is a violation of the Law of Demeter, because the `Car` class needs to know that the `Context` object has a `getDriver` method. If we want to test this constructor, we need to get hold of a valid `Context` object before calling the constructor. If the `Context` object has a lot of variables and methods, we could be forced to use mock objects (see chapter 7) to simulate the context.

The proper solution is to apply the Principle of Least Knowledge and pass references to methods and constructors only when we need to do so. In our example, we should pass the `Driver` to the `Car` constructor, as in the following:

```
Car(Driver driver) {
    this.driver = driver;
}
```

That illustrates a key concept: *Require objects, don't search for objects, and ask only for objects that your application requires.*

5.2.5 *Avoid hidden dependencies and global state*

Be careful with global state because global state makes it possible for many clients to share the global object. This can have unintended consequences if the global object is not coded for shared access or if clients expect exclusive access to the global object.

For instance, consider the example in listing 5.4.

Listing 5.4 Global state in action

```
public void reserve() {
    DBManager manager = new DBManager();
```

```
    manager.initDatabase();
    Reservation r = new Reservation();
    r.reserve();
}
```

The `DBManager` implies a global state. Without instantiating the database first, you won't be able to make a reservation. Internally, the `Reservation` uses the `DBManager` to access the database. Unless documented, the `Reservation` class hides its dependency on the database manager from the programmer because the API doesn't give us a clue. Listing 5.5 provides a better implementation.

Listing 5.5   Avoiding global state

```
public void reserve() {
    DBManager manager = new DBManager();
    manager.initDatabase();
    Reservation r = new Reservation (manager);
    r.reserve();
}
```

In this example, the `Reservation` object is constructed with a given database manager. Strictly speaking, the `Reservation` object should be able to function only if it has been configured with a database manager.

Avoid global state; when you provide access to a global object, you share not only that object but also any object to which it refers.

As Miško Hevery[2] says in his blog:

> *You can live in a society where everyone (every class) declares who their friends (collaborators) are. If I know that Joe knows Mary but neither Mary nor Joe knows Tim, then it is safe for me to assume that if I give some information to Joe he may give it to Mary, but under no circumstances will Tim get hold of it. Now, imagine that everyone (every class) declares some of their friends (collaborators), but other friends (collaborators which are singletons) are kept secret. Now you are left wondering how in the world did Tim got hold of the information you gave to Joe.*
>
> *Here is the interesting part. If you are the person who built the relationships (code) originally, you know the true dependencies, but anyone who comes after you is baffled, since the friends which are declared are not the sole friends of objects, and information flows in some secret paths which are not clear to you. You live in a society full of liars.*

5.2.6   Singletons pros and cons

Although we just discouraged you from using global state, the Singleton[3] is a useful design pattern that ensures a class has only one instance. You can extend the concept

---

[2] http://misko.hevery.com/about/

[3] You can find more on the Singleton pattern in *Design Patterns: Elements of Reusable Object-Oriented Software*, by Erich Gamma, Richard Helm, Ralph Johnson, and John M. Vlissides.

of singleton to provide several instances of a class. Most often, the implementation defines a private constructor and a static variable. For example, the simplest singleton implementation is

```
public class Singleton {
  public static final Singleton INSTANCE = new Singleton();
  private  Singleton() {}
}
```

Here, you access the singleton with the static final field INSTANCE. Alternatively, the class can use lazy initialization to create the instance, for example:

```
public class Singleton {
  private  static Singleton INSTANCE;
  private  Singleton() {}
  public static Singleton getInstance() {
     if(INSTANCE == null) {
        INSTANCE = new Singleton();
     }
     return INSTANCE;
  }
}
```

The Singleton design pattern needs to make sure the object is instantiated only once. To ensure this, we hide the constructor by making it private. As with a private method, you can't call and test a private constructor explicitly. You have a choice: you can rely on code coverage to check that all private methods are tested, or you change access modifiers to open the class to explicit testing of those methods.

The obvious drawback of a singleton is that it introduces global state into your application. The INSTANCE field in the first example is a global variable. Use this design pattern with care.

5.2.7   *Favor generic methods*

Static methods, like factory methods, are useful, but large groups of utility static methods can introduce issues of their own. Recall that unit testing is testing in isolation. In order to achieve isolation you need some articulation points in your code, where you can easily substitute your code with the test code. These points use polymorphism. With polymorphism (the ability of one object to appear as another object) the method you're calling isn't determined at compile time. You can easily use polymorphism to substitute application code with the test code to force certain code patterns to be tested.

The opposite situation occurs when you use nothing but static methods. Then you practice procedural programming, and all of your method calls are determined at compile time. You no longer have articulation points that you can substitute.

Sometimes the harm of static methods to your test isn't big, especially when you choose some method that ends the execution graph, like Math.sqrt(). On the other hand, you can choose a method that lies in the heart of your application logic. In that case, every method that gets executed inside that static method becomes hard to test.

Static code and the inability to use polymorphism in your application affect your application and tests equally. No polymorphism means no code reuse for both your application and your tests. This can lead to code duplication in the application and tests, something we try to avoid.

5.2.8 *Favor composition over inheritance*

Many people choose inheritance as a code-reuse mechanism. We think composition can be easier to test. At runtime, code can't change an inheritance hierarchy, but we can compose objects differently. We strive to make our code as flexible as possible at runtime. This way we can be sure that it's easy to switch from one state of our objects to another, and that makes our code easily testable.

For example, because we consider it bad practice for all servlets to extend `AuthenticatedServlet`, we always need to instantiate the credentials for a test user in our tests. On the other hand, we could add a `Credentials` instance variable to those servlets that need it and make our classes easier to test by instantiating the `Credentials` variable only when we need it.

5.2.9 *Favor polymorphism over conditionals*

As mentioned previously, we do only the following in our tests:

- Instantiate the class to test
- Set the class into a particular state
- Assert the final state of the class

Difficulties may arise at any of these points. For example, it could be difficult to instantiate our class if it's too complex.

One of the main ways to decrease complexity is to try to avoid long `switch` and `if` statements. Consider listing 5.6.

> **Listing 5.6 Example of a bad design with conditionals**

```
public class DocumentPrinter {
  [...]
    public void printDocument() {
        switch (document.getDocumentType()) {
            case Documents.WORD_DOCUMENT:
                printWORDDocument();
                break;
            case Documents.PDF_DOCUMENT:
                printPDFDocument();
                break;
            case Documents.TEXT_DOCUMENT:
                printTextDocument();
                break;
```

```
        default:
            printBinaryDocument();
            break;
        }
    }
  [...]
}
```

This implementation is awful for several reasons. This code is hard to test and maintain. Every time we want to add a new document type, we add additional case clauses. If that happens often in your code, you'll have to change it in every place that it occurs.

Every time you see a long conditional statement, think of polymorphism. Polymorphism is a natural object-oriented way to avoid long conditionals, by breaking a class into several smaller classes. Several smaller components are easier to test than one large complex component.

In the given example, we can avoid the conditional by creating different document types like WordDocument, PDFDocument, and XMLDocument, each one implementing a printDocument() method. This will decrease the complexity of our code and will make it easier to read.

5.3   *Test-driven development*

In chapter 3, we designed an application controller and quickly wrote some tests to validate your design. As we wrote the tests, the tests helped improve the initial design. As you write more unit tests, positive reinforcement encourages you to write them earlier. As you design and implement, it becomes natural to wonder about how you'll test a class. Following this methodology, more developers are making the leap from test-friendly designs to test-driven development.

> **DEFINITION**   *Test-driven development* (TDD) is a programming practice that instructs developers to write new code only if an automated test has failed *and* to eliminate duplication. The goal of TDD is "clean code that works."

Let's move on and see how we can adapt our development lifecycle to enforce the test-driven development approach.

5.3.1   *Adapting the development cycle*

When you develop code, you design an application programming interface (API) and then implement the behavior promised by the interface. When you unit test code, you verify the promised behavior through a method's API. The test is a client of the method's API, just as your domain code is a client of the method's API.

The conventional development cycle goes something like this: code, *test*, (repeat), commit. Developers practicing TDD make a seemingly slight but surprisingly effective adjustment: *test*, code, (repeat), commit. (More on this later.) The test drives the design and becomes the method's first client.

Listing 5.7 illustrates how unit tests can help design the implementation. The `get-BalanceOk` method shows that the `getBalance` method of `Account` returns the account balance as a `long` and that this balance can be set in the `Account` constructor. At this point, the implementation of `Account` is purely hypothetical, but writing the unit tests allows you to focus on the design of the code. As soon as you implement the class, you can run the test to prove that the implementation works. If the test fails, then you can continue working on the implementation until it passes the test. When the test passes, you know that your code fulfills the contract.

Listing 5.7   Unit tests as a design guide

```java
import org.junit.Test;
import static org.junit.Assert.assertEquals;

public class TestAccount {
   @Test
   public void getBalanceOk () {
      long balance = 1000;
      Account account = new Account(balance);
      long result = account.getBalance();

      assertEquals(balance, result);
   }
}
```

When you use the test as the method's first client, it becomes easier to focus purely on the API. Writing the tests first provides the following:

- Means to design the code
- Documentation as to how the code works
- Unit tests for the code

Someone new to the project can understand the system by studying the functional test suite (high-level UML diagrams also help). To analyze a specific portion of the application in detail, they can drill down into individual unit tests.

5.3.2   *The TDD two-step*

Earlier, we said that TDD tweaks the development cycle to go something like test, code, (repeat), and ship. The problem with this chant is that it leaves out a key step. It should go more like this: test, code, *refactor*, (repeat), and ship. The core tenets of TDD are to

1 Write a failing automatic test before writing new code
2 Eliminate duplication

Eliminating duplication ensures that you write code that's not only testable but also *maintainable*. When you eliminate duplication, you tend to increase cohesion and decrease dependency. These are hallmarks of code that's easier to maintain over time.

Other coding practices have encouraged us to write maintainable code by anticipating change. In contrast, TDD encourages us to write maintainable code *by* eliminating duplication. Developers following this practice have found that test-backed, well-factored code is, by its very nature, easy and safe to change. TDD gives us the confidence to solve today's problems today and tomorrow's problems tomorrow. Carpe diem!

> **JUnit best practice: write failing tests first**
>
> If you take the TDD development pattern to heart, an interesting thing happens: before you can write any code, *you must write a test that fails.* Why does it fail? *Because you have not written the code to make it succeed.*
>
> Faced with this situation, most of us begin by writing a simple implementation to let the test pass. Now that the test succeeds, you could stop and move on to the next problem. Being a professional, you'd take a few minutes to refactor the implementation to remove redundancy, clarify intent, and optimize the investment in the new code. But as long as the test succeeds, technically you've finished.
>
> The end game? If you always test first, you'll never write a line of new code without a failing test.

Now that we've described the cycle—test, code, *refactor,* (repeat), and ship—of test-driven development, we show next how testing fits into development overall.

5.4   *Testing in the development cycle*

Testing occurs at different places and times during the development cycle. We first introduce a development lifecycle and then use it as a base for deciding what types of tests are executed when. Figure 5.5 shows a typical development cycle we've used effectively in both small and large teams.

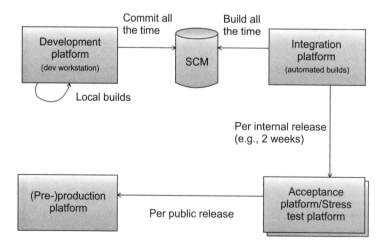

Figure 5.5   A typical application development lifecycle using the continuous integration principle

We divide the lifecycle into the following platforms:

- *Development platform*—This is where coding happens, on developers' workstations. One important rule is usually to commit (aka check in), up to several times per day, to your Source Control Management (SCM) system (SVN, CVS, ClearCase, and the like). Once you commit, others can begin using your work. But it's important to commit only something that "works." To ensure this, you run a local build with Ant or Maven. You can also watch the results of an automated build based on the latest changes to the SCM repository (see chapters 9, 10, and 11.)

- *Integration platform*—This platform builds the application from its various components (which may have been developed by different teams) and ensures that they all work together. This step is extremely valuable, because problems are often discovered here. It's so valuable that we want to automate it. It's then called continuous integration (see http://www.martinfowler.com/articles/continuousIntegration.html) and can be achieved by automatically building the application as part of the build process (more on that in chapter 11 and later).

- *Acceptance platform/stress test platform*—Depending on the resources available to your project, this can be one or two platforms. The stress test platform exercises the application under load and verifies that it scales correctly (with respect to size and response time). The acceptance platform is where the project's customers accept (sign off on) the system. It's highly recommended that the system be deployed on the acceptance platform as often as possible in order to get user feedback.

- *(Pre-)production platform*—The preproduction platform is the last staging area before production. It's optional, and small or noncritical projects can do without it.

We now show how testing fits in the development cycle. Figure 5.6 highlights the different types of tests you can perform on each platform.

- On the *development platform*, you execute logic unit tests (tests that can be executed in isolation from the environment). These tests execute quickly, and you usually execute them from your IDE to verify that any change you've brought to the code has not broken anything. They're also executed by your automated build before you commit the code to your SCM. You could also execute integration unit tests, but they often take much longer, because they need some part of the environment to be set up (database, application server, and the like). In practice, you'd execute only a subset of all integration unit tests, including any new integration unit tests you've written.

- The *integration platform* usually runs the build process automatically to package and deploy the application and then executes unit and functional tests.

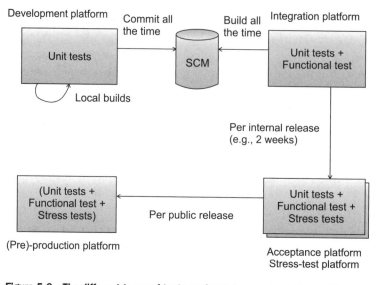

Figure 5.6   The different types of tests performed on each platform of the development cycle

Usually, only a subset of all functional tests is run on the integration platform, because compared to the target production platform, it's a simple platform that lack elements (for example, it may be missing a connection to an external system being accessed). All types of unit tests are executed on the integration platform (logic unit tests, integration unit tests, and functional unit tests). Time is less important, and the whole build can take several hours with no impact on development.

- On the *acceptance platform/stress test platform,* you reexecute the same tests executed by the integration platform; in addition, you run stress tests (performance and load tests). The acceptance platform is extremely close to the production platform, and more functional tests can also be executed.

- It's always a good habit to try to run on the (*pre-*)*production platform* the tests you ran on the acceptance platform. Doing so acts as a sanity check to verify that everything is set up correctly.

Human beings are strange creatures, always tending to neglect details. In a perfect world, we'd have all four platforms to run our tests on. In the real world, however, most of the software companies try to skip some of the platforms we listed—or the concept of testing as a whole. As a developer who bought this book, you already made the right decision: more tests, less debugging!

Now, again, it's up to you. Are you going to strive for perfection, stick to everything that you learned so far, and let your code benefit from that?

> ### JUnit best practice: continuous regression testing
>
> Most tests are written for the here and now. You write a new feature, and you write a new test. You see whether the feature plays well with others and whether the users like it. If everyone is happy, you can lock the feature and move on to the next item on your list. Most software is written in a progressive fashion: you add one feature and then another.
>
> Most often, each new feature is built over a path paved by existing features. If an existing method can service a new feature, you reuse the method and save the cost of writing a new one. It's never quite that easy. Sometimes you need to change an existing method to make it work with a new feature. When this happens, you need to confirm that all the old features still work with the amended method.
>
> A strong benefit of JUnit is that the test cases are easy to automate. When a change is made to a method, you can run the test for that method. If that test passes, then you can run the rest. If any fail, you can change the code (or the tests) until all tests pass again.
>
> Using old tests to guard against new changes is a form of regression testing. Any kind of test can be used as a regression test, but running unit tests after every change is your first, best line of defense.
>
> The best way to ensure that regression testing takes place is to automate your test suites. See part 3 of the book for more about automating JUnit.

5.5   Summary

This chapter was mainly dedicated to some advanced techniques in unit testing: checking your test coverage and improving it, designing your code to be easily testable, and practicing test-driven development (TDD). These advanced techniques come naturally once you've completed the introduction to testing (chapters 1 and 2) and have learned about software testing (chapter 3) and software tests (chapter 4).

The next chapter will take you to the next level of testing your code. This next level involves using not only JUnit as a testing framework but also including other frameworks and tools, and it introduces the concept of mocking.

Coarse-grained testing
with stubs

And yet it moves.

—Galileo

This chapter covers

- Introducing stubs
- Using an embedded server in place of a real web server
- Unit testing an HTTP connection with stubs

As you develop your applications, you'll find that the code you want to test depends on other classes, which themselves depend on other classes, which then depend on the environment. For example, you might be developing an application that uses JDBC to access a database, a Java EE application (one that relies on a Java EE container for security, persistence, and other services), an application that accesses a file system, or an application that connects to some resource using HTTP, SOAP, or another protocol.

In the previous chapters, we introduced the JUnit framework. Starting in this chapter, we look at using JUnit to test an application that depends on external resources.

84

For applications that depend on a specific runtime environment, writing unit tests is a challenge. Your tests need to be stable, and when run repeatedly, they need to yield the same results. You need a way to control the environment in which the tests run. One solution is to set up the real required environment as part of the tests and run the tests from within that environment. In some cases, this approach is practical and brings real benefits (see chapter 8, which discusses in-container testing). But it works well only if you can set up the real environment on your development and build platforms, which isn't always feasible.

For example, if your application uses HTTP to connect to a web server provided by another company, you usually won't have that server application available in your development environment. Therefore, you need a way to simulate that server so you can still write and run tests for your code.

Alternatively, suppose you're working with other developers on a project. What if you want to test your part of the application, but the other part isn't ready? One solution is to simulate the missing part by replacing it with a fake that behaves the same way.

There are two strategies for providing these fake objects: stubbing and using mock objects. Stubs, the original solution, are still very popular, mostly because they allow you to test code without changing it to make it testable. This isn't the case with mock objects. This chapter is dedicated to stubbing, whereas chapter 7 covers mock objects.

6.1 *Introducing stubs*

Stubs are a mechanism for faking the behavior of real code or code that isn't ready yet. Stubs allow you to test a portion of a system even if the other part isn't available. Stubs usually don't change the code you're testing but instead adapt to provide seamless integration.

> **DEFINITION** A *stub* is a piece of code that's inserted at runtime in place of the real code, in order to isolate the caller from the real implementation. The intent is to replace a complex behavior with a simpler one that allows independent testing of some part of the real code.

Here are some examples of when you might use stubs:

- When you can't modify an existing system because it's too complex and fragile
- For coarse-grained testing, such as integration testing between different subsystems

Stubs usually provide high confidence in the tested system. With stubs, you aren't modifying the objects under test, and what you are testing is the same as what will execute in production. A build or developer usually executes tests involving stubs in their running environment, providing additional confidence.

On the downside, stubs are usually hard to write, especially when the system to fake is complex. The stub needs to implement the same logic as the code it's replacing, and that's difficult to get right for complex logic. Here are some cons of stubbing:

- Stubs are often complex to write and need debugging themselves.
- Stubs can be difficult to maintain because they're complex.
- Stubs don't lend themselves well to fine-grained unit testing.
- Each situation requires a different stubbing strategy.

In general, stubs are better adapted for replacing coarse-grained portions of code.

You usually use stubs to replace a full-blown external system such as a file system, a connection to a server, a database, and so forth. Stubs can replace a method call to a single class, but it's more difficult. (We demonstrate how to do this with mock objects in chapter 7.)

6.2   *Stubbing an HTTP connection*

To demonstrate what stubs can do, let's build some stubs for a simple application that opens an HTTP connection to a URL and reads its content. Figure 6.1 shows the sample application (limited to a `WebClient.getContent` method) opening an HTTP connection to a remote web resource. The remote web resource is a servlet, which generates an HTML response. The web resource in figure 6.1 is what we called the "real code" in the stub definition.

Our goal in this chapter is to unit test the `getContent` method by stubbing the remote web resource, as demonstrated in figure 6.2. You replace the servlet web resource with the stub, a simple HTML page returning whatever you need for the `TestWebClient` test case. This approach allows you to test the `getContent` method independently of the implementation of the web resource (which in turn could call several other objects down the execution chain, possibly down to a database).

The important point to notice with stubbing is that we didn't modify `getContent` to accept the stub. The change is transparent to the application under test. In order to allow stubbing, the target code needs to have a well-defined interface and allow plugging in of different implementations (a stub, in our case). In the figure 6.1 example, the interface is the public abstract class `java.net.URLConnection`, which cleanly isolates the implementation of the page from its caller.

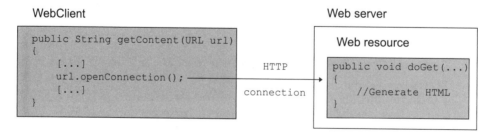

Figure 6.1   The sample application opens an HTTP connection to a remote web resource. The web resource is the "real code" in the stub definition.

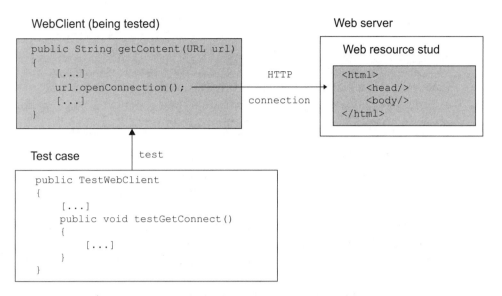

Figure 6.2 Adding a test case and replacing the real web resource with a stub

Let's look at a stub in action using the simple HTTP connection example. Listing 6.1 from the example application demonstrates a code snippet opening an HTTP connection to a given URL and reading the content found at that URL. Imagine the method is one part of a bigger application that you want to unit test.

Listing 6.1 Sample method opening an HTTP connection

```
[...]
import java.net.URL;
import java.net.HttpURLConnection;
import java.io.InputStream;
import java.io.IOException;

public class WebClient {
    public String getContent(URL url) {
        StringBuffer content = new StringBuffer();
        try {
            HttpURLConnection connection = (HttpURLConnection)      ❶
                url.openConnection();
            connection.setDoInput(true);
            InputStream is = connection.getInputStream();
            byte[] buffer = new byte[2048];
            int count;                                              ❷
            while (-1 != (count = is.read(buffer))) {
                content.append(new String(buffer, 0, count));
            }
        } catch (IOException e) {
            return null;                                        ⬅❸
        }
```

```
    return content.toString();
    }
}
```

We start ❶ by opening an HTTP connection using the `HttpURLConnection` class. We then read the stream content until there's nothing more to read ❷. If an error occurs, we return `null` ❸. One might argue that a better implementation should throw an exception. But for testing purposes, returning `null` is fine.

6.2.1   *Choosing a stubbing solution*

There are two possible scenarios in the example application: the remote web server (see figure 6.1) could be located outside the development platform (such as on a partner site), or it could be part of the platform where you deploy the application. But in both cases, you need to introduce a server into your development platform in order to be able to unit test the `WebClient` class. One relatively easy solution would be to install an Apache test server and drop some test web pages in its document root. This is a typical, widely used stubbing solution.

But it has several drawbacks, listed in table 6.1.

Table 6.1   Drawbacks of the chosen stubbing solution

Drawback	Explanation
Reliance on the environment	You need to be sure the full environment is up and running before the test starts. If the web server is down and you execute the test, it'll fail and you'll spend time debugging the failure. You'll discover that the code is working fine and it's only a setup issue generating a false failure. When you're unit testing, it's important to be able to control as much as possible of the environment in which the tests execute, such that test results are reproducible.
Separated test logic	The test logic is scattered in two separate locations: in the JUnit test case and in the test web page. You need to keep both types of resources in sync for the tests to succeed.
Difficult tests to automate	Automating the execution of the tests is difficult because it involves deploying the web pages on the web server, starting the web server, and then running the unit tests.

Fortunately, an easier solution exists using an embedded web server. Because we're testing in Java, the easiest solution is to use a Java web server that you can embed in the test case. You can use the free and open source Jetty server for this exact purpose. In this book, we use Jetty to set up our stubs. For more information about Jetty, visit http://www.eclipse.org/jetty/.

We use Jetty because it's fast (important when running tests), it's lightweight, and your test cases can programmatically control it. In addition, Jetty is a very good web, servlet, and JSP container that you can use in production. You seldom need this for most tests, but it's always nice to use best-of-breed technology.

Using Jetty allows you to eliminate the drawbacks outlined previously: the JUnit test case starts the server, you write the tests in Java in one location, and automating the test suite is a nonissue. Thanks to Jetty's modularity, the real point of the exercise is to stub only the Jetty handlers and not the whole server from the ground up.

6.2.2 *Using Jetty as an embedded server*

In order to understand how to set up and control Jetty from your tests, let's implement a simple example. Listing 6.2 shows how to start Jetty from Java and how to define a document root (/) from which to start serving files.

Listing 6.2 Starting Jetty in embedded mode—`JettySample` class

```
[...]
import org.mortbay.jetty.Server;
import org.mortbay.jetty.handler.ResourceHandler
import org.mortbay.jetty.servlet.Context;

public class JettySample {
    public static void main(String[] args) throws Exception {
        Server server = new Server(8080);                    ◁─❶

        Context root = new Context(server, "/");             ❷
        root.setResourceBase("./pom.xml");
        root.setHandler(new ResourceHandler());

        server.start();                              ◁─❸
    }
}
```

We start by creating the Jetty `Server` object ❶ and specifying in the constructor which port to listen to for HTTP requests (port 8080). Next, we create a `Context` object ❷ that processes the HTTP requests and passes them to various handlers. We map the context to the already-created server instance and to the root (/) URL. The set-ResourceBase method sets the document root from which to serve resources. On the next line, we attach a `ResourceHandler` handler to the root to serve files from the file system. Because this handler will return an HTTP 403-Forbidden error if we try to list the content of a directory, we specify the resource base to be a file. In this example, we specify the file pom.xml in the project's directory. Finally, we start the server ❸.

If you start the program from listing 6.2 and navigate your browser to http://localhost:8080, you should be able to see the content of the pom.xml file (see figure 6.3).

Figure 6.3 displays the results of running the code in listing 6.2 after opening a browser on http://localhost:8080.

Now that you've seen how to run Jetty as an embedded server, we show next how to stub the server's resources.

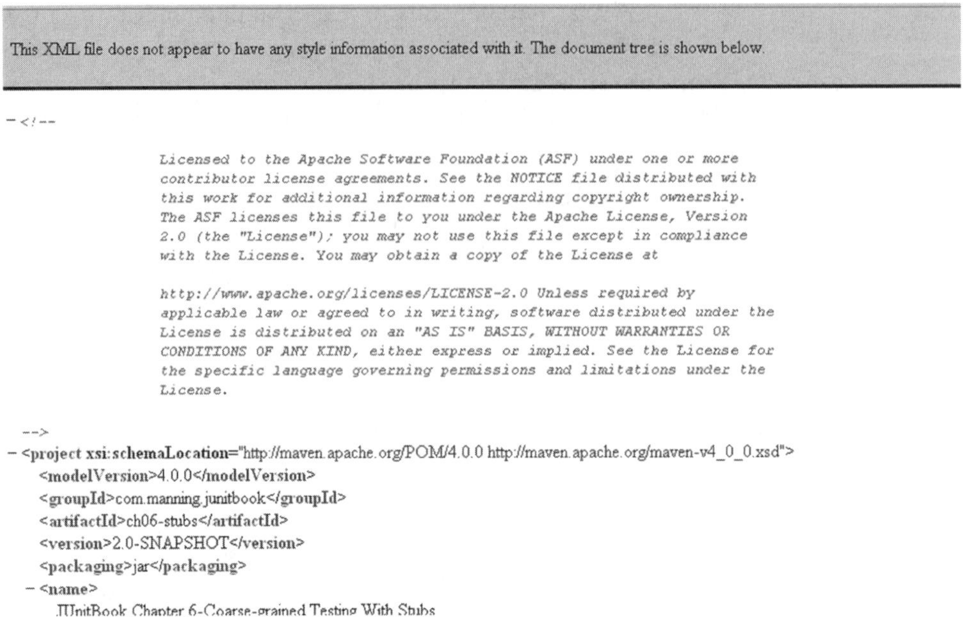

This XML file does not appear to have any style information associated with it. The document tree is shown below.

```
- <!--

          Licensed to the Apache Software Foundation (ASF) under one or more
          contributor license agreements. See the NOTICE file distributed with
          this work for additional information regarding copyright ownership.
          The ASF licenses this file to you under the Apache License, Version
          2.0 (the "License"); you may not use this file except in compliance
          with the License. You may obtain a copy of the License at

          http://www.apache.org/licenses/LICENSE-2.0  Unless required by
          applicable law or agreed to in writing, software distributed under the
          License is distributed on an "AS IS" BASIS, WITHOUT WARRANTIES OR
          CONDITIONS OF ANY KIND, either express or implied. See the License for
          the specific language governing permissions and limitations under the
          License.

  -->
 - <project xsi:schemaLocation="http://maven.apache.org/POM/4.0.0 http://maven.apache.org/maven-v4_0_0.xsd">
      <modelVersion>4.0.0</modelVersion>
      <groupId>com.manning.junitbook</groupId>
      <artifactId>ch06-stubs</artifactId>
      <version>2.0-SNAPSHOT</version>
      <packaging>jar</packaging>
    - <name>
      JUnitBook Chapter 6-Coarse-grained Testing With Stubs
```

Figure 6.3   Testing the `JettySample` class in a browser

6.3 *Stubbing the web server's resources*

You now know how to easily start and configure Jetty, so let's focus on the HTTP connection unit test. You'll write a first test that verifies you can call a valid URL and get its content.

6.3.1 *Setting up the first stub test*

To verify that the `WebClient` works with a valid URL, you need to start the Jetty server before the test, which you can implement in a test case `setUp` method. You can also stop the server in a `tearDown` method. Listing 6.3 shows the code.

Listing 6.3   First test to verify that `WebClient` works with a valid URL

```
[...]
import java.net.URL;
import org.junit.test;
import org.junit.Before;
import org.junit.After;

public class TestWebClientSkeleton {

    @Before
    public void setUp() {

    }
```

```
@After
public void tearDown() {
   // Stop Jetty.
}

@Test
public void testGetContentOk() throws Exception {
   WebClient client = new WebClient();
   String result = client.getContent(new URL(
      "http://localhost:8080/testGetContentOk"));

   assertEquals ("It works", result);
}
}
```

In order to implement the @Before and @After methods, you have two options. You can prepare a static page containing the text "It works", which you put in the document root (controlled by the call to context.setResourceBase(String) in listing 6.2). Alternatively, you can configure Jetty to use your own custom Handler that returns the string "It works" instead of getting it from a file. This is a much more powerful technique, because it lets you unit test the case when the remote HTTP server returns an error code to your WebClient client application.

CREATING A JETTY HANDLER
Listing 6.4 shows how to create a Jetty Handler that returns the string "It works".

Listing 6.4 Create a Jetty `Handler` that returns `"It works"` when called

```
private class TestGetContentOkHandler extends AbstractHandler {        ◄┐

   @Override                                                           ◄┤
   public void handle(String target, HttpServletRequest request,       ❶
         HttpServletResponse response, int dispatch) throws IOException { ◄┘

      OutputStream out = response.getOutputStream();                   ❷
      ByteArrayISO8859Writer writer = new ByteArrayISO8859Writer();
      writer.write("It works");                                       ❸
      writer.flush();
      response.setIntHeader(HttpHeaders.CONTENT_LENGTH, writer.size());
      writer.writeTo(out);                                            ❹
      out.flush();
   }
}
```

This class creates a handler ❶ by extending the Jetty AbstractHandler class and implementing a single method, handle. Jetty calls the handle method to forward an incoming request to our handler. After that, we use the Jetty ByteArrayISO-8859Writer class ❷ to send back the string "It works", which we write in the HTTP response ❸. The last step is to set the response content length to be the length of the string written to the output stream (this is required by Jetty) and then send the response ❹.

Now that this handler is written, you can tell Jetty to use it by calling context.set-Handler(new TestGetContentOkHandler()). You're almost ready to run your test.

The last issue to solve is the one involving the `@Before` and `@After` methods. The solution shown in listing 6.3 isn't optimal because JUnit will start and stop the server for every test method. Even though Jetty is fast, this process isn't necessary. A better solution is to start the server only once for all the tests by using the JUnit annotations we described in the second chapter of the book: `@BeforeClass` and `@AfterClass`. These annotations let you execute code before and after all `@Test` methods in a class.

Isolating each test versus performance considerations

In previous chapters, we went to great lengths to explain why each test should run in a clean environment (even to the extent of using a new class loader instance). But sometimes there are other considerations to take into account. Performance is a typical one. In the case of Jetty, even if starting the server takes only 1 second, once you have 300 tests, it will add an overhead of 300 seconds (5 minutes). Test suites that take a long time to execute are a handicap; you'll be tempted not to execute them often, which negates the regression feature of unit testing. You must be aware of this tradeoff. Depending on the situation, you may choose to have longer-running tests that execute in a clean environment or instead tune the tests for performance by reusing some parts of the environment. In the example at hand, you use different handlers for different tests, and you can be fairly confident they won't interfere with each other.

WRITING THE TEST CLASS

We can now easily write the test class using the `@BeforeClass` annotation, as demonstrated in listing 6.5.

Listing 6.5   Putting it all together

```
[...]
import java.net.URL;
[...]

public class TestWebClient {

    @BeforeClass
    public static void setUp() throws Exception() {
        Server server = new Server(8080);

        TestWebClient t = new TestWebClient();

        Context contentOkContext = new Context(server, "/testGetContentOk");
        contentOkContext.setHandler(t.new TestGetContentOkHandler());

        server.setStopAtShutDown(true);
        server.start();

    }

    @Test
    public void testGetContentOk() throws Exception {
        WebClient client = new WebClient();
        String result = client.getContent(new URL(
```

```
          "http://localhost:8080/testGetContentOk"));
      assertEquals("It works", result);
   }

   @AfterClass
   public static void tearDown() {
      //Empty
   }

   private class TestGetContentOkHandler extends AbstractHandler {
      //Listing 6.4 here.
   }

}
```

The test class has become quite simple. The @BeforeClass setUp method constructs the Server object the same way as in listing 6.2. Then come the @Test methods, and we leave our @AfterClass method empty intentionally because we programmed the server to stop at shutdown.

If you run the test in Eclipse, you'll see the result in figure 6.4—our test passes.

So far, so good—our tests have been testing the good side of our code. But it seems logical to test the behavior of what would happen if the server crashed or the application deployed in the server crashed. The next section answers exactly those questions.

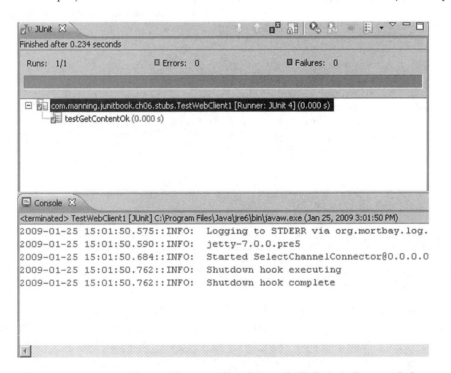

Figure 6.4 Result of the first working test using a Jetty stub. JUnit starts the server before the first test, and the server shuts itself down after the last test.

6.3.2   *Testing for failure conditions*

Now that you have the first test working, let's see how to test for server failure conditions. The `WebClient.getContent(URL)` method returns a `null` value when a failure occurs. You need to test for this possibility too. With the infrastructure you've put in place, you need to create a new Jetty `Handler` class that returns an error code and register it in the `@Before` method of the `TestWebClientSetup1` class.

Let's add a test for an invalid URL—a URL pointing to a file that doesn't exist. This case is quite easy, because Jetty already provides a `NotFoundHandler` handler class for that purpose. You only need to modify the `TestWebClient` `setUp` method as follows (changes are in bold):

```
@BeforeClass
public static void setUp() throws Exception {
    Server server = new Server(8080);
    TestWebClient t = new TestWebClient();

    Context contentOkContext = new Context(server, "/testGetContentOk");
    contentOkContext.setHandler(t.new TestGetContentOkHandler());

    Context contentNotFoundContext = new Context(server,
                                       "/testGetContentNotFound");
    contentNotFoundContext.setHandler(t.new
                            TestGetContentNotFoundHandler());

    server.start();
}
```

Here's the code for the `TestGetContentNotFoundHandler` class:

```
private class TestGetContentNotFoundHandler extends AbstractHandler {
    public void handle(String target, HttpServletRequest request,
            HttpServletResponse response, int dispatch) throws IOException {
        response.sendError(HttpServletResponse.SC_NOT_FOUND);
    }
}
```

Adding a new test in `TestWebClient` is also a breeze:

```
@Test
public void testGetContentNotFound() throws Exception {
    WebClient client = new WebClient();
    String result = client.getContent(new URL(
        "http://localhost:8080/testGetContentNotFound"));
    assertNull(result);
}
```

In similar fashion, you can easily add a test to simulate the server having trouble. Returning a 5xx HTTP response code indicates this problem. To do so, you'll need to write a Jetty `Handler` class, using `HttpServletResponse.SC_SERVICE_UNAVAILABLE`, and register it in the `@Before` method of the `TestWebClientSetup1` class.

A test like this would be very difficult to perform if you didn't choose an embedded web server like Jetty.

6.3.3 *Reviewing the first stub test*

You've now been able to fully unit test the getContent method in isolation by stubbing the web resource. What have you really tested? What kind of test have you achieved? You've done something quite powerful: you've unit tested the method, but at the same time, you've executed an integration test. In addition, not only have you tested the code logic, but you've also tested the connection part that's outside the code (through the Java HttpURLConnection class).

The drawback to this approach is that it's complex. It can take a Jetty novice half a day to learn enough about Jetty to set it up correctly. In some instances, you'll have to debug stubs to get them to work properly. Keep in mind that the stub must remain simple and not become a full-fledged application that requires tests and maintenance. If you spend too much time debugging your stubs, a different solution may be called for.

In these examples, you need a web server—but another example and stub will be different and will need a different setup. Experience helps, but different cases usually require different stubbing solutions.

The example tests are nice because you can both unit test the code and perform some integration tests at the same time. But this functionality comes at the cost of complexity. More solutions that are lightweight focus on unit testing the code without performing integration tests. The rationale is that although you need integration tests, they could run in a separate test suite or as part of functional tests.

In the next section, we look at another solution that can still qualify as stubbing. It's simpler in the sense that it doesn't require you to stub a whole web server. It brings you one step closer to the mock object strategy, which is described in the following chapter.

6.4 *Stubbing the connection*

So far, you've stubbed the web server's resources. Next, we stub the HTTP connection instead. Doing so will prevent you from effectively testing the connection, but that's fine because it isn't your real goal at this point. You want to test your code in isolation. Functional or integration tests will test the connection at a later stage.

When it comes to stubbing the connection without changing the code, we benefit from Java's URL and HttpURLConnection classes, which let us plug in custom protocol handlers to process any kind of communication protocol. You can have any call to the HttpURLConnection class redirected to your own class, which will return whatever you need for the test.

6.4.1 *Producing a custom URL protocol handler*

To implement a custom URL protocol handler, you need to call the URL method setURLStreamHandlerFactory and pass it a custom URLStreamHandlerFactory. Whenever the URL openConnection method is called, the URLStreamHandlerFactory class is called to return a URLStreamHandler. Listing 6.6 shows the code to perform this feat.

The idea is to call the URL static method setURLStreamHandlerFactory in the JUnit setUp method. (A better implementation would use a TestSetup class, such that this is performed only once during the whole test suite execution.)

Listing 6.6   Providing custom stream handler classes for testing

```
[...]
import java.net.URL;
import java.net.URLStreamHandlerFactory;
import java.net.URLStreamHandler;
import java.net.URLConnection;
import java.io.IOException;

public class TestWebClient1 {

    @BeforeClass
    public static void setUp() {
        TestWebClient1 t = new TestWebClient1();
        URL.setURLStreamHandlerFactory(t.new StubStreamHandlerFactory());
    }
    private class StubStreamHandlerFactory implements
        URLStreamHandlerFactory {

        public URLStreamHandler createURLStreamHandler(String protocol) {
            return new StubHttpURLStreamHandler();
        }
    }
    private class StubHttpURLStreamHandler extends URLStreamHandler {
        protected URLConnection openConnection(URL url)
            throws IOException {
            return new StubHttpURLConnection(url);
        }
    }
    @Test
    public void testGetContentOk() throws Exception {
        WebClient client = new WebClient();
        String result = client.getContent(new URL("http://localhost"));
        assertEquals("It works", result);
    }
}
```

- ❶ (points to `URL.setURLStreamHandlerFactory(t.new StubStreamHandlerFactory());`)
- ❷ (points to StubStreamHandlerFactory block)
- ❸ (points to StubHttpURLStreamHandler block)

We use several (inner) classes (❷ and ❸) to be able to use the StubHttpURL-Connection class. We start by calling setURLStreamHandlerFactory ❶ with our first stub class, StubStreamHandlerFactory. In StubStreamHandlerFactory, we override the createURLStreamHandler method ❷, in which we return a new instance of our second private stub class, StubHttpURLStreamHandler. In StubHttpURLStreamHandler, we override one method, openConnection, to open a connection to the given URL ❸.

You could also use anonymous inner classes for conciseness, but that approach would make the code more difficult to read. Note that you haven't written the StubHttpURLConnection class yet, which is the topic of the next section.

6.4.2 *Creating a JDK HttpURLConnection stub*

The last step is to create a stub implementation of the HttpURLConnection class so you can return any value you want for the test. Listing 6.7 shows a simple implementation that returns the string "It works" as a stream to the caller.

Listing 6.7 Stubbed HttpURLConnection class

```
[...]
import java.net.HttpURLConnection;
import java.net.ProtocolException;
import java.net.URL;
import java.io.InputStream;
import java.io.IOException;
import java.io.ByteArrayInputStream;

public class StubHttpURLConnection extends HttpURLConnection {
    private boolean isInput = true;
    protected StubHttpURLConnection(URL url) {
        super(url);
    }
    public InputStream getInputStream() throws IOException {      ◁─❶
        if (!isInput) {
            throw new ProtocolException(
                "Cannot read from URLConnection"
                + " if doInput=false (call setDoInput(true))");
        }
        ByteArrayInputStream bais = new ByteArrayInputStream(
            new String("It works").getBytes());
        return bais;
    }
    public void disconnect() {}
    public void connect() throws IOException {}
    public boolean usingProxy() {
        return false;
    }
}
```

HttpURLConnection is an abstract public class that doesn't implement an interface, so you extend it and override the methods wanted by the stub. In this stub, you provide an implementation for the getInputStream method because it's the only method used by your code under test. Should the code to test use more APIs from HttpURLConnection, you'd need to stub these additional methods. This is where the code would become more complex—you'd need to reproduce completely the same behavior as the real HttpURLConnection. For example, at ❶, you test that if set-DoInput(false) has been called in the code under test, then a call to the get-InputStream method returns a ProtocolException. (This is the behavior of HttpURLConnection.) Fortunately, in most cases, you need to stub only a few methods and not the whole API.

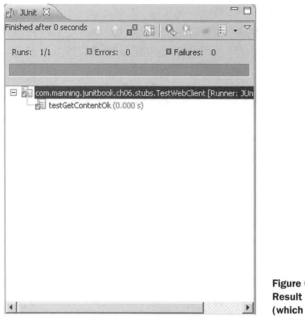

Figure 6.5
Result of executing `TestWebClient1`
(which uses the `StubHttpURLConnection`)

6.4.3   Running the test

Let's run the `TestWebClient1` test, which uses the `StubHttpURLConnection`. Figure 6.5 shows the result of the execution of the test in Eclipse.

As you can see, it's much easier to stub the connection than to stub the web resource. This approach doesn't bring the same level of testing (you aren't performing integration tests), but it enables you to more easily write a focused unit test for the `WebClient` logic.

6.5   Summary

In this chapter, we demonstrated how using a stub has helped us unit test code accessing a remote web server using the Java `HttpURLConnection` API. In particular, we showed how to stub the remote web server by using the open source Jetty server. Jetty's embeddable nature lets you concentrate on stubbing only the Jetty HTTP request handler, instead of having to stub the whole container. We also demonstrated a more lightweight solution by stubbing the Java `HttpURLConnection` class.

The next chapter demonstrates a technique called mock objects that allows fine-grained unit testing, which is completely generic, and (best of all) forces you to write good code. Although stubs are very useful in some cases, some consider them more a vestige of the past, when the consensus was that tests should be a separate activity and shouldn't modify existing code. The new mock objects strategy not only allows modification of code but favors it. Using mock objects is more than a unit testing strategy; it's a completely new way of writing code.

Testing with mock objects

7

Programming today is a race between software engineers striving to build bigger and better idiot-proof programs, and the Universe trying to produce bigger and better idiots. So far, the Universe is winning.

—Rich Cook

This chapter covers

- Introducing and demonstrating mock objects
- Performing different refactorings
- Practicing on the HTTP connection sample application
- Introducing the EasyMock and the JMock libraries

Unit testing each method in isolation from the other methods or the environment is certainly a nice goal. How do you perform this feat? You saw in chapter 6 how the stubbing technique lets you unit test portions of code by isolating them from the environment (for example, by stubbing a web server, the file system, a database, and so on). What about fine-grained isolation, like being able to isolate a method call to another class? Is that possible? Can you achieve this without deploying huge amounts of energy that would negate the benefits of having tests?

Yes! It's possible. The technique is called mock objects. Tim Mackinnon, Steve Freeman, and Philip Craig first presented the mock objects concept at XP2000. The mock objects strategy allows you to unit test at the finest-possible level and develop method by method, while providing you with unit tests for each method.

7.1   *Introducing mock objects*

Testing in isolation offers strong benefits, such as the ability to test code that has not yet been written (as long as you at least have an interface to work with). In addition, testing in isolation helps teams unit test one part of the code without waiting for all the other parts.

The biggest advantage is the ability to write focused tests that test only a single method, without side effects resulting from other objects being called from the method under test. Small is beautiful. Writing small, focused tests is a tremendous help; small tests are easy to understand and don't break when other parts of the code are changed. Remember that one of the benefits of having a suite of unit tests is the courage it gives you to refactor mercilessly—the unit tests act as a safeguard against regression. If you have large tests and your refactoring introduces a bug, several tests will fail; that result will tell you that there's a bug somewhere, but you won't know where. With fine-grained tests, potentially fewer tests will be affected, and they'll provide precise messages that pinpoint the exact cause of the breakage.

Mock objects (or *mocks* for short) are perfectly suited for testing a portion of code logic in isolation from the rest of the code. Mocks replace the objects with which your methods under test collaborate, offering a layer of isolation. In that sense, they're similar to stubs. But this is where the similarity ends, because mocks don't implement any logic: they're empty shells that provide methods to let the tests control the behavior of all the business methods of the faked class.

We discuss when to use mock objects in section 7.6 at the end of this chapter, after we show them in action on some examples.

7.2   *Unit testing with mock objects*

In this section, we present an application and a test using mock objects. Imagine a simple use case where you want to be able to make a bank transfer from one account to another (figure 7.1 and listings 7.1 and 7.2).

The `AccountService` class offers services related to `Accounts` and uses the `AccountManager` to persist data to the database (using JDBC, for example). The service that interests us is materialized by the `AccountService.transfer` method, which makes the transfer. Without mocks, testing the `AccountService.transfer` behavior would imply setting up a database, presetting it with test data, deploying the code inside the container (Java EE application server, for example), and so forth. Although this process is required to ensure the application works end to end, it's too much work when you want to unit test only your code logic.

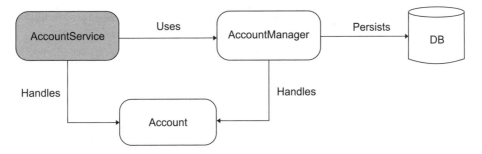

Figure 7.1 **In this simple bank account example, we use a mock object to test an account transfer method.**

Listing 7.1 presents a simple Account object with two properties: an account ID and a balance.

Listing 7.1 `Account.java`

```
[...]
public class Account {
   private String accountId;
   private long balance;
   public Account(String accountId, long initialBalance) {
      this.accountId = accountId;
      this.balance = initialBalance;
   }
   public void debit(long amount) {
      this.balance -= amount;
   }
   public void credit(long amount) {
      this.balance += amount;
   }
   public long getBalance() {
      return this.balance;
   }
}
```

The AccountManager interface that follows manages the lifecycle and persistence of Account objects. (We're limited to finding accounts by ID and updating accounts.)

```
[...]
  public interface AccountManager {
     Account findAccountForUser(String userId);
           void updateAccount(Account account);
  }
```

Listing 7.2 shows the transfer method for transferring money between two accounts. It uses the AccountManager interface we previously defined to find the debit and credit accounts by ID and to update them.

Listing 7.2 `AccountService.java`

```
[...]
public class AccountService {
   private AccountManager accountManager;
   public void setAccountManager(AccountManager manager) {
      this.accountManager = manager;
   }
 public void transfer(String senderId, String beneficiaryId, long amount) {
      Account sender = this.accountManager.findAccountForUser(senderId);
      Account beneficiary =
                 this.accountManager.findAccountForUser(beneficiaryId);

      sender.debit(amount);
      beneficiary.credit(amount);
      this.accountManager.updateAccount(sender);
      this.accountManager.updateAccount(beneficiary);
   }
}
```

We want to be able to unit test the `AccountService.transfer` behavior. For that purpose, we use a mock implementation of the `AccountManager` interface (listing 7.3). We do this because the transfer method is using this interface, and we need to test it in isolation.

Listing 7.3 `MockAccountManager.java`

```
[...]
import java.util.HashMap;
public class MockAccountManager implements AccountManager {

   private Map<String, Account> accounts = new HashMap<String, Account>();

      public void addAccount(String userId, Account account) {        ❶
      this.accounts.put(userId, account);
   }

   public Account findAccountForUser(String userId) {                 ❷
      return this.accounts.get(userId);
   }

   public void updateAccount(Account account) {                       ❸
      // do nothing
   }
}
```

The `addAccount` method uses an instance variable to hold the values to return ❶. Because we have several account objects that we want to be able to return, we store the `Account` objects to return in a `HashMap`. This makes the mock generic and able to support different test cases: one test could set up the mock with one account, another test could set it up with two accounts or more, and so forth.

In ❷ we implement a method to retrieve the account from the `accounts` map—we can retrieve only accounts that have been added before that. The `updateAccount`

JUnit best practices: don't write business logic in mock objects

The most important point to consider when writing a mock is that it shouldn't have any business logic. It must be a dumb object that does only what the test tells it to do. It's driven purely by the tests. This characteristic is exactly the opposite of stubs, which contain all the logic (see chapter 6).

There are two nice corollaries. First, mock objects can be easily generated, as you'll see in following chapters. Second, because mock objects are empty shells, they're too simple to break and don't need testing themselves.

---

method updates an account but doesn't return any value ❸. We do nothing. When it's called by the transfer method, it will do nothing, as if the account had been correctly updated.

We're now ready to write a unit test for `AccountService.transfer`. Listing 7.4 shows a typical test using a mock.

Listing 7.4 Testing transfer with `MockAccountManager`

```
[...]
public class TestAccountService {

  @Test
  public void testTransferOk() {
      MockAccountManager mockAccountManager = new MockAccountManager();
      Account senderAccount = new Account("1", 200);
      Account beneficiaryAccount = new Account("2", 100);          ❶
      mockAccountManager.addAccount("1", senderAccount);
      mockAccountManager.addAccount("2", beneficiaryAccount);
      AccountService accountService = new AccountService();
      accountService.setAccountManager(mockAccountManager);
      accountService.transfer("1", "2", 50);                       ◄—❷

      assertEquals(150, senderAccount.getBalance());               ❸
      assertEquals(150, beneficiaryAccount.getBalance());
  }
}
```

As usual, a test has three steps: the test setup ❶, the test execution ❷, and the verification of the result ❸. During the test setup, we create the `MockAccountManager` object and define what it should return when called for the two accounts we manipulate (the sender and beneficiary accounts). We've succeeded in testing the `AccountService` code in isolation of the other domain object, `AccountManager`, which in this case didn't exist, but which in real life could have been implemented using JDBC.

At this point in the chapter, you should have a reasonably good understanding of what a mock is. In the next section, we show you that writing unit tests with mocks leads to refactoring your code under test—and that this process is a good thing!

> ### JUnit best practices: test only what can possibly break
>
> You may have noticed that we didn't mock the `Account` class. The reason is that this data access object class doesn't need to be mocked—it doesn't depend on the environment, and it's simple. Our other tests use the `Account` object, so they test it indirectly. If it failed to operate correctly, the tests that rely on `Account` would fail and alert us to the problem.

7.3   *Refactoring with mock objects*

Some people used to say that unit tests should be totally transparent to your code under test, and that you should not change runtime code in order to simplify testing. *This is wrong!* Unit tests are first-class users of the runtime code and deserve the same consideration as any other user. If your code is too inflexible for the tests to use, then you should correct the code.

For example, what do you think of the following piece of code?

```
[...]
import java.util.PropertyResourceBundle;
import java.util.ResourceBundle;
import org.apache.commons.logging.Log;
import org.apache.commons.logging.LogFactory;
[...]
public class DefaultAccountManager implements AccountManager {
    private static final Log LOGGER =                          Create
        LogFactory.getLog(AccountManager.class);              a Log

    public Account findAccountForUser(String userId) {
        LOGGER.debug("Getting account for user [" + userId + "]");
        ResourceBundle bundle =                                Retrieve a SQL
            PropertyResourceBundle.getBundle("technical");    command
        String sql = bundle.getString("FIND_ACCOUNT_FOR_USER");
        // Some code logic to load a user account using JDBC
        [...]
    }
    [...]
}
```

Does the code look fine to you? We can see two issues, both of which relate to code flexibility and the ability to resist change. The first problem is that it isn't possible to decide to use a different `Log` object, because it's created inside the class. For testing, for example, you probably want to use a `Log` that does nothing, but you can't.

As a rule, a class like this should be able to use whatever `Log` it's given.

The goal of this class isn't to create loggers but to perform some JDBC logic. The same remark applies to the use of `PropertyResourceBundle`. It may sound okay right now, but what happens if you decide to use XML to store the configuration? Again, it shouldn't be the goal of this class to decide what implementation to use.

An effective design strategy is to pass to an object any other object that's outside its immediate business logic. The choice of peripheral objects can be controlled by someone higher in the calling chain. Ultimately, as you move up in the calling layers, the decision to use a given logger or configuration should be pushed to the top level. This strategy provides the best possible code flexibility and ability to cope with changes. And, as we all know, change is the only constant.

7.3.1   Refactoring example

Refactoring all code so that domain objects are passed around can be time consuming. You may not be ready to refactor the whole application just to be able to write a unit test. Fortunately, there's an easy refactoring technique that lets you keep the same interface for your code but allows it to be passed domain objects that it shouldn't create. As a proof, let's see how the refactored `DefaultAccountManager` class could look. See listing 7.5; modifications are shown in bold.

Listing 7.5   Refactoring `DefaultAccountManager` for testing

```
public class DefaultAccountManager implements AccountManager {
    private Log logger;                                            ❶
    private Configuration configuration;

    public DefaultAccountManager() {
        this(LogFactory.getLog(DefaultAccountManager.class),
        new DefaultConfiguration("technical"));
    }
    public DefaultAccountManager(Log logger, Configuration configuration) {
        this.logger = logger;
        this.configuration = configuration;
    }

    public Account findAccountForUser(String userId) {
        this.logger.debug("Getting account for user [" + userId + "]");
        this.configuration.getSQL("FIND_ACCOUNT_FOR_USER");
        // Some code logic to load a user account using JDBC
    [...]
    }
[...]
}
```

Notice that at ❶, we swap the `PropertyResourceBundle` class from the previous listing in favor of a new `Configuration` interface. This makes the code more flexible because it introduces an interface (which will be easy to mock), and the implementation of the `Configuration` interface can be anything we want (including using resource bundles). The design is better now because we can use and reuse the `Default-AccountManager` class with any implementation of the `Log` and `Configuration` interfaces (if we use the constructor that takes two parameters). The class can be controlled from the outside (by its caller). Meanwhile, we haven't broken the existing interface, because we've only added a new constructor. We kept the original default constructor that still initializes the `logger` and `configuration` field members with default implementations.

With this refactoring, we've provided a trapdoor for controlling the domain objects from your tests. We retain backward compatibility and pave an easy refactoring path for the future. Calling classes can start using the new constructor at their own pace.

Should you worry about introducing trapdoors to make your code easier to test? Here's how Extreme Programming guru Ron Jeffries explains it:

> *My car has a diagnostic port and an oil dipstick. There is an inspection port on the side of my furnace and on the front of my oven. My pen cartridges are transparent so I can see if there is ink left.*
>
> *And if I find it useful to add a method to a class to enable me to test it, I do so. It happens once in a while, for example in classes with easy interfaces and complex inner function (probably starting to want an Extract Class).*
>
> *I just give the class what I understand of what it wants, and keep an eye on it to see what it wants next.*[1]

Design patterns in action: Inversion of Control

Applying the IoC pattern to a class means removing the creation of all object instances for which this class isn't directly responsible and passing any needed instances instead. The instances may be passed using a specific constructor, using a setter, or as parameters of the methods needing them. It becomes the responsibility of the calling code to correctly set these domain objects on the called class.[2]

IoC makes unit testing a breeze. To prove the point, let's see how easily we can now write a test for the `findAccountByUser` method:

```
public void testFindAccountByUser() {
    MockLog logger = new MockLog();                                    ← 1
    MockConfiguration configuration = new MockConfiguration();           2
    configuration.setSQL("SELECT * [...]");
    DefaultAccountManager am = new DefaultAccountManager(logger,        3
                                                  configuration);
    Account account = am.findAccountForUser("1234");
    // Perform asserts here
    [...]
}
```

---

[1] Ron Jeffries, on the TestDrivenDevelopment mailing list: http://groups.yahoo.com/group/testdrivendevelopment/message/3914.

[2] See the Jakarta Avalon framework for a component framework implementing the IoC pattern (http://avalon.apache.org).

At ❶, we use a mock logger that implements the `Log` interface but does nothing. Next, we create a `MockConfiguration` instance ❷ and set it up to return a given SQL query when `Configuration.getSQL` is called. Finally, we create the instance of `Default-AccountManager` ❸ that we test, passing to it the `Log` and `Configuration` instances.

We've been able to completely control our logging and configuration behavior from outside the code to test, in the test code. As a result, our code is more flexible and allows for any logging and configuration implementation to be used. You'll see more of these code refactorings in this chapter and later ones.

One last point to note is that if you write your test first, you'll automatically design your code to be flexible. Flexibility is a key point when writing a unit test. If you test first, you won't incur the cost of refactoring your code for flexibility later.

7.4 *Mocking an HTTP connection*

To see how mock objects work in a practical example, let's use the simple application that opens an HTTP connection to a remote server and reads the content of a page. In chapter 6 we tested that application using stubs. Let's now unit test it using a mock object approach to simulate the HTTP connection.

In addition, you'll learn how to write mocks for classes that don't have a Java interface (namely, the `HttpURLConnection` class). We show a full scenario in which you start with an initial testing implementation, improve the implementation as you go, and modify the original code to make it more flexible. We also show how to test for error conditions using mocks.

As you dive in, you'll keep improving both the test code and the sample application, exactly as you might if you were writing the unit tests for the same application. In the process, you'll learn how to reach a simple and elegant testing solution while making your application code more flexible and capable of handling change.

Figure 7.2 introduces the sample HTTP application.

This application consists of a simple `WebClient.getContent` method performing an HTTP connection to a web resource executing on a web server. We want to be able to unit test the `getContent` method in isolation from the web resource.

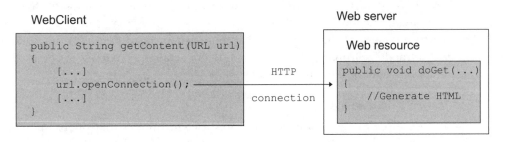

Figure 7.2 The sample HTTP application before introducing the test

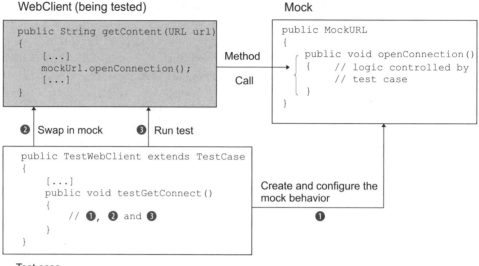

Figure 7.3   The steps involved in a test using mock objects

7.4.1   *Defining the mock objects*

Figure 7.3 illustrates the definition of a mock object. The MockURL class stands in for the real URL class, and all calls to the URL class in getContent are directed to the Mock-URL class. As you can see, the test is the controller: it creates and configures the behavior the mock must have for this test; it (somehow) replaces the real URL class with the MockURL class; and it runs the test.

Figure 7.3 shows an interesting aspect of the mock objects strategy: the need to be able to swap the mock into the production code. The perceptive reader will have noticed that because the URL class is final, it's not possible to create a MockURL class that extends it.

In the coming sections, we demonstrate how to perform this feat in a different way (by mocking at another level). In any case, when using the mock objects strategy, swapping in the mock instead of the real class is the hard part. This may be viewed as a negative point for mock objects, because we usually need to modify our code to provide a trapdoor. Ironically, modifying code to encourage flexibility is one of the strongest advantages of using mocks, as explained in section 7.3.1.

7.4.2   *Testing a sample method*

The example in listing 7.6 demonstrates a code snippet that opens an HTTP connection to a given URL and reads the content found at that URL. Let's imagine that it's one method of a bigger application that we want to unit test, and let's unit test that method.

> **Listing 7.6   A sample method that opens an HTTP connection**

```
[...]
import java.net.URL;
import java.net.HttpURLConnection;
import java.io.InputStream;
import java.io.IOException;
public class WebClient {
    public String getContent(URL url) {
        StringBuffer content = new StringBuffer();
        try {
            HttpURLConnection connection =
                (HttpURLConnection) url.openConnection();        Open an HTTP
            connection.setDoInput(true);                        connection
            InputStream is = connection.getInputStream();
            int count;
            while (-1 != (count = is.read())) {
                content.append( new String( Character.toChars( count ) ) );
            }
        } catch (IOException e) {
            return null;                                         Read all
        }                                                       contents
        return content.toString();
    }
}
```

If an error occurs, we return null. Admittedly, this isn't the best possible error-handling solution, but it's good enough for the moment. (And our tests will give us the courage to refactor later.)

7.4.3   First attempt: easy method refactoring technique

The idea is to be able to test the getContent method independently of a real HTTP connection to a web server. If you map the knowledge you acquired in section 7.2, it means writing a mock URL in which the url.openConnection method returns a mock HttpURLConnection. The MockHttpURLConnection class would provide an implementation that lets the test decide what the getInputStream method returns. Ideally, you'd be able to write the following test:

```
@Test                                                   Create a mock
public void testGetContentOk() throws Exception {       HttpURLConnection
    MockHttpURLConnection mockConnection = new MockHttpURLConnection();
    mockConnection.setupGetInputStream(
                    new ByteArrayInputStream("It works".getBytes()));
    MockURL mockURL = new MockURL();                        Create a
    mockURL.setupOpenConnection(mockConnection);            mock URL
    WebClient client = new WebClient();
    String result = client.getContent(mockURL);     ←┘ Test the getContent method
    assertEquals("It works", result);               ←┐ Assert the result
}
```

Unfortunately, this approach doesn't work! The JDK URL class is a final class, and no URL interface is available. So much for extensibility. We need to find another solution and, potentially, another object to mock. One solution is to stub the URL-StreamHandlerFactory class. We explored this solution in chapter 6, so let's find a technique that uses mock objects: refactoring the getContent method. If you think about it, this method does two things: it gets an HttpURLConnection object and then reads the content from it. Refactoring leads to the class shown in listing 7.7 (changes from listing 7.6 are in bold). We've extracted the part that retrieved the HttpURLConnection object.

Listing 7.7 Extracting retrieval of the connection object from getContent

```
public class WebClient {
   public String getContent(URL url) {
      StringBuffer content = new StringBuffer();
      try {
         HttpURLConnection connection = createHttpURLConnection(url);
         InputStream is = connection.getInputStream();
         int count;
         while (-1 != (count = is.read())) {
            content.append( new String( Character.toChars( count ) ) );
         }
      }
      catch (IOException e) {
         return null;                                        Refactoring  ❶
      }
      return content.toString();
   }
   protected HttpURLConnection createHttpURLConnection(URL url)
                                          throws IOException {
      return (HttpURLConnection) url.openConnection();
   }
}
```

In the listing, we call createHttpURLConnection ❶ to create the HTTP connection.

How does this solution let us test getContent more effectively? We can now apply a useful trick, which consists of writing a test helper class that extends the WebClient class and overrides its createHttpURLConnection method, as follows:

```
private class TestableWebClient extends WebClient {
   private HttpURLConnection connection;
   public void setHttpURLConnection(HttpURLConnection connection) {
      this.connection = connection;
   }
   public HttpURLConnection createHttpURLConnection(URL url)
                                          throws IOException {
      return this.connection;
   }
}
```

In the test, we can call the setHttpURLConnection method, passing it the mock HttpURLConnection object. The test now becomes the following (differences are shown in bold):

```
@Test
public void testGetContentOk() throws Exception {
    MockHttpURLConnection mockConnection = new MockHttpURLConnection();
    mockConnection.setExpectedInputStream(
        new ByteArrayInputStream("It works".getBytes()));
    TestableWebClient client = new TestableWebClient();
    client.setHttpURLConnection(mockConnection);
    String result = client.getContent(new URL("http://localhost"));
    assertEquals("It works", result);
}
```

①

◁—**②**

In this code, we configure `TestableWebClient` **①** so that the `createHttpURLConnection` method returns a mock object. Next, the `getContent` method is called **②**.

This is a common refactoring approach called *method factory* refactoring, which is especially useful when the class to mock has no interface. The strategy is to extend that class, add some setter methods to control it, and override some of its getter methods to return what we want for the test. In the case at hand, this approach is okay, but it isn't perfect. It's a bit like the Heisenberg uncertainty principle: the act of subclassing the class under test changes its behavior, so when we test the subclass, what are we truly testing?

This technique is useful as a means of opening up an object to be more testable, but stopping here means testing something that's similar to (but not exactly the same as) the class we want to test. It isn't as if we're writing tests for a third-party library and can't change the code—we have complete control over the code to test. We can enhance it and make it more test friendly in the process.

7.4.4   *Second attempt: refactoring by using a class factory*

Let's apply the Inversion of Control pattern, which says that any resource we use needs to be passed to the `getContent` method or `WebClient` class. The only resource we use is the `HttpURLConnection` object. We could change the `WebClient.getContent` signature to

```
public String getContent(URL url, HttpURLConnection connection)
```

This means we're pushing the creation of the `HttpURLConnection` object to the caller of `WebClient`. But the URL is retrieved from the `HttpURLConnection` class, and the signature doesn't look nice. Fortunately, there's a better solution that involves creating a `ConnectionFactory` interface, as shown in listings 7.8 and 7.9. The role of classes implementing the `ConnectionFactory` interface is to return an `InputStream` from a connection, whatever the connection might be (HTTP, TCP/IP, and so on). This refactoring technique is sometimes called a *class factory* refactoring.[3]

---

[3] J. B. Rainsberger calls it Replace Subclasses with Collaborators: http://www.diasparsoftware.com/template.php?content=replaceSubclassWithCollaborator.

Listing 7.8   `ConnectionFactory.java`

```
[...]
import java.io.InputStream;
public interface ConnectionFactory {
   InputStream getData() throws Exception;
}
```

The WebClient code then becomes as shown in listing 7.9. (Changes from the initial implementation in listing 7.6 are shown in bold.)

Listing 7.9   Refactored `WebClient` using `ConnectionFactory`

```
[...]
import java.io.InputStream;

public class WebClient {
   public String getContent(ConnectionFactory connectionFactory) {
      StringBuffer content = new StringBuffer();
      try {
         InputStream is = connectionFactory.getData();
         int count;
         while (-1 != (count = is.read())) {
            content.append( new String( Character.toChars( count ) ) );
         }
      }
      catch (Exception e) {
         return null;
      }
      return content.toString();
   }
}
```

This solution is better because we've made the retrieval of the data content independent of the way we get the connection. The first implementation worked only with URLs using HTTP. The new implementation can work with any standard protocol (`file://`, `http://`, `ftp://`, `jar://`, and so forth) or even your own custom protocol. For example, listing 7.10 shows the ConnectionFactory implementation for HTTP.

Listing 7.10   `HttpURLConnectionFactory.java`

```
[...]
import java.io.InputStream;
import java.net.HttpURLConnection;
import java.net.URL;

public class HttpURLConnectionFactory implements ConnectionFactory {
   private URL url;
   public HttpURLConnectionFactory(URL url) {
      this.url = url;
   }
   public InputStream getData() throws Exception {
      HttpURLConnection connection =
         (HttpURLConnection) this.url.openConnection();
```

```
    return connection.getInputStream();
  }
}
```

Now we can easily test the `getContent` method by writing a mock for `Connection-Factory` (see listing 7.11).

Listing 7.11 `MockConnectionFactory.java`

```
[...]
import java.io.InputStream;

  public class MockConnectionFactory implements ConnectionFactory {
    private InputStream inputStream;

    public void setData(InputStream stream) {
      this.inputStream = stream;
    }
    public InputStream getData() throws Exception {
      return this.inputStream;
    }
  }
```

As usual, the mock doesn't contain any logic and is completely controllable from the outside (by calling the `setData` method). We can now easily rewrite the test to use `MockConnectionFactory`, as demonstrated in listing 7.12.

Listing 7.12 Refactored `WebClient` test using `MockConnectionFactory`

```
[...]
import java.io.ByteArrayInputStream;

public class TestWebClient {

  @Test
  public void testGetContentOk() throws Exception {
    MockConnectionFactory mockConnectionFactory =
                                      new MockConnectionFactory();
    mockConnectionFactory.setData(
                new ByteArrayInputStream("It works".getBytes()));

    WebClient client = new WebClient();
    String result = client.getContent(mockConnectionFactory);
    assertEquals("It works", result);
  }
}
```

We've achieved our initial goal: to unit test the code logic of the `WebClient.get-Content` method. In the process we had to refactor it for the test, which led to a more extensible implementation that's better able to cope with change.

7.5   *Using mocks as Trojan horses*

Mock objects are Trojan horses, but they're not malicious. Mocks replace real objects from the inside, without the calling classes being aware of it. Mocks have access to internal information about the class, making them quite powerful. In the examples so far, we've used them only to emulate real behaviors, but we haven't mined all the information they can provide.

It's possible to use mocks as probes by letting them monitor the method calls the object under test makes. Let's take the HTTP connection example. One of the interesting calls we could monitor is the close method on the InputStream. We haven't been using a mock object for InputStream so far, but we can easily create one and provide a verify method to ensure that close has been called. Then, we can call the verify method at the end of the test to verify that all methods that should have been called were called (see listing 7.13). We may also want to verify that close has been called exactly once and raise an exception if it was called more than once or not at all. These kinds of verifications are often called *expectations*.

DEFINITION   *Expectation*—When we're talking about mock objects, an *expectation* is a feature built into the mock that verifies whether the external class calling this mock has the correct behavior. For example, a database connection mock could verify that the close method on the connection is called exactly once during any test that involves code using this mock.

To see an example of an expectation, look at listing 7.13.

Listing 7.13   Mock `InputStream` with an expectation on close

```
[...]
import java.io.IOException;
import java.io.InputStream;
public class MockInputStream extends InputStream {
   private String buffer;
   private int position = 0;
   private int closeCount = 0;
   public void setBuffer(String buffer) {          Tell mock what
      this.buffer = buffer;                         read method
   }                                                 should return
   public int read() throws IOException {
      if (position == this.buffer.length()) {
         return -1;
      }
      return this.buffer.charAt(this.position++);
   }
   public void close() throws IOException {          Count number of
      closeCount++;                               ◁─┘ times close is called
      super.close();
   }
   public void verify() throws java.lang.AssertionError {
      if (closeCount != 1) {                                    Verify
         throw new AssertionError ("close() should "            expectations
                     + "have been called once and once only");  are met
      }
   }
}
```

In the case of the MockInputStream class, the expectation for close is simple: we always want it to be called once. But most of the time, the expectation for closeCount depends on the code under test. A mock usually has a method like setExpected-CloseCalls so that the test can tell the mock what to expect.

Let's modify the TestWebClient.testGetContentOk test method to use the new MockInputStream:

```
[...]
public class TestWebClient {

    @Test
    public void testGetContentOk() throws Exception {
        MockConnectionFactory mockConnectionFactory =
            new MockConnectionFactory();

        MockInputStream mockStream = new MockInputStream();
        mockStream.setBuffer("It works");
        mockConnectionFactory.setData(mockStream);
        WebClient client = new WebClient();
        String result = client.getContent(mockConnectionFactory);

        assertEquals("It works", result);
        mockStream.verify();
    }
}
```

Instead of using a real ByteArrayInputStream as in previous tests, we now use the MockInputStream. Note that we call the verify method of MockInputStream at the end of the test to ensure that all expectations are met. The result of running the test is shown in figure 7.4.

The test fails with the message close() should have been called once and once only.

Why? Because we haven't closed the input stream in the WebClient.getContent method. The same error would be raised if we were closing it twice or more, because the test verifies that it's called once and only once.

Let's correct the code under test (see listing 7.14).

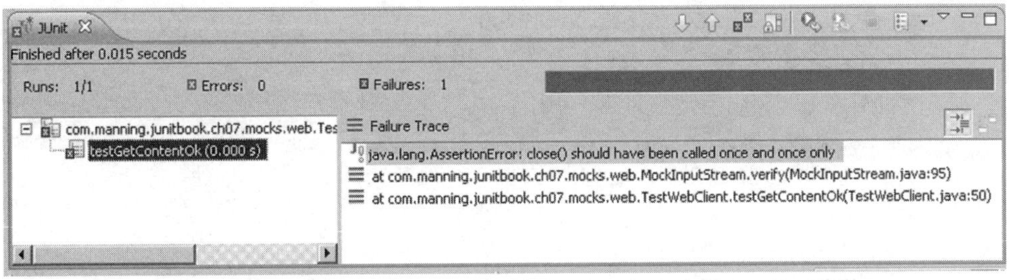

Figure 7.4 Running TestWebClient with the new close expectation

Listing 7.14   WebClient closing the stream

```java
public class WebClient {
    public String getContent(ConnectionFactory connectionFactory)
                                            throws IOException {
        String result;
        StringBuffer content = new StringBuffer();
        InputStream is = null;
        try {
            is = connectionFactory.getData();
            int count;
            while (-1 != (count = is.read())) {
                content.append( new String( Character.toChars( count ) ) );
            }
            result = content.toString();
        }
        catch (Exception e) {
            result = null;
        }

        // Close the stream
        if (is != null) {
            try {
                is.close();
            }
            catch (IOException e) {
                result = null;
            }
        }
        return result;
    }
}
```

> **Close stream and return null if error occurs**

We now get a nice green bar (figure 7.5).

There are other handy uses for expectations. For example, if you have a component manager calling different methods of your component lifecycle, you might expect them to be called in a given order. Or, you might expect a given value to be passed as a parameter to the mock. The general idea is that, aside from behaving the way you want during a test, your mock can also provide useful feedback on its usage.

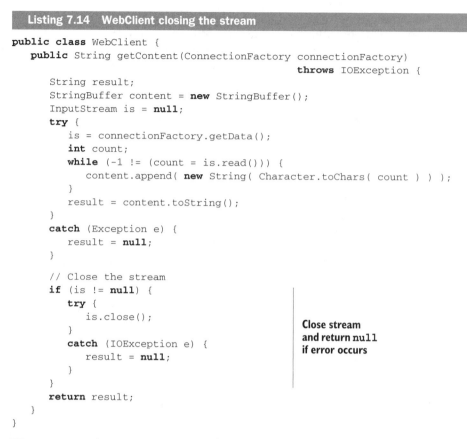

Figure 7.5   Working WebClient that closes the input stream

The next section demonstrates the use of some of the most popular open source mocking frameworks—they're powerful enough for our needs, and we don't need to implement our mocks from the beginning.

7.6 Introducing mock frameworks

So far we've been implementing the mock objects we need from scratch. As you can see, it's not a tedious task but rather a recurring one. You might guess that we don't need to reinvent the wheel every time we need a mock. And you're right—there are many good projects already written that can help us facilitate the usage of mocks in our projects. In this section we take a closer look at two of the most widely used mock frameworks: the EasyMock and the JMock. We try to rework the example HTTP connection application so that we can demonstrate how to use the two frameworks.

7.6.1 Using EasyMock

EasyMock (http://easymock.org/) is an open source framework that provides useful classes for mocking objects. To use the framework you need to download the zip archive from the website of the project, unpack it somewhere, and include the contained easymock.jar in your classpath.

To show you how easy it is to construct mock objects in your test cases using Easy-Mock, we revise some of the mocks we constructed in the previous sections. We start with a simple one: reworking the `AccountService` test from listing 7.2. See listing 7.15.

> **Listing 7.15 Reworking the `TestAccountService` test using EasyMock**

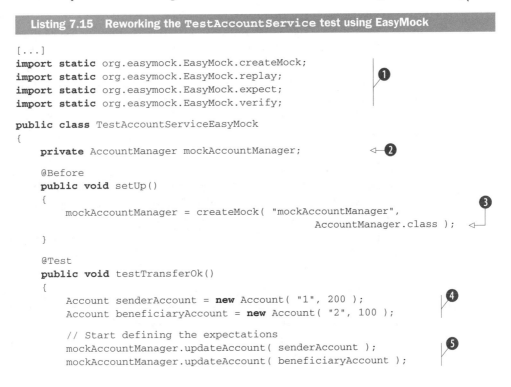

```
[...]
import static org.easymock.EasyMock.createMock;
import static org.easymock.EasyMock.replay;               ❶
import static org.easymock.EasyMock.expect;
import static org.easymock.EasyMock.verify;

public class TestAccountServiceEasyMock
{
    private AccountManager mockAccountManager;            ◁━❷

    @Before
    public void setUp()
    {                                                                    ❸
        mockAccountManager = createMock( "mockAccountManager",
                                    AccountManager.class );  ◁━┘
    }

    @Test
    public void testTransferOk()
    {
        Account senderAccount = new Account( "1", 200 );         ❹
        Account beneficiaryAccount = new Account( "2", 100 );

        // Start defining the expectations
        mockAccountManager.updateAccount( senderAccount );       ❺
        mockAccountManager.updateAccount( beneficiaryAccount );
```

```
        expect( mockAccountManager.findAccountForUser( "1" ) )
                            .andReturn( senderAccount );         ◁──
        expect( mockAccountManager.findAccountForUser( "2" ) )       ❻
                            .andReturn( beneficiaryAccount );   ◁──┘

        // we're done defining the expectations
        replay( mockAccountManager );                       ◁──❼

        AccountService accountService = new AccountService();
        accountService.setAccountManager( mockAccountManager );
        accountService.transfer( "1", "2", 50 );            ◁──❽

        assertEquals( 150, senderAccount.getBalance() );          ❾
        assertEquals( 150, beneficiaryAccount.getBalance() );
    }

    @After
    public void tearDown()
    {
        verify( mockAccountManager );      ◁──❿
    }
}
```

As you see, listing 7.15 is pretty much the same size as listing 7.4, but we are spared the writing of any additional mock classes. We start the listing by defining the imports from the EasyMock library that we need ❶. EasyMock relies heavily on the static-import feature of Java 5+. In ❷ we declare the object that we'd like to mock. Notice that our AccountManager is an interface. The reason behind this is simple: the core EasyMock framework can mock only interface objects. In ❸ we call the createMock method to create a mock of the class that we want. In ❹, as in listing 7.4, we create two account objects that we're going to use in our tests. After that we start declaring our expectations. With EasyMock we declare the expectations in two ways. When the method return type is void, we call it on the mock object (as in ❺), or when the method returns any kind of object, then we need to use the expect and andReturn methods from the EasyMock API ❻. Once we've finished defining the expectations, we need to call the replay method to announce it ❼. In ❽ we call the transfer method to transfer some money between the two accounts, and in ❾ we assert the expected result. The @After method, which gets executed after every @Test method, holds the verification of the expectations. With EasyMock we can call the verify method with any mock object ❿, to verify that the method-call expectations we declared were triggered.

That was pretty easy, wasn't it? So how about moving a step forward and revising a more complicated example? No problem; listing 7.16 shows the reworked WebClient test from listing 7.12.

What we'd like is to test the getContent method of the WebClient. For this purpose we need to mock all the dependencies to that method. In this example we have two dependencies: one is the ConnectionFactory and one is the InputStream. It looks like there's a problem because EasyMock can mock only interfaces, and the InputStream is a class.

JUnit best practices: EasyMock object creation

Here is a nice-to-know tip on the `createMock` method. If you check the API of Easy-Mock, you'll see that the `createMock` method comes with numerous signatures. The signature that we use is

```
createMock(String name, Class claz);
```

But there's also

```
createMock(Class claz);
```

So which one should you use? The first one is better. If you use the second one and your expectations aren't met, then you'll get an error message like the following:

```
java.lang.AssertionError:
  Expectation failure on verify:
    read(): expected: 7, actual: 0
```

As you can see, this message isn't as descriptive as we want it to be. If we use the first signature instead, and we map the class to a given name, we get something like the following:

```
java.lang.AssertionError:
  Expectation failure on verify:
    name.read(): expected: 7, actual: 0
```

To be able to mock the `InputStream` class, we're going to use the Class Extension of EasyMock. Class Extension is an extension project of EasyMock that lets you generate mock objects[4] for classes and interfaces. You can download it separately from the Easy-Mock website.

Listing 7.16   Reworking the `WebClient` test using EasyMock

```
[...]
import static org.easymock.classextension.EasyMock.createMock;       ❶
import static org.easymock.classextension.EasyMock.replay;
import static org.easymock.classextension.EasyMock.verify;

public class TestWebClientEasyMock
{
    private ConnectionFactory factory;        ❷
    private InputStream stream;

    @Before
    public void setUp()
    {
        factory = createMock( "factory", ConnectionFactory.class );    ❸
        stream = createMock( "stream", InputStream.class );
    }
```

---

[4] Final and private methods can't be mocked.

```
@Test
public void testGetContentOk() throws Exception
{
    expect( factory.getData() ).andReturn( stream );
    expect( stream.read() ).andReturn( new Integer( (byte) 'W' ) );
    expect( stream.read() ).andReturn( new Integer( (byte) 'o' ) );
    expect( stream.read() ).andReturn( new Integer( (byte) 'r' ) );
    expect( stream.read() ).andReturn( new Integer( (byte) 'k' ) );
    expect( stream.read() ).andReturn( new Integer( (byte) 's' ) );
    expect( stream.read() ).andReturn( new Integer( (byte) '!' ) );
    expect( stream.read() ).andReturn( -1 );
    stream.close();

    replay( factory );
    replay( stream );

    WebClient2 client = new WebClient2();
    String result = client.getContent( factory );

    assertEquals( "Works!", result );
}

[...]
    @Test
    public void testGetContentCannotCloseInputStream() throws Exception {
        expect( factory.getData() ).andReturn( stream );
        expect( stream.read() ).andReturn( -1 );
        stream.close();
        expectLastCall().andThrow(new IOException("cannot close"));

        replay( factory );
        replay( stream );
        WebClient2 client = new WebClient2();
        String result = client.getContent( factory );

        assertNull( result );
    }

    @After
    public void tearDown()
    {
        verify( factory );
        verify( stream );
    }
}
```

④ ⑤ ⑥ ⑦ ⑧ ⑨ ⑩

We start the listing by importing the objects that we need ❶. Notice that because we use the `classextensions` extension of EasyMock, we now need to import the `org.easymock.classextension.EasyMock` object instead of `org.easymock.EasyMock`. That's it! Now we're ready to create mock objects of classes and interfaces using the statically imported methods of `classextensions`. In ❷, as in the previous listings, we declare the objects that we want to mock, and in ❸ we call the `createMock` method to initialize them.

In ❹ we define the expectation of the stream when the `read` method is invoked (notice that to stop reading from the `stream`, the last thing to return is `-1`), and in

❺ we expect the close method to be called on the stream. Now we need to denote that we've finished declaring our expectations; we do this by calling the replay method ❻. The rest is invoking the method under test ❼ and asserting the expected result ❽.

We also add another test to simulate a condition when we can't close the Input-Stream. We define an expectation where we expect the close method of the stream to be invoked ❾, and on the next line we declare that an IOException should be raised if this call occurs ❿.

As the name of the framework suggests, using EasyMock is easy, and you should use it whenever possible. But to make you aware of the entire mocking picture, we'd like to introduce another framework, so you have a better taste of what mocking is.

7.6.2   Using JMock

So far we showed how to implement our own mock objects and how to use the Easy-Mock framework. In this section we introduce the JMock framework (http://jmock.org/), so that we can have a full view of the different mocking techniques. As in the previous section, we start with a simple example: reworking listing 7.4 by means of JMock. See listing 7.17.

Listing 7.17   Reworking the `TestAccountService` test using JMock

```
[...]
import org.jmock.Expectations;
import org.jmock.Mockery;                                          ❶
import org.jmock.integration.junit4.JMock;
import org.jmock.integration.junit4.JUnit4Mockery;

@RunWith( JMock.class )                                         ◁─❷
public class TestAccountServiceJMock
{
    private Mockery context = new JUnit4Mockery();              ◁─❸

    private AccountManager mockAccountManager;                  ◁─❹

    @Before
    public void setUp()
    {
        mockAccountManager = context.mock( AccountManager.class );   ◁─❺
    }

    @Test
    public void testTransferOk()
    {
        final Account senderAccount = new Account( "1", 200 );       ❻
        final Account beneficiaryAccount = new Account( "2", 100 );

        context.checking( new Expectations()                    ◁─❼
        {
            {
                oneOf( mockAccountManager ).findAccountForUser( "1" );   ❽
                will( returnValue( senderAccount ) );
```

```
                oneOf( mockAccountManager ).findAccountForUser( "2" );
                will( returnValue( beneficiaryAccount ) );

                oneOf( mockAccountManager ).updateAccount( senderAccount );
                oneOf( mockAccountManager )
                            .updateAccount( beneficiaryAccount );
        }
    } );

        AccountService accountService = new AccountService();
        accountService.setAccountManager( mockAccountManager );
        accountService.transfer( "1", "2", 50 );                    ◁─❾

        assertEquals( 150, senderAccount.getBalance() );           ◁─❿
        assertEquals( 150, beneficiaryAccount.getBalance() );
    }
}
```

As always, we start the listing by importing all the necessary objects we need ❶. As you can see, unlike EasyMock, the JMock framework doesn't rely on any static import features. Luckily enough, the JMock framework provides a JUnit 4 runner[5] that will facilitate a lot. In ❷ we instruct JUnit to use the JMock runner that comes with the framework. In ❸ we declare the context `Mockery` object that will serve us to create mocks and to define expectations. In ❹ we declare the `AccountManager` that we'd like to mock. Just like EasyMock, the core JMock framework provides mocking only of interfaces. In the `@Before` method, which gets executed before each of the `@Test` methods, we create the mock by means of the context object ❺. As in any of the previous listings, we declare two accounts that we're going to use to transfer money between ❻. Notice that this time the accounts are declared `final`. This is because we use them in an inner class defined in a different method. In ❼ we start declaring the expectations by constructing a new `Expectations` object. In ❽ we declare the first expectation, each expectation having the following form:

```
invocation-count (mock-object).method(argument-constraints);
    inSequence(sequence-name);
    when(state-machine.is(state-name));
    will(action);
    then(state-machine.is(new-state-name));
```

All the clauses are optional, except for the bold ones: `invocation-count` and `mock-object`. We need to specify how many invocations will occur and on which object. After that, in case the method returns some object, we can declare the return object by using the `will(returnValue())` construction.

In ❾ we start the transfer from one account to the other, and after that we assert the expected results ❿. It's as simple as that! But wait; what happened with the verification of the invocation count? In all of the previous examples we needed to verify that the invocations of the expectations happened the expected number of times.

---

[5] You can see how to implement a custom JUnit runner in appendix B of the book.

Well, with JMock you don't have to do that; the JMock JUnit runner takes care of this, and in case any of the expected calls were not made, the test will fail.

Following the pattern from the previous section about EasyMock, let's rework listing 7.12, shown in listing 7.18, showing the WebClient test, this time using JMock.

Listing 7.18 Reworking the `TestWebClient` test using JMock

```
[...]
@RunWith( JMock.class )                                          ←①
public class TestWebClientJMock
{
    private Mockery context = new JUnit4Mockery()
    {
        {
            setImposteriser( ClassImposteriser.INSTANCE );      ②
        }
    };

    @Test
    public void testGetContentOk() throws Exception
    {
        final ConnectionFactory factory =
                        context.mock( ConnectionFactory.class ); ←┐
        final InputStream mockStream =                            ③
                        context.mock( InputStream.class );       ←┘

        context.checking( new Expectations()
        {
            {
                oneOf( factory ).getData();                      ④
                will( returnValue( mockStream ) );

                atLeast( 1 ).of( mockStream ).read();
                will( onConsecutiveCalls(
                        returnValue( new Integer( (byte) 'W' ) ),
                        returnValue( new Integer( (byte) 'o' ) ),
                        returnValue( new Integer( (byte) 'r' ) ), ⑤
                        returnValue( new Integer( (byte) 'k' ) ),
                        returnValue( new Integer( (byte) 's' ) ),
                        returnValue( new Integer( (byte) '!' ) ),
                        returnValue( -1 ) ) );

                oneOf( mockStream ).close();
            }
        } );

        WebClient2 client = new WebClient2();
        String result = client.getContent( factory );           ←⑥

        assertEquals( "Works!", result );                        ←⑦
    }

    @Test
    public void testGetContentCannotCloseInputStream() throws Exception
    {
```

```
final ConnectionFactory factory =
                    context.mock( ConnectionFactory.class );
final InputStream mockStream = context.mock( InputStream.class );

context.checking( new Expectations()
{
    {
        oneOf( factory ).getData();
        will( returnValue( mockStream ) );
        oneOf( mockStream ).read();
        will( returnValue( -1 ) );
        oneOf( mockStream ).close();                        ◄─❽
        will( throwException(
                new IOException( "cannot close" ) ) );     ◄─❾
    }
} );

WebClient2 client = new WebClient2();

String result = client.getContent( factory );

assertNull( result );
    }
}
```

Once again, we start the test case by instructing JUnit to use the JMock test runner
❶. This will save us the explicit verification of the expectations. To tell JMock to create mock objects not only for interfaces but also for classes, we need to set the
imposteriser property of the context ❷. That's all; now we can continue creating
mocks the normal way. In ❸ we declare and initialize the two objects we'd like to
create mocks of. In ❹ we start the declaration of the expectations. Notice the fine
way we declare the consecutive execution of the read() method of the stream ❺
and also the returned values. In ❻ we call the method under test, and in ❼ we
assert the expected result.

For a full view of how to use the JMock mocking library, we also provide another
@Test method, which tests our WebClient under exceptional conditions. In ❽ we
declare the expectation of the close() method being triggered, and in ❾ we instruct
JMock to raise an IOException when this trigger happens.

As you can see, the JMock library is as easy to use as the EasyMock one. Whichever
you prefer to use is up to you, as long as you remember that what increases your software quality isn't the framework you use but rather how much you use it.

7.7   Summary

This chapter described a technique called *mock objects* that lets you unit test code in
isolation from other domain objects and from the environment. When it comes to
writing fine-grained unit tests, one of the main obstacles is to extract yourself from
the executing environment. We've often heard the following remark: "I haven't
tested this method because it's too difficult to simulate a real environment." Well, not
any longer!

In most cases, writing mock object tests has a nice side effect: it forces you to rewrite some of the code under test. In practice, code is often not written well. You hardcode unnecessary couplings between the classes and the environment. It's easy to write code that's hard to reuse in a different context, and a little nudge can have a big effect on other classes in the system (similar to the domino effect). With mock objects, you must think differently about the code and apply better design patterns, like interfaces and Inversion of Control.

Mock objects should be viewed not only as a unit testing technique but also as a design technique. A new rising star among methodologies called test-driven development (TDD) advocates writing tests before writing code. With TDD, you don't have to refactor your code to enable unit testing: the code is already under test! (For a full treatment of the TDD approach, see Kent Beck's book *Test Driven Development: By Example*.[6] For a brief introduction, see chapter 5.)

Although writing mock objects is easy, it can become tiresome when you need to mock hundreds of objects. In the following chapters, we present several open source frameworks that automatically generate ready-to-use mocks for your classes, making it a pleasure to use the mock objects strategy.

---

[6] Kent Beck, *Test Driven Development: By Example* (Boston: Addison-Wesley, 2003).

In-container testing 8

The secret of success is sincerity. Once
you can fake that you've got it made.

—Jean Giraudoux

> **This chapter covers**
> - The drawbacks of mock objects
> - In-container testing
> - Comparing stubs, mock objects, and
>   in-container testing

This chapter examines one approach to unit testing components in an application container: in-container unit testing, or integration unit testing. We discuss in-container testing pros and cons and show what can be achieved using the mock objects approach introduced in chapter 7, where mock objects fall short, and how in-container testing enables you to write integration unit tests. Finally, we compare the stubs, mock objects, and in-container approaches we've already covered in this second part of this book.

8.1 Limitations of standard unit testing

Let's start with the example servlet in listing 8.1, which implements the `Http-Servlet` method `isAuthenticated`, the method we want to unit test.

Listing 8.1   Servlet implementing `isAuthenticated`

```
[...]
import javax.servlet.http.HttpServlet;
import javax.servlet.http.HttpServletRequest;
import javax.servlet.http.HttpSession;

public class SampleServlet extends HttpServlet {
    public boolean isAuthenticated(HttpServletRequest request) {
        HttpSession session = request.getSession(false);
        if (session == null) {
            return false;
        }
        String authenticationAttribute =
            (String) session.getAttribute("authenticated");
        return Boolean.valueOf(authenticationAttribute).booleanValue();
    }
}
```

This servlet, although simple enough, allows us to show the limitation of standard unit testing. In order to test the method `isAuthenticated`, we need a valid `Http-ServletRequest`. Because `HttpServletRequest` is an interface, we can't just call a new `HttpServletRequest`. The `HttpServletRequest` lifecycle and implementation are provided by the container (in this case, a servlet container.) The same is true for other server-side objects like `HttpSession`. JUnit alone isn't enough to write a test for the `isAuthenticated` method and for servlets in general.

> **DEFINITION**   *Component* and *container*—In this chapter, a *component* executes in a container. A *container* offers services for the components it's hosting, such as lifecycle, security, transaction, distribution, and so forth.

In the case of servlets and JSPs, the container is a servlet container like Jetty or Tomcat. There are other types of containers, for example, EJB, database, and OSGi containers.

As long as a container creates and manages objects at runtime, we can't use standard JUnit techniques to test those objects.

8.2   *The mock objects solution*

We look at several solutions for in-container testing. The first solution for unit testing the `isAuthenticated` method (listing 8.1) is to mock the `HttpServletRequest` class using the approach described in chapter 7. Although mocking works, we need to write a lot of code to create a test. We can achieve the same result more easily using the open source EasyMock[1] framework (see chapter 7), as listing 8.2 demonstrates.

---

[1]   http://easymock.org/

Listing 8.2   Testing a servlet with EasyMock

```
[...]
import javax.servlet.http.HttpServletRequest;
import static org.easymock.EasyMock.createStrictMock;
import static org.easymock.EasyMock.expect;
import static org.easymock.EasyMock.replay;                          ❶
import static org.easymock.EasyMock.verify;
import static org.easymock.EasyMock.eq;
import static org.junit.Assert.assertFalse;
import static org.junit.Assert.assertTrue;
[...]
public class EasyMockSampleServletTest {

    private SampleServlet servlet;
    private HttpServletRequest mockHttpServletRequest;               ❷
    private HttpSession mockHttpSession;

    @Before
    public void setUp() {
        servlet = new SampleServlet();
        mockHttpServletRequest =                                     ❸
            createStrictMock(HttpServletRequest.class);
        mockHttpSession = createStrictMock(HttpSession.class);
    }

    @Test
    public void testIsAuthenticatedAuthenticated() {
        expect(mockHttpServletRequest.getSession(eq(false)))
            .andReturn(mockHttpSession);
        expect(mockHttpSession.getAttribute(eq("authenticated")))    ❹
            .andReturn("true");
        replay(mockHttpServletRequest);                              ❺
        replay(mockHttpSession);
        assertTrue(servlet.isAuthenticated(mockHttpServletRequest));    ❻
    }

    @Test
    public void testIsAuthenticatedNotAuthenticated() {
        expect(mockHttpSession.getAttribute(eq("authenticated")))
            .andReturn("false");
        replay(mockHttpSession);
        expect(mockHttpServletRequest.getSession(eq(false)))
            .andReturn(mockHttpSession);
        replay(mockHttpServletRequest);
        assertFalse(servlet.isAuthenticated(mockHttpServletRequest));
    }

    @Test
    public void testIsAuthenticatedNoSession() {
        expect(mockHttpServletRequest.getSession(eq(false))).andReturn(null);
        replay(mockHttpServletRequest);
        replay(mockHttpSession);
        assertFalse(servlet.isAuthenticated(mockHttpServletRequest));
    }
}
```

```
@After
public void tearDown() {                    ◄──❼
    verify(mockHttpServletRequest);                ❽
    verify(mockHttpSession);
    }
}
```

We start by importing the necessary classes and methods using Java 5 static imports ❶. We use the EasyMock class extensively, which has similar syntax to the JUnit Hamcrest matchers. Next, we declare instance variables for the objects ❷ we want to mock, HttpServletRequest and HttpSession. The setUp method annotated with @Before ❸ runs before each call to @Test methods; this is where we instantiate all of our mock objects. Next, we implement our tests following this pattern:

1 Set our expectations using the EasyMock API ❹.
2 Invoke the replay method to finish declaring our expectations ❺.
3 Assert test conditions on the servlet ❻.

Finally, at ❼ the @After method (executed after each @Test method) calls the Easy-Mock verify API ❽ to check whether the mocked objects met all of our programmed expectations.

Mocking a minimal portion of a container is a valid approach to testing components. But mocking can be complicated and require a lot of code. As with other kinds of tests, when the servlet changes, the test expectations must change to match. Next, we look at easing this task.

8.3   In-container testing

Another approach to testing the SampleServlet is to run the test cases where the HttpsServletRequest and HttpSession objects live, in the container itself. This avoids the need to mock any objects; we access the objects and methods we need in the real container.

For our example, we need HttpServletRequest and HttpSession to be real objects managed by the container. Using a mechanism to deploy and execute our tests in a container, we have in-container testing. Next, we see what options are available to implement in-container tests.

8.3.1   Implementation strategies

We have two architectural choices to drive in-container tests: server-side and client-side. As we stated previously, we can drive the tests directly by controlling the server-side container and the unit tests. Alternatively, we can drive the tests from the client side, as shown in figure 8.1.

Once the tests are packaged and deployed in the container and to the client, the JUnit test runner executes the test classes on the client (1). A test class opens a connection via a protocol like HTTP(S) and calls the same test case on the server side (2). The server-side test case operates on server-side objects, which are normally available (such as HttpServletRequest, HttpServletResponse, HttpSession, BundleContext,

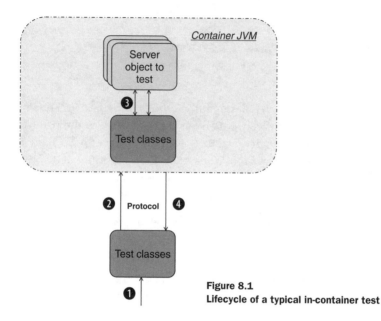

Figure 8.1
Lifecycle of a typical in-container test

and so on), and tests our domain objects (3). The server returns the result from the tests back to the client (4), which an IDE or Ant or Maven can gather.

8.3.2 *In-container testing frameworks*

As you just saw, in-container testing is applicable when code interacts with a container and tests can't create valid container objects (HttpServletRequest in the previous example).

Our example uses a servlet container, but there are many different types of containers: servlet, database, OSGi, SIP, and the like. In all of these cases, we can apply the in-container testing strategy. In the third part of the book, we present different open source projects that use this strategy. Table 8.1 lists the types of containers and the testing frameworks we use in later chapters.

Although the open source world offers other projects, we cover the more mature projects listed in the table. Next, we compare stubs, mock objects, and in-container testing.

Table 8.1 Containers and testing frameworks

Container type	In-container testing framework to use	Chapter with detailed description
HTTP container	Cactus (for testing servlets, JSPs, tag libraries, filters, and EJBs)	Chapter 14
HTTP container	JSFUnit (for testing JSF components)	Chapter 15
OSGi container	JUnit4OSGi (for testing OSGi modules)	Chapter 16
Database container	DBUnit	Chapter 17

8.4   *Comparing stubs, mock objects, and in-container testing*

In this section we compare[2] the different approaches we presented to test components. This section draws from the many questions in forums and mailing lists asking about the pros and cons of stubs, mock objects, and in-container testing.

8.4.1   *Stubs pros and cons*

We introduced stubs as our first out-of-container testing technique in chapter 6. Stubs work well to isolate a given class for testing and asserting the state of its instances. For example, stubbing a servlet container allows us to track how many requests were made, what the state of the server is, or what URLs where requested.

Using mocks, however, we can test the state of the server and its behavior. When using mock objects, we code and verify expectations; we check at every step to see whether tests execute domain methods and how many times tests call these methods.

One of the biggest advantages of stubs over mocks is that stubs are easier to understand. Stubs isolate a class with little extra code compared to mock objects, which require an entire framework to function. The drawback of stubs is that they rely on external tools and hacks, and they don't track the state objects they fake.

Going back to chapter 6, we easily faked a servlet container with stubs; doing so with mock objects would be much harder because we'd need to fake container objects with state and behavior. Here's a summary of stubs pros and cons.

Pros:

- They're fast and lightweight.
- They're easy to write and understand.
- They're powerful.
- Tests are coarser grained.

Cons:

- Specialized methods are required to verify state.
- They don't test the behavior of faked objects.
- They're time consuming for complicated interactions.
- They require more maintenance when the code changes.

8.4.2   *Mock objects pros and cons*

The biggest advantage of mock objects[3] over in-container testing is that mocks don't require a running container in order to execute tests. Tests can be set up quickly and run quickly. The main drawback is that the tested components don't

---

[2] For an in-depth comparison of the stubs and mocks technology, see "Mocks Aren't Stubs" by Martin Fowler: http://martinfowler.com/articles/mocksArentStubs.html.

[3] For an in-depth comparison of the mocks and in-container testing, see "Mock Objects vs. In-Container Testing": http://jakarta.apache.org/cactus/mock_vs_cactus.html.

run in the container in which you'll deploy them. The tests can't verify the interaction between components and container. The tests also don't test the interaction between the components themselves as they run in the container.

You still need a way to perform integration tests. Writing and running functional tests could achieve this. The problem with functional tests is that they're coarse grained and test only a full use case—you lose the benefits of fine-grained unit testing. You won't be able to test as many different cases with functional tests as you will with unit tests.

There are other disadvantages to mock objects. For example, you may have many mock objects to set up, which may prove to be considerable overhead. Obviously, the cleaner the code (small and focused methods), the easier tests are to set up.

Another important drawback to mock objects is that in order to set up a test, you usually must know exactly how the mocked API behaves. It's easy to know the behavior of your own API, but it may not be so easy for another API, such as the Servlet API.

Even though containers of a given type all implement the same API, not all containers behave the same way. For example, consider the following servlet method:

```
public void doGet(HttpServletRequest request,
                  HttpServletResponse response) {
    response.setContentType("text/xml");
}
```

This example seems simple enough, but if you run it in Tomcat (http://tomcat.apache.org/) and in Orion prior to version 1.6.0 (http://www.orionserver.com/), you'll notice different behaviors. In Tomcat, the returned content type is text/xml, but in Orion, it's text/html.

This is an extreme example; all servlet containers implement the Servlet API in pretty much the same way. But the situation is far worse for the various Java EE APIs—especially the EJB API. Implementers can interpret an API specification differently, and a specification can be inconsistent, making it difficult to implement. In addition, containers have bugs; the previous example may have been a bug in Orion 1.6.0. Although it's unfortunate, you'll have to deal with bugs, tricks, and hacks for various third-party libraries in any project.

To wrap up this section, we summarize the drawbacks of unit testing with mock objects:

- This approach doesn't test interactions with the container or between the components. It doesn't test the deployment of components.
- It requires excellent knowledge of the API to mock, which can be difficult (especially for external libraries).
- It doesn't provide confidence that the code will run in the target container.
- It's more fine grained, which may lead you to being swamped with interfaces.
- Like stubs, it requires maintenance when code changes.

8.4.3 *In-container testing pros and cons*

So far, we've described the advantages of in-container unit testing. But there are also a few disadvantages, which we now discuss.

SPECIFIC TOOLS REQUIRED

A major drawback is that although the concept is generic, the tools that implement in-container unit testing are specific to the tested API, such as Apache Jakarta Cactus for Java EE testing. If you wish to write integration unit tests for another component model, chances are such a framework exists. With mock objects, because the concept is generic, you can test almost any API.

NO GOOD IDE SUPPORT

A significant drawback of most of the in-container testing frameworks is the lack of good IDE integration. In most cases, you can use Ant or Maven to execute tests, which also provides the ability to run a build in a continuous integration server (CIS, see chapter 11). Alternatively, IDEs can execute tests that use mock objects as normal JUnit tests.

We strongly believe that in-container testing falls in the category of integration testing. This means that you don't need to execute your in-container tests as often as normal unit tests and will most likely run them in a CIS, alleviating the need for IDE integration.

LONGER EXECUTION TIME

Another issue is performance. For a test to run in a container, you need to start and manage the container, which can be time consuming. The overhead in time (and memory) depends on the container: Jetty can start in less than 1 second, Tomcat in 5 seconds, and WebLogic in 30 seconds. The startup overhead isn't limited to the container. For example, if a unit test hits a database, the database must be in an expected state before the test starts (see database application testing in chapter 17). In terms of execution time, integration unit tests cost more than mock objects. Consequently, you may not run them as often as logic unit tests.

COMPLEX CONFIGURATION

The biggest drawback to in-container testing is that tests are complex to configure. Because the application and its tests run in a container, your application must be packaged (usually as a WAR or EAR file) and deployed to the container. You must then start the container and run the tests.

On the other hand, because you must perform these exact same tasks for production, it's a best practice to automate this process as part of the build and reuse it for testing purposes. As one of the most complex tasks of a Java EE project, providing automation for packaging and deployment becomes a win-win situation. The need to provide in-container testing will drive the creation of this automated process at the beginning of the project, which will also facilitate continuous integration.

To further this goal, most in-container testing frameworks include support for build tools like Ant and Maven. This will help hide the complexity involved in building various runtime artifacts as well as with running tests and gathering reports.

8.4.4   *In-container versus out-of-container testing*

A standard design goal is to separate presentation from business layers. For example, you should implement the code for a tag that retrieves a list of customers from a database with two classes. One class implements the tag and depends on the Taglib API, whereas the other implements the database access and depends not on the Taglib API but on database classes like JDBC.

The separation-of-concerns strategy not only permits the reuse of classes in more than one context, but it also simplifies testing. You can test the business logic class with JUnit and mock objects and use in-container testing to validate the tag class.

In-container testing requires more setup than mock objects but is well worth the effort. You may not run the in-container tests as often, but they can confirm that your tags will work in the target environment. Although you may be tempted to skip testing a component, such as a taglib, reasoning that functional tests will eventually test the tag as a side effect, we recommend that you fight this temptation. *All components benefit from unit testing*. We outline these benefits here:

- Fine-grained tests can be run repeatedly and tell you when, where, and why your code breaks.

- You have the ability to test completely your components, not only for normal behavior but also for error conditions. For example, when testing a tag accessing a database, you should confirm that the tag behaves as expected when the connection with the database is broken. This would be hard to test in automated functional tests, but it's easy to test when you combine in-container testing and mock objects.

8.5   *Summary*

When it comes to unit testing an application in a container, we've shown that standard JUnit tests come up short. Although testing with mock objects works, it misses some scenarios like integration tests to verify component interactions in and with a container. In order to verify behavior in a container, we need a technique that addresses testing from an architectural point of view: in-container testing.

Although complex, in-container testing addresses these issues and provides developers with the confidence necessary to change and evolve their applications. This chapter provided the foundation for the last part of this book, where we continue to explore such testing frameworks.

Next, we start the third part of this book by integrating JUnit into the build process, a tenet of test-driven development.

Part 3

JUnit and the build process

This part of the book deals with a very important aspect in the development cycle of every project: the build process. The importance of the build process is reconsidered more often these days, especially in large projects. That's why we dedicate a whole part of this book to integration between JUnit and two of the most important build tools: Ant and Maven.

The ninth chapter gives you a quick introduction to Ant and its terminology: tasks, targets, and builds. We discuss how to start your tests as part of your Ant build lifecycle, and we also show how to produce some fancy reports with the results of the JUnit execution. This chapter serves as a basis for most of the rest of the book, because you need a good knowledge of Ant to be able to grasp all of the Ant integration sections in the latter chapters.

The tenth chapter guides you through the same concepts, but this time by means of another popular tool called Maven. We show you how to include the execution of your tests in the Maven build lifecycle and how to produce nice HTML reports by means of some of the Maven plug-ins.

The last chapter in this part of the book is devoted to continuous integration (CI) tools. This practice is highly recommended by extreme programmers and helps you maintain a code repository and automate the build on it. This is helpful in building large projects that depend on several other projects that change often (as any open source project does).

Running JUnit tests
from Ant

It's supposed to be automatic, but
you still have to press the button.

—John Brunner

This chapter covers

- Introducing Ant and Ivy
- Running Ant JUnit tasks
- Creating reports

In this chapter, we look at Apache Ant[1] or *Ant* for short, a free and open source build tool with direct support for JUnit. You can use Ant with any Java programming environment. We show you how to be more productive with JUnit by running tests as part of the build. We also show you how to set up your environment to build Java projects, manage JAR file dependencies, execute JUnit tests, and generate JUnit reports.

---

[1] http://ant.apache.org/

137

9.1   *A day in the life*

For unit tests to be effective, they must be part of the development routine. Most development cycles begin by checking out code from the source code repository. Before making any changes, prudent developers first run all unit test suites. Many teams have a rule that all unit tests in the repository must pass. Before starting any development, you should check to make sure all tests pass. You should always be sure that your work starts from a known stable baseline.

The next step is to write the code for a new use case (or modify an existing one.) If you're a test-driven development (TDD) practitioner, you'll start by writing new tests for the use case (for more about TDD, see chapter 5). In general, the tests will show that your use case isn't supported by not compiling or failing when executed. Once you write the code to implement (correctly) the use case, the tests pass, and you can check in your code. Non-TDD practitioners implement the use case first and then write the tests. Once the tests pass, the developer checks in the code.

Before you move on to code the next feature, you should have tests to prove the feature works. After you implement the feature, you can run the tests for the entire project, ensuring that the new feature didn't break any existing tests. If the existing code needs to change to accommodate the new feature, you should update the tests first and then make the changes.

If you test rigorously, both to help you write new code (TDD) and to ensure existing code works with new features (regression testing[2]), you must continually run the unit tests as a normal part of the development cycle. You need to be able to run these tests automatically and effortlessly throughout the day.

In chapter 1, section 1.4, we discussed running JUnit from the command line. Running a single JUnit test case against a single class isn't difficult. But it isn't practical to run continuous tests in a project with hundreds or even thousands of classes.

A project that's fully tested can have as many test classes as production classes. You can't expect developers to run an entire set of regression tests every day manually. Therefore, you need a way to run tests easily and automatically.

Because you're writing so many tests, you need to write and run tests in the most effective way possible. Ant is the de facto standard tool for building Java applications; it's an excellent tool for managing and automating JUnit tests.

9.2   *Running tests from Ant*

Compiling and testing a single class, like the `DefaultController` class from chapter 3, isn't difficult. Compiling a larger project with multiple classes can be a huge headache if your only tool is the `javac` command-line compiler. When the number of classes goes up, more classes need to be on the compiler classpath. Usually, in any one build you'll have changed only a few classes, which leads us to the issue of minimizing how

---

[2] For more about regression testing, see chapter 4.

much to rebuild. Rerunning your JUnit tests by hand after each build can be equally inconvenient for the same reasons.

Ant can solve both problems. Ant is not only an essential tool for building applications but also a great way to run your JUnit tests.

9.3   *Introducing and installing Ant*

One reason for Ant's popularity is that it's more than a tool: Ant is a framework for running code. In addition to using Ant to configure and launch a Java compiler, you can use it to copy files, run JUnit test suites, and create reports.

You configure Ant through an XML document called a *build file*, which is named build.xml by default. The Ant build file describes each task that you want to perform in your project. A build file can have several *targets*, or entry points, so that you can run a single target or chain several targets together. Let's look at using Ant to run tests automatically as part of the build. If you don't have Ant installed, see the following sidebar. For full details, consult the Ant manual (http://ant.apache.org/manual/).

Now that you're familiar with Ant and have it installed, let's get started with a project.

Installing Ant on Windows

To install Ant on Windows:

1 Unzip the zip distribution file to a local directory (for example, C:\Ant). In this directory, Unzip creates a subdirectory for the Ant distribution, for example, C:\Ant\apache-ant-1.8.0.

2 Add an `ANT_HOME` variable to your environment with this directory as the value, for example:

Variable name: `ANT_HOME`
Variable value: `C:\Ant\apache-ant-1.8.0`

3 Edit your `PATH` environment variable to include the %ANT_HOME%\bin folder:

Variable name: `PATH`
Variable value: `%ANT_HOME%\bin;%PATH%`

4 We recommend that you specify the location of your Java Development Kit (JDK) as the `JAVA_HOME` environment variable:

Variable name: `JAVA_HOME`
Variable value: `C:\jdk1.6.0_14`

This value, like the others, may vary depending on where you installed the JDK on your system.

5 To enable Ant's JUnit task, copy the file junit.jar to the %ANT_HOME%\lib folder. Ant will add the JAR file to the classpath for your build. We look at other options later.

Installing Ant on UNIX (Bash)

To install Ant on UNIX (or Linux), follow these steps:

1 Untar the Ant tarball to a local directory (for example, /opt/ant). In this directory, tar creates a subdirectory for the Ant distribution, for example, /opt/ant/apache-ant-1.7.1.

2 Add this directory to your environment as ANT_HOME, for example:

```
export ANT_HOME=/opt/ant/apache-ant-1.8.0
```

3 Add the ANT_HOME/bin folder to your system's command path:

```
export PATH=${PATH}:${ANT_HOME}/bin
```

4 We recommend that you specify the location of your JDK as the JAVA_HOME environment variable:

```
export JAVA_HOME=/usr/java/jdk1.6.0_14/
```

5 To enable Ant's JUnit task, copy the file junit.jar to the ${ANT_HOME}/lib folder. Ant will add the JAR file to the classpath for your build. We look at other options later.

9.4 Ant targets, projects, properties, and tasks

When you build a project, you often want to produce more than binary code. For a distribution, you may also want to generate Javadocs. For an internal development build, you might skip Javadoc generation. At times, you may want to run a build from scratch. You may also want to compile only the classes that have changed. To help you manage the build process, a build file may have several targets, encapsulating the different tasks needed to create your application and related resources.

To make the build files easier to configure and reuse, Ant lets you define property elements (similar to a constant in programming, or a final field in Java). The core Ant concepts are as follows:

- *Build file*—Each build file is usually associated with a particular development project. Ant uses the project XML tag as the root element in a build file to define the project. It also lets you specify a default target, so you can run Ant without any parameters.

- *Target*—When you run Ant, you can specify one or more targets to execute. Targets can optionally declare dependencies on other targets. If you ask Ant to run one target, Ant will execute its dependent targets *first*. This lets you create, for example, a distribution target that depends on other targets, like clean, compile, javadoc, and war.

- *Property elements*—Because many of the targets within a project share the same settings, Ant lets you create property elements to encapsulate specific settings and reuse them throughout a build file. To refer to a property in a build file, you use the notation ${property}. To refer to the property named target.dir, you'd write ${target.dir}.

As we mentioned, Ant isn't so much a tool as a framework for running tools. You can use `property` elements to set the parameters a tool needs and a *task* to run that tool. A great number of tasks come bundled with Ant, but you can also write your own custom tasks. For more about developing with Ant, we recommend reading *Ant in Action*[3] and exploring the Ant website.

Listing 9.1 shows the start of the build file for the example project from chapter 3. This segment of the build file sets the default target and the properties your targets and tasks will use.

Listing 9.1 Start of an Ant build file

```
<project name="example" default="test">        ←❶    ❷
    <property file="build.properties"/>              ←
    <property name="src.dir" location="src"/>
    <property name="src.java.dir" location="${src.dir}/java"/>    ❸
    <property name="src.test.dir" location="${src.dir}/test"/>
    <property name="target.dir" location="target"/>       ←
    <property name="target.classes.java.dir"
          location="${target.dir}/classes/java"/>          ←
    <property name="target.classes.test.dir"               ❹
        location="${target.dir}/classes/test"/>            ←
[...]
```

The listing starts ❶ by giving the project the name `example` and setting the default target to `test`. The `test` target appears in listing 9.3.

Next, we include the build.properties file ❷. Because programmers may store JAR files in different locations, it's a good practice to use a build.properties file to define their locations. Many open source projects provide a sample build.properties file you can copy and edit to match your environment.

We use the `property` Ant task to define the directories for production and test source code ❸ as well as the location of the directories for compiled production and test code ❹. It's a good practice to define source and test directories in separate locations for both source and compiled code. In our example, we end up with four property definitions. Splitting out compiled production and test code makes it easy to build other artifacts such as JAR files because all compiled production code is rooted in its own directory.

An important aspect of Ant properties is that they're immutable. Once you set a property value, you can't change it. If you try to redefine the value with another `property` element, Ant ignores the request.

9.4.1   *The javac task*

For simple projects, running the javac compiler from the command line is easy enough. For products with multiple packages and source directories, the configuration of the javac compiler becomes more complicated. The `javac` Ant task allows a

---

[3] http://manning.com/loughran/

build file to invoke the compiler so you no longer need to rely on the command line. Ant provides a task for almost all build-related jobs that you'd otherwise do on the command line, including dealing with repositories like CVS. You can also find tasks not defined by Ant itself that deal with just about anything. We mentioned CVS, but if you're using Subversion for revision control, you can use SvnAnt[4] out of the Subclipse project.

A standard practice is to create `compile` targets in your build file to invoke the Ant `javac` task to compile production and source code. The `javac` task lets you set all compiler options, such as the source and destination directories, through task attributes.

Listing 9.2 shows the production and test compile targets that call the Java compiler.

> **Listing 9.2   The build file compile targets**

```
<target name="compile.java">                                    ← ❶
    <mkdir dir="${target.classes.java.dir}"/>               ← ❷   ❸
    <javac destdir="${target.classes.java.dir}">            ←
        <src path="${src.java.dir}"/>                        ←
    </javac>                                                       ❹
</target>

<target name="compile.test" depends="compile.java">
    <mkdir dir="${target.classes.test.dir}"/>                    ❺
    <javac destdir="${target.classes.test.dir}">
        <src path="${src.test.dir}"/>
        <classpath>
            <pathelement location="${target.classes.java.dir}"/>  ❻
        </classpath>
    </javac>
</target>

<target name="compile" depends="compile.java, compile.test"/>  ←  ❼
```

First, we declare the target `compile.java` ❶ to make sure that the destination directory exists ❷ and compile the production sources ❸. Ant resolves the property `target.classes.java.dir` set at the top of the build file (in listing 9.1) and inserts it in place of `${target.classes.java.dir}`. The `mkdir` task creates a directory ❷, but if it already exists, Ant continues quietly. The build then calls the Java compiler with `javac`, giving it the destination ❸ and source ❹ directories.

The `compile.test` target has a dependency on the `compile.java` target, specified with the `depends` attribute ❺ (depends="compile.java"). When you call the `compile.test` target, if Ant hasn't called the `compile.java` target yet, it does so immediately.

You may have noticed that you don't explicitly add the JUnit JAR to the classpath. Remember that when you installed Ant, you copied the JUnit JAR file to the ${ANT_HOME}/lib directory in order to use the `junit` Ant task. Because junit.jar is

---

[4] http://subclipse.tigris.org/svnant.html

already on your classpath, you don't need to specify it in the `javac` task to compile your tests.

You need to add a nested `classpath` element ❻ in order to add the production classes you just compiled to the classpath because the test classes call the production classes.

Last, we have a `compile` target ❼ that depends on the `compile.java` and `compile.test` targets.

9.4.2 *The JUnit task*

In chapter 3, we ran the `DefaultController` tests manually. To test changes, we had to do the following:

- Compile the source code.
- Run the `TestDefaultController` test case against the compiled classes.

We can get Ant to perform both steps as part of the same `build` target. Listing 9.3 shows the `test` target.

Listing 9.3   The build file `test` target

```
<target name="test" depends="compile">                                    ←❶
   <junit printsummary="yes" haltonerror="yes" haltonfailure="yes"         ❷
       fork="yes">
      <formatter type="plain" usefile="false"/>                           ←❸
      <test name="junitbook.example.TestDefaultController"/>
         <classpath>                                                       ❹
            <pathelement location="${target.classes.java.dir}"/>           ←
            <pathelement location="${target.classes.test.dir}"/>           ←
         </classpath>                                                      ❺
   </junit>
</target>
```

We declare the `test` target and define it to depend on the `compile` target ❶. If we ask Ant to run the `test` target, it'll run the `compile` target before running the `test` target (unless Ant has already called `compile`). The only task defined in this target is to call `junit` ❷. The `junit` `printsummary` attribute causes the task to print a one-line summary at the end of the test. Setting `fork` to `yes` forces Ant to use a separate Java Virtual Machine for each test. Although this is a performance hit, it's a good practice if you're worried about interference between test cases. The `haltonfailure` and `haltonerror` attributes direct the build to stop if any test returns an error or a failure. In Ant, an error is an unexpected error, like an exception, whereas a failure is a failed assert call. We configure the `junit` task formatter to use plain text and output the test result to the console ❸. The `test name` attribute defines the class name of the test to run ❹. Finally, we extend the classpath to use for this task to include the production and test classes we just compiled ❺.

This makes up our first `test` target; next, we run the Ant build.

```
C:\WINDOWS\system32\cmd.exe                                    _ □ x

compile.test:

compile:

test:
    [junit] Running com.manning.junitbook.ch09.ant.TestDefaultController
    [junit] Testsuite: com.manning.junitbook.ch09.ant.TestDefaultController
    [junit] Tests run: 5, Failures: 0, Errors: 0, Time elapsed: 0.047 sec
    [junit] Tests run: 5, Failures: 0, Errors: 0, Time elapsed: 0.047 sec
    [junit]
    [junit] Testcase: testAddHandler took 0 sec
    [junit] Testcase: testProcessRequest took 0 sec
    [junit] Testcase: testProcessRequestAnswersErrorResponse took 0 sec
    [junit] Testcase: testGetHandlerNotDefined took 0 sec
    [junit] Testcase: testAddRequestDuplicateName took 0 sec

BUILD SUCCESSFUL
Total time: 0 seconds
C:\junitbook2\ch09-ant>
```

Figure 9.1   Running the build file from the command line

9.5   *Putting Ant to the task*

Now that you've assembled the build file, you can run it from the command line by changing to your project directory and typing ant. Figure 9.1 shows the Ant console output.

We can now build and test the project at the same time. If any of the tests fail, the haltonfailure and haltonerror settings will stop the build, bringing the problem to our attention.

Running the junit optional task

The junit task is an optional component bundled in Ant's ant-junit.jar file, which should already be in your ${ANT_HOME}/lib directory. Ant doesn't bundle a copy of JUnit, so you must ensure that junit.jar is on your classpath or in the ${ANT_HOME}/lib directory. The ant-junit.jar file contains the task itself. For more information on installing Ant, see section 9.3, "Introducing and installing Ant." If you have any trouble running the Ant build files presented in this chapter, make sure the ant-junit.jar file is in the ${ANT_HOME}/lib folder and junit.jar is either on your classpath or in the ${ANT_HOME}/lib folder.

So far, we've looked at one way to execute tests with Ant. We now look at another aspect of the build process: dependency management. In order to automate management of dependencies for Ant projects, we introduce and use the Apache Ivy[5] project.

---

[5] http://ant.apache.org/ivy/

9.6 *Dependency management with Ivy*

When your project is small, it can be easy to deal with the JAR files your code depends on. In our previous example, we depended on only one JAR file, junit.jar. For larger projects, your build may end up depending on dozens of libraries. These dependencies can trip up new developers or downstream developers of the project. Having to know what the JAR dependencies are and where to get them on the web should not be an impediment to developers using your project.

The Apache Maven project first introduced dependency management for Java projects (see the next chapter for coverage of the Maven build tool.) Maven dependency management is based on the concept of one or more (internet, network, or local) repositories containing JARs from many projects from all over the open source world. The developer lists dependencies for a project in a configuration file and lets Maven download the right files to a local repository cache on your machine. You can then add the JARs to your classpath based on their location in the local repository.

Apache Ivy[6] is a popular open source dependency management tool (used for recording, tracking, resolving, and reporting dependencies), focusing on flexibility and simplicity. Although available as a standalone tool, Ivy works particularly well with Ant, providing a number of powerful Ant tasks ranging from dependency resolution to reporting and publication. It's out of the scope of this book to cover Ivy in depth, but we rework our build file with dependency management using Ivy.

The installation of Ivy is straightforward; download the zip file from the website, extract it, and copy the ivy-vvv.jar (where *vvv* stands for the Ivy version) to the ${ANT_HOME}/lib directory.

Ivy works in the same manner as Maven and even uses Maven repositories for resolving and downloading dependencies. You specify the dependencies for your project in a file named, by default, ivy.xml. Ivy will download all the dependencies listed in the ivy.xml file into a local cache directory.

Listing 9.4 shows the build file with changes highlighted in bold.

Listing 9.4   Adding the Ivy changes to the build file

```
<project name="example" default="test"
    xmlns:ivy="antlib:org.apache.ivy.ant">          ◁-❶
    <property file="build.properties"/>

    [...]
    <ivy:retrieve file="./ivy.xml" sync="true"/>          ◁-❷

    <property name="junit.jar" location="lib/junit-4.6.jar"/>          ◁-❸
    [...]

    <target name="compile.test" depends="compile.java">
        <mkdir dir="${target.classes.test.dir}"/>
        <javac destdir="${target.classes.test.dir}">
```

---

[6] http://ant.apache.org/ivy/

```
        <src path="${src.test.dir}"/>
        <classpath>
            <pathelement location="${target.classes.java.dir}"/>
            <pathelement location="${junit.jar}"/>                    ◄-❹
        </classpath>
    </javac>
</target>
[...]

<target name="test" depends="compile">
    <junit printsummary="yes" haltonerror="yes" haltonfailure="yes"
        fork="yes">
        <formatter type="plain" usefile="false"/>
        <test name="junitbook.example.TestDefaultController"/>
        <classpath>
            <pathelement location="${target.classes.java.dir}"/>
            <pathelement location="${target.classes.test.dir}"/>
            <pathelement location="${junit.jar}"/>                    ◄-❺
        </classpath>
    </junit>
</target>
[...]
```

We start by declaring the `ivy` namespace ❶ and calling the Ivy Ant task to retrieve the
dependencies listed in the ivy.xml file from the public repository ❷. After we retrieve
the junit.jar with Ivy, the archive is in the lib folder of our project. Next, we define the
`junit.jar` property to point to the JAR file we just downloaded ❸. We include the JAR
in the classpath of the `javac` task ❹ and in the classpath of the `junit` task ❺. We no
longer need the junit.jar in the ${ANT_HOME}/lib folder, so we can delete it.

The file ivy.xml defines the project dependencies as shown in listing 9.5.

Listing 9.5 The ivy.xml file with the listed dependencies

```
<ivy-module version="2.0">                                      ◄-❶
    <info organisation="junitbook" module="example-ivy"/>       ◄-❷
    <dependencies>                                              ◄-❸
        <dependency org="junit" name="junit" rev="4.6"/>
    </dependencies>
</ivy-module>
```

First, the root tag `ivy-module` ❶ defines the version of Ivy we want to use (in this case
2.0). Then, the `info` tag ❷ defines the organization and the module name for which
we're defining dependencies. Finally, the `dependencies` nested element ❸ is where
we specify our dependencies. Our module has only one dependency listed: JUnit.

Invoking Ant again gives us the same result (figure 9.2) as when junit.jar was in
the ${ANT_HOME}/lib folder, but this time we see Ivy invoked and resolve the proj-
ect dependencies.

In the next section, we try out another kind of report.

```
C:\WINDOWS\system32\cmd.exe                                    _ □ ×
 ::
:: loading settings :: url = jar:file:/D:/apache/apache-ant-1.7.0/lib/ivy-2.0.0-
beta1.jar!/org/apache/ivy/core/settings/ivysettings.xml
[ivy:retrieve] :: resolving dependencies :: junitbook#sampling-ivy;working@WM-AM
S-PET
[ivy:retrieve]  confs: [default]
[ivy:retrieve]  found junit#junit;4.5 in public
[ivy:retrieve] :: resolution report :: resolve 94ms :: artifacts dl 0ms
       ┌──────────────┬───────────────────────────┬┬────────────────┐
       ¦              ¦         modules           ¦¦    artifacts   ¦
       ¦     conf     ¦ number¦ search¦dwnlded¦evicted¦¦ number¦dwnlded¦
       ├──────────────┼───────────────────────────┼┼────────────────┤
       ¦    default   ¦    1  ¦   0   ¦   0   ¦   0   ¦¦    1  ¦   0   ¦
       └──────────────┴───────────────────────────┴┴────────────────┘
[ivy:retrieve] :: retrieving :: junitbook#sampling-ivy [sync]
[ivy:retrieve]  confs: [default]
[ivy:retrieve]  0 artifacts copied, 1 already retrieved (0kB/15ms)

compile.java:

compile.test:

compile:

test:
    [junit] Running com.manning.junitbook.ch09.ant.TestDefaultController
    [junit] Testsuite: com.manning.junitbook.ch09.ant.TestDefaultController
    [junit] Tests run: 5, Failures: 0, Errors: 0, Time elapsed: 0.047 sec
    [junit] Tests run: 5, Failures: 0, Errors: 0, Time elapsed: 0.047 sec
    [junit]
    [junit] Testcase: testAddHandler took 0 sec
    [junit] Testcase: testProcessRequest took 0 sec
    [junit] Testcase: testProcessRequestAnswersErrorResponse took 0 sec
    [junit] Testcase: testGetHandlerNotDefined took 0 sec
    [junit] Testcase: testAddRequestDuplicateName took 0 sec

BUILD SUCCESSFUL
Total time: 0 seconds
C:\junitbook2\ch09-ant>
```

Figure 9.2 Ant output with Ivy at work

9.7 *Creating HTML reports*

The console output from figure 9.1 might be acceptable when you're running tests interactively, but you can't use the output if you want to examine the results later. A (cron) job or a continuous integration server (see chapter 11) might run the tests automatically every day such that the console output might not be available.

The junit task can produce XML documents detailing the results of various test runs. Another optional Ant task, junitreport, transforms this XML into HTML using an XSL stylesheet. The result is a report you can view with any web browser. Figure 9.3 shows a report page for the example project.

Listing 9.6 shows the changes necessary (in bold) to the build file to generate this report.

> **Listing 9.6   Adding a JUnitReport task to the build file**

```
<project name="example" default="test">
[...]
    <property name="target.report.dir" location="${target.dir}/report"/>   ◁─┐
[...]
```
❶

```
    <target name="test" depends="compile">
        <mkdir dir="${target.report.dir}"/>                              ←② 
        <junit printsummary="yes" haltonerror="yes" haltonfailure="yes"
            fork="yes">
            <formatter type="xml"/>                                      ←③ 
            <test name="junitbook.example.TestDefaultController"
                todir="${target.report.dir}"/>                           ←④ 
                <classpath>
                    <pathelement location="${target.classes.java.dir}"/>
                    <pathelement location="${target.classes.test.dir}"/>
                </classpath>
        </junit>
    </target>
    <target name="report" depends="test">                         ⑤ ⑥
        <mkdir dir="${target.report.dir}/html"/>
        <junitreport todir="${target.report.dir}">                       ←⑦ 
            <fileset dir="${target.report.dir}">
                <include name="TEST-*.xml"/>                             ←⑧ 
            </fileset>
            <report todir="${target.report.dir}/html"/>                  ←⑨ 
        </junitreport>
    </target>
</project>
```

First, we define a property for the location where the report will be generated ❶ and then create that directory ❷. We modify the junit task to output the test results as

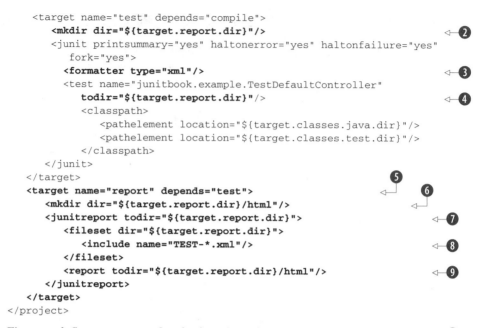

Figure 9.3   Ant JUnit HTML report

XML ❸ instead of plain text. The junitreport transforms the XML test results into an HTML report using XSL. We change the junit task to create an XML report file in the ${target.report.dir} directory ❹ and then create a new report target that generates the HTML report ❺.

We begin the report target by creating the directory where the HTML report will be generated ❻. We call the junitreport task to create the report ❼. The task scans the XML test results specified as an Ant fileset ❽ and generates the HTML report to our specified location ❾.

The next step is learning how to batch tests.

The future of JUnit reports

The Ant junit task produces XML output containing detailed results of the execution of JUnit tests. This task isn't the only tool to produce XML documents of this format; so does Maven's Surefire plug-in. Several tools also consume this format in addition to junitreport, like maven-surefire-reports, and different CI servers.

As of Ant 1.7.1, the generated HTML reports don't list skipped tests because Ant doesn't use JUnit 4 features. Note that in the previous version of JUnit there was no special status for skipped tests. We should expect the XML schema for JUnit reports to evolve, a topic currently under discussion on the Apache Ant[7] wiki.

9.8   *Batching tests*

Our current build file calls the junit task through the test target to invoke specific test cases. Although this is fine for a small set of test classes, it may become unwieldy for larger sets of classes. One way to remedy this situation is to group tests together in a test suite and invoke the test suite from Ant.

Alternatively, you can direct Ant to batch tests together by using wildcards to find tests by class names. The batchtest element uses a fileset with wildcards to find test classes, as shown in listing 9.7 (with changes from listing 9.4 in bold).

Listing 9.7   Using batchtest to find test cases

```
<project name="example" default="test">
   [...]
   <target name="test" depends="compile">
      <mkdir dir="${target.report.dir}"/>
      <property name="tests" value="Test*"/>                    ◁─❶
      <junit printsummary="yes" haltonerror="yes" haltonfailure="yes"
         fork="yes">
         <formatter type="plain" usefile="false"/>
         <formatter type="xml"/>
```

---

[7] http://wiki.apache.org/ant/Proposals/EnhancedTestReports

```
            <batchtest todir="${target.report.dir}">
                <fileset dir="${src.test.dir}">                        ❷
                    <include name="**/${tests}.java"/>
                    <exclude name="**/Test*All.java"/>
                </fileset>
            </batchtest>
            <classpath>
                <pathelement location="${target.classes.java.dir}"/>
                <pathelement location="${target.classes.test.dir}"/>
            </classpath>
        </junit>
    </target>
    [...]
    <target name="clean">
        <delete dir="${target.dir}"/>
    </target>
</project>
```

The tests property defines ❶ the class name pattern used by the batchtest element ❷ later in the listing. Defining this property allows us to override it from the command line or by another property definition. This allows us, for instance, to run a single test case or provide a value that runs a narrower set of tests. This technique provides us a shortcut to run the test for any given class we're working on while leaving the default value to execute the full set of tests. The following example executes only the TestDefaultController test case:

```
ant –Dtests=TestDefaultController test
```

The batchtest element ❷ makes the test target and our build more flexible. It's always a good practice to include a clean target to remove all build-generated files. Doing so lets us build from first principles (in our case, Java source files), removing potential side effects from obsolete classes. Typically, a dist (for *distribution*) target generates all project distributable files and depends on the clean target.

You should give thought to your test class names such that you can match them using a reasonable pattern. Depending on your language background, you may choose to prefix or postfix your class names with Test or TestCase, for example, DatabaseAccessorTest.

Are automated unit tests a panacea?

In brief, no. Although automated tests can find a significant number of bugs, manual testing is still required to find as many bugs as possible. In general, automated regression tests catch 15–30 percent of all bugs found; manual testing finds the other 70–85 percent.

Are you sure about that?

Some test-first enthusiasts are now reporting remarkably low numbers of bug counts, approximately one to two per month or fewer. Formal studies need to substantiate these reports. Your mileage will definitely vary.

9.9 *Summary*

In this chapter, we introduced Apache Ant, one of the best tools for building Java software. We looked at the basics of an Ant build file and described key tasks: `javac` `junit` and `junitreport`. These tasks allow you to compile Java code, run JUnit tests, and create HTML test reports. We also introduced Apache Ivy to manage with ease your project's JAR file dependencies. Ivy resolves and downloads JAR file dependencies for your build.

In the following chapters, we continue to explore the continuous integration paradigm with Maven, another tool for building software. We start with core Maven concepts and explore two important plug-ins: `maven-surefire` and `maven-surefire-report`. We also look at how Maven handles dependency management in comparison to Ivy.

10
Running JUnit tests from Maven 2

The conventional view serves to protect
us from the painful job of thinking.
—John Kenneth Galbraith

This chapter covers

- Introduction to Maven
- Dependency management the Maven way
- Maven Surefire plug-in
- Maven Surefire Report plug-in

In this chapter we discuss and reveal another common build system tool called Maven. We show you how Maven differs from Ant. We also present a brief introduction to this build system, which will be useful if you're new to it or need a way to start your tests continuously.

People sometimes come to Maven thinking that it will be something like Ant. Once they discover that it's totally different, they get frustrated. Don't worry; you're not alone. This is why we spend the first few pages of this chapter explaining what's most essential in order to understand Maven: how it's different from Ant. After that, we present some real-world examples of compiling your test cases and running them as well as producing fancy reports.

By the end of this chapter, you'll know how to set up your environment on your machine to build Java projects with Maven, including managing their dependencies, executing JUnit tests, and generating JUnit reports.

10.1 Maven's features

Once you've used Ant on several projects, you'll notice that projects almost always need the same Ant scripts (or at least a good percentage of them). These scripts are easy enough to reuse through cutting and pasting, but each new project requires a bit of fussing to get the Ant buildfiles working just right. In addition, each project usually ends up having several subprojects, each of which requires you to create and maintain an Ant buildfile. Maven (http://maven.apache.org/) picks up where Ant leaves off, making it a natural fit for many teams. Like Ant, Maven is a tool for running other tools, but Maven is designed to take tool reuse to the next level. If Ant is a source-building framework, then Maven is a source-building *environment*.

In order to understand better how Maven works, you need to understand the key points (principles) behind Maven. Maven was designed to take the build systems to the next level, beyond Ant. You need to become familiar with the things that the Maven community didn't like in Ant and how it tried to avoid them in designing Maven, that is, the core reason for starting Maven as a whole new project.

From the beginning of the Maven project, certain ground rules were in place for the entire software architecture of the project. These rules aim to simplify development with Maven and to make it easier for developers to implement the build system. One of the fundamental ideas of Maven is that the build system should be as simple as possible—software engineers should not spend a lot of time implementing the build system. It should be easy enough to start a new project from scratch and then rapidly begin developing the software, not spend valuable time designing and implementing a build system.

In this section we describe each of the core Maven principles in detail, and we explain what they mean to us, from a developer's point of view.

10.1.1 Convention over configuration

This feature is a software design principle that aims to decrease the number of configurations a software engineer needs to make, in favor of introducing a number of conventional rules that the developers need to follow. This way you, as a developer, can skip the tedious configuration required for every single project, and you can focus on the more important parts of your work.

Convention over configuration is one of the strongest principles of the Maven project. As an example of its application, let's look at the directory structure of the build process. When the Maven project was started, some of the initial Maven developers noticed that for every Ant buildfile, the person who writes the buildfile has to design the directory structure: declare the source directories, the build directories, and many other directories needed for the build itself. And although the Ant community tries to imply some directory names and directory structure, there's still no official specification (convention) of how a directory should be named. For instance, many people declare the `target.dir` property to denote the directory that holds their compiled classes, whereas others may be accustomed to using the `build.dir` property and it seems unnatural to them to use `target.dir`. Also, many people place their source code in the src/ directory, but others put it in the src/java/ directory. The Maven team decided that instead of allowing the software engineers to choose the build structure every time themselves, they'd introduce a convention for this. This resulted in what's now called the "Maven convention of directory structure." With Maven, instead of defining all the directories you need, they're defined for you. For example, the src/ main/java/ directory is the Maven convention for where the Java code for the project resides, src/main/test/ is where the unit tests for the project reside, target is the build directory, and so on. And it isn't just the directory structure. Later on when we discuss the plug-ins themselves, you'll see how every plug-in has a default state already defined, so you don't need to define it again.

That sounds great, but aren't we losing some of the flexibility of the project? What if we want to use Maven, and our source code resides in another directory? Maven is great at this. It provides the convention, but you still can, at any point, override the convention and use the configuration of your choice.

10.1.2   *Strong dependency management*

This is the second key point that Maven introduced. At the time the project was started, the de facto build system for Java projects was Ant. With Ant you have to distribute the dependencies of your project with the project itself. Maven introduced the notion of a *central repository*—a location on the internet where all kinds of artifacts (dependencies) are stored. The Maven build tool resolves them by reading your project's build descriptor, downloading the necessary versions of the artifacts, and then including them in the classpath of your application. This way you only need to list your dependencies in the dependencies section of your build descriptor, as shown here:

```
<dependencies>
    <dependency>
        <groupId>junit</groupId>
        <artifactId>junit</artifactId>
        <version>4.5</version>
    </dependency>
    <dependency>
        <groupId>jmock</groupId>
        <artifactId>jmock</artifactId>
        <version>1.0.1</version>
    </dependency>
</dependencies>
```

Then you're free to build the software on any other machine. There's no need to bundle the dependencies with your project and so forth.

But Maven introduced also the concept of the local repository. This is a directory on your hard disk (~/.m2/repository/ on UNIX and C:\Documents and Settings\<User-Name>\.m2\repository\ on Windows) where Maven keeps the artifacts that it has just downloaded from the central repository. Also, after you've built your project, your artifacts are installed in the local repository for later use by some other projects—simple and neat.

10.1.3 *Maven build lifecycles*

Another strong principle in Maven is the *build lifecycle*. The Maven project is built around the idea of defining the process of building, testing, and distributing a particular artifact. Maven projects can produce *only one* artifact. This way we can use Maven for building the project's artifact, or cleaning the project's directory structure, or generating the project's documentation. The activities we use Maven for define the three built-in lifecycles of Maven:

- *Default*—For generating the project's artifact
- *Clean*—For cleaning the project
- *Site*—For generating the project's documentation

Each of these lifecycles comprises several *phases*, and in order to pass through a certain lifecycle, the build must follow its phases.

Here's a list of all the phases of the default lifecycle:

- *Validate*—Validate that the project is correct and all necessary information is available.
- *Compile*—Compile the source code of the project.
- *Test*—Test the compiled source code using a suitable unit-testing framework. These tests should not require the code to be packaged or deployed.
- *Package*—Package the compiled code in its distributable format, such as a JAR.
- *Integration test*—Process and deploy the package if necessary into an environment where integration tests can be run.
- *Verify*—Run any checks to verify that the package is valid and meets quality criteria.
- *Install*—Install the package into the local repository for use as a dependency in other projects locally.
- *Deploy*—In an integration or release environment, copy the final package to the remote repository for sharing with other developers and projects.

If you remember, with Ant we had targets with almost the same names. And yes, the targets in Ant are the analogue of the phases in Maven, with one exception. In Ant *you* write the targets and *you* specify which target depends on which other target. With Maven, we see again the convention-over-configuration principle here. These phases are already defined for us in the order in which we listed them. And Maven invokes these phases in a strict order: they get executed sequentially in the order listed to complete the lifecycle. This means that if you invoke any of them, for example, if you type

```
mvn compile
```

on the command line in your project's home directory, Maven will first *validate* the project and then try to *compile* the sources of your project.

One last thing—it's useful to think of all these phases as extension points. At any moment you can attach additional Maven plug-ins to the phases and orchestrate the order and the way these plug-ins are executed.

10.1.4 *Plug-in-based architecture*

The last feature of Maven that we'll mention is its plug-in-based architecture. At the beginning of this chapter, we said that Ant is a source-building framework and Maven is a source-building environment. More specifically, Maven is a plug-in, execution, source-building environment. The core of the project is small, but the architecture of the project allows multiple plug-ins to be attached to the core, and so Maven builds an environment where different plug-ins can get executed.

Each of the phases in a given lifecycle has a number of plug-ins attached to that phase, and Maven invokes them when passing through the given phase in the order in which the plug-ins are declared. Here are some of the core Maven plug-ins:

- *Clean plug-in*—Cleans up after the build
- *Compiler plug-in*—Compiles Java sources
- *Deploy plug-in*—Deploys the built artifact to the remote repository
- *Install plug-in*—Installs the built artifact into the local repository
- *Resources plug-in*—Copies the resources to the output directory for inclusion in the JAR
- *Site plug-in*—Generates a site for the current project
- *Surefire plug-in*—Runs the JUnit tests in an isolated classloader
- *Verifier plug-in*—Useful for integration tests; verifies the existence of certain conditions

Apart from these core Maven plug-ins, there are also dozens of other Maven plug-ins for every kind of situation you may need—WAR plug-in, Javadoc plug-in, AntRun plug-in—you name it.

Plug-ins are declared in the `plugins` section of your build configuration file, for instance:

```
<build>
    <plugins>
      <plugin>
          <groupId>org.apache.cactus</groupId>
```

```
        artifactId>cactus.integration.maven2</artifactId>
        <version>1.8.1-SNAPSHOT</version>
    </plugin>
    </plugins>
  </build>
```

As you can see, every plug-in declaration specifies `groupId`, `artifactId`, and version. With this the plug-ins look like dependencies, don't they? Yes, they do, and they're handled the same way—they're downloaded into your local repository the same way dependencies are. When specifying a plug-in, the `groupId` and version are optional parameters; if you don't declare them, Maven will look for a plug-in with the specified `artifactId` and one of the following `groupId`s: `org.apache.maven.plugins` or `org.codehaus.mojo`. The version is optional. If you're using a Maven version pre-2.0.9, Maven will try to download the latest version available. But as of Maven version 2.0.9, the versions of most plug-ins are locked down in the Super POM, so it won't download the latest version anymore. Locking down plug-in versions is highly recommended to avoid autoupdating and nonreproducible builds.

Tons of additional plug-ins are available outside the Maven project but can be used with Maven. The reason for this is that it's extremely easy to write plug-ins for Maven.

10.1.5 *The Maven Project Object Model*

If you remember, Ant has a buildfile, by default named build.xml, that holds all of the information for our build. In that buildfile we specify all the things that we want to accomplish in the form of tasks and targets.

What's the analogue in Maven of Ant's build.xml? Maven also has a build descriptor that's by default called pom.xml, shortened from Project Object Model (POM). In contrast to Ant, in Maven's project descriptor we don't specify the things we want to do; we specify general information for the project itself, as in listing 10.1.

Listing 10.1   Simple pom.xml

```
<project>
    <modelVersion>4.0.0</modelVersion>
    <groupId>com.manning.junitbook</groupId>
    <artifactId>example-pom</artifactId>
    <packaging>jar</packaging>
    <version>2.0-SNAPSHOT</version>
</project>
```

It looks simple, doesn't it? But one big question arises at this moment: "How is even Maven capable of building our source code with so little information?"

The answer lies in the inheritance feature of the pom.xmls: every simple pom.xml inherits most of its functionality from a Super POM. As in Java, where every object inherits certain methods from the `java.lang.Object` object, the Super POM empowers each of our pom.xmls with the Maven features.

You see the similarity between Java and Maven. This analogue goes even further: Maven pom.xmls can inherit from each other, just as in Java some classes can act as parents for others. For instance, if we want to use the pom from listing 10.1 for our parent, all we have to do is change its packaging value to pom. Parent and aggregation (multimodule) projects can have only pom as a packaging value. We also need to define in our parent the child modules, as shown in listing 10.2.

Listing 10.2   Child modules for parent pom.xml

```
<project>
    <modelVersion>4.0.0</modelVersion>
    <groupId>com.manning.junitbook</groupId>
    <artifactId>example-pom</artifactId>
    <packaging>pom</packaging>                  <-1
    <version>2.0-SNAPSHOT</version>

    <modules>
        <module>example-module</module>        <-2
    </modules>
</project>
```

This listing is an extension of listing 10.1. We declare that this pom is an aggregation module by declaring the package to be of pom type ❶ and adding a modules section ❷. The modules section lists all the child modules that our module has, by providing the relative path to the project directory (example-module).

Listing 10.3 shows the child pom.xml.

Listing 10.3   Pom.xml that inherits the parent pom.xml

```
<project>
    <modelVersion>4.0.0</modelVersion>
    <parent>
        <groupId>com.manning.junitbook</groupId>
        <artifactId>example-pom</artifactId>
        <version>2.0-SNAPSHOT</version>
    </parent>
    <artifactId>example-child</artifactId>
</project>
```

Remember that this pom.xml resides in the directory that the parent pom.xml has declared (example-module).

There are two things are worth noticing here. First, because we inherit from some other pom, there's no need to specify groupId and version for the child pom; Maven expects they're the same as the parent's.

Going with the similarity to Java, it seems reasonable to ask, "What kind of objects can poms inherit from their parents?" Here's a list of all the elements that a pom can inherit from its parent:

- Dependencies
- Developers and contributors
- Plug-in lists
- Reports lists

- Plug-in executions with matching IDs
- Plug-in configurations

And again, each of these elements specified in the parent pom get automatically specified in the child pom.

We discuss the poms further in the upcoming sections.

10.2 *Setting up a Maven project*

Now that you've seen the differences between Ant and Maven, it's time to move on and start building our projects with Maven. But first, let's examine the installation process.

Installing Maven

Installing Maven is a three-step process:

1 Download the latest distribution from http://maven.apache.org/ and unzip/ untar it in the directory of your choice (for example, C:\maven on Windows or /opt/maven on UNIX).

2 Define an M2_HOME environment variable pointing to where you've installed Maven.

3 Add M2_HOME\bin (M2_HOME/bin on UNIX) to your PATH environment variable so that you can type mvn from any directory.

You're now ready to use Maven. The first time you execute a plug-in, make sure your internet connection is on, because Maven will automatically download from the web all the third-party JARs the plug-in requires.

Let's navigate to the c:\junitbook2\ directory. This is our work directory, and here we set up the Maven examples. Type the following on the command line:

```
mvn archetype:create -DgroupId=com.manning.junitbook
    -DartifactId=maven-sampling -DarchetypeArtifactid=maven-artifact-mojo
```

After you press Enter and wait for appropriate artifacts to download, you should see a directory named *maven-sampling* being created. If you look inside that directory, you should see the directory structure being created, as shown in figure 10.1.

What happened here? We invoked the maven-archetype-plugin from the command line and told it to create a new project from scratch with the given parameters. As a result, this Maven plug-in created a new project with a new directory structure, following the convention of the directory structure. Further, it created a sample App.java class with a main method and a corresponding AppTest.java file that's a unit test for our application. Now, most likely, after looking at this directory structure, you're quite familiar with which files stay in src/main/java and which files stay in src/test/java.

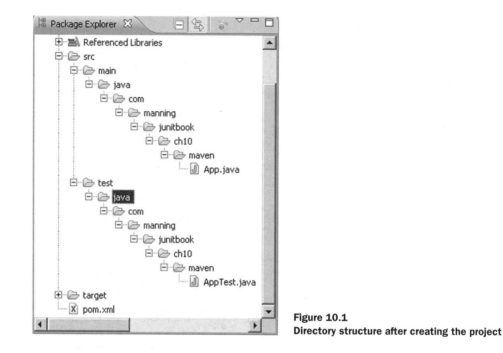

Figure 10.1
Directory structure after creating the project

But it gets even more automated. The Maven plug-in also generated a pom.xml file for us. Let's open it and examine the different parts of the descriptor, shown in listing 10.4.

Listing 10.4   Pom.xml for the `maven-sampling` project

```
<project xmlns="http://maven.apache.org/POM/4.0.0"
        xmlns:xsi=http://www.w3.org/2001/XMLSchema-instance
        xsi:schemaLocation="http://maven.apache.org/POM/4.0.0
        http://maven.apache.org/maven-v4_0_0.xsd">

  <modelVersion>4.0.0</modelVersion>
  <groupId>com.manning.junitbook</groupId>
  <artifactId>maven-sampling</artifactId>
  <packaging>jar</packaging>
  <version>1.0-SNAPSHOT</version>
  <name>maven-sampling</name>
  <url>http://maven.apache.org</url>
  <dependencies>
    <dependency>
      <groupId>junit</groupId>
      <artifactId>junit</artifactId>
      <version>3.8.1</version>
      <scope>test</scope>
    </dependency>
  </dependencies>
</project>
```

This is the build descriptor for our project. It starts with a global `<project>` tag with the appropriate namespaces, inside which we place all of our components:

- `modelVersion`—The model version of the `pom` being used. Currently the only supported version is 4.0.0.
- `groupId`—The group ID of our project. Notice that this is the value that we provided on the command line when invoking Maven. The `groupId` acts as the Java packaging in the filesystem; it groups together different projects from one organization, company, group of people, and so on.
- `artifactId`—The artifact ID of our project. Again, the value here is the one we specified on the command line. The `artifactId` represents the name the project is known by.
- `packaging`—What kind of artifact packaging will our project use? We specify here `jar`, but it also could be `pom`, `ear`, or `war`.
- `version`—The current version of our project (or our project's artifact). Notice the `-SNAPSHOT` ending. This ending denotes that this artifact is still in development mode; we haven't released it yet.
- `dependencies`—This section is used to list the dependencies.

Now that we have our project descriptor, let's improve it a little, as shown in listing 10.5. First, we need to change the version of the JUnit dependency, because we're using 4.6, and the one that the plug-in generated is 3.8.1. After that, we can make some additional information in the pom.xml more descriptive, like adding a `developers` section. This information not only makes the pom.xml more descriptive, but it will also be included later on when we build the website.

> **Listing 10.5 Additional metadata for the pom.xml**

```
<developers>
      <developer>
      <name>Petar Tahchiev</name>
      <id>ptahchiev</id>
      <organization>Apache Software Foundation</organization>
      <roles>
         <role>Java Developer</role>
      </roles>
   </developer>
   <developer>
      <name>Gary Gregory</name>
      <id>ggregory</id>
       <organization>Apache Software Foundation</organization>
       <roles>
          <role>Java Developer</role>
       </roles>
   </developer>
   <developer>
       <name>Felipe Leme</name>
       <id>felipeal</id>
       <organization>Apache Software Foundation</organization>
```

```
        <roles>
            <role>Java Developer</role>
        </roles>
    </developer>
</developers>
```

Listing 10.6 continues the previous one, showing the `organization`, `description`, and `inceptionYear` elements.

Listing 10.6   Description elements for the pom.xml

```
<description>
    "JUnit in Action II" book, the sample project for the "Running Junit
    tests from Maven" chapter.
</description>
<organization>
    <name>Manning Publications</name>
    <url>http://manning.com/</url>
</organization>
<inceptionYear>2008</inceptionYear>
```

Now let's move on and start developing our software. We want to use our favorite Java IDE: Eclipse or IntelliJ IDEA. No problem—Maven offers additional plug-ins to import the project into our favorite IDE. For instance, we use Eclipse to show you how this import happens. Again, open a terminal and navigate to the directory that contains your project descriptor (pom.xml). Once there, type the following and hit Enter:

```
mvn eclipse:eclipse -DdownloadSources=true
```

This will invoke the `maven-eclipse-plugin`, which, after downloading the necessary artifacts, will produce the two files (.project and .classpath) that Eclipse needs in order to recognize your project as an Eclipse project. The `downloadSources` parameter that we specify in the command line is optional. By using it we instruct the plug-in to also download source attachments. You can also download the Javadoc attachments by setting the optional `downloadJavadocs` parameter to `true` on the command line. Now you can import your project into Eclipse and examine it; you'll notice that all of the dependencies that are listed in the pom.xml file are now added to your `build-path`. Amazing, isn't it?

To continue, let's generate some documentation for the project. But wait a second, how are we supposed to do that? We don't have any files to generate the documentation from. This is another one of Maven's great features—with the little configuration and description that we have, we can produce a fully functional website skeleton. Type

```
mvn site
```

on the command line where your pom.xml is. Maven should start downloading its plug-ins, and after their successful installation, it will produce the nice website you see in figure 10.2.

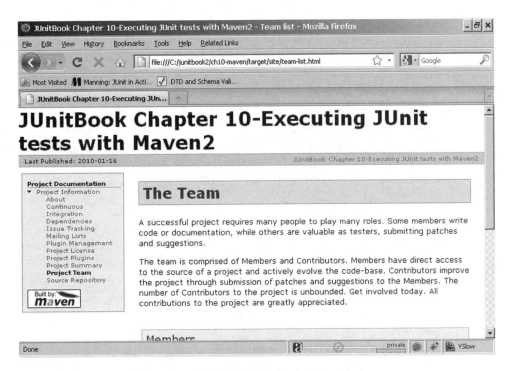

Figure 10.2   Maven produces nice website documentation for the project.

This website is generated in Maven's build directory—another convention. Maven uses the target/ directory for all the needs of the build itself. The convention continues even beneath this directory: source code is compiled in the target/classes/ directory, and the documentation is generated in target/site/.

After you examine the project, you'll probably notice that this website is more like a skeleton of a website. That's true, but remember that we entered only a small amount of data to begin with. We could enter more data and web pages in the src/site directory, and Maven will include it in the website, generating full documentation.

10.3   *Introduction to Maven plug-ins*

So far, so good. You've seen what Maven is and how to use it to start a project from scratch. You've also seen how to generate the project's documentation and how to import our project in Eclipse.

To continue, we can get the source code from the first part of the book and place it in the src/main/java directory, where Maven expects it to be. Also, we can get the tests for the sampling project and place them in the src/test/java directory (again a convention). Now it's time to invoke Maven and instruct it to compile the source code and tests and also to execute the tests.

But first we need to clean the project from our previous activities:

```
mvn clean
```

This will cause Maven to go through the clean phase and invoke all of the plug-ins that are attached to this phase, in particular the `maven-clean-plugin`, which will delete the target/ directory, where our generated site resides.

10.3.1 *Maven Compiler plug-in*

Like any other build system, Maven is supposed to build your projects—compile your software and package in an archive. As we mentioned at the beginning of the chapter, every task in Maven in done by an appropriate plug-in, the configuration of which happens in the `<plugins>` section of our project descriptor. To compile your source code, all you need to do is invoke the compile phase on the command line:

```
mvn compile
```

This will cause Maven to execute all of the plug-ins that are attached to the *compile* phase (in particular it will invoke the `maven-compiler-plugin`). But before invoking the compile phase, as already discussed, Maven will go through the *validate* phase and will download all of the dependencies that are listed in the pom.xml and include them in the classpath of the project. Once the compilation process is completed, you can go to the target/classes/ directory, and you should see the compiled classes there.

Let's move on and try to *configure* the Compiler plug-in. Notice the italics in the previous sentence? Yeah, that's right—we'll escape from the convention-over-configuration principle and will try to configure the Compiler plug-in.

So far, we've used the conventional Compiler plug-in, and everything worked well. But what if we need to include the -source and -target attributes in the compiler invocation to generate class files for a specific version of the JVM? We should add the lines in listing 10.7 to the `<build>` section of our buildfile.

> **Listing 10.7   Configuring the `maven-compiler-plugin`**

```xml
<build>
   <plugins>
      <plugin>
         <artifactId>maven-compiler-plugin</artifactId>
         <configuration>
            <source>1.4</source>
            <target>1.4</target>
         </configuration>
      </plugin>
   </plugins>
</build>
```

This is a general way to configure each one of your Maven plug-ins; you enter a `<plugins>` section into your `<build>` section. There you list each of the plug-ins that you want to configure. In our case, it's the `maven-compiler-plugin`. You need to enter the configuration parameters in the plug-in's `configuration` section. You can get a list of parameters for every plug-in from the Maven website.

As you can see in the declaration of the `maven-compiler-plugin` in the previous listing, we haven't set the `groupId` parameter. That's because the `maven-compiler-plugin` is one of the core Maven plug-ins that has a `org.apache.maven.plugins` `groupId`, and as we mentioned at the beginning of the chapter, plug-ins with such a `groupId` can skip it.

10.3.2 *Maven Surefire plug-in*

Ant uses the `javac` task to compile the tests that we've selected, the same way Maven uses the `maven-compiler-plugin` to compile *all* of the source code that's in src/main/java/. The same thing happens with the process of unit testing your project; Ant uses the `junit` task and executes the test cases that we've *selected*, whereas Maven uses—guess what?— a plug-in. The Maven plug-in that *executes the unit tests* is called `maven-surefire-plugin`. Notice the italics in the previous sentence; the Surefire plug-in is used to execute the unit tests for your code, but these unit tests aren't necessarily JUnit tests. There are also other frameworks for unit testing, and the Surefire plug-in can execute their tests, too.

The *conventional* way to start the `maven-surefire-plugin` is simple. All you need to do is invoke the test phase of Maven. This way Maven will first invoke all of the phases that are supposed to come before the test phase (validate and compile phases) and then invoke all of the plug-ins that are attached to the test phase, thus invoking the `maven-surefire-plugin`. So by calling

```
mvn clean test
```

Maven first cleans the target/ directory, then compiles the source code and the tests, and finally executes all of the tests that are in the src/test/java directory (remember the convention). The output should be similar to that shown in figure 10.3.

That's great, but what if we don't want to execute all of our tests? What if we want to execute only a single test case? Well, this is something *unconventional,* so we need to configure the `maven-surefire-plugin` to do it. Hopefully there's a parameter for the plug-in that allows us to specify a pattern of test cases that we want to be executed. The configuration of the Surefire plug-in is done in the same way as the configuration of the Compiler plug-in, and it's shown in listing 10.8.

> **Listing 10.8 Configuration of the `maven-surefire-plugin`**

```
<build>
   <plugins>
   [...]
      <plugin>
         <artifactId>maven-surefire-plugin</artifactId>
         <configuration>
            <includes>**/Test*.java</includes>
         </configuration>
      </plugin>
   [...]
   </plugins>
</build>
```

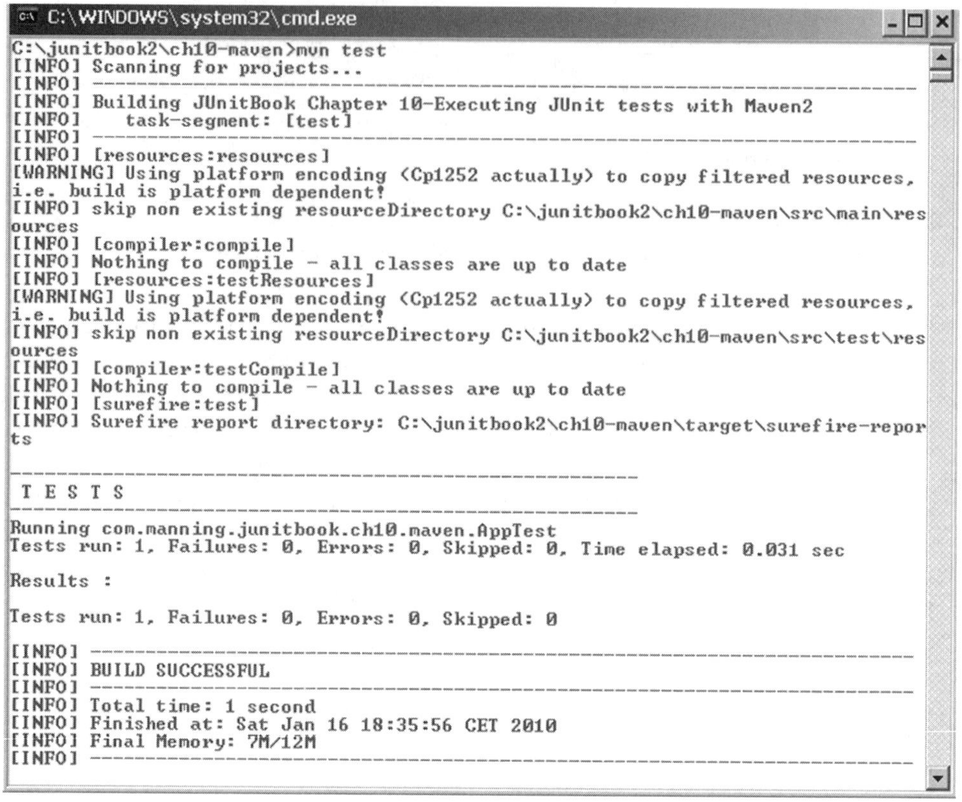

```
C:\WINDOWS\system32\cmd.exe
C:\junitbook2\ch10-maven>mvn test
[INFO] Scanning for projects...
[INFO] ------------------------------------------------------------------------
[INFO] Building JUnitBook Chapter 10-Executing JUnit tests with Maven2
[INFO]    task-segment: [test]
[INFO] ------------------------------------------------------------------------
[INFO] [resources:resources]
[WARNING] Using platform encoding (Cp1252 actually) to copy filtered resources,
i.e. build is platform dependent!
[INFO] skip non existing resourceDirectory C:\junitbook2\ch10-maven\src\main\res
ources
[INFO] [compiler:compile]
[INFO] Nothing to compile - all classes are up to date
[INFO] [resources:testResources]
[WARNING] Using platform encoding (Cp1252 actually) to copy filtered resources,
i.e. build is platform dependent!
[INFO] skip non existing resourceDirectory C:\junitbook2\ch10-maven\src\test\res
ources
[INFO] [compiler:testCompile]
[INFO] Nothing to compile - all classes are up to date
[INFO] [surefire:test]
[INFO] Surefire report directory: C:\junitbook2\ch10-maven\target\surefire-repor
ts

-------------------------------------------------------
 T E S T S
-------------------------------------------------------
Running com.manning.junitbook.ch10.maven.AppTest
Tests run: 1, Failures: 0, Errors: 0, Skipped: 0, Time elapsed: 0.031 sec

Results :

Tests run: 1, Failures: 0, Errors: 0, Skipped: 0

[INFO] ------------------------------------------------------------------------
[INFO] BUILD SUCCESSFUL
[INFO] ------------------------------------------------------------------------
[INFO] Total time: 1 second
[INFO] Finished at: Sat Jan 16 18:35:56 CET 2010
[INFO] Final Memory: 7M/12M
[INFO] ------------------------------------------------------------------------
```

Figure 10.3 Execution of JUnit tests with Maven2

As you can see, we've specified the `includes` parameter to denote that we want only the test cases matching the given pattern to be executed. Yes, but how do we know what parameters the `maven-surefire-plugin` accepts? No one knows all the parameters by heart, but you can always consult the `maven-surefire-plugin` documentation (and any other plug-in documentation) on the Maven website (http://maven.apache.org/).

10.3.3 HTML JUnit reports with Maven

As you saw in the previous chapter, Ant has a task for generating nice reports out of JUnit's XML output. The same thing applies for Maven. And because Maven, by default, produces plain and XML-formatted output (by convention it goes into the target/surefire-reports directory), we don't need any other configuration to produce HTML Surefire Reports for the JUnit tests.

As you've already guessed, the job for producing these reports is done by a Maven plug-in. The name of the plug-in is `maven-surefire-report-plugin`, and by default, it isn't attached to any of the core phases that we already know (many people don't need HTML reports every time they build their software). This means that we can't

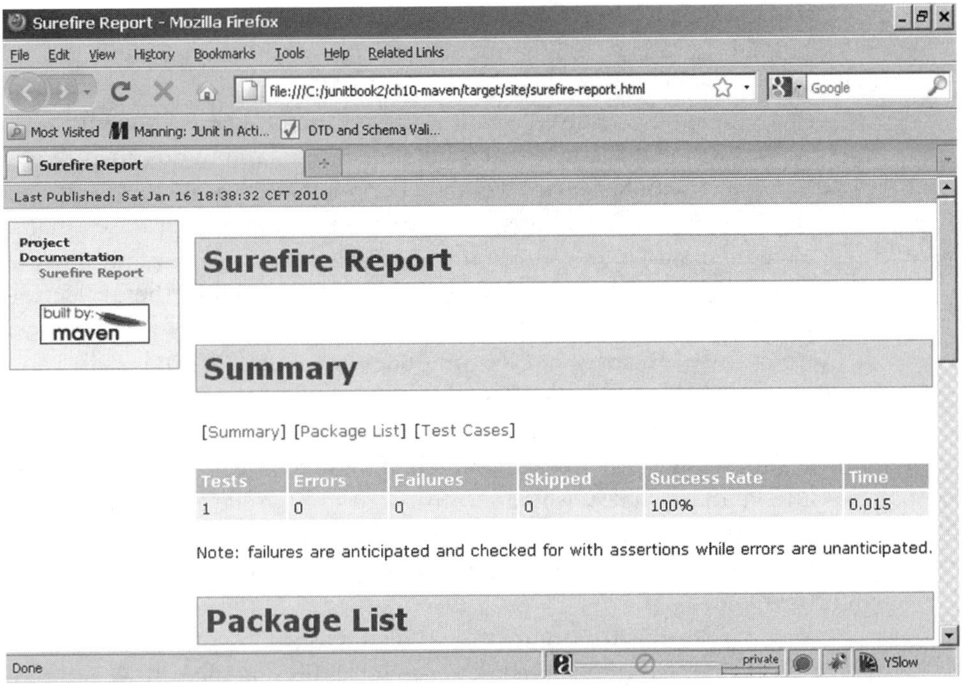

Figure 10.4 HTML report from the Maven Surefire Report plug-in

invoke it by running a certain phase (as we did with both the Compiler plug-in and the Surefire plug-in), but instead we have to call it directly from the command line:

```
mvn surefire-report:report
```

When we do so, Maven will try to compile the source files and the test cases and then invoke the Surefire plug-in to produce the plain text and XML-formatted output of the tests. After that the Surefire Report plug-in will try to transform all of the XML reports from the target/surefire-reports/ directory into an HTML report that will be placed in the target/site directory (remember that the convention for the directory is to keep all of the generated documentation of the project, and the HTML reports are considered documentation).

If you try to open the generated HTML report, it should look something like the one shown in figure 10.4.

In the next section, we cover some of Maven's weaker points.

10.4 *The bad side of Maven*

So far, we've discussed Maven as the tool that's going to take the place of Ant. But as with all other things in life, it's not all a bed of roses. Maven has its bad sides, too. Before you get too excited, just think about it. Maven has been out since 2002, and still Ant is the de facto standard for building software.

All of the people who've used Maven agree that it's easy to start up with it. And the idea behind the project is amazing. But things seem to break when you need to do some of the *unconventional* things.

What's great about Maven is that it will set up a frame for you and will constrain you to think inside that frame—to think the Maven way and do things the Maven way. When you work with Maven for a certain period of time, you'll inevitably need to copy a file from one place to another. We think you'll be surprised to see that there's no copy plug-in in Maven, in contrast with Ant, which has the copy task. You have to deal with the situation, and if you investigate further and think "the Maven way," it may turn out that you never needed to copy that file.

In most cases Maven won't let you do any nonsense. It will restrict you and show you the way things need to be done. Ant works the other way: it's a powerful tool, and you can do whatever you need to do. But it can be dangerous in inappropriate hands. And again, it's up to you to decide which of these tools you want to use. Some companies hire build engineers, who are considered to have the appropriate knowledge, so for them Ant is no danger at all—it's just a powerful tool.

To finish this chapter we'll tell you a story. We have a friend who once had a job interview.

"Well, is it possible for Ant to do …?" he was asked.

Without even letting the interviewer to finish his sentence, my friend replied, "Yes, it is."

We're not sure what his answer would have been if he'd been asked about Maven.

10.5   Summary

In this chapter we briefly introduced you to what Maven is and how to use it in a development environment to build your source code. We discussed in detail all of the features of Maven that make it unique compared to any other build system. We also looked at two of Maven's plug-ins in detail: the Compiler plug-in and the Surefire plug-in. With this information you should be able not only to start and execute your tests but also to produce nice HTML reports of the test results.

In the next chapter we close the automation part of the book, by introducing different continuous integration build tools, such as CruiseControl and Hudson. We show you the benefits of using such tools and also how to install and configure these tools.

11

Continuous integration tools

Life is a continuous exercise in creative problem solving.

—Michael J. Gelb

This chapter covers

- Practicing continuous integration
- Introduction to CruiseControl
- Introduction to Hudson

In the two previous chapters we described ways to execute our tests automatically by using tools such as Ant and Maven. Our tests were then triggered by the build. Now it's time to go to the next level: automatically executing the build and the tests at a regular interval by using some other popular tools. In this chapter we introduce the paradigm of continuous integration and show you how to schedule your project to be built automatically in a certain timeframe.

11.1 *A taste of continuous integration*

Integrating the execution of JUnit tests as part of your development cycle—code : run : test : code (or test : code : run : test if you're test-first inclined)—is an important concept in the sense that JUnit tests are unit tests, that is, they test a single component of your project in isolation. A great many of the projects out there, however, have modular architecture, where different developers on the team work on different modules of the project. Each developer takes care of developing their own module and their own unit tests to make sure their module is well tested.

Modules interact with each other, so we need to have all the different modules assembled to see how they work together. In order for the application to be test proven, we need another sort of test: integration or functional tests. As you already saw in chapter 3, these tests test the interaction between different modules.

But almost always integration tests are time consuming, and as a single developer you may not have all the modules built on your machine. Therefore, it makes no sense to run all the integration tests during development. That's because at development we're focused on only our module, and all we want to know is that it works as a single unit. During development we care mostly that if we provide the right input data, the module not only behaves as expected but also produces the expected result.

Test-driven development taught us to test early and test often. Executing all our unit, integration, and functional tests every time we make a small change would slow us immensely. To avoid this, we execute at development time only the unit tests—as early and as often as reasonable. What happens to the integration tests?

11.1.1 *Continuous integration testing*

Integration tests should be executed independently from the development process. The best way is to execute them at a regular interval (say, 15 minutes). This way, if something gets broken, you'll hear about it within 15 minutes, and there's a better chance for you to fix it.

> **DEFINITION**[1] *Continuous integration (CI)*—Continuous integration is a software development practice whereby members of a team integrate their work frequently. Usually each person integrates at least daily, leading to multiple integrations per day. Each integration is verified by an automated build (including a test) to detect integration errors as quickly as possible. Many teams find that this approach leads to significantly reduced integration problems and allows for the development of cohesive software more rapidly.

To get the integration tests executed at a regular interval, we also need to have the modules of the system prepared and built. After the modules are built and the integration tests are executed, we'd like to see the results of the execution as quickly as possible.

---

[1] This definition is taken from a marvelous article by Martin Fowler and Matthew Foemmel. It can be found here: http://www.martinfowler.com/articles/continuousIntegration.html.

We need a software tool to do all of the following steps automatically:

1 Check out the project from the source control system.

2 Build each of the modules and execute all of the unit tests to verify that the different modules work as expected in isolation.

3 Execute integration tests to verify that the modules integrate with each other in the expected way.

4 Publish the results from the tests executed in step 3.

Several questions may arise at this point. First, what's the difference between a human executing all these steps and a tool doing so? The answer is, there's no difference and there shouldn't be! Apart from the fact that no one can bear doing such a job, if you take a close look at the first item in the list, you'll see that we check out the project from the source control system. We do that as if we were new members of the team and just started with the project—with a clean checkout in an empty folder. Then, before moving on, we want to make sure that all of the modules work properly in isolation, because if they don't, it makes little sense to test whether they integrate well with the other modules. The last step in the proposed scenario is to notify the developers about the test results. The notification could be done with an email, or an ICQ message, or by publishing the reports from the tests on a web server.

This overall interaction is shown in figure 11.1. The CI tool interacts with the source control system to get the project (1). After that it uses the build tool that your project is using, builds your project, and executes different kinds of tests (2 and 3). Finally (4), the CI tool publishes the results and blows the whistle so that everybody can see them.

The four steps are general and could be greatly improved. For instance, it would be better to check to see if any changes have been made in the source control system

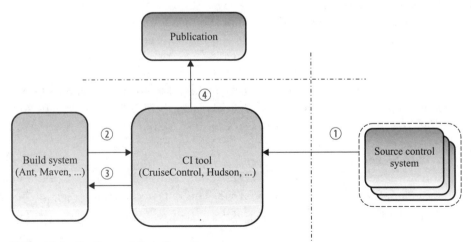

Figure 11.1 Continuous integration scheme

before we start building. Otherwise, we waste the CPU power of our machine, knowing for sure that we'll get the same results.

Now that we agree that we certainly need a tool to continuously integrate our projects, let's see which open source solutions we might want to use (there's no sense in reinventing the wheel when there are good tools already made for us).

11.2   CruiseControl to the rescue

The first open source[2] project we're going to look at is called CruiseControl (CC) (http://cruisecontrol.sourceforge.net/) and is currently the de facto standard when it comes to continuous build process. This project was created by a company called ThoughtWorks and was the first continuous integration server available.

11.2.1   Getting started with CruiseControl

The first thing to do before we can start building our code continuously is to manage our resources. By this we mean finding a suitable host machine for our CruiseControl server. We need to manage the resources we have in such manner as to dedicate a separate machine to continuous integration. We may not need this at the beginning, but with time our project will get bigger, and the CI build will take longer, so it's always better to have a separate machine for the integration build.

Another good practice is to create an ad hoc user on the host machine for the CC server. This user will have the right permissions to start the continuous server and execute the builds.

Once you find the host for the CruiseControl server, it's time to install it. The installation procedure is pretty simple. You go to the CruiseControl website (http://cruisecontrol.sourceforge.net/) and download the zip distribution of your choice. As this book is being written, the latest version of CruiseControl is 2.8.3, and we use the binary distribution.

Once you download the distribution, you need to extract it into a folder (probably the best place to extract the zip is in the home directory of the CC user you just created), which from now on we refer to as $CC_HOME. In the $CC_HOME directory, you should see the content we shown in table 11.1.

There are several things to notice in the folder structure within the $CC_HOME folder. As you can see, the CruiseControl package comes with an Apache Ant distribution. But this doesn't mean that you can't use Maven as a build system. You can use whichever one you like best. We talk further on this topic later on.

Another thing that's worth mentioning is the projects folder. This folder is where you store the projects you want to build continuously. If you look in that folder you'll see a sample project called connectfour. This is a checked-out project, so before moving on it's good to take a brief look at it.

---

[2]   The CruiseControl framework is distributed under its own BSD-style license. The software is an OSI-certified open source solution.

Table 11.1 Default content of the $CC_HOME folder

File/folder	Used for
apache-ant-distribution	Distribution of the Apache Ant project that comes bundled with the CruiseControl server distribution. You could choose to use this distribution or any later version.
docs	Documentation of the CruiseControl project.
lib	Various third-party libraries for the project.
logs	The logs of the continuous builds.
projects	The projects you build continuously. By default there's a sample project already set up in this folder called connectfour.
webapp	Used to store a GUI to the build server.
config.xml	The main configuration file of CruiseControl.
cruisecontrol script	This .bat or .sh script (depending on the architecture you're using) is used to start CruiseControl.

Now that we've found a host for our CruiseControl installation and we've seen how the project is structured, let's start using it by setting up a project to build.

11.2.2 *Setting up a sample project*

Setting up a project in CruiseControl is straightforward. You need to do only three things:

- Check out your project in the projects folder.
- Configure CruiseControl for the project's build.
- Start CruiseControl.

Let's look at these steps one by one.

Usually we keep the source in a central repository using a source control system, and that system has responsibility for managing the version of your software. If you're using Subversion as your revision control system, you can easily check out your project by first navigating to the $CC_HOME\projects folder and then executing the following command there:

```
svn co http://url.of.your.repository.here/ theNameOfMyProject
```

You need to specify the URL of your source repository and also the name of the folder in which to check out the project. Then Subversion will check out a local copy of your project in the *theNameOfMyProject* folder.

11.2.3 *The CruiseControl config file explained*

Now that we have the project checked out in the projects folder, it's time to configure CruiseControl to build it the way we want. The configuration itself is done with a file called config.xml. You can find the config script in the $CC_HOME folder, and if you look at it, you should see something like listing 11.1.

Listing 11.1 CruiseControl's config.xml

```
<cruisecontrol>                                              ←❶
  <project name="connectfour">                                ←❷

    <listeners>                                               ←❸
      <currentbuildstatuslistener
        file="logs/${project.name}/status.txt"/>
    </listeners>

    <bootstrappers>                                          ←❹
      <antbootstrapper                                       ←❺
          anthome="apache-ant-1.7.0"
          buildfile="projects/${project.name}/build.xml"
          target="clean" />
    </bootstrappers>                                         ❻

    <modificationset quietperiod="30">

      <!-- touch any file in connectfour project to trigger a build -->
      <filesystem folder="projects/${project.name}"/>

    </modificationset>

    <schedule interval="300">                                ←❼
      <ant anthome="apache-ant-1.7.0"
          buildfile="projects/${project.name}/build.xml"/>
    </schedule>

    <log>                                                    ←❽
      <merge dir="projects/${project.name}/target/test-results"/>
    </log>

    <publishers>                                             ←❾
      <onsuccess>
        <artifactspublisher
          dest="artifacts/${project.name}"
          file="projects/${project.name}/target/${project.name}.jar"/>
      </onsuccess>
    </publishers>

  </project>
</cruisecontrol>
```

This config file describes the build for the connectfour project. We'll walk through it and explain what the different parts mean, so that later you can modify the script with your project's configurations.

We start with a global cruisecontrol tag ❶, which is required, and inside that global tag we list all the projects we want to build ❷. We can have multiple projects being built, but that means that we must give all the projects a distinct name (using the name attribute of the project tag).

The `listeners` element ❸ is used mainly to enlist different pluggable listener instances. These listeners are notified of every project build event (like the start or end of the project). For instance, in our config.xml we define a `currentbuild-statuslistener`, which we use to write the project's statuses in a file, specified by the `file` attribute.

Listeners in CruiseControl are interesting creatures, so we'd like here to spend a few lines on them. As you've probably noticed, building the project on a regular schedule wastes a lot of resources. CruiseControl is smart in that it doesn't fire a new build unless it detects some changes in the source control system. Otherwise, the build would be pointless, because we'd get the same results. But how do we distinguish whether the CruiseControl server was up and skipped the build because there were no changes in the source control system or the server was down? The solution is the listeners. You can configure CruiseControl's listeners to log everything in a file, somewhere on the filesystem. The upside is that the events that activate the listeners are triggered regardless of the state of the source control system. This way you can keep track of whether a build was attempted.

The next thing in our config.xml is the `bootstrappers` element ❹. This is a container element to define some actions that need to be taken before the build is executed. Again, the `bootstrappers` are run regardless of whether a build is necessary or not. In our config file we've specified an `antbootstrapper` ❺ that will invoke the `clean` target of our project's build descriptor and will clean all the resources we've used during the previous build.

The `modificationset` element ❻ defines the sets of files and folders that Cruise-Control will monitor for changes. One thing to remember here is that the build is attempted only when a change is detected on any of the sets listed in the `modificationset` element.

The `schedule` element ❼ is the one that schedules the build. The `interval` parameter specifies the build time interval (in seconds), and inside the `schedule` element we list the type of build system we're using. We need to specify the home folder of the build system and also the buildfile to execute. In our config file we've specified Ant, but you can use Maven without any problems as well.

The `log` section ❽ is optional and is used to specify where the logs of the execution should be stored. The `merge` element inside it tells CruiseControl which logs of the build execution are valuable and should be stored in the log directory of the CruiseControl execution. In our example, we only care about the .xml files from the JUnit execution, so we're going to store them in the log folder.

The last section is the `publishers` section ❾, and it's used to make the final steps of the scheduled build. The same ways the bootstrappers are executed every time *before* the build, the publishers are executed every time *after* the build, regardless of the result of the build. In `publishers` we can specify what whistles are blown as the build finishes. It could be sending an email, publishing the produced artifacts somewhere on the internet, or posting a message on the Jabber Messenger. In the example shown previously, we publish the result from the build (the .jar file from the target folder) into the artifacts folder. We do that only if the result from the execution is successful (see the onsuccess element).

So far, so good—we're able to start CruiseControl, and according to the configuration in the listing, it will build our project every 300 seconds (if there's a change in the source control system). So let's do it. Navigate to the $CC_HOME folder and start the CruiseControl server by issuing the following command:

```
cruisecontrol.bat
```

Or in case of UNIX,[3] execute

```
./cruisecontrol.sh
```

CruiseControl will be executed and will look for the config.xml file to read. If you've done everything right, after execution you should see something similar to figure 11.2.

Now it's time to make a change in the repository, and hopefully after 300 seconds you'll see the build being executed again.

Here's an interesting question: how often should you build your projects? This is a tough question, and it all depends on you and on the time you need to make a new build. It makes little sense to make a build every minute when you need more than a minute to execute the build itself. Keep in mind that this is a book about software testing, and we all propagate a lot of testing, using not only JUnit but also all kinds of integration and functional testing tools. This means that production builds tend to be time consuming.

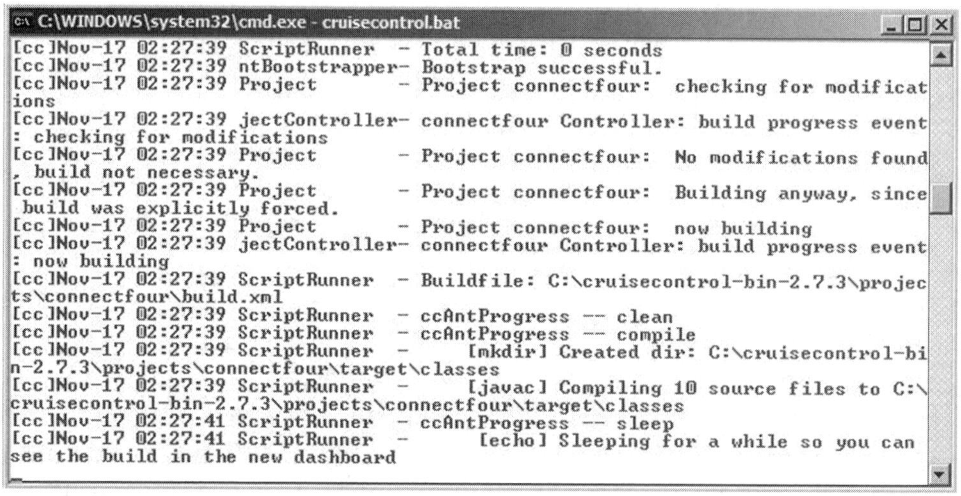

Figure 11.2 Executing CruiseControl for the first time

---

[3] You need to check to make sure that the .sh script has executable modifiers set.

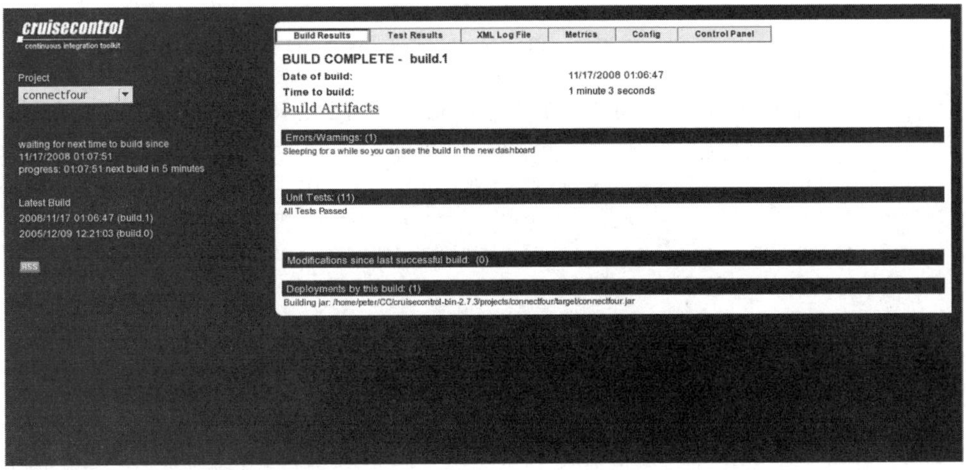

Figure 11.3 CruiseControl control panel in the browser

CruiseControl also provides a way to control your scheduled builds through a nice GUI, by starting a Jetty instance. By default, this Jetty instance is started on port 8080, but you can change it (in case that port is already taken). To do so you need to change the `port` property in your jetty.xml file in the etc folder. For our purposes we start CC on port 8888. You can check the GUI by visiting http://localhost:8888/cruisecontrol/ in a browser. You should be able to see something like the screen displayed in figure 11.3. As you can see, there some nice details on how many builds were iterated, some detailed statistics on how many of them failed, and, of course, the JUnit logs. There's also an RSS feed that you could subscribe to, to get the results from the execution.

Let's move on. Some things are working, but currently the way they are doesn't give us much data. If we look in the console or the GUI, we can see that the build is going well, but it's a tedious task to look there all the time. What if we had some way to get the results from the execution directly into our email or, even better, get the email from CruiseControl only in case things go bad?

This is possible, and all we have to do is add another publisher in our config.xml. The section we want to add is shown in listing 11.2.

> **Listing 11.2 CruiseControl's `htmlemail` notification**

```
<htmlemail
    mailhost="your.company.smtp.host"                                    ← 1     2
    returnaddress="cruisecontrol@yourcompany.com"                          ←
    buildresultsurl="http://localhost:8888/buildresults/connectfour/"
    css="/home/peter/my-very-own-css/cruisecontrol.css"                    ← 3
    logdir="logs/connectfour">                                             ←
  <map alias="developers" address="connectfour-team@mycompany.com" />            4
  <map alias="manager" address="boss@mycompany.com" />
```

```
    <always address="manager" />
    <failure address="developers" reportWhenFixed="true" />
</htmlemail>
```

The `htmlemail` publisher defines the notification emails to be sent. We start by defining the `mailhost` to use for sending the emails ❶ and also from what address the emails are coming ❷. These two, along with the `buildresultsurl` parameter (the location at which our build results reside), are required. All the rest of the parameters are optional. We're able to specify a custom CSS stylesheet ❸ and the path to our logs ❹.

The last touch would be to create aliases to which persons the notifications should go. We use the `map` element to map the alias to an email. After that, we specify on what occasion we want those guys to receive email notifications. By default, CruiseControl delivers notification on both success and failure. But that's too much information for the development team, and that's why we've listed them to receive only emails on failure and when the problems get fixed.

Now it's time to restart the CruiseControl server and break the build on purpose. Commit something that's breaking the build! In only 300 seconds, you should get an email, looking like the one shown in figure 11.4.

As you can see, the report gives you information on not only which JUnit test failed but also the last guy to make a commit in the source control system. It's pretty easy to determine which member of the team gets the blame for breaking the integration.

CruiseControl has a pluggable architecture, and as you saw, you can plug different listeners, or bootstrappers, to do things before, during, or after the build execution. You can also specify different publishers for different ways of notifying the results from the build execution. Along with the `htmlemail` method we already covered, there's a publisher to send an instant message on Yahoo! Messenger or on Jabber Messenger or by posting the results on a blog and collecting them through an RSS feed.

View results here -> http://localhost:8080/buildresults/connectfour/?log=log20081125160807Lbuild.3

	BUILD COMPLETE - build.3	
Date of build:	11/25/2008 16:08:07	
Time to build:	1 minute 1 second	
Last changed:	11/25/2008 16:07:36	
Last log entry:		

Errors/Warnings: (1)
Sleeping for a while so you can see the build in the new dashboard

Unit Tests: (11)
All Tests Passed

Modifications since last successful build: (1)
change User projects/connectfour/test/net/sourceforge/cruisecontrol/sampleproject/connectfour/CellTest.java   11/25/2008 16:07:36

Deployments by this build: (1)
Building jar: /home/peter/CC/cruisecontrol-bin-2.7.3/projects/connectfour/target/connectfour.jar

Figure 11.4   Email notification from CruiseControl server

Let's move on and take a look at another continuous integration server called Hudson. After we've covered both of them, you can compare them and choose whichever one you want to use.

11.3 Another neat tool—Hudson

As we mentioned in the beginning of the chapter, CruiseControl was probably one of the first continuous integration servers available. But there are a whole bunch of other software tools out there, trying to compete with CruiseControl by introducing some interesting new features. Some of those tools aren't even free (like AntHill Pro, Hudson, or Cruise[4]), and those include not only the product you purchase but also training and support.

For the sake of completeness, we need to cover another tool. This way you can choose whichever tool you like. Remember, your software quality will improve not from the tool you choose to use but rather from the fact that you decided to practice continuous integration!

11.3.1 Introducing Hudson

Hudson (http://hudson-ci.org/) is an open source project for continuous build. Like any other software for continuous build, it's based on the idea of being able to continuously poll the source code from the source control system and, in case it detects changes, to fire up a build. Why do we cover it in this chapter? First, because it has become popular, and second, because it's very different from CruiseControl.

11.3.2 Installation

Before installing Hudson, make sure you have J2SE version 1.5 or higher already installed. Also make sure your JAVA_HOME environment variable points to where you've installed Java.

The installation procedure itself is easy. You go to the project's website and download the latest version of Hudson. At the time this book is being written, the latest version is 1.352. The Hudson distribution comes as a single WAR file, as opposed to CruiseControl, where the distribution is a zip. You don't need to extract the WAR file, because Hudson comes with a Winstone servlet container. You can start the server from the command line with the following command:

```
java -jar hudson.war --httpPort=8888
```

Note first that we start Hudson on a port other than 8080 (simply because the examples in the book require this port to be free), and second, if you start Hudson this way, all of your logs will go to the console.

In order to start using the server, you need to navigate to http://localhost:8888/. If no errors occur, you should see something similar to what is shown in figure 11.5.

---

[4] Cruise and CruiseControl aren't the same! Although they both originated from the same company, Thought-Works, CruiseControl was open sourced and is free to use. Cruise is still commercial software.

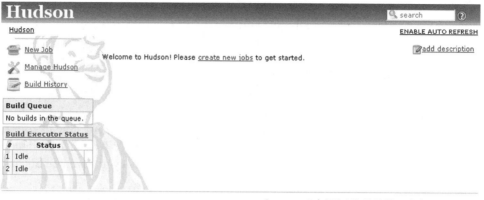

Figure 11.5 Hudson initial startup screen

There's also a way to specify different command-line parameters, such as the one to redefine the port on which the server is started or the root under which the application is started.

Also, if you don't want to use the Winstone servlet container, you can use any other servlet container you want. If you stick with that solution, you'll be forced to follow the installation procedures specific to the servlet container you use.

11.3.3 *Configuring Hudson*

Hudson's advantage over CruiseControl is easier configuration, which is done through the web interface. Once you've installed Hudson, it's time to start the configuration. Open a browser and navigate to http://localhost:8888/. You should see the Hudson welcome screen, and there should be a Manage Hudson link on the left side. Click it, and you'll be given a list of additional links leading to the parts of the installation you want to configure. Click Configure System, and it will open a web page similar to the one shown in figure 11.6.

As you already saw, Hudson, in contrast to CruiseControl, comes with no Ant installation, so the tool needs to know where you've installed Ant, Maven, JDK, and the like. You need to specify this information on the configuration page shown in figure 11.6.

The first line on the configuration page is Home Directory. The home directory of Hudson is an interesting creature, so we devote a subsection to it.

HUDSON HOME DIRECTORY

The home directory of Hudson is used to maintain the source, perform builds, and hold some archives. By default it's located in $USER_HOME/.hudson ($USER_HOME is interpreted as /home/<username> in UNIX systems and as C:\Documents and Settings\<username>\ in Windows).

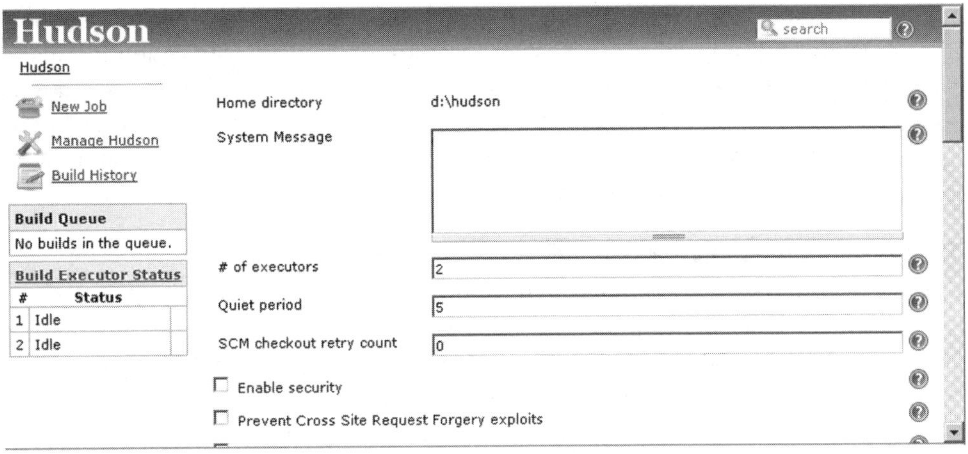

Figure 11.6 Hudson configuration screen

You can change the default location of the Hudson home directory either by setting the HUDSON_HOME environment variable or by setting the HUDSON_HOME servlet-container property.

If you take a sneak peek in the HUDSON_HOME directory, you should see a folder structure similar to the one shown in listing 11.3.

Listing 11.3 Hudson home directory folder structure

```
[HUDSON_HOME]
+- config.xml      (hudson root configuration)          <-- 1
+- fingerprints    (stores fingerprint records)
+- plugins         (stores plugins)                     <-- 2
+- jobs                                                  <--
   +- [JOBNAME]       (sub directory for each job)          3
      +- config.xml     (job configuration file)
      +- workspace      (working directory for the version control
                                                    system)
      +- latest         (symbolic link to the last successful build)
      +- builds
         +- [BUILD_ID]     (for each build)
            +- build.xml      (build result summary)
            +- log            (log file)
            +- changelog.xml  (change log)
```

Inside the home directory, Hudson keeps a configuration file ❶, various plug-ins ❷, and all the jobs that it runs ❸. The jobs, as they're known in Hudson, are different projects that you build. Each job can have multiple builds, so you can easily follow which one failed and the cause for the failure.

Moving forward in the configuration page, there are also some options to specify the path to your Ant installation (in case the project you want to build uses Ant) or your Maven installation (in case your project is being built by Maven). You can also specify a JDK installation, a CVS installation, and email notification installations (such as the email server, username, and password). Take note here that you don't specify the path to your build.xml files, but instead you point to the place where Ant was installed, so that later on Hudson can to talk to that Ant installation and issue the `ant -f build.xml` command.

11.3.4 Configuring a project in Hudson

Now that you've configured Hudson to find the installations of Ant, Maven, and the others, you can move on and configure a new job. To configure a new job with Hudson, first navigate to the main screen and select the New Job link from the list on the left side. After that you'll be presented with a sample form to fill in. You need to specify a name for the job, and make sure you choose one of the presented build options. If your build is Maven2-based, make sure you select Build A Maven2 Project; otherwise, go with the Build A Free-style Software Project option. Click OK, and you'll be presented the job-configuration screen shown on figure 11.7.

Here you're given the ability to configure the way you want to build your job. You use the first lines to specify or change the name and the description of the job. After that are some options regarding the source control management (SCM) system you use (Subversion, CVS, and the like).

The next section tunes the settings for the build triggers—on what occasion you want to trigger your build. You're presented with several options: poll the SCM system to check whether a build is needed, build the project periodically, build it after some dependent projects were built, and so on. Let's select the Poll The SCM trigger; a field opens where we need to specify on what interval of time we want the poll to happen. This field uses a nice syntax that follows the syntax of the UNIX cron tool. We'd like to have our project executed every hour, so we specify `@hourly` in the

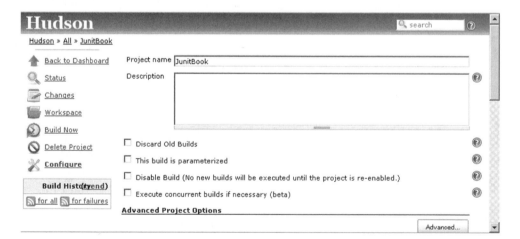

Figure 11.7   Job-configuration screen in Hudson

field. You can learn more about the cron syntax if you click the corresponding question mark next to the trigger.

The next section deals with invoking the build itself. You can specify to execute a shell script, a Windows batch file, an Ant build file, or a Maven build file. On any of these you can specify any parameters, targets, goals, and so on. You can also arrange multiple build steps, such as first invoking a shell script and then running Ant. There's also the option to rearrange all these steps by dragging and dropping.

The last section configures the post-build triggers. The options listed there will help you publish the artifact, publish the Javadoc, build some other project, send an email with the build results, or anything else you need. There's also the option to select multiple triggers.

After doing all this, you should save the job configuration. This will lead you to the project's home page (shown in figure 11.8).

From the job's home page you can keep track of the current job. From the menu on the left side, you can choose to see the changes someone has made on the job, inspect the workspace of the job, delete the project, configure it, or schedule another build. You can also subscribe to the build results RSS feeds.

We don't want to wait another hour for the build to be triggered, so let's execute it right now. On the job's home page, click the Build Now link and wait for the build to finish.

Now you can see the results of the build execution on the job's home page. You can see not only when the last build was run, but also when the last successful build happened. Clicking any build number lets you explore the build itself: which modules were built, which tests failed or succeeded, and, most important, why (see figure 11.9).

Once you spend some time using Hudson, you'll probably find it a lot easier to use. Its entire configuration is done through a nice web interface, and it's relatively

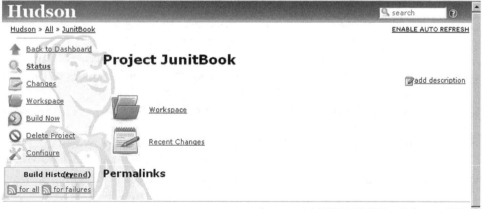

Figure 11.8 Hudson job home page

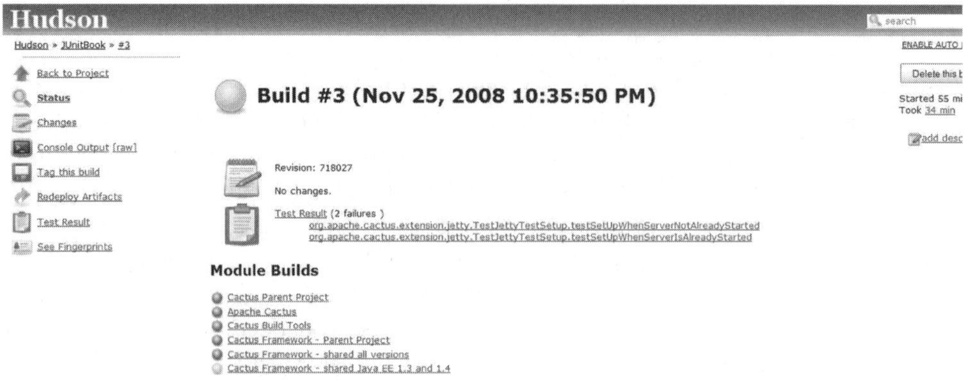

Figure 11.9   Hudson build results

easy to do. But the nicest thing is that the web interface is intuitive. That's why we don't cover Hudson in detail. Another reason for this is that Hudson is currently undergoing rapid development. It's a mature project with a large community of developers who constantly improve the codebase. From that point of view, it'll be interesting to see how the project will evolve in time.

11.4   *Benefits of continuous integration*

In general, the software tests are there to help you find your own errors. You execute the unit tests every time you make any changes on the code you develop. This way, they cover your back and will alert you whenever you introduce a new bug into the system.

The continuous integration servers have exactly the same purpose: they cover your back and alert you the moment you break the integration with the other modules of the system. And because you can't run the CI tools manually every time you make a small change in the system, they run on a separate host and try to continuously integrate your software. But again, they protect you and will alert you to a change that breaks the integration.

We've heard many excuses from people as to why you shouldn't use CI tools, and the winner is this one: "I don't see the profit in using it." And usually this comes from people who've never used a CI server.

We all make errors—face it! You and we, and everybody else—it's human to err. And no matter how good you are, you'll sometimes make a mistake and introduce a bug into the system. Knowing this, it seems reasonable to have something notify you when those errors occur. The software tests and CI tools are exactly this. Once you start using a CI tool, no matter which one—CruiseControl or Hudson or anything else— you'll see how good it is to know that something is watching your back and that an empty mailbox means that nothing is broken.

To sum up we'd say:

- *CI tools*—Free
- *Installation and configuration*—A couple of hours work
- *Knowing your build is well integrated*—Priceless

11.5 Summary

In this chapter we looked at two of the most popular CI tools: CruiseControl and Hudson. As you probably noticed, they're totally different. So why do we cover those tools?

The reason is to make you understand that continuous integration is an important concept in the modern software development lifecycle and that it makes absolutely no difference which tool you use, but it makes a great difference whether you use CI or not.

With this chapter we close the part of the book that deals with integrating JUnit with the build process. You should now be ready to run your build and execute your tests with Ant or Maven and also to set up a continuous integration build and execute your builds and tests on a scheduled basis.

This way you have JUnit tests that protect your modules from new bugs, and you also have a workspace where you continuously execute your build and run your tests to see if anything got broken during the integration. You're now fully automated and ready to move on with the next chapters.

The next part of the book deals with testing different layers of your application. We look at some examples of how to execute tests against the presentation layer and also against the database and persistence layers. We show how to test your GUI components, and you can include those tests and run them in the continuous integration environment you just learned about. Let's move on!

Part 4

JUnit extensions

This last part of the book deals with different kinds of JUnit extensions. We cover all types of external projects that try to extend JUnit to the point where the testing framework falls short. They test different aspects and layers of an enterprise application.

We start by introducing the HTMLUnit and Selenium projects in chapter 12. We show you how to test your presentation layer with these projects. We go into details of not only how to set up your projects but also some best practices in testing your presentation layer. Chapter 13 is dedicated, again, to testing your front end. In that chapter we discuss how to test the Ajax part of your application. We also introduce the JsUnit project and give some special hints on testing a Google Web Toolkit (GWT) application.

Chapters 14 and 15 are dedicated to testing your server-side Java code. Chapter 14 introduces the Cactus project, which focuses on testing your Java EE core components (JSPs, servlets, EJBs, and the like). Chapter 15 describes the JSFUnit project, which tests your JSF-based applications.

Chapter 16 is a small chapter that concentrates on testing component-oriented applications. We describe various techniques for testing your OSGi services.

Chapters 17 and 18 are both dedicated to testing the persistence layer. These chapters talk about the DBUnit project and give recipes for testing the JPA part of an application.

The last chapter describes how to create your own extensions by means of the Unitils and JUnit-addons projects.

Presentation-layer testing

If debugging is the process of removing software bugs, then programming must be the process of putting them in.

—Edsger Dijkstra

This chapter covers

- Introducing presentation-layer testing
- Testing with HtmlUnit
- Testing with Selenium

Simply stated, *presentation-layer testing* means finding bugs in the graphical user interface (GUI) of an application. Finding errors here is as important as finding errors in other application tiers. A bad user experience can cost you a customer or discourage a web surfer from visiting your site again. Furthermore, bugs in the user interface may cause other parts of the application to malfunction.

Because of its nature and interaction with a person, GUI testing presents unique challenges and requires its own set of tools and techniques. This chapter covers testing web application user interfaces.

We address here what can be objectively, or programmatically, asserted about the GUI. Outside the scope of this discussion are whether the choice of subjective elements like fonts, colors, and layout cause an application to be difficult or impossible to use.

What we can test is the content of web pages to any level of detail (we could include spelling), the application structure or navigation (following links to their expected destination, for example), and the ability to verify user stories with acceptance tests.[1] We can also verify that the site works with required browsers and operating systems.

12.1 Choosing a testing framework

We look at two free open source tools to implement presentation-layer tests within JUnit: HtmlUnit and Selenium.

HtmlUnit is a 100 percent Java headless browser framework that runs in the same virtual machine as your tests. Use HtmlUnit when your application is independent of operating system features and browser-specific implementations not accounted for by HtmlUnit, like JavaScript, DOM, CSS, and so on.

Selenium drives various web browsers programmatically and checks the results from JUnit. Selenium also provides a simple IDE to record and play back tests and can generate test code. Use Selenium when you require validation of specific browsers and operating systems, especially if the application takes advantage of or depends on a browser's specific implementation of JavaScript, DOM, CSS, and the like. Let's start with HtmlUnit.

12.2 Introducing HtmlUnit

HtmlUnit is an open source Java headless browser framework. It allows tests to imitate programmatically the user of a browser-based web application. HtmlUnit tests don't display a user interface. The framework lets you test all aspects of a web application. We describe here the most common tasks; for the rest, you'll find the API quite intuitive and easy to use.

In the remainder of this HtmlUnit section when we talk about "testing with a web browser," it's with the understanding that we're testing by emulating a specific web browser.

To install HtmlUnit, see appendix E, "Installing software."

12.2.1 A live example

Let's jump in with the example in listing 12.1. You can test now, assuming you can connect to the internet. The test will go to the HtmlUnit website, navigate the Javadoc, and make sure a class has the proper documentation.

---

[1] Extreme programming acceptance tests: http://www.extremeprogramming.org/rules/functionaltests.html

Listing 12.1   Our first HtmlUnit example

```
[...]
public class JavadocPageTest {

@Test
public void testClassNav() throws IOException {          ❶
    WebClient webClient = new WebClient();               ◄─┐
    HtmlPage mainPage = (HtmlPage) webClient.getPage(      ❷
        "http://htmlunit.sourceforge.net/apidocs/index.html");
    HtmlPage packagePage = (HtmlPage) mainPage.getFrameByName(  ❸
        "packageFrame").getEnclosedPage();
    HtmlPage bVerPage = packagePage.getAnchorByHref(      ❹
        "com/gargoylesoftware/htmlunit/BrowserVersion.html").click();
    HtmlParagraph p = (HtmlParagraph) bVerPage.getElementsByTagName(  ❺
        "p").item(0);                                     ❻
    Assert.assertTrue("Unexpected text", p.asText().startsWith(  ◄─┐
        "Objects of this class represent one specific version of a given"));
    webClient.closeAllWindows();                          ◄─┐
}                                                          ❼
}
```

Let's step through the example. We always start by creating an HtmlUnit web client ❶, which gives us an Internet Explorer 7 web client by default. We get to the home page from the web client ❷ and then to the list of classes on the page in the bottom-left frame ❸. Next, we get the link for the class we're interested in and click it as a user would ❹. This gives us a new page for the link we clicked, which we then query for the first paragraph element ❺. Finally, we check that the paragraph starts with the text we expect should be there ❻ and release resources ❼.

This example covers the basics: getting a web page, navigating the HTML object model, and asserting results. You'll notice a lack of standard JUnit assertions in the code that navigates the HTML model. If HtmlUnit doesn't find an element or encounters a problem, it will throw an exception on our behalf.

12.3   *Writing HtmlUnit tests*

When you write an HtmlUnit test, you write code that simulates the action of a user sitting in front of a web browser: You get a web page, enter data, read text, and click buttons and links. Instead of manually manipulating the browser, you programmatically control an emulated browser. At each step, you can query the HTML object model and assert that values are what you expect. The framework will throw exceptions if it encounters a problem, which allows your test cases to avoid checking for these errors, thereby reducing clutter.

12.3.1   *HTML assertions*

As you're familiar with by now, JUnit provides a class called Assert to allow tests to fail when they detect an error condition. Assert is the bread and butter of any unit test.

HtmlUnit provides a class in the same spirit called WebAssert, which contains standard assertions for HTML like assertElementPresent, assertLinkPresent, and assertTextPresent. HtmlUnit itself uses `WebAssert notNull` extensively to guard against null parameters. Make sure to check the `WebAssert` class before you write code that may duplicate its functionality.

If a method you need is absent, you should consider creating your own assert class for additional HTML assertions. You should also consider creating an application-specific assertion class to reuse across your unit tests. Remember, code duplication is the enemy.

12.3.2 *Testing for a specific web browser*

HtmlUnit, as of version 2.7, supports the browsers shown in table 12.1.

Table 12.1   HtmlUnit-supported browsers

Web browser and version	HtmlUnit `BrowserVersion` constant
Firefox 2 (deprecated)	`BrowserVersion.FIREFOX_2`
Firefox 3	`BrowserVersion.FIREFOX_3`
Internet Explorer 6	`BrowserVersion.INTERNET_EXPLORER_6`
Internet Explorer 7	`BrowserVersion.INTERNET_EXPLORER_7`
Internet Explorer 8	`BrowserVersion.INTERNET_EXPLORER_8`

By default, `WebClient` emulates Internet Explorer 7. In order to specify which browser to emulate, you provide the `WebClient` constructor with a `BrowserVersion`. For example, for Firefox 3 use

```
WebClient webClient = new WebClient(BrowserVersion.FIREFOX_3);
```

12.3.3 *Testing more than one web browser*

You'll probably want to test your application with the most common version of Internet Explorer and Firefox. For our purposes, we define our test matrix to be all HtmlUnit-supported web browsers.

Listing 12.2 uses the JUnit `Parameterized` feature to drive the same test with all browsers in our text matrix.

Listing 12.2   Testing for all HtmlUnit-supported browsers

```
[...]
@RunWith(value = Parameterized.class)                                  ①
public class JavadocPageAllBrowserTest {

    private BrowserVersion browserVersion;                             ②

    @Parameters
    public static Collection<BrowserVersion[]> getBrowserVersions() {  ③
        return Arrays.asList(new BrowserVersion[][]{
            {BrowserVersion.FIREFOX_2},
```

```
                {BrowserVersion.FIREFOX_3},
                {BrowserVersion.INTERNET_EXPLORER_6},
                {BrowserVersion.INTERNET_EXPLORER_7}});
    }

    public JavadocPageAllBrowserTest(BrowserVersion browserVersion) {      ◁━❹
        this.browserVersion = browserVersion;
    }
                                                                          ❺
    @Test
    public void testSearchPage() throws Exception {                       ◁┘
        WebClient webClient = new WebClient(this.browserVersion);
        // same as before...
    }
}
```

Based on our previous example, we made the following changes: We used the `Parameterized` JUnit test runner ❶. We added a BrowserVersion instance variable ❷ to track the browser context. We added the method `getBrowserVersions` ❸ to return a list of BrowserVersion objects corresponding to the browsers we want to test. The signature of this method must be `@Parameters public static java.util. Collection`, without parameters. The `Collection` elements must be arrays of identical lengths. This array length must match the number of arguments of the only public constructor. In our case, each array contains one element because the public constructor has one argument.

Now let's step through the test. JUnit calls the static method `getBrowserVersions` ❷. JUnit loops for each array in the `getBrowserVersions` collection ❸. JUnit calls the only public constructor ❹. If there's more than one public constructor, JUnit will throw an assertion error. JUnit calls the constructor with an argument list built from the array elements. In our case, JUnit calls the one argument constructor with the only element in the array. JUnit then calls each `@Test` method ❺ as usual. We repeat the process for the next array in the `getBrowserVersions` collection ❸.

When you compare the test results with the previous example, you'll see that instead of running one test, the parameterized JUnit test runner ran the same method four times, once for each value in our `@Parameters` collection.

12.3.4 Creating standalone tests

You may not always want to use actual URL addressed pages as test fixtures, HTTP, files, or otherwise. Next, we show you how to embed and run HTML in the unit test code itself.

The framework allows you to plug a mock[2] HTTP connection into a web client. In listing 12.3, we set up a mock connection with a default HTML response string. The test can then get this default page by using any URL value.

---

[2] See chapter 7, "Testing with mock objects."

Listing 12.3 Configuring a standalone test

```
[...]
public class InLineHtmlFixtureTest {

@Test
public void testInLineHtmlFixture() throws Exception {
    final String expectedTitle = "Hello 1!";
    String html = "<html><head><title>" + expectedTitle +
                                        "</title></head></html>";    ❶
    WebClient webClient = new WebClient();
    MockWebConnection conn = new MockWebConnection();
    conn.setDefaultResponse(html);                                   ❷
    webClient.setWebConnection(conn);
    HtmlPage page = webClient.getPage("http://page");
    Assert.assertEquals(expectedTitle, page.getTitleText());         ❸
    webClient.closeAllWindows();
}
[...]
```

We start by defining our expected HTML page title and HTML test fixture. Then we create the web client, a `MockWebConnection` ❶, and install the HTML fixture as the default response for the mock connection ❷. We can then set the web client's connection to our mock connection ❸. We're now ready to go, and we get the test page. Any URL will do here because we set up our HTML fixture as the default response. Finally we check that the page title matches our HTML fixture.

To configure a test with multiple pages, you call one of the `MockWebConnection` `setResponse` methods for each page. The code in listing 12.4 sets up three web pages in a mock connection.

Listing 12.4 Configuring a test with multiple page fixtures

```
@Test
public void testInLineHtmlFixtures() throws Exception {
    WebClient webClient = new WebClient();
    final URL page1Url = new URL("http://Page1/");
    final URL page2Url = new URL("http://Page2/");
    final URL page3Url = new URL("http://Page3/");

    MockWebConnection conn = new MockWebConnection();
    conn.setResponse(page1Url,
        "<html><head><title>Hello 1!</title></head></html>");
    conn.setResponse(page2Url,
        "<html><head><title>Hello 2!</title></head></html>");    ❶
    conn.setResponse(page3Url,
        "<html><head><title>Hello 3!</title></head></html>");
    webClient.setWebConnection(conn);

    HtmlPage page1 = webClient.getPage(page1Url);                 ❷
    Assert.assertEquals("Hello 1!", page1.getTitleText());
                                                                 ❸
    HtmlPage page2 = webClient.getPage(page2Url);
    Assert.assertEquals("Hello 2!", page2.getTitleText());
```

```
      HtmlPage page3 = webClient.getPage(page3Url);
      Assert.assertEquals("Hello 3!", page3.getTitleText());
      webClient.closeAllWindows();
}
```

This example installs three pages ❶ in the mock connection and tests getting each page ❷ and verifying each page title ❸.

> **Common pitfall**
> Don't forget the trailing slash (/) in the URL; "http://Page1/" will work but "http://Page1" won't be found in the mock connection and will therefore throw an exception.

12.3.5 Navigating the object model

HtmlUnit provides an object model that parallels the HTML object model. You'll use it to navigate through your application's web pages. Let's explore it now.

To get to an HTML page, you always start with a `WebClient` and call `getPage`:

```
WebClient webClient = new WebClient();
HtmlPage page = (HtmlPage) webClient.getPage("http://www.google.com");
```

HtmlPage is HtmlUnit's model of an HTML page returned from a server. Once you have a page, you access its contents in one of three ways:

- Call methods reflecting specific HTML concepts like forms, anchors, and frames.
- Call methods that address HTML elements by references using names and IDs.
- Call methods using XPath, a web standard for addressing XML document nodes.

Let's now look at each technique.

12.3.6 Accessing elements by specific element type

The HtmlPage API provides methods reflecting the HTML element model: for anchors, `getAnchorByName`, `getAnchors`, and others; for a body, `getBody`; for forms, `getForm-ByName`, `getForms`; for frames, `getFrameByName`, `getFrames`; for meta tags, `getMeta-Tags`. We explore specifically how to work with form and frame elements in the following sections.

12.3.7 Accessing elements by name versus index

This discussion applies to all methods that return a `List`: `getAnchors`, `getForms`, and `getFrames`. You should consider the implication of addressing these lists with indexes. For example, consider the following snippet:

```
HtmlForm form = page.getForms().get(0);
```

The index access creates an assumption in your test that the HTML form you want to test will always be the first form in the list. If the page changes and the search form changes position, your test will fail, even though the page's functionality may not have changed. By addressing the form by index, you're explicitly testing the form order on the page. Address an element only through a list index if you want to test the order of an element in that list.

To make the code resistant to list-order change, replace

```
HtmlForm form = page.getForms().get(0);
```

with

```
HtmlForm form = page.getFormByName("f");
```

Well, you might say, now you have a dependency on the form name "f" instead of on form position 0. The benefit is that when you change the form order on a page, the form name doesn't have to change, but the form index must change.

Lists are useful when the order of its elements matter. You may want to assert that an anchor list is alphabetical or that a product list is in ascending price order.

12.3.8 *Accessing elements with references*

As you just saw, HtmlPage allows you to get specific elements by name. HtmlPage also lets you get to any element by name, ID, or access key with any of the methods starting with getElementBy such as getElementById, getElementsByName, and others. These methods allow you to ask generic questions about the HTML model. For example, when we wrote

```
HtmlForm form = page.getFormByName("f");
```

we ask specifically for a form named "f". We can also write

```
HtmlForm form = (HtmlForm) page.getElementsByName("f").get(0);
```

which asks for all elements named "f" and then asks for the first element of that list. Note two changes in the code: First, we cast the result to the desired type unless we can work with an HtmlElement. Second, because element names aren't unique in a page, getElementsByName returns a list of HtmlElement, which is why we have the call to get.

If you can address the desired element by ID, you can use getElementById and do away with the get call.

Calling get introduces some brittleness to this test because we're introducing a dependency on the list order. If we wanted a more resilient test, and the element didn't contain an ID, we'd need to resort to one of the following:

- Traverse the list until we find the right element.
- Use getChildren or getChildNodes to navigate down to the desired element.

Neither option is appealing, so the lesson here is to use HTML IDs if you can. This will allow you to create tests that are more resistant to change.

In general, for each HTML {Element}, there's a class called Html{Element}, for example, HtmlForm. Some class names are more explicit than their HTML element names: for the HTML element "a", the class is `HtmlAnchor`; for "h1", the class is `HtmlHeading1`.

12.3.9 *Using XPath*

Use XPath[3] for complex searches to reduce test code complexity. XPath is a language specified by the W3C for querying nodes in an XML document. We won't cover the XPath language itself here; we focus on its usage in HtmlUnit to perform two types of tasks: getting to a specific element and gathering data.

ACCESSING ELEMENTS WITH XPATH

You call one of two methods to run an XPath query: `getByXPath` returns a list of elements and `getFirstByXPath` returns a single element. Because `DomNode` implements both methods, it's accessible not only to HtmlPage but to all `DomNode` subclasses, which include the HTML classes.

Knowing which XPath expression to use can involve a lot of trial and error. Fortunately, you can inspect any website with XPath Checker[4] or Firebug,[5] free open source Firefox add-ons, and create an XPath from the current selection. For example, to access the text input field on Google's home page, use `/html/body/center/form/table/tbody/tr/td[2]/input[2]`.

Note that expressions generated automatically from such tools usually suffer from the same indexing issue we discussed earlier in section 12.3.7 "Accessing elements by name versus index." By inspecting the code, you can create the following expression, which is more resilient to changes in the page:

```
//input[@name='q']
```

We all know there's no such thing as a free lunch,[6] and this expression's gain in page-change resilience and brevity comes with a small performance price: XPath must find all input elements on the page that match the criteria `[@name='q']` and then give us the first one. This is in contrast to the first expression, which drills down to a known spot in the page or fails along the way if an element is missing. To run this XPath query, the call is

```
page.getFirstByXPath("//input[@name='q']");
```

We look next at a powerful XPath feature supported by the HtmlUnit API: the ability to collect data.

DATA GATHERING WITH XPATH

An extremely powerful feature of XPath is its ability to return a set of nodes. This feature allows us to perform, with one expression, a query that returns a data set. This is

---

[3] XPath 1.0: http://www.w3.org/TR/xpath
[4] XPath Checker: http://slesinsky.org/brian/code/xpath_checker.html
[5] Firebug: http://getfirebug.com/
[6] TANSTAAFL: http://en.wikipedia.org/wiki/TANSTAAFL

a great way to gather values on a page, whether or not the values are formally present in a list-like structure like an HTML table, list, or form.

For example, this expression returns an anchor list from the Java 6 Javadoc page for all package names:

```
//a[contains(@href, 'package-frame.html') and @target='packageFrame']
```

To see this XPath expression in action, go to the Java 6 Javadoc page:

```
client = new WebClient();
mainPage = (HtmlPage) client.getPage
➥("http://java.sun.com/javase/6/docs/api/index.html");
```

Then go to the package list page:

```
HtmlPage packageListPage = (HtmlPage) mainPage.getFrameByName
➥("packageListFrame").getEnclosedPage();
```

From that page, we can gather all links that point to a Java package:

```
List<DomNode> anchors = (List<DomNode>) packageListPage.getByXPath
➥("//a[contains(@href, 'package-frame.html') and @target='packageFrame']");
```

Beware that there's an XPath version 1.0[7] and 2.0[8] specification. HtmlUnit includes the Apache Xalan XPath implementation, which supports only 1.0. If you want to use XPath 2.0 features, you need to get an XPath 2.0 engine, which usually means an XSL 2.0 engine, like Saxon. You'll also need to write some code, an advanced endeavor.

12.3.10 *Test failures and exceptions*

Tests check for error conditions with the JUnit `Assert` class and the HtmlUnit `Web-Assert` class and by letting the HtmlUnit API throw unchecked exceptions. We already covered the `WebAssert` class in section 12.3.1, "HTML assertions." For example, if you query for a form with an invalid name by calling `HtmlPage getFormByName`, you'll get the exception

```
com.gargoylesoftware.htmlunit.ElementNotFoundException:
➥elementName=[form] attributeName=[name] attributeValue=[unknown_element]
```

If you call `WebClient getPage` and the page doesn't exist, you'll get the exception

```
java.net.UnknownHostException: unknown_page
```

HtmlUnit defines exceptions like `ElementNotFoundException` in the package `com.gargoylesoftware.htmlunit`. To verify that a method throws an expected exception, annotate the method with the expected attribute:

```
@Test(expected = ElementNotFoundException.class)
```

Because these exceptions are all unchecked, you don't have to throw them from your methods, but you'll need to remember to catch them if you want to examine

---

[7] XPath 1.0: http://www.w3.org/TR/1999/REC-xpath-19991116
[8] XPath 2.0: http://www.w3.org/TR/xpath20/

the particular state of a failure. For example, the exception `ElementNotFound-Exception` contains specific information as to what exactly caused the failure: the name of the element, the name of attribute, and the attribute value.

Although not explicitly documented in the `WebAssert` Javadoc, `WebAssert` methods will throw exceptions for unexpected conditions. Many `WebAssert` methods throw `ElementNotFoundException`.

JavaScript and ScriptException

By default, all JavaScript errors will throw a `ScriptException` and cause your unit test to fail. This may not be acceptable, especially if you're testing integration with third-party sites or if the exception is due to a shortcoming in the Mozilla JavaScript library or in HtmlUnit itself. You can avoid aborting your unit test on a JavaScript error by calling `setThrowExceptionOnScriptError` on a web client:

```
webClient.setThrowExceptionOnScriptError(false);
```

Logging

You'll notice that HtmlUnit logs warnings on the console whenever it encounters problems. To disable these messages, you need to tell the logger to skip warnings and report only severe problems. The following example sets all HtmlUnit loggers to the severe level:

```
@BeforeClass
public static void setUpLogging() {
  Logger.getLogger("com.gargoylesoftware.htmlunit").setLevel(Level.SEVERE);
}
```

HtmlUnit uses Apache Commons Logging to do its logging, which in turns uses the JRE logging facility by default. Our example reconfigures a JRE `Logger` instance directly. Apache Commons Logging doesn't allow you to reconfigure logs generically; you must do so with the actual log implementation.

12.3.11 Application and internet navigation

You can navigate through an application and the web in general by getting an HTML page and then clicking a link or clicking a user interface element like a button. The API can perform all forms of navigation. Let's look at various types of navigation.

Page navigation

Getting a page is done with the `WebClient` `getPage()` methods. You can get a page by URL or URL string, for example:

```
WebClient webClient = new WebClient();
webClient.setThrowExceptionOnScriptError(false);
HtmlPage page = (HtmlPage) webClient.getPage("http://www.google.com");
HtmlPage page2 = (HtmlPage) webClient.getPage
➥(new URL("http://www.yahoo.com"));
```

If a page is absent or isn't reachable, the API throws an exception. See section 12.3.10, "Test failures and exceptions."

CLICK NAVIGATION

The `click` and `dblClick` methods conveniently navigate through a link or any click-able user interface element. For example, continuing from the previous example, we enter a web query and click the Search button:

```
HtmlForm form = page.getFormByName("f");
HtmlTextInput queryText = (HtmlTextInput) form.getInputByName("q");
queryText.setValueAttribute("Manning Publications Co.");
HtmlSubmitInput searchButton = (HtmlSubmitInput) form.getInputByName("btnG");
HtmlPage resultPage = (HtmlPage) searchButton.click();
```

You can call the `click` and `dblClick` methods on all classes descending from `Html-Element`. Click methods simulate clicking an element (remember, HtmlUnit is an emulator) and return the page in the window that has the focus after the element has been clicked.

The HTML 4.01 specification[9] defines clickable HTML elements. `HtmlElement` is the base class for all HTML elements except frame and iframe.

See the `HtmlElement` Javadoc[10] or select `HtmlElement` in Eclipse and hit F4 to display the class hierarchy.

KEYBOARD NAVIGATION

To simulate the user hitting the Enter key instead of clicking the Search button, replace getting and clicking the search button with the following:

```
HtmlPage resultPage = (HtmlPage) queryText.type('\n');
```

You can code the Enter key with the `'\n'` character. You can also simulate the user tabbing around the page with the HtmlPage methods `tabToNextElement` and `tabTo-PreviousElement`. Hitting the Enter key or any key may not be enough or the right process to test. You can set the focus to any element with the HtmlPage method `set-FocusedElement`. Be aware that this will trigger any `onfocus` and `onblur` event handlers. Let's now put these concepts together with another example and test forms.

12.3.12 *Testing forms with HtmlUnit*

HTML form support is built into the HtmlPage API, where form elements can be accessed with `getForms` (returns `List<HtmlForm>`) to get all form elements and `get-FormByName` to get the first HtmlForm with a given name. You can call one of the Html-Form `getInput` methods to get HTML input elements and then simulate user input with `setValueAttribute`.

The following example focuses on the HtmlUnit mechanics of driving a form. First, we create a simple page to display a form with an input field and Submit button. We include form validation via JavaScript alerts in listing 12.5 as a second path to test. The section "Testing JavaScript alerts" describes this in more detail.

---

[9] http://www.w3.org/TR/html401/

[10] http://htmlunit.sourceforge.net/apidocs/com/gargoylesoftware/htmlunit/html/HtmlElement.html

Listing 12.5   Example form page

```
<!DOCTYPE html PUBLIC "-//W3C//DTD XHTML 1.0 Transitional//EN"
➥"http://www.w3.org/TR/xhtml1/DTD/xhtml1-transitional.dtd">
<html xmlns="http://www.w3.org/1999/xhtml">
<head>
<script type="text/javascript">
function validate_form(form) {
    if (form.in_text.value=="") {
        alert("Please enter a value.");
        form.in_text.focus();
        return false;
    }
}
</script>
<title>Form</title></head>
<body>
<form name="validated_form" action="submit.html"
➥onsubmit="return validate_form(this);" method="post">
  Value:
  <input type="text" name="in_text" id="in_text" size="30"/>
  <input type="submit" value="Submit" id="submit"/>
</form>
</body>
</html>
```

This form looks like figure 12.1 when you click the button without input.

We test normal user interaction with the form in listing 12.6.

Value: | Submit

[JavaScript Application]   ⚠ Please enter a value.   OK

Figure 12.1   Sample form and alert

Listing 12.6   Testing a form

```
@Test
public void testForm() throws IOException {
    WebClient client = new WebClient();
    HtmlPage page = (HtmlPage)
                client.getPage("file:src/main/webapp/formtest.html");
    HtmlForm form = page.getFormByName("validated_form");
    HtmlTextInput input =(HtmlTextInput) form.getInputByName("in_text");
    input.setValueAttribute("typing...");
    HtmlSubmitInput submitButton = (HtmlSubmitInput)
                                        form.getInputByName("submit");
    HtmlPage resultPage = (HtmlPage) submitButton.click();
    WebAssert.assertTitleEquals(resultPage, "Result");
    // more asserts...
}
```

❶ ❷

Let's work through this example. We create the web client, get the page containing the form, and get the form. Next, we get the input text field from the form, emulate the user typing in a value ❶, and then get and click the Submit button ❷. We get a page back from clicking the button, and we make sure it's the expected page.

If at any step, the framework doesn't find an object, the API throws an exception and the test automatically fails. This allows you to focus on the test and let the framework handle failing your test if the page or form isn't as expected. The section "Testing JavaScript alerts" completes this example.

12.3.13 Testing frames

HTML frame support is built into the HtmlPage API, where frames can be accessed with getFrames (returns List<FrameWindow>) to get all iframes and frames and get-FrameByName to get the first iframe or frame with a given name. You then call FrameWindow getEnclosedPage to get the HTML page in that frame. Listing 12.7 navigates through the Java 6 Javadoc.

Listing 12.7   Page navigation through frames

```
@Test
public void testFramesByNames() throws IOException {
    WebClient webClient = new WebClient();
    HtmlPage mainPage = (HtmlPage)
     webClient.getPage("http://java.sun.com/javase/6/docs/api/index.html");

    // Gets page of the first Frame (upper left)
    HtmlPage packageListPage = (HtmlPage)
       mainPage.getFrameByName("packageListFrame").getEnclosedPage();
    packageListPage.getAnchorByHref("java/lang/package-
                                              frame.html").click();

    // get page of the Frame named 'packageFrame' (lower left)
    HtmlPage packagePage = (HtmlPage)
       mainPage.getFrameByName("packageFrame").getEnclosedPage();
    packagePage.getAnchors().get(1).click();

    // get page of the Frame named 'classFrame' (right)
    HtmlPage classPage = (HtmlPage)
                mainPage.getFrameByName("classFrame").getEnclosedPage();
    webClient.closeAllWindows();
}
```

This example uses getFrameByName to get frames and then calls getEnclosedPage. Unit tests can use the list API getFrames as well, but we point you to the issues discussed in section 12.3.7, "Accessing elements by name versus index," earlier in this chapter.

The intermediary FrameWindow returned by getFrameByName isn't used in this example. Note that it represents the actual web window for a frame or iframe and provides APIs to dig deeper through the GUI such as getFrameElement, which returns a BaseFrame. BaseFrame in turn provides access to attributes like longdesc, noresize, scrolling, and so on.

By now, you should have the hang of using the API, so let's move on to JavaScript, CSS, and other topics.

12.3.14 *Testing JavaScript*

HtmlUnit processes JavaScript automatically. Even when, for example, HTML is generated with `Document.write()`, you follow the usual pattern: call `getPage`, find an element, call `click` on it, and check the result.

You can toggle JavaScript support on and off in a web client by calling `setJavaScriptEnabled`. HtmlUnit enables JavaScript support by default. You can also set how a long a script is allowed to run before being terminated with `setJavaScriptTimeout` and passing it a timeout in milliseconds.

To deal with JavaScript alert and confirm calls, you can provide the framework with callbacks routines. We explore these next.

TESTING JAVASCRIPT ALERTS

Your tests can check which JavaScript alerts have taken place. We reuse our form example from section 12.3.12, "Testing forms with HtmlUnit," which includes JavaScript validation code to alert the user of empty input values.

The test in listing 12.8 loads our form page and checks calling the alert when the form detects an error condition. In a second example, we enhance our existing test from section 12.3.12 to ensure that normal operation of the form doesn't raise any alerts. Our test will install an alert handler that gathers all alerts and checks the result after the page has been loaded. The stock class `CollectingAlertHandler` saves alert messages for later inspection.

Listing 12.8 Asserting expected alerts

```
@Test
public void testFormAlert() throws IOException {                               ①
    WebClient webClient = new WebClient();
    CollectingAlertHandler alertHandler = new CollectingAlertHandler();
    webClient.setAlertHandler(alertHandler);                                   ②
    HtmlPage page = (HtmlPage)
            webClient.getPage("file:src/main/webapp/formtest.html");
    HtmlForm form = page.getFormByName("validated_form");
    HtmlSubmitInput submitButton = (HtmlSubmitInput)                           ③
                              form.getInputByName("submit");
    HtmlPage resultPage = (HtmlPage) submitButton.click();
    assertEquals(resultPage.getTitleText(), page.getTitleText());
    assertEquals(resultPage, page);
    List<String> collectedAlerts = alertHandler.getCollectedAlerts();
    List<String> expectedAlerts =                                             ④
                Collections.singletonList("Please enter a value.");
    assertEquals(expectedAlerts, collectedAlerts);
    webClient.closeAllWindows();
}
```

Let's work through the example: We start by creating the web client and alert handler ①, which we install in the web client ②. Next, we get the form page, get the form object, get the Submit button, and click it ❸. This invokes the JavaScript, which calls the alert. Clicking the button returns a page object, which we use to check that the page has not changed by comparing current and previous page titles. We also check that the page has not changed by comparing current and previous page objects. Note that this comparison uses Object equals, so we're really asking whether the page objects are identical. This might not be a great test if a future version of the framework implements equals in an unexpected manner. Finally, we get the list of alert messages that were raised ❹, create a list of expected alert messages, and compare the expected and actual lists.

> **JUnit tip**
>
> When using any assertion that use the equals methods, make sure you understand the semantics of the equals implementation of the objects you're comparing. The default implementation of equals in Object returns true if the objects are the same.

Next, listing 12.9 rewrites the original form test to make sure that normal operation raises no alerts.

Listing 12.9   Asserting no alerts under normal operation

```java
@Test
public void testFormNoAlert() throws IOException {
    WebClient webClient = new WebClient();
    CollectingAlertHandler alertHandler = new CollectingAlertHandler();   ❶
    webClient.setAlertHandler(alertHandler);
    HtmlPage page = (HtmlPage)
            webClient.getPage("file:src/main/webapp/formtest.html");
    HtmlForm form = page.getFormByName("validated_form");
    HtmlTextInput input = (HtmlTextInput) form.getInputByName("in_text");
    input.setValueAttribute("typing...");
    HtmlSubmitInput submitButton = (HtmlSubmitInput)
            form.getInputByName("submit");                                ❷
    HtmlPage resultPage = (HtmlPage) submitButton.click();
    WebAssert.assertTitleEquals(resultPage, "Result");                   ❸
    assertTrue("No alerts expected",
            alertHandler.getCollectedAlerts().isEmpty());
    webClient.closeAllWindows();
}
```

The differences with the original test are that at the beginning of the test ❶ we install a CollectingAlertHandler in the web client, we simulate a user entering a value ❷, and at the end of the test we check that the alert handler's list of messages is empty ❸.

To customize the alert behavior, you need to implement your own AlertHandler. Listing 12.10 will cause your test to fail when a script raises the first alert.

Listing 12.10   Custom alert handler

```
client.setAlertHandler(new AlertHandler() {
        public void handleAlert(final Page page, final String message) {
                fail("JavaScript alert: " + message);
        }
});
```

You can apply the same principles to test JavaScript confirm calls by installing a confirm handler in the web client with `setConfirmHandler`.

12.3.15 *Testing CSS*

You can toggle CSS support on and off in a web client by calling `setCssEnabled`. By default, HtmlUnit enables CSS support.

When calling APIs, the standard HtmlUnit behavior is to throw an exception when encountering a problem. In contrast, when HtmlUnit detects a CSS problem, it doesn't throw an exception; instead, it reports problems to the log through the Apache Commons Logging[11] library. You can customize this behavior in a `WebClient` with an `org.w3c.css.sac.ErrorHandler`. Two `ErrorHandler` implementations are provided with HtmlUnit:

- `DefaultCssErrorHandler` is the default handler and logs all CSS problems.
- `SilentCssErrorHandler` ignores all CSS problems.

To install an error handler, use the `setCssErrorHandler` method on a web client. For example, the following causes all CSS problems to be ignored:

```
webClient.setCssErrorHandler(new SilentCssErrorHandler());
```

If you want any CSS problem to cause test failures, create an error handler that always rethrows the `CSSException` it's given.

12.3.16 *SSL errors*

You'll find that many websites have expired or incorrectly configured SSL certificates. By default, the Java runtime throws exceptions if it detects errors. If this gets in the way of your testing, you can call `WebClient.setUseInsecureSSL(true)` to allow the test to proceed. Using this API causes HtmlUnit to use an insecure SSL handler, which trusts everyone.

Now, that we've covered testing from the client point of view, let's go to the server side and examine how HtmlUnit can be used for in-container testing with the Cactus framework.

---

[11] Apache Commons Logging: http://commons.apache.org/logging/

12.4   *Integrating HtmlUnit with Cactus*

Cactus[12] is a free, open source test framework for unit testing server-side Java code including servlets, EJBs, and much more. Chapter 14, "Server-side Java testing with Cactus," discusses Cactus in detail.

Where does HtmlUnit fit in? Let's look at the various opportunities to test an application from the inside out:

- JUnit can test the data tier.
- Cactus testing takes place in the business middle tier by extending JUnit.
- HtmlUnit lives in the presentation tier.

In the standard HtmlUnit unit test scenario, HtmlUnit drives the test. More specifically, JUnit invokes your unit test classes and methods, from which you call HtmlUnit to emulate a web browser to test your application.

Cactus unit testing manages a different interaction; Cactus calls your HtmlUnit unit tests at just the right time to verify that the web pages returned to the client. The main difference here is that HtmlUnit unit testing takes place in-container instead of through an emulated web client.

To install HtmlUnit in Cactus, see appendix E. For details on managing Cactus tests with tools like Ant and Maven, we refer you to chapter 14.

12.4.1   *Writing tests in Cactus*

Because HtmlUnit tests normally work with HtmlPage objects, we need to plug into the Cactus test execution at the point where a page is about to be returned to the client. Cactus tests for Java-based code like servlets are subclasses of `org.apache.cactus.ServletTestCase`. If the test class contains a method whose name starts with `end`, Cactus will call this method with a `WebResponse`, which contains the contents of the server's response. Take great care to import the appropriate `WebResponse` class for your tests, because three variations are supported:

- `com.meterware.httpunit.WebResponse` for HtmlUnit 1.6
- `com.gargoylesoftware.htmlunit.WebResponse` for HtmlUnit 2.7
- `org.apache.cactus.WebResponse` for Cactus itself

Your boilerplate test class should look like listing 12.11.

Listing 12.11   Boilerplate HtmlUnit `ServletTestCase` subclass

```
[...]
public class HtmlUnitServletTestCase extends ServletTestCase {
    public static Test suite() {
        return new TestSuite(HtmlUnitServletTestCase.class);
    }
```

---

[12] Cactus site: http://jakarta.apache.org/cactus/

```
public HtmlUnitServletTestCase(String name) {
    super(name);
}

public void end(WebResponse webResponse) {
    // asserts
}

public void test() throws ServletException {
    SampleServlet servlet = new SampleServlet();
    servlet.init(this.config);
    // asserts
}
}
```

There are a couple of things to note in this example:

- The `ServletTestCase` provides the following instance variables for your use:

  ```
  AbstractServletConfigWrapper config
  AbstractHttpServletRequestWrapper request
  HttpServletResponse response
  HttpSession session
  ```

- The test method creates the servlet to test and initializes it.
- Cactus integrates with JUnit 3; it doesn't provide JUnit 4 niceties.

Cactus tip

If your test class doesn't contain a begin method, the end method name must be end. If your test class includes a begin method, the end method name *must* match, for example, `beginFoo` and `endFoo`; otherwise the end method won't be called.

Next, let's create the simple servlet in listing 12.12.

Listing 12.12 A simple servlet

```
[...]
public class SampleServlet extends HttpServlet {
    public void doGet(HttpServletRequest request,
        HttpServletResponse response) throws ServletException, IOException {
        response.setContentType("text/html");
        PrintWriter out = response.getWriter();
        out.println("<html><head><title>Hello
            World</title></head><body><p>Hello World</p></body></html>");
    }
}
```

This servlet returns an HTML document with a title and a single paragraph. The next step is to flesh out our end method; we need to get an HtmlPage from the `WebResponse` argument and validate its contents. Getting an HtmlPage from a `WebResponse` requires parsing the HTML. To do so, we use the HtmlUnit `HTMLParser` class:

```
public void end(WebResponse webResponse) throws IOException {
    WebClient webClient = new WebClient();
    HtmlPage page = HTMLParser.parse(webResponse,
                                    webClient.getCurrentWindow());
    WebAssert.assertTitleEquals(page, "Hello World");
    webClient.closeAllWindows();
}
```

We create a `WebClient` only to fulfill the needs of the HTMLParser API, which requires a `WebWindow`, which the `WebClient` holds.

> **Cactus tip**
>
> In Cactus, you don't use `getPage` to get an `HtmlPage`. Instead, you parse it from the `WebResponse` with `HTMLParser.parse`.

Once you have an HtmlPage, you're back to using the standard HtmlUnit API.

We've finished covering HtmlUnit for this chapter; the API is intuitive and straightforward, so we invite you to explore the rest on your own. Let's now look at Selenium, a testing framework that differs from HtmlUnit in a fundamental way: instead of emulating a web browser, Selenium drives a real web browser process.

12.5   *Introducing Selenium*

Selenium[13] is a free open source tool suite used to test web applications. Selenium's strength lies in its ability to run tests against a real browser on a specific operating system. This is unlike HtmlUnit, which emulates the browser in the same VM as your tests. This strength comes at a cost: the complexity of setting up and managing the Selenium runtime. Although Selenium provides many components, we consider the following components: the Selenium Remote Control (RC) server, IDE, and client driver API.

The Selenium IDE is a Firefox add-on used to record, play back, and generate tests in many languages, including Java. The Selenium client driver API is what tests call to drive the application; it communicates to the remote control server, which in turns drives the web browser.

The client driver connects to the server over TCP/IP; the server doesn't need to run in the JVM or even on the same physical machine. Selenium recommends[14] running the server on many different machines, with different operating systems and browser installations. A test connects to a server by specifying a hostname and port number to the `DefaultSelenium` class.

Figure 12.2 shows the main Selenium IDE (1.0 Beta 2) window. The IDE generates code against the client driver API but doesn't support change management. You

---

[13] Selenium site: http://seleniumhq.org/
[14] Selenium Server setup: http://seleniumhq.org/documentation/remote-control/languages/java.html

Figure 12.2   The main Selenium IDE window

should consider the IDE a one-way, use-once tool you use to get started for any given test case. You must handle any change in the application by manually changing the generated tests.

To use the IDE, start by choosing a language (in the menu Options > Format > Format Java (JUnit)), click the red record button, use the browser as a user would, and click the record button again to stop. Because the IDE records everything you do, you should plan in advance which user stories you want to verify and create one or more test cases for each. At any point in the recording, you can ask the IDE to generate an assertion from the browser's context menu; the current web page selection determines the choices. Figure 12.3 shows an example context menu.

To install Selenium, see appendix E, "Installing software." Once you've done that, we can start generating Selenium tests.

```
open /
verifyTextPresent
assertTitle Google
verifyValue q
verifyElementPresent q
Show All Available Commands        ▶
```

Figure 12.3   Selenium IDE context menu

12.6   Generating Selenium tests

The Selenium IDE is a great way to get up and running fast. Before you record a test, edit the package name and class name in the IDE Source pane to match the directory and Java filename you desire. Note that the generated code is JUnit 3 code, and as such it subclasses the Selenium class `SeleneseTestCase`.

12.6.1   A live example

The same user interaction as in our first HtmlUnit test generated the following example. Go to Google, enter a query, and click to go to the expected site. Listing 12.13 shows our first Selenium example.

Listing 12.13   Our first Selenium example

```
[...]
public class FirstTestJUnit3 extends SeleneseTestCase {
    @Override
    public void setUp() throws Exception {                        ←─❶
        setUp("http://www.google.com/", "*iexplore");
    }

    public void testSearch() throws Exception {
        selenium.open("/");                                      ←─❷    ❸
        assertEquals("Google", selenium.getTitle());
        selenium.type("q", "Manning Publishing Co.");           ←─
        selenium.click("btnG");                                 ←─
        selenium.waitForPageToLoad("30000");                          ❹
        assertEquals("Manning Publishing Co. - Google Search",
                                        selenium.getTitle());
        selenium.click("link=Manning Publications Co.");        ←─
        selenium.waitForPageToLoad("30000");                          ❺
        assertEquals("Manning Publications Co.", selenium.getTitle());
    }
}
```

First, the `setUp` method ❶ calls the superclass's `setUp` method with the base URL for the tests and the browser launcher to use, in this case, Internet Explorer (see section 12.8 1, "Testing for a specific web browser" for other settings). This initializes the `selenium` instance variable to a `DefaultSelenium` instance.

In the test method, we start by opening the home page ❷. Next, we set the value of the input field ❸, as if a user had typed it in, and we click the Search button ❹. The `click` argument is a Selenium locator, which here is the button name (more on the locator concept later). We wait for the new page to load and assert the opened page's title. Then, we click a link ❺ using a Selenium link locator. Again, we wait for the new page to load and assert the opened page's title.

Selenium tests subclass `SeleneseTestCase`, which in turn subclasses JUnit's `Test-Case` class. You'll note that methods aren't annotated; Selenium-generated tests are JUnit 3 tests.

The immediate issue raised by running within the JUnit 3 framework is the performance of a test class. Each time JUnit calls a test method, JUnit also calls the `setUp` and `tearDown` methods; this means starting and stopping a web browser, which is slow. We remedy this performance problem in section 12.7.2, "Running Selenium tests with JUnit 4."

Another issue to consider when using the Selenium IDE is that you're recording tests in Firefox 3. If your browser requirements are different from Firefox 3, what you recorded may not play back the same in a different browser. Web pages can behave differently, sometimes in a subtle manner, from browser to browser. In addition, pages can contain scripts to customize behavior based on the host browser. Server-side code can customize replies based on the agent making the request. Consider these issues before generating code from Firefox with the Selenium IDE; you may need to write the tests from scratch, a la HtmlUnit, if your application has code paths for a non-Firefox browser, such as Internet Explorer or Safari.

Next, we look at what it takes to run Selenium tests.

12.7   Running Selenium tests

Now that you know the basic concepts surrounding a Selenium test case, we describe the setup and mechanics of running Selenium tests: managing a Selenium server and integrating Selenium with JUnit 4.

12.7.1   Managing the Selenium server

To run Selenium tests, you must use the Selenium server included in the Selenium Remote Control download.

> **Selenium: under the hood**
> The Selenium server launches the web browser and acts as a proxy server to your tests; the server then runs the tests on your behalf. This architecture works for any browser and operating system combination; you can also use it to test Ajax applications. This proxy server setup is why you may get certificate warnings.

To start the server manually, open a command-line window in the server directory, for example: selenium-remote-control-1.0-beta-2\selenium-server-1.0-beta-2. Assuming the JVM is on your `PATH`, type the following:

```
java -jar selenium-server.jar
```

You'll see, for example:

```
22:14:11.367 INFO - Java: Sun Microsystems Inc. 11.2-b01
22:14:11.382 INFO - OS: Windows XP 5.1 x86
22:14:11.382 INFO - v1.0-beta-2 [2571], with Core v1.0-beta-2 [2330]
22:14:11.539 INFO - Version Jetty/5.1.x
22:14:11.554 INFO - Started HttpContext[/selenium-server/driver,/
          ➥selenium-server/driver]
```

```
22:14:11.554 INFO - Started HttpContext[/selenium-server,/selenium-server]
22:14:11.554 INFO - Started HttpContext[/,/]
22:14:11.570 INFO - Started SocketListener on 0.0.0.0:4444
22:14:11.585 INFO - Started org.mortbay.jetty.Server@109a4c
```

You're now ready to run tests. When you run tests, you'll see two browser windows open and close. The first will contain the tested application; the second will display commands sent to the browser and log entries if you have logging enabled.

If you're building with Ant or Maven, you can manage the lifecycle of the Selenium server from these tools. We recommend that you manage the server from the test class or suite directly, as we show next. This allows you, as a developer, to run the tests directly from the command line or an IDE like Eclipse.

12.7.2 Running Selenium tests with JUnit 4

The Selenium requirement for JUnit is version 3; as of Selenium version 1.0 Beta 2, there's no out-of-the-box integration with JUnit 4. This is a problem because the performance associated with a default `SeleneseTestCase` is bad; JUnit starts and stops a browser around each test method invocation through the `setUp` and `tearDown` methods.

We present a two-stage solution to this problem by first managing a server for all test methods in a given class and then managing a server for all classes in a test suite. To do so, you'll need to add the server JAR file to your classpath, for example, selenium-remote-control-1.0-beta-2\selenium-server-1.0-beta-2\selenium-server.jar.

In our first solution, JUnit starts and stops the server once per class run in the `@BeforeClass` and `@AfterClass` methods, as listing 12.14 demonstrates.

Listing 12.14   Managing the Selenium server from a test

```
[...]
public class ManagedSeleniumServer {
    protected static Selenium selenium;              ⟵❶

    private static SeleniumServer seleniumServer;    ⟵❷

    @BeforeClass
    public static void setUpOnce() throws Exception {   ⟵❸
        startSeleniumServer();
        startSeleniumClient();
    }

    public static void startSeleniumClient() throws Exception {
        selenium = new DefaultSelenium("localhost", 4444, "*iexplore",
                                       "http://www.google.com/");
        selenium.start();
    }

    public static void startSeleniumServer() throws Exception {
        seleniumServer = new SeleniumServer();
        seleniumServer.start();
    }
```

```
    public static void stopSeleniumClient() throws Exception {
        if (selenium != null) {
            selenium.stop();
            selenium = null;
        }
    }

    public static void stopSeleniumServer() throws Exception {
        if (seleniumServer != null) {
            seleniumServer.stop();
            seleniumServer = null;
        }
    }

    @AfterClass
    public static void tearDownOnce() throws Exception {          ◁─❹
        stopSeleniumClient();
        stopSeleniumServer();
    }
}
```

Let's examine this code. The test manages two static variables: a Selenium client driver ❶ and a Selenium server ❷. The @BeforeClass method starts the Selenium server and then the Selenium client ❸. The @AfterClass method stops the client and then the server ❹. We can now run tests from ManagedSeleniumServer subclasses, as this next example demonstrates.

This class doesn't subclass SeleneseTestCase to avoid inheriting its setUp and tearDown methods, which respectively start and stop a web browser. If you want to subclass SeleneseTestCase, make sure you override the setUp and tearDown methods to do nothing. Let's look at an example of a managed test:

```
public class ManagedTestJUnit4v2 extends ManagedSeleniumServer {
    @Test
    public void testSearch() {
        // test...
    }
}
```

As a ManagedSeleniumServer subclass, this class needs only test methods. JUnit will call the @BeforeClass methods declared in superclasses before those of the current class and will call the @AfterClass methods in superclasses after those of the current class.

If you aren't going to manage a Selenium server farm for different browsers and operating systems, using this class as a superclass for tests offers a simple solution to get you up and running managing the Selenium server within your tests and VM.

The drawback to this approach is that JUnit starts and stops the Selenium server for each test class. To avoid this, you could create a test suite with first and last test classes that start and stop the server, but you'll need to remember to do this for each suite, and you'll also need to share the Selenium server through what amounts to a global variable. We take care of this problem next.

Our second solution, in listing 12.15, creates a JUnit Suite class to manage a Selenium server. This custom suite will start the Selenium server, run all the test classes in the suite, and then stop the server.

Listing 12.15   A test suite to manage a Selenium server

```
[...]
public class ManagedSeleniumServerSuite extends Suite {
    private static SeleniumServer seleniumServer;

    public static void startSeleniumServer() throws Exception {        ←─❶
        ManagedSeleniumServerSuite.stopSeleniumServer();
        seleniumServer = new SeleniumServer();
        seleniumServer.start();
    }

    public static void stopSeleniumServer() {                          ←─❷
        if (seleniumServer != null) {
            seleniumServer.stop();
            seleniumServer = null;
        }
    }

    public ManagedSeleniumServerSuite(Class<?> klass, Class<?>[]       ←─┐
        suiteClasses) throws InitializationError {
        super(klass, suiteClasses);
    }

    public ManagedSeleniumServerSuite(Class<?> klass, List<Runner>     ←─┤
        runners) throws InitializationError {
        super(klass, runners);                                              ❸
    }

    public ManagedSeleniumServerSuite(Class<?> klass, RunnerBuilder    ←─┤
        builder) throws InitializationError {
        super(klass, builder);
    }

    public ManagedSeleniumServerSuite(RunnerBuilder builder, Class<?>  ←─┤
        klass, Class<?>[] suiteClasses) throws InitializationError {
        super(builder, klass, suiteClasses);
    }

    public ManagedSeleniumServerSuite(RunnerBuilder builder, Class<?>[] ←─┘
        classes) throws InitializationError {
        super(builder, classes);
    }
                                                                           ❹
    @Override
    public void run(final RunNotifier notifier) {                      ←─┘
        EachTestNotifier testNotifier = new EachTestNotifier(notifier,
                                              this.getDescription());
        try {
            ManagedSeleniumServerSuite.startSeleniumServer();         ←─┐
            Statement statement = this.classBlock(notifier);               ❺
            statement.evaluate();
```

```
      } catch (AssumptionViolatedException e) {
         testNotifier.fireTestIgnored();
      } catch (StoppedByUserException e) {
         throw e;
      } catch (Throwable e) {
         testNotifier.addFailure(e);
      } finally {
         ManagedSeleniumServerSuite.stopSeleniumServer();          ◁─❻
      }
   }
}
```

The key to this class is our implementation of the run method ❹. We clone the method from the superclass and insert calls to our methods to start ❺ and stop ❻ the Selenium server. The startSeleniumServer ❶ and stopSeleniumServer ❷ methods are straightforward enough. The rest of the code consists of duplicating constructors from the superclass ❸. This allows us to write our test suite simply and succinctly as follows:

```
@RunWith(ManagedSeleniumServerSuite.class)
@SuiteClasses( {
   UnmanagedFirstTestJUnit3.class, UnmanagedFirstTestJUnit4.class })
public class ManagedExampleSuiteTest {}
```

Each test class in the suite is responsible for connecting to the local server. Check that classes, like UnmanagedFirstTestJUnit4, connect to the server with the hostname "localhost" and the default port 4444. You can further enhance the suite to customize these settings.

Now that we can generate and run Selenium tests, let's focus on writing our own.

12.8   *Writing Selenium tests*

With an efficient test infrastructure in place, we can now explore writing individual tests with Selenium. We look at how to test for multiple browsers and how to navigate the object model, and we work through some example tests.

12.8.1   *Testing for a specific web browser*

Selenium, as of version 1.0 Beta 2, supports the browser launch strings shown in table 12.2.

Table 12.2   Selenium browser launcher strings

Web browser	SeleneseTestCase and DefaultSelenium browser strings
Chrome	`*googlechrome`
Firefox	`*firefox`
Firefox	`*firefoxproxy`

Table 12.2   Selenium browser launcher strings *(continued)*

Web browser	`SeleneseTestCase` and `DefaultSelenium` browser strings
Firefox Chrome URL[15]	`*chrome`
Internet Explorer	`*iexplore`
Internet Explorer HTML application[16]	`*iehta`
Internet Explorer	`*iexploreproxy`
Opera	`*opera`
Safari	`*safari`
Specific executable	`c:\\path\\to\\a\\browser.exe"`

If you don't call `SeleneseTestCase`'s `setUp(String,String)`, the default web browser launch string used on Windows is `*iexplore`, and it's `*firefox` for all other operating systems. If you use the class `DefaultSelenium`, you must provide a browser launch string, for example:

```
selenium = new DefaultSelenium("localhost", 4444, "*iexplore",
    "http://www.google.com/");
```

Note that experimental[17] browser launchers exist for elevated security privileges and proxy injection.

12.8.2 *Testing multiple browsers*

We can apply the same JUnit `@Parameterized` feature we used with HtmlUnit in order to run the same test class with more than one browser. In listing 12.16, we rework our previous example with class-level and instance-level JUnit initialization in order to combine the ability to run all tests with one client driver instance and then repeat the test for different browsers.

Listing 12.16   Running the test class for multiple browsers

```
[File 1]
@RunWith(ManagedSeleniumServerSuite.class)
@SuiteClasses({UnmanagedAllBrowsersTest.class})
public class ManagedAllBrowsersSuiteTest {}
```

---

[15] Chrome URL: https://developer.mozilla.org/En/XUL

[16] IE HTML application: http://msdn.microsoft.com/en-us/library/ms536496(VS.85).aspx

[17] Experimental browser launchers: http://seleniumhq.org/documentation/remote-control/experimental.html

```
[File 2]
@RunWith(value = Parameterized.class)                              ❶
public class UnmanagedAllBrowsersTest {
    private static Map<String, Selenium> SeleniumMap;              ◄—❷

    @Parameters                                                      ❸
    public static Collection getBrowsers() {                       ◄—
        return Arrays.asList(new String[][]{{"*iexplore"}, {"*firefox"}});
    }

    private static Selenium getSelenium(String key) {              ◄—┐
        Selenium s = getSeleniumMap().get(key);                       │
        if (s != null) {                                           ❹│
            return s;
        }
        stopDrivers(); // only let one driver run                 ◄—❺
        s = new DefaultSelenium("localhost", 4444, key, "http://
 www.google.com/");
        getSeleniumMap().put(key, s);
        s.start();
        return s;
    }

    private static Map<String, Selenium> getSeleniumMap() {
        if (SeleniumMap == null) {
            SeleniumMap = new HashMap<String, Selenium>();
        }
        return SeleniumMap;
    }

    @AfterClass
    public static void stopDrivers() {                            ◄—❻
        for (Selenium s : getSeleniumMap().values()) {
            s.stop();
        }
        SeleniumMap = null;
    }

    private String browserStartCommand;
    private Selenium selenium;                                     ◄—❼

    public UnmanagedAllBrowsersTest(String browserStartCommand) {
        this.browserStartCommand = browserStartCommand;
    }

    @Before                                                        ◄—❽
    public void setUp() throws Exception {
        this.selenium = getSelenium(this.browserStartCommand);
    }

    @Test
    public void testGoogleSearch() {
        this.selenium.open("/");
        SeleneseTestCase.assertEquals("Google", this.selenium.getTitle());
        this.selenium.type("q", "Manning Publishing Co.");
        this.selenium.click("btnG");
        this.selenium.waitForPageToLoad("30000");
```

```
        SeleneseTestCase.assertEquals("Manning Publishing Co. - Google
                                      Search", this.selenium.getTitle());
    this.selenium.click("link=Manning Publications Co.");
    this.selenium.waitForPageToLoad("30000");
        SeleneseTestCase.assertEquals("Manning Publications Co.",
                                      this.selenium.getTitle());
    }
}
```

Let's examine this more complex setup. The test class is annotated with `@Run-`
`With(value = Parameterized.class)` ❶, which directs JUnit to run the test class as
many times as there are values returned from our `@Parameters` method `getBrowsers`
❸. By contract with JUnit, this method must return a `Collection` of arrays; in our
case, we return a list of browser launch strings, one for each browser we want to test.

JUnit will run all test methods with the test class initialized with `"*iexplore"` and
then do it all over again with `"*firefox"`. You'll need to have both browsers installed
on your machine for this to work.

Let's walk through this JUnit subtlety more carefully. When running the test class,
JUnit creates test class instances for the cross product of the test methods and the test
collection elements. One instance of the class is created for `"*iexplore"` and for a single `@Test` method in the class. JUnit runs that `@Test` method and repeats the process
for all `@Test` methods in the class. JUnit then repeats that whole process with `"*fire-`
`fox"` and so on for all elements in the `@Parameters` collection ❸.

We no longer have a `@BeforeClass` method; instead we use a `@Before` method ❽
to initialize the `selenium` instance variable ❼ for each test method. The `selenium`
instance variable gets its value from a lazy-initialized static variable ❷. This can work
only by using a `@Before` method and lazy initializing our client driver. Remember, we
want our test class to reuse the same driver instance for each test method in a given
parameterized run.

We have an `@AfterClass` method ❻ to clean up the driver at the end of the class
run. Even though we use a static `Map` ❷ to save our driver across test runs, there's only
one driver in the map at any given time. The `getSelenium` method ❹ can safely stop
❺ the current driver when creating a new driver because we know that JUnit finished
one of its parameterized runs.

Now that you know how to run tests efficiently for a browser suite, let's survey the
API used to navigate an application.

12.8.3 *Application and internet navigation*

Unlike HtmlUnit, there's no Selenium HTML object model to navigate; instead, you
call the `com.thoughtworks.selenium.Selenium` interface, using a locator string to
address elements (see section 12.8.4, "Accessing elements with references"). This
interface contains more than 140 methods and provides all of the services and setting
toggles needed to write tests. Although there's no object model per se, the API provides some methods to work with certain types of elements. For example, `getAll-`
`Fields` returns the IDs of all input fields on a page.

Here's a brief sample of how tests can manipulate page elements:

- Call `click` and `doubleClick` to click an element and get the resulting page.
- Call `check` and `uncheck` to toggle a radio button or check box.
- Call `type` to set the value of an input field.

We now look at the different ways to access elements.

12.8.4 Accessing elements with references

In our first example, we saw HTML elements referred to by locators. Selenium provides a `String` format to address elements with different schemes. The two locators we saw are the default `scheme`, `id`, and `link` used to find anchor elements. The format for API arguments that take a locator is `LocatorType=Argument`. Table 12.3 describes the different locators and their formats.

Table 12.3 Locators and their formats

Locator type	Argument	Example
css	W3C CSS2 and CSS3 selectors	`css=a[href="#AnId"]`
dom	JavaScript expression	`dom=document.forms['f1'].intxt`
id	@id attribute	`id=AnId`
identifier	@id attribute or the first element where the @name attribute equals id	`identifier=AnId`
link	Anchor element matching the text	`link=I'm feeling lucky`
name	First element with the @name attribute	`name=lucky`
ui	Uses a Selenium UI-Element	`ui=loginPages::loginButton()`
xpath	XPath expression	`xpath=//*[text()="lucky"]`

To get the value of a field, for example, you'd write

```
String actualMsg = selenium.getText("name=serverMessage");
```

If you run into XPath cross-browser compatibility issues, you can either refactor tests with browser-specific XPath expressions or call `allowNativeXpath(false)` to force expressions to be evaluated in Selenium's JavaScript library.

12.8.5 Failing tests with exceptions

Although a generated test method throws an exception, it doesn't throw any checked exceptions, nor do APIs you use to write tests. The generated code and APIs throw unchecked exceptions to make sure your tests fail under the proper conditions. Even though Selenium defines `SeleniumException` and `SeleniumCommandTimedOut-Exception` as unchecked exceptions, some APIs also throw `RuntimeException`.

Let's now look at various examples of using the API and navigating an application.

12.8.6 *Testing forms with Selenium*

The API doesn't provide explicit support for forms; instead, you work with forms as you would any other elements, calling APIs for typing, clicking, and pressing keys.

The following example recasts the HtmlUnit example from the "Testing forms with HtmlUnit" section to the Selenium API. To remind you, in the HtmlUnit section, we created a simple page to display a form with an input field and a Submit button. We included form validation via JavaScript alerts in the example as a second path to test, as described in the section "Testing JavaScript alerts."

We test normal user interaction with the form as follows:

```
@Test
public void testForm() throws IOException {
    selenium.open("file:///C:/path/to/src/main/webapp/formtest.html");
    selenium.type("id=in_text", "typing...");
    selenium.click("id=submit");
    SeleneseTestCase.assertEquals("Result", selenium.getTitle());
}
```

Let's step through the example. We open the form page, type in a value, and click the Submit button to go to the next page. Finally, we make sure we land on the right page.

If at any step Selenium can't find an object, the framework throws an exception and your test automatically fails. This allows you to focus on the test and let the framework handle failing your test if the page or form is not as expected.

12.8.7 *Testing JavaScript alerts*

A test can check to see whether a JavaScript alert has taken place. We reuse our form example from section 12.3.12, "Testing forms with HtmlUnit," which includes JavaScript validation code to alert the user of empty input values.

The following test loads our form page and checks that the browser raised the alert when the error condition occurred. The key method is `getAlert`, which returns the most recent JavaScript alert message. Calling `getAlert` has the same effect as clicking OK in the dialog box.

```
@Test
public void testFormAlert() throws IOException {
    selenium.open("file:///C:/path//to/src/main/webapp/formtest.html");
    String title = selenium.getTitle();
    selenium.click("id=submit");
    SeleneseTestCase.assertEquals("Please enter a value.",
                                  selenium.getAlert());              ◄─❶
    SeleneseTestCase.assertEquals(title, selenium.getTitle());
}
```

Let's look at this example. We open the form page, save the current page title, and click the Submit button. This raises the alert because we didn't type in a value. Next, we call getAlert ❶ to check whether the code raised the correct alert. Finally, we make sure we're still on the same page by comparing the new page title with the saved title.

> **Selenium tip**
>
> As of version Selenium 1.0 Beta 2, JavaScript alerts won't pop up a visible alert dialog box. JavaScript alerts generated from a page's onload event handler aren't supported. If this happens, JavaScript will open a visible dialog box, and Selenium will wait until someone clicks the OK button.

We don't need to create a test to check whether an alert has taken place during normal operation of our page. If the test generates an alert but getAlert doesn't consume it, the next Selenium action will throw a SeleniumException, for example:

```
com.thoughtworks.selenium.SeleniumException:
ERROR: There was an unexpected Alert! [Please enter a value.]
```

12.8.8 *Capturing a screen shot for a JUnit 3 test failure*

Selenium provides the ability to capture a screen shot at the time of failure to subclasses of SeleneseTestCase. Selenium disables this feature by default; to enable it, call setCaptureScreenShotOnFailure(true). By default, the screen shot is written to a PNG file in the Selenium server directory with the same name as the test name given to the SeleneseTestCase String constructor.

12.8.9 *Capturing a screen shot for a JUnit 4 test failure*

To access this feature from a JUnit 4 test case, you'll need to modify the search example as shown in listing 12.17.

Listing 12.17 Capturing a screen shot on JUnit 4 test failure

```
private void captureScreenshot(Throwable t) throws Throwable {        ◀─❶
    if (selenium != null) {
        String filename = this.getClass().getName() + ".png";          ❷
        try {
            selenium.captureScreenshot(filename);                      ◀─┘
            System.out.println("Saved screenshot " + filename + " for " +
                                                        t.toString());
        } catch (Exception e) {
            System.err.println("Exception saving screenshot " + filename +
                            " for " + t.toString() + ": " + e.toString());
            e.printStackTrace();
        }
        throw t;
    }
}
```

```
public void testSearch() {
    // Same as before...
}

@Test
public void testSearchOnErrSaveScreen() throws Throwable {        ◄—❸
    try {
        this.testSearch();
    } catch (Throwable t) {
        this.captureScreenshot(t);
    }
}
```

We've added a new method called `captureScreenshot` ❶, which takes a `Throwable` argument and calls the Selenium `captureScreenshot` method ❷. We refactored our test method by creating a new method `testSearchOnErrSaveScreen` ❸, removing `@Test` from `testSearch`, and adding it to the new method instead.

To avoid repeating this code pattern in every method that wants to capture a screen shot on failure requires extending JUnit, which is beyond the scope of this section.

This concludes our Selenium survey; next, we contrast and compare HtmlUnit and Selenium before presenting our chapter summary.

12.9   *HtmlUnit versus Selenium*

Here's a recap of the similarities and differences you'll find between HtmlUnit and Selenium.

The similarities are that both are free and open source and both require Java 5 as the minimum platform requirement.

The major difference between the two is that HtmlUnit emulates a specific web browser, whereas Selenium drives a real web browser process. When using Selenium, the browser itself provides support for JavaScript. In HtmlUnit 2.7, Mozilla's Rhino[18] 1.7 Release 2 engine provides JavaScript support, and specific browser behavior is emulated.

Use HtmlUnit when

Use HtmlUnit when your application is independent of operating system features and browser-specific implementations not accounted for by HtmlUnit, like Java-Script, DOM, SCC, and so on.

Use Selenium when

Use Selenium when you require validation of specific browsers and operating systems, especially if the application takes advantage of or depends on a browser's specific implementation of JavaScript, DOM, CSS, and the like.

---

[18] Mozilla Rhino: http://www.mozilla.org/rhino/

The HtmlUnit pros are that it's a 100 percent Java solution, it's easy to integrate in a build process, and Cactus can integrate HtmlUnit code for in-container testing, as can other frameworks. HtmlUnit provides an HTML object model, which can validate web pages to the finest level of detail. HtmlUnit also supports XPath to collect data; Selenium XPath support is limited to referencing elements.

The Selenium pros are that the API is simpler and drives native browsers, which guarantees that the behavior of the tests is as close as possible to a user installation.

12.10 Summary

In this chapter, we examined presentation-layer testing and explored the use of two free open source tools to test the user interface of a web application: HtmlUnit and Selenium.

HtmlUnit is a 100 percent Java solution with no external requirements; it offers a complete HTML object model, which, although creating rather verbose test code, offers great flexibility.

Selenium is a more complex offering; it includes a simple IDE and many complementary components. The IDE generates test code but doesn't maintain it. The strength of the product comes from its architecture, which allows the embeddable Selenium Remote Control server to control different browsers on assorted operating systems. The Selenium API is much simpler and flatter than with HtmlUnit, resulting in more concise test code.

Use HtmlUnit when your application is independent of operating system features and browser-specific implementations of JavaScript, DOM, CSS, and so on.

Use Selenium when you require validation of specific browsers and operating systems, especially if the application takes advantage of or depends on a browser's specific implementation of JavaScript, DOM, CSS, and so on.

In the next chapter, we add a layer of complexity by considering Ajax technologies in our applications and test cases.

Ajax testing

Should array indices start at 0 or 1?
My compromise of 0.5 was rejected without,
I thought, proper consideration.

—Stan Kelly-Bootle

This chapter covers

- Introducing Ajax testing
- Testing the Ajax stack
- Testing JavaScript
- Testing server services
- Testing Google Web Toolkit applications

This chapter covers testing Ajax applications. It's a continuation of chapter 12, which discusses presentation-layer testing in general and introduces two of the libraries and tools used in this chapter: HtmlUnit and Selenium. As in the previous chapter, our goal is finding bugs in the graphical user interface of an application. We describe a divide-and-conquer approach by breaking up tests into three groups: functional testing, testing client-side scripts, and testing server services. We present the technologies relevant to testing each tier. We end by looking at the unique testing challenges presented by Google Web Toolkit (GWT) applications. We start by reviewing Ajax and why testing is difficult.

13.1 Why are Ajax applications difficult to test?

In 2005, the article "A New Approach to Web Applications"[1] coined the term *Ajax* to describe the architecture of a new generation of web applications like Google Maps[2] and Google Suggest.[3] These new applications were richer, more interactive, and more responsive than their predecessors. Critical to the user experience, they left behind the need to constantly reload or refresh an entire web page to keep any portion of its information updated. Although still browser based, these applications started to give the web the look and feel of what had been strictly the domain of desktop applications.

Although Ajax is often associated with its all-uppercase sibling AJAX, the acronym, it's today much more than Asynchronous JavaScript and XML. You build an Ajax application by combining the following technologies: CSS, DOM, JavaScript, server-side scripting, HTML, HTTP, and web remoting (XMLHttpRequest).

Beyond its associated technologies, Ajax reflects the mindset of a new breed of web applications built on standards and designed to give users a rich and interactive experience. In this chapter, we study how to test these applications.

To understand the challenge of testing an Ajax application, let's look at a web-classic interaction and then step through the stages of an Ajax application interaction.

13.1.1 Web-classic interaction

In a web-classic interaction, the user opens the browser on a page, and each time the page needs data, it asks the server for a new page. Figure 13.1 illustrates this process.

13.1.2 Ajax interaction

In an Ajax application, the page communicates with the server to get data for the part of the page that needs updating and then updates only that part of the page. Figure 13.2 illustrates this process.

The user starts by opening an Ajax application's start page in a browser; this causes the HTML page to load. The browser displays the HTML using any associated CSS and runs client-side JavaScript code to set up the page's event handlers. The page is now ready to respond to user interactions. The user interacts with the page, triggering a JavaScript event handler. In an application like Google Suggest, each keystroke creates a server request for a list of suggestions that are displayed in a drop-down list box. The JavaScript event handler builds an XHR object and calls the server with a specific request using HTTP. The XHR object includes a JavaScript

---

[1] http://www.adaptivepath.com/ideas/essays/archives/000385.php
[2] http://maps.google.com/
[3] http://www.google.com/webhp?complete=1&hl=en

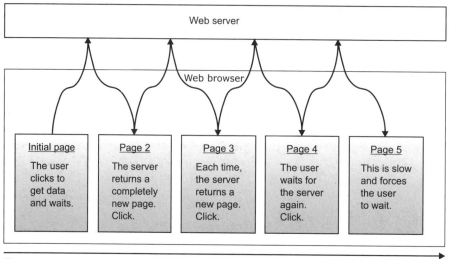

Figure 13.1   New pages are downloaded for each interaction in a web-classic application.

callback function the browser will invoke when results are ready. The server processes the request and returns a response using HTTP. The browser invokes the XHR callback and uses the data returned by the server, in the form of XML or text, to update the page in the browser. In order to update the page, the callback function uses the DOM API to modify the model, which the browser displays immediately.

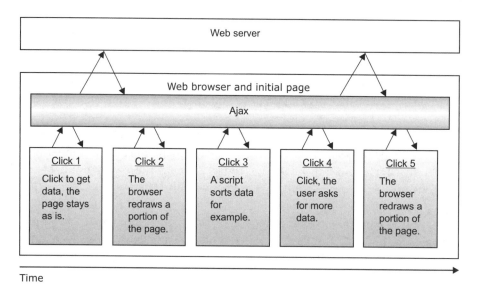

Figure 13.2   Relevant portions of a page downloaded for each Ajax web application interaction

13.1.3 *A brave new world*

This interaction is quite different from the web-classic architecture where a page is loaded, a user interacts with the page causing another page to load, and then the cycle repeats. With Ajax, the page is loaded once, and everything happens within that page. JavaScript code runs in the page to perform I/O with the server and updates the in-memory DOM of the page, which the browser displays to the user.

13.1.4 *Testing challenges*

The challenge in writing tests for the application interaction described previously is the asynchronous aspect of HTTP communications and the DOM manipulation by JavaScript code. The difficulty is how to drive a self-changing application when those changes are asynchronous to the test itself.

In addition to testing the traditional page state described in chapter 12, you should also test an Ajax application's best practices. Tests should exercise features[4] like drag and drop, form validation and submission, event handling, back button, refresh button, undo and redo commands, fancy navigation, state management and caching, and user friendliness (latency, showing progress, timing out, and multiple clicks).

Further complicating matters, different implementations of Ajax component technologies like JavaScript, DOM, and XMLHttpRequest exist in different browsers from different vendors. Although various free and open source libraries abstract these differences away, an application is nonetheless more complicated to test. You may want to ensure test coverage for all code paths for all supported browsers on all supported operating systems.

Next, we split up testing this complex application stack into more manageable tiers through functional testing, testing client-side scripts, and testing server services.

13.2 *Testing patterns for Ajax*

Before we jump into test code, we survey the testing patterns we use to verify the various aspects of an Ajax application. We can orchestrate testing with three types of tests:

- Functional testing drives the whole application from the client-browser and usually ends up exercising all application layers.
- Client-side script unit testing covers the JavaScript scripts running in the browser. The application page hosting the script isn't tested.
- Service testing verifies services provided by the server and accessed from JavaScript XHR objects.

Let's look at these types of tests in more detail before we turn to implementation.

13.2.1 *Functional testing*

Functional testing drives the whole application from the client browser and usually ends up exercising all application layers. As we discussed in chapter 12, a functional

---

[4] See *Ajax in Action*: http://www.manning.com/crane/.

test simulates a user and checks the state of visited web pages. You can choose to have the tests emulate a web browser (HtmlUnit) or drive a live web browser (Selenium.) As always with browser-emulation software, the key is how well it supports JavaScript.

13.2.2 *Client-side script unit testing*

Here we divide the scripts into two piles: the ones that use XHR to manipulate a DOM and the ones that don't.

Although we can test some script functions and libraries independently from their hosting page where scripts call XHR objects and modify the DOM of the current page, we need a JavaScript engine and browser; the browser in turn may be emulated or live. For these scripts, we should use a functional test.

For other scripts, we're testing a library of functions, and we prefer to deliver these functions in standalone files as opposed to embedded in HTML pages.

We can test all scripts through functional tests of the pages that call on them, but we want to provide a lighter-weight test pass that's more along the line of a true unit test. Heavier-weight and slower functional tests using web browsers should ideally be reserved for when scripts can't be otherwise verified.

Let's look at JavaScript unit testing. What should you look for in a JavaScript testing framework? From the TDD point of view, the most important feature is the ability to automate tests. We must be able to integrate JavaScript testing in our Ant or Maven build. Second, we want the ability to run the tests from JUnit. You'll find many JavaScript frameworks that provide for creating and running tests by embedding test invocation in an HTML page (JsUnit,[5] JsUnitTest,[6] script.aculo.us[7]), whereas others do it all from JavaScript (RhinoUnit).[8] The best integration for our purposes must include support for JUnit. Although JUnit or Ant integration can be custom coded for a specific JavaScript testing framework, JsUnit provides this functionality out of the box. JsUnit is a free, open source framework integrated with JUnit that goes one step further by providing advanced Selenium-type distributed configuration options.

JsUnit is to JavaScript testing what Selenium is to web application testing. JsUnit allows you to test JavaScript, from JUnit, by controlling a web browser process on a local or remote machine. We discuss JsUnit in action in the section "JavaScript testing with JsUnit."

13.2.3 *Service testing*

Service testing verifies services provided by the server and accessed from JavaScript XHR objects. The HTML page and JavaScript aren't tested. Because HTTP is the standard used by XHR objects to communicate with the server, we can use any HTTP client to test the service independently of XHR and the browser. Free, open source Java

---

[5] http://www.jsunit.net/
[6] http://jsunittest.com/
[7] http://script.aculo.us/
[8] http://code.google.com/p/rhinounit/

HTTP libraries suitable for unit testing include HtmlUnit, HttpUnit, and Apache Commons HttpClient. We examine HttpClient in action in the section "Testing services with HttpClient."

In this chapter, we test *server services for Ajax applications*, which we distinguish from testing *web services*, a different web standard.

We now examine each technique in more detail with implementation examples. We start with functional testing with Selenium and HtmlUnit.

13.3 Functional testing

We now look at testing the application stack by continuing our demonstration of Selenium and HtmlUnit started in the previous chapter on presentation layer testing. We show you how to use Selenium and HtmlUnit to write the same kind of tests. We show how to deal with the asynchronous aspect of an Ajax application before going on to test specific components that make up the stack, such as JavaScript libraries and server-provided services (as opposed to web services). The key aspect of writing tests for an Ajax application is to know when an action causes a change in the DOM. We show how to do this and create functional tests using Selenium and then HtmlUnit.

13.3.1 Functional testing with Selenium

If you're not familiar with Selenium, please consult the previous chapter to get an understanding of the fundamentals we build on here. We pick up Selenium where we left off, this time testing Ajax, a more advanced task.

Once a page is loaded in the browser, Selenium sees that version of the page. To see the updated DOM, you must use a different API than what we showed you in the previous chapter.

Let's take as an example the form in figure 13.3. When you click the Get Message button, the page queries the server and returns a simple text message: Hello World. JavaScript code then updates the DOM with the message, and the browser displays the input field value, as you can see in the screenshot.

Listing 13.1 shows the HTML source for the page, which includes the JavaScript to perform the HTTP XML Request.

Figure 13.3 A simple Ajax form

Listing 13.1   testform.html—a simple form (client)

```html
<html>
<body>
<script type="text/javascript">
function newXHR() {                                        ←❶
    if (window.XMLHttpRequest) {
        return new XMLHttpRequest();
    } else if (window.ActiveXObject) {
        return new ActiveXObject("Microsoft.XMLHTTP");
    } else {
        alert("This browser does not support XMLHTTP.");
    }
}
function setMessage() {                                    ←❷
    var xhr = newXHR();
    xhr.onreadystatechange=function() {
        if(xhr.readyState == 4) {
            document.helloForm.serverMessage.value=xhr.responseText;   ←❸
        }
    }
    xhr.open("GET","hello-world.asp", true);
    xhr.send(null);                                        ←❹
}
</script>                                                      ❺
<form name="helloForm"><input value="Get Message" type="button"  ←
    name="getMsgBtn" onclick="setMessage();" /> Message: <input
    type="text" name="serverMessage" /></form>
</body>
</html>
```

Let's examine the key elements in the HTML. The form ❺ defines a button, which when clicked invokes the JavaScript function setMessage ❷. The first thing the set-Message function does is call newXHR ❶, which creates a new HTTP XML request object. setMessage then calls the server ❹ and updates the DOM ❸ when the response is ready.

The following shows the server-side source for this example (hello-world.asp).

```
<%
response.expires=-1
response.write("Hello World")              ←❶
%>
```

The response is the string "Hello World" ❶. To run this example locally with IIS, you'll need to create a virtual directory for the example webapp directory and use the IIS Permission Wizard to grant it default rights.

In order to test the form and check that the message is what we expect it to be, we use the same JUnit scaffolding from the previous chapter and first set up a test suite to manage the Selenium server:

```
[...]
@RunWith(ManagedSeleniumServerSuite.class)
@SuiteClasses( { UnmanagedFormTester.class })
```

```
public class ManagedFormTest {
    // See annotations.
}
```

This code shows the test suite `ManagedFormTest` that runs the test case `Unmanaged-FormTester` containing the `@Test` methods. The JUnit test runner `ManagedSelenium-ServerSuite` manages the Selenium server and drives the unit test.

Without knowing anything about Ajax, you might create the test method `test-FormNo` in listing 13.2.

Listing 13.2 UnmanagedFormTester.java bad test method

```
/**
 * Tests a form. The Selenium server must be managed elsewhere.
 * To test the form in IE, create a virtual directory in IIS and point your
 * browser and tests to http://localhost/webapp/formtest.html
 */
public class UnmanagedFormTester {
    private static final String APP_WINDOW =
        "selenium.browserbot.getCurrentWindow()";

    private static final String EXPECTED_MSG = "Hello World";

    /**
     * The directory /ch13-ajax/src/main/webapp has been configured as
     * an IIS virtual directory for this test.
     */
    private static final String TEST_URL = "http://localhost/webapp/";

    private static final String TEST_PAGE = "formtest.html";

    private static Selenium selenium;

    @BeforeClass
    public static void setUpOnce() throws Exception {
        selenium = new DefaultSelenium("localhost", 4444, "*iexplore",
            TEST_URL);
        selenium.start();
    }

    @AfterClass
    public static void tearDownOnce() throws Exception {
        if (selenium != null) {
            selenium.stop();
        }
        selenium = null;
    }

    @Test
    public void testFormNo() throws IOException {
        selenium.open(TEST_PAGE);
        selenium.click("name=getMsgBtn");
        String actualMsg = selenium.getText("name=serverMessage");   ◀─❶
        // The message is not there!
        Assert.assertFalse(EXPECTED_MSG.equals(actualMsg));          ◀─❷
    }
}
```

All is well from the beginning of the file UnmanagedFormTester.java until the call to
getText ❶. The call takes a Selenium locator to retrieve the content of the element
named serverMessage. The return value is the empty string ❷ because the DOM
model in the object model isn't up to date. Perhaps we need to wait for the server to do
its work and the result to come back. Calling waitForPageToLoad doesn't work because
the code doesn't reload the page. Recall that this is an Ajax application; pages don't
reload. Calling Thread.sleep after clicking the button doesn't work either. Fortunately, Selenium provides a single powerful API for this purpose: waitForCondition.
Here it is in action in the class UnmanagedFormTester:

```
@Test
public void testFormWithJavaScript() throws IOException {
    selenium.open(TEST_PAGE);
    selenium.click("name=getMessageButton");
    selenium.waitForCondition(APP_WINDOW +
        ".document.helloForm.serverMessage.value=='" + EXPECTED_MSG + "'",
        "1000");
}
```

Alternatively, without the refactoring, the JavaScript expression in the first argument
to waitForCondition reads:

```
selenium.browserbot.getCurrentWindow().document.helloForm.serverMessage.
value == 'Hello World'
```

The waitForCondition method waits for a given condition to become true or a timeout to expire. The method takes two arguments: the first is JavaScript code where the
last expression must evaluate to a Boolean; the second is a timeout String expressed
in milliseconds.

> ### Wait for condition API tip
> In order for JavaScript to access the application window, you must use the follow-
> ing expression:
>
> ```
> selenium.browserbot.getCurrentWindow()
> ```
>
> For example, to get to the document, use
>
> ```
> selenium.browserbot.getCurrentWindow().document
> ```

The art of testing Ajax with Selenium is about embedding JavaScript in your JUnit
code. This can be confusing because you're embedding JavaScript in Java, but it's
what's required because the Selenium server controlling the web browser will run the
JavaScript for you. In contrast, let's go back to HtmlUnit and see how this test looks in
that framework.

13.3.2 *Functional testing with HtmlUnit*

We return now to testing with HtmlUnit, which we document in chapter 12. Though the HtmlUnit API is more verbose than that of Selenium, you write tests entirely in Java. Listing 13.3 tests the form with HtmlUnit.

> **Listing 13.3 Testing the same form with HtmlUnit**

```
public class AjaxFormTest {

private static final String EXPECTED_MSG = "Hello World";

private static final String TEST_URL =
    "http://localhost/webapp/formtest.html";

@Test
public void testAjaxForm() throws IOException {
    WebClient webClient = new WebClient();
    try {
        webClient.setAjaxController(new                          ❶
            NicelyResynchronizingAjaxController());
        HtmlPage page = (HtmlPage) webClient.getPage(TEST_URL);
        HtmlButtonInput button = (HtmlButtonInput)              ❷
            page.getFirstByXPath("/html/body/form/input[1]");
        HtmlPage newPage = button.click();                      ❸
        HtmlInput reply = (HtmlInput)
            newPage.getFirstByXPath("/html/body/form/input[2]");
        Assert.assertTrue(EXPECTED_MSG.equals(reply.asText())); ❹
    } finally {
        webClient.closeAllWindows();
    }
}
}
```

Let's walk through this example. As usual, we start by creating an HtmlUnit web client and getting the application's start page ❷. We get our button, we click it, and the result is a new page ❸. From this page, we get the entry field that was updated through the DOM by the XHR call and assert that the contents are what we expect ❹.

The general pattern with HtmlUnit is to get a page, find the element, click it, and check the resulting page contents.

Because the test thread can finish before HtmlUnit reads the Ajax response from the server, you must synchronize the test code with the response to guarantee predictable results from run to run. Although a simple approach is to sleep the thread for a while, HtmlUnit provides APIs to guarantee that Ajax tests are synchronous and predictable. This example illustrates this with the call to setAjaxController ❶.

The setAjaxController method and the NicelyResynchronizingAjaxController class work together to turn asynchronous Ajax calls into synchronous Ajax calls. The class NicelyResynchronizingAjaxController is the only subclass of the Ajax-Controller class delivered with HtmlUnit. By default, a web client initializes itself with an instance of AjaxController, which leaves Ajax calls asynchronous.

> **HtmlUnit tip**
>
> Create predictable tests by synchronizing Ajax calls. To do so, set the web client's Ajax controller to an instance of `NicelyResynchronizingAjaxController`:
>
> ```
> webClient.setAjaxController(new NicelyResynchronizingAjaxController());
> ```

If you want finer-grained control over the behavior of tests, the framework provides experimental[9] APIs to wait for various JavaScript tasks to complete. The method `wait-ForBackgroundJavaScript` waits for all background JavaScript tasks to complete execution, defined as tasks scheduled for execution via `window.setTimeout`, `window.setInterval`, and asynchronous `XMLHttpRequest`. For example, you call `waitForBackgroundJavaScript` after an action invokes a script with a timeout in milliseconds:

```
HtmlPage newPage = button.click();
int jobs = this.webClient.waitForBackgroundJavaScript(1000);
```

The return value is the number of jobs still executing or scheduled for execution. If you have an idea of when your background JavaScript is supposed to start executing, but you're not necessarily sure how long it will take to execute, use the method `wait-ForBackgroundJavaScriptStartingBefore`. You should use the wait methods instead of the methods internal to HtmlUnit provided by `JavaScriptJobManager`.

You've now seen how to create functional tests with Selenium and HtmlUnit. Although this can prove that an application works from the perspective of a client, it doesn't assert the quality of the underlying building blocks. It's now time to dive deeper into testing by dealing with testing these building blocks: JavaScript and server services. We start with JavaScript.

13.4   JavaScript testing

Here, you face the same choice you had between HtmlUnit and Selenium: do you want to emulate a browser or drive a live browser? We look next at two JavaScript testing frameworks, RhinoUnit and JsUnit. RhinoUnit is like HtmlUnit, a 100 percent Java solution, and JsUnit is akin to Selenium in that it drives local or remote web browsers. To wrap up JavaScript testing, we use JSLint to check our code against best practices.

13.4.1   JavaScript testing with RhinoUnit

RhinoUnit allows you to run JavaScript unit tests from Ant. You write unit tests in JavaScript and invoke them from Ant with the help of the Java Scripting Framework and the Mozilla Rhino JavaScript engine included in Java 6. If you're on an older version of Java, you'll need the Apache Bean Scripting Framework[10] (BSF) and the Mozilla Rhino JavaScript engine as documented in appendix E, "Installing software."

---

[9] HtmlUnit 2.5 Javadoc warns that these APIs may change behavior or may not exist in future versions.
[10] http://jakarta.apache.org/bsf/

As a bonus, RhinoUnit includes JSLint,[11] which allows you to check from Ant that your JavaScript code follows best practices. Download and unzip RhinoUnit.[12] If you're on Java 6, you've finished; if not, some additional steps are documented in appendix E.

Let's create a simple function to test; the following code defines a factorial function (factorial.js.)

```javascript
function factorial(n) {
    if ((n === 0) || (n === 1)) {
        return 1;
    }
    return n * factorial(n - 1);
}
```

The following JavaScript unit tests the factorial function (test-example.js.)

```javascript
eval(loadFile("src/main/webapp/factorial.js"));        ← ❶
testCases(test,                                          ← ❷
    function test15() {
        assert.that(factorial(15), eq(1307674368000));  ← ❸
    },

    function test16() {
        assert.that(factorial(16), eq(20922789888000)); ← ❹
    }
);
```

We start the test by including the library of functions we want to test ❶ with a call to eval. Note that the path to the file is relative to where we're running the test from; in this case, it's the project's root directory. Next, we must call testCases, passing in test as the first variable ❷, followed by our test functions. You can pass in any number of functions; note the comma separating the test functions. For this simple test, we call our factorial function from two different tests and make sure that the computation results in the expected value ❸ ❹, for example, checking that calling factorial(15) yields 1307674368000 ❸. The assert.that call is how to make an assertion in RhinoUnit. The first value is the value we're testing, the *actual value*; the second value, the *predicate*, defines the actual test. Here we use eq to test for equality to its argument, 1307674368000. The general format is

```javascript
assert.that(actual, predicate)
```

The RhinoUnit site lists[13] the functions you can use in addition to eq; these are the most widely used:

- The function eq(expected) uses === to compare actual and expected values.
- The function matches(regExp) tests the actual value against the given regular expression.

---

[11] http://www.JSLint.com/
[12] http://code.google.com/p/rhinounit/
[13] http://code.google.com/p/rhinounit/wiki/APIDescription

- The function `isTrue(message)` tests that the actual value is `true`, displaying an optional message if it isn't.
- The function `isFalse(message)` tests that the actual value is `false`, displaying an optional message if it isn't.
- The function `not(predicate)` inverts the predicate.
- The function `isNull(message)` tests that the actual value is `null`, returning the message if it isn't.

The following example shows how to match regular expressions:

```
var actual = "JUnit in Action";
assert.that(actual, matches(/in/));          ◀—❶
assert.that(actual, not(matches(/out/)));        ◀—❷
```

The example calls the `match` function first to assert that "in" is in the test string ❶ and then to check that "out" isn't ❷.

The `assert` object contains other useful functions: `fail` is like the JUnit `fail` method. The various `mustCall` functions check that the tests causing the given functions have or have not been invoked.

In order to run the tests, you'll need an Ant build script. Listing 13.4 is the sample build script used to run our examples.

Listing 13.4   Ant build.xml for JavaScript unit tests

```
<project name="ch13-ajax-rhinounit" basedir="." default="run-all-tests">

<target name="run-all-tests" depends="run-unit-tests, run-js-lint" />

<property name="src.dir" value="src/main/webapp" />
<property name="test.dir" value="src/test/webapp" />
<property name="rhinounit.dir" value="rhinounit_1_2_1" />          ❶
<property name="rhinounit.src" value="${rhinounit.dir}/src" />
<property name="JSLint.src" value="${rhinounit.dir}/JSLint" />

<!-- Requires Java 6 or Java 5 + BSF -->
<scriptdef name="rhinounit" src="${rhinounit.src}/rhinoUnitAnt.js"          ◀—❷
language="javascript">
    <attribute name="options" />
    <attribute name="ignoredglobalvars" />
    <attribute name="haltOnFirstFailure" />
    <attribute name="rhinoUnitUtilPath" />
    <element name="fileset" type="fileset" />
</scriptdef>

<target name="run-unit-tests">
    <rhinounit options="{verbose:true, stackTrace:true}"          ◀—❸
ignoredglobalvars="rhinounit"
rhinoUnitUtilPath="${rhinounit.src}/rhinoUnitUtil.js">
        <fileset dir="${test.dir}">
            <include name="*.js" />
        </fileset>
    </rhinounit>
</target>
```

```
<scriptdef name="JSLintant" src="${JSLint.src}/JSLintant.js"              ◁━④
    language="javascript">
    <attribute name="options" />
    <attribute name="JSLintpath" />
    <element name="fileset" type="fileset" />
</scriptdef>

<target name="run-js-lint">
    <JSLintant options="{eqeqeq : true, white: true, plusplus : false,    ◁━⑤
bitwise : true, evil: true, passfail: false}"
JSLintpath="${JSLint.src}/fullJSLint.js">
        <fileset dir="${src.dir}" />
    </JSLintant>
</target>

</project>
```

We start our Ant script by defining properties for the locations of directories and files ❶ relative to where we run the Ant build. Next, we define a rhinounit Ant script ❷ and its arguments by loading its source from rhinoUnitAnt.js. We call the script ❸ with a fileset pointing to our JavaScript unit test source, where we include all files with the js extension. In the same way that we defined a script for rhinounit and ran our tests, we define a script for JSLint ❹ to help us detect scripting issues, and we finish by running this JSLint script ❺ on our source directory. For more on JSLint, please see section 13.6, "Checking best practices with JSLint."

> ### RhinoUnit tip
> When you invoke the rhinounit Ant script, make sure you point the rhino-UnitUtilPath argument to the location of the rhinoUnitUtil.js file, for example:
>
> rhinoUnitUtilPath="${rhinounit.src}/rhinoUnitUtil.js"

This takes care of JavaScript unit testing in the build file; please consult the Rhino-Unit[14] website for additional documentation. Next, we look at the alternative to RhinoUnit and browser emulation with JsUnit, a framework that drives a web browser á la Selenium.

13.4.2 JavaScript testing with JsUnit

JsUnit[15] is a JavaScript unit-testing framework written in JavaScript and in Java. We use it from Ant to drive a web browser in order to validate the same JavaScript we just tested in the previous section. JsUnit is similar to Selenium in that it controls a web browser and the tests run in that browser's JavaScript engine.

---

[14] RhinoUnit: http://code.google.com/p/rhinounit/
[15] http://www.jsunit.net/

Let's start by showing how to run a test from JsUnit and then automating the test from Ant. The source code for this chapter includes a copy of JsUnit; for details please see appendix E.

13.4.3 *Writing JsUnit tests*

You write a JsUnit test by creating an HTML page containing JavaScript test functions. You then run the test from a web browser. You use HTML only as the container for the JavaScript. Listing 13.5 is our factorial test.

Listing 13.5   jsFactorialTests.html

```
<!DOCTYPE HTML PUBLIC "-//W3C//DTD HTML 4.01 Transitional//EN"
    "http://www.w3.org/TR/html4/loose.dtd">
<html>
<head>
    <meta http-equiv="Content-Type" content="text/html; charset=UTF-8">
    <title>JsUnit Factorial Tests - Chapter 13</title>
    <link rel="stylesheet" type="text/css"
        href="../../../jsunit/css/jsUnitStyle.css">
    <script type="text/javascript"
        src="../../../jsunit/app/jsUnitCore.js"></script>
    <script type="text/javascript"
        src="../../../src/main/webapp/factorial.js"></script>
    <script type="text/javascript">

        function test15() {
            assertEquals(factorial(15), 1307674368000);
        }

        function testRegEx() {
            var actual = "JUnit in Action";
            assertTrue(actual, /in/.test(actual));
            assertFalse(actual, /out/.test(actual));
        }

    </script>
</head>
<body>
    <h1>JsUnit Chapter 13 Tests</h1>
    <p>This page contains tests for the Chapter 13 examples.</p>
    <p>To see the tests, view the source for this page.</p>
</body>
</html>
```

① ② ③ ④

You define the JsUnit test in the HTML head element and start with the references needed to bring in the JsUnit framework ① and the JavaScript code to test ②.

JsUnit tip

The references in the `link href` and `script src` attributes are relative to the location of the HTML test file.

A JavaScript `script` element defines the test functions for our factorial **❸** and regular expression **❹** tests. As with JUnit 3, we define test functions with the function name prefix `test`. The set of JsUnit `assert` functions is smaller than the set of JUnit `assert` methods and is listed here. Like JUnit, the API defines a version of `assert` functions with and without a message argument. The square brackets in the following list denote that the argument is optional.

- `assert([message,] booleanValue)`
- `assertTrue([message,] booleanValue)`
- `assertFalse([message,] booleanValue)`
- `assertEquals([message,] expectedValue, actualValue)`
- `assertNotEquals([message,] expectedValue, actualValue)`
- `assertNull([message,] value)`
- `assertNotNull([message,] value)`
- `assertUndefined([message,] value)`
- `assertNotUndefined([message,] value)`
- `assertNaN([message,] value)`
- `assertNotNaN([message,] value)`
- `fail(message)`

Like JUnit, JsUnit lets you use `setUp` and `tearDown` functions. JsUnit calls your `setUp` function before each test function and your `tearDown` function after each test function.

JsUnit supports an equivalent to `@BeforeClass` if you define a function called `setUpPage`. JsUnit calls `setUpPage` once after the page is loaded but before it calls any test functions. When your `setUpPage` function ends, it must set the variable `setUpPageStatus` to `'complete'` to indicate to JsUnit that it can proceed to execute the page.

> **JsUnit versus JUnit**
>
> JsUnit differs from JUnit in that JsUnit doesn't define the order of test function invocation; in JUnit, the order of methods in the source file defines the invocation order.
>
> In addition, although JUnit creates a new test object instance to invoke each method, JsUnit doesn't use a corresponding action, like reloading the page, which means that JsUnit preserves page-variable values across test function invocations.

13.4.4 *Writing JsUnit test suites*

As in JUnit, you can group JsUnit tests into a suite of related tests. Listing 13.6 wraps our previous test page into a test suite.

Listing 13.6   jsUnitTestSuite.html

```
<!DOCTYPE HTML PUBLIC "-//W3C//DTD HTML 4.01 Transitional//EN"
    "http://www.w3.org/TR/html4/loose.dtd">
<html>
<head>
    <meta http-equiv="Content-Type" content="text/html; charset=UTF-8">
    <title>JsUnit Test Suite - Chapter 13</title>
    <link rel="stylesheet" type="text/css"
        href="../../../jsunit/css/jsUnitStyle.css">
    <script type="text/javascript"
        src="../../../jsunit/app/jsUnitCore.js"></script>
    <script type="text/javascript">
        function suite() {                                      ←❶
            var newsuite = new JsUnitTestSuite();
            newsuite.addTestPage(                               ←❷
                "../src/test/webapp/jsFactorialTests.html");
            return newsuite;
        }
    </script>
</head>
<body>
    <h1>JsUnit Test Suite for Chapter 13</h1>
    <p>This page contains a suite of tests for testing JsUnit.</p>
    <p>To see the tests, view the source for this page.</p>
</body>
</html>
```

To define a test suite, create a function called suite ❶, which returns a JsUnitTestSuite object. You then build up a suite object by adding test pages or other suite objects. In our example, we add one page ❷, the page we previously defined by calling the addTest-Page function. The rest of the code in this HTML page is the same as our previous example with the exception that we don't need to refer to our JavaScript factorial library.

JsUnit addTestPage tip

The addTestPage argument is a location relative to the test runner page you'll use. In our examples, we use the test runner jsunit/testRunner.html.

To add a test suite to another test suite, create a new JsUnitTestSuite object, and call the addTestSuite API. This allows you to organize your tests just as you can in JUnit. Listing 13.7 defines and adds two test suites to a main test suite.

Listing 13.7   Building a JsUnit test suite

```
function featureASuite() {
    var result = new JsUnitTestSuite();
    result.addTestPage("../tests/featureA/Test1.html");
    result.addTestPage("../tests/featureA/Test2.html");
    return result;
}
```

```
function featureBSuite() {
    var result = new JsUnitTestSuite();
    result.addTestPage("../tests/featureB/Test1.html");
    result.addTestPage("../tests/featureB/Test2.html");
    return result;
}

function suite() {
    var newsuite = new JsUnitTestSuite();
    newsuite.addTestSuite(featureASuite());
    newsuite.addTestSuite(featureASuite());
    return newsuite;
}
```

We now show you how to run the tests manually during development and then through Ant for builds.

13.4.5 *Running JsUnit tests manually*

To run your tests manually, open a web browser on jsunit/testRunner.html, enter into the file entry field a URL (file:// or http://) or file reference (c:\path\to\a\file) to an HTML test page for a test or a suite, and click the Run button. In figure 13.4, we show the result of running our test suite with the familiar green bar.

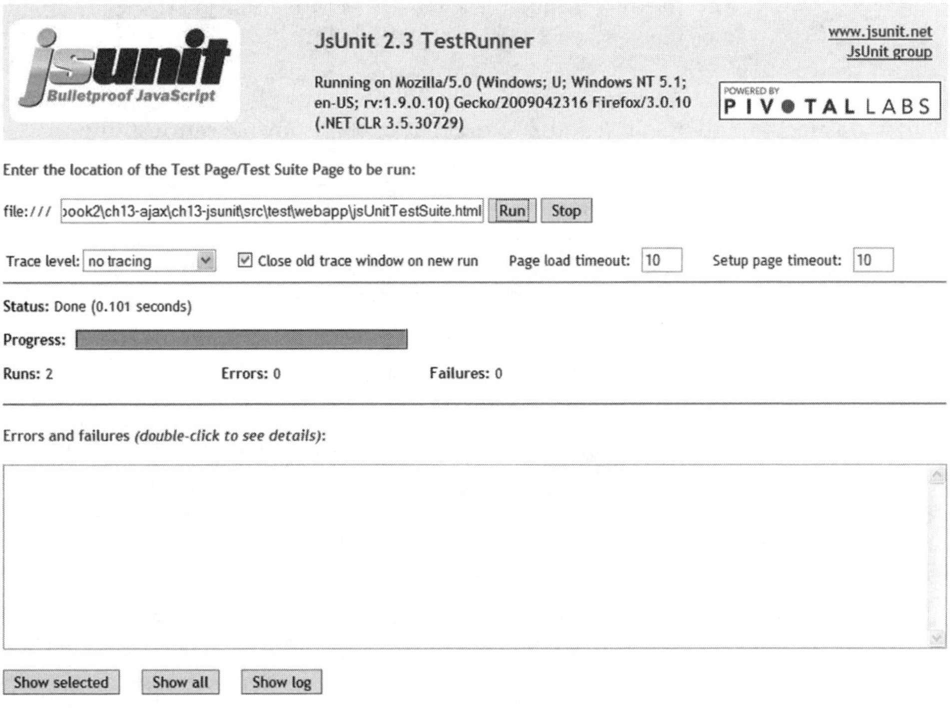

Figure 13.4 The JsUnit test runner

You can run a self-test on JsUnit itself by running the test suite jsunit/tests/jsUnitTest-
Suite.html. The result will show you the green bar with 90 successful tests.

JsUnit tip: Status `Aborted` or tests time out

JsUnit doesn't give you much feedback when something goes wrong. If you see
`Aborted` in the JsUnit Status field, check your paths starting with `link href` and
`script src` and then `addTestPage`.

Now that we have a manual way to run tests, let's move on to automating tests with Ant.

13.4.6 *Running JsUnit tests with Ant*

JsUnit includes the file jsunit/build.xml, which you can use as a template to call JsUnit
tests from Ant. The Ant build file will manage web browsers, invoke tests, and create reports.

JsUnit tip: Java 6 runtime requirement

The version of JsUnit tested here, version 2.2, will run only with Java 6 or greater.
If you use an earlier version of Java you will see the error `java.lang.Unsupported-
ClassVersionError: Bad version number in .class file`.

Listing 13.8 shows the build.xml file that excerpts invoke our test suite.

Listing 13.8   JsUnit build.xml excerpts

```xml
<?xml version="1.0" encoding="utf-8"?>
<project name="JsUnit" default="standalone_test" basedir=".">
    <property name="jsunit.dir" value="jsunit"/>                          ❶

    <property name="browserFileNames"                                     ❷
        value="c:\program files\internet explorer\iexplore.exe"/>

    <property id="logsDirectory" name="logsDirectory" value="logs"/>      ❸

    <property id="timeoutSeconds" name="timeoutSeconds" value="60"/>      ❹ ❺

    <property id="url" name="url"
value="http://localhost:8080/jsunit/jsunit/testRunner.html?testPage=http://
    localhost:8080/jsunit/src/test/webapp/jsUnitTestSuite.html"/>

    <property name="bin" location="${jsunit.dir}/java/bin"/>
    <property name="lib" location="${jsunit.dir}/java/lib"/>
    <property name="loggingPropertiesFile" location="logging.properties"/>

    <path id="classpath">
        <fileset dir="${lib}">                                           ❻
            <include name="*.jar"/>
            <include name="*/*.jar"/>
        </fileset>
```

```
        <fileset dir="${bin}">
            <include name="jsunit.jar"/>
        </fileset>
    </path>

    <target name="standalone_test"                                      ◄─❼
        description="Runs tests on the local machine">
        <junit showoutput="true" haltonerror="true" haltonfailure="true">
            <formatter type="plain" usefile="false"/>
            <classpath refid="classpath"/>
            <sysproperty key="java.util.logging.config.file"
                value="${loggingPropertiesFile}"/>
            <sysproperty key="browserFileNames"
                value="${browserFileNames}"/>
            <sysproperty key="description" value="${description}"/>
            <sysproperty key="closeBrowsersAfterTestRuns"
                value="${closeBrowsersAfterTestRuns}"/>
            <sysproperty key="logsDirectory" value="${logsDirectory}"/>
            <sysproperty key="port" value="${port}"/>
            <sysproperty key="resourceBase" value="${resourceBase}"/>
            <sysproperty key="timeoutSeconds" value="${timeoutSeconds}"/>
            <sysproperty key="url" value="${url}"/>
            <test name="net.jsunit.StandaloneTest"/>
        </junit>
    </target>

    <target name="jsunit_self_test"                                     ◄─❽
        description="Runs JsUnit self-tests on the local machine">
        <junit showoutput="true" haltonerror="true" haltonfailure="true">
            <formatter type="plain" usefile="false"/>
            <classpath refid="classpath"/>
            <sysproperty key="java.util.logging.config.file"
                value="${loggingPropertiesFile}"/>
            <sysproperty key="browserFileNames"
                value="${browserFileNames}"/>
            <sysproperty key="description" value="${description}"/>
            <sysproperty key="closeBrowsersAfterTestRuns"
                value="${closeBrowsersAfterTestRuns}"/>
            <sysproperty key="logsDirectory" value="${logsDirectory}"/>
            <sysproperty key="port" value="${port}"/>
            <sysproperty key="resourceBase" value="${resourceBase}"/>
            <sysproperty key="timeoutSeconds" value="${timeoutSeconds}"/>
            <sysproperty key="url"
                value="http://localhost:8080/jsunit/jsunit/
                testRunner.html?testPage=http://localhost:8080/jsunit/
                jsunit/tests/jsUnitTestSuite.html"/>
            <test name="net.jsunit.StandaloneTest"/>
        </junit>
    </target>

</project>
```

We start our build.xml file by defining the location of the JsUnit installation directory
❶; in this case, it's a subdirectory of the directory containing our example build.xml.
Then we define which web browsers JsUnit will use to test our code with the property
browserFileNames ❷. This property is a comma-separated list of browser executable

paths. Next, we define `logsDirectory` ❸ to hold the directory location for test report XML files. The property `timeoutSeconds` ❹ is a timeout in seconds to wait for a test run to complete; if absent, the default value is 60 seconds. The `url` property ❺ defines which test runner to use and which test or test suite it should invoke. It's worth breaking down this URL into its component parts. The example URL is http://localhost:8080/jsunit/jsunit/testRunner.html?testPage=http://localhost:8080/jsunit/src/test/webapp/jsUnitTestSuite.html.

The URL starts with http://localhost:8080 because we're running our tests locally. The next segment, jsunit, specifies the jsunit servlet and from there the location to the JsUnit stock test runner, relative to build.xml, which is jsunit/testRunner.html. All of this yields the first part of the URL: http://localhost:8080/jsunit/jsunit/testRunner.html. The testPage URL parameter points to the test page or suite page to run. It too starts with the same local server plus the jsunit servlet prefix and is followed by the path to the test suite page relative to where the test is run. Put it all together and we have the complete URL.

Next, we give Ant all of the JAR files needed to run JsUnit ❻, and then we can proceed to running our test with the target `standalone_test` ❼, which we invoke from the command line in the build.xml directory with a simple call to Ant by typing the following in a console:

```
ant standalone_test
```

Ant starts, and you'll see the web browser open, run the tests in the test runner page, and close. You'll also see a couple of pages of Ant and JsUnit output on the console detailing the test run, too much to reproduce here. We can look for the next-to-last line of Ant output for the familiar BUILD SUCCESSFUL message.

You can even add to your test run the JsUnit self-tests as a sanity check by adding the target `jsunit_self_test` ❽ to your Ant invocation:

```
ant jsunit_self_test standalone_test
```

For the self-test to work in your build, make sure that your `jsunit_self_test` target points to the JsUnit test suite located in jsunit/tests/jsUnitTestSuite.html, as our example build.xml does.

We wrap up this section by noting that more advanced test configurations are possible with JsUnit because it provides support for driving farms of JsUnit servers. A JsUnit server is what allows tests to be performed from Ant; it acts under the covers of our examples to drive web browsers on the local machine or on remote machines and also creates the result logs.

> ### JsUnit Firefox tip: permission denied
> If you get a permission denied error in Firefox, set the `security.fileuri.strict_origin_policy` to `false`.

13.5   *RhinoUnit versus JsUnit*

Should you use RhinoUnit or JsUnit? The answer to this question is quite similar to the HtmlUnit versus Selenium question, which we presented in the previous chapter. The similarity is that both are free and open source.

The major difference between the two is that RhinoUnit emulates a web browser, whereas JsUnit drives a real web browser process. When using JsUnit, the browser itself provides support for JavaScript. In RhinoUnit, Java 6 or Apache BSF plus the Mozilla Rhino[16] engine provide JavaScript support.

The RhinoUnit pros are that it's a 100 percent Java solution and is easy to integrate in a build process. The JsUnit pros are that it drives native browsers and can manage a farm of JsUnit test servers.

> **Use RhinoUnit when**
>
> Use RhinoUnit when your application is independent of operating system features and browser-specific implementations of JavaScript, DOM, CSS, and so on.
>
> **Use JsUnit when**
>
> Use JsUnit when you require validation of specific browsers and operating systems, especially if the application takes advantage of or depends on a browser's specific implementation of JavaScript, DOM, CSS, and so on.

You've seen how to test client-side scripts with RhinoUnit and JsUnit. Next, we show how you can check best practices with JSLint.

13.6   *Checking best practices with JSLint*

We now move on to checking our code for best practices with JSLint.[17] As we did for the unit-testing script, we use scripts to define and run JSLint from Ant:

```
<scriptdef name="JSLintant" src="${JSLint.src}/JSLintant.js"
    language="javascript">
    <attribute name="options" />
    <attribute name="JSLintpath" />
    <element name="fileset" type="fileset" />
</scriptdef>

<target name="run-js-lint">
    <JSLintant options="{eqeqeq : true, white: true, plusplus : false,
bitwise : true, evil: true, passfail: false}"
JSLintpath="${JSLint.src}/fullJSLint.js">
        <fileset dir="${src.dir}" />
    </JSLintant>
</target>
```

❶

❷

---

[16] http://www.mozilla.org/rhino/
[17] JSLint: http://www.JSLint.com/

> **JSLint tip**
>
> When you invoke the `JSLintant` Ant script, make sure you point the `JSLintpath` argument to the location of the full JSLint.js file, for example:
>
> `JSLintpath="${JSLint.src}/fullJSLint.js"`

We start by defining an Ant script for JSLint ❶ and then call the script ❷ and pass it the source location to our JavaScript library directory.

You run this example script by typing `ant` on the command line in the ch13-ajax-rhinounit directory for this chapter example, which displays the results shown in listing 13.9.

Listing 13.9   Ant build results

```
Buildfile: build.xml

run-unit-tests:
[rhinounit] Testsuite: test-all-valid.js
[rhinounit] Tests run: 17, Failures: 0, Errors: 0
[rhinounit]
[rhinounit] Testsuite: test-example.js
[rhinounit] Tests run: 2, Failures: 0, Errors: 0
[rhinounit]

run-js-lint:
[JSLintant] Attribute options = {eqeqeq : true, white: true, plusplus :
false, bitwise : true, evil: true, passfail: false}
[JSLintant] JSLint: No problems found in ch13-
rhinounit\src\main\webapp\factorial.js

run-all-tests:

BUILD SUCCESSFUL
Total time: 0 seconds
```

JSLint is quite verbose and comprehensive in its output; please see the JSLint[18] website for details.

We started by looking at functional testing from the client perspective. Next, we dove into testing one of the underlying building blocks of an Ajax application: client-side scripts with RhinoUnit and JsUnit. We also checked these scripts for best practices with JSLint. Next, we move to the server side and another building block: testing server-side services with HttpClient.

---

[18] http://www.JSLint.com/

13.7 Testing services with HttpClient

The idea behind testing the application services layer separately is to validate each service independently from HTML, JavaScript, and DOM and how the application uses the data. An application calls a service from JavaScript through the XMLHttpRequest object. Here, we use XMLHttpRequest to refer to the standard JavaScript XMLHttp-Request object and to the Microsoft ActiveX XMLHTTP objects Microsoft.XMLHTTP and Msxml2.XMLHTTP. Our goal is to emulate an XMLHttpRequest object by using HTTP as the transport mechanism and XML and JSON as example data formats. We use the Apache Commons HttpClient to provide HTTP support, Java's built-in XML support, and jslint4java to check that JSON documents are well formed.

13.7.1 Calling an XML service

To simplify this example, we've made the chapter's example webapp directory an IIS virtual directory so that we can run the unit tests from Ant locally. A production Ant build would start and stop a web container like Jetty around the unit test invocations. Our first XML service test in listing 13.10 makes sure that we're getting back from the server the expected XML document. A second test validates the document.

Listing 13.10 An XML service test

```
@Test
public void testGetXmlBasicCheck() throws IOException {
    HttpClient httpClient = new HttpClient();                        ← 1
    GetMethod get = new GetMethod(                                     2
        "http://localhost/ch13personal/personal.xml");
    String responseString;
    try {
        httpClient.executeMethod(get);                                3
        InputStream input = get.getResponseBodyAsStream();
        responseString = IOUtils.toString(input, "UTF-8");          ← 4
    } finally {
        get.releaseConnection();                                    ← 5
    }
    Assert.assertTrue(responseString, responseString.startsWith(     6
        "<?xml version=\"1.0\" encoding=\"UTF-8\"?>"));
    // more...
}
```

The test starts by creating an Apache Commons HttpClient ❶ and defining the HTTP GET method ❷ with a URL for our XML document fixture. The URL specified in the GetMethod constructor is application specific and must include parameters if appropriate for a given test. The test then executes the HTTP GET method ❸ and reads the data back from the server. Note the use of the Apache Commons IO API IOUtils.toString to read the response stream in a string as a one-liner ❹. The code does this synchronously, unlike a standard Ajax application. We then guarantee that HttpClient resources are freed by calling releaseConnection from a finally block ❺. We can now check that the data from the server is as expected. For this first test, all we do is a simple string comparison of the start of the document ❻. You could also use Java regular expressions to do some further XML string-based checks; next, we use an important XML feature: XML validation.

13.7.2 *Validating an XML response*

If you can parse an XML document, you know that it's *well formed,* meaning that the XML syntax is obeyed, nothing more. XML provides a standard called XML Schema, which you use to define a *vocabulary* of XML, specifying which elements and attributes make up a *valid* document. In this next example, the schema is stored in a file called personal.xsd. Listing 13.11 uses the standard Java XML APIs to validate the XML document returned from a server call against an XML Schema.

Listing 13.11   A validating XML service test

```
@Test
public void testGetXmlAndValidateXmlSchema() throws
  IOException, ParserConfigurationException, SAXException {
    HttpClient httpClient = new HttpClient();
    GetMethod get = new GetMethod(
        "http://localhost/ch13personal/personal.xml");
    Document document;
    try {
        httpClient.executeMethod(get);
        InputStream input = get.getResponseBodyAsStream();
        // Parse the XML document into a DOM tree
        DocumentBuilder parser = DocumentBuilderFactory
            .newInstance().newDocumentBuilder();                        ❶
        document = parser.parse(input);
    } finally {
        get.releaseConnection();
    }

    // Create a SchemaFactory capable of understanding XSD schemas
    SchemaFactory factory = SchemaFactory.newInstance(                  ❷
        XMLConstants.W3C_XML_SCHEMA_NS_URI);

    // Load the XSD schema in a Schema instance
    Source schemaFile = new StreamSource(new File(
        "src/main/webapp/personal.xsd"));                               ❸
    Schema schema = factory.newSchema(schemaFile);

    // Create a Validator, which we use to validate the document
    Validator validator = schema.newValidator();                       ❹
    validator.validate(new DOMSource(document));
}
```

This example starts as the previous one did, but after the test executes the HTTP GET method, we read the server response directly with an XML parser ❶. If the DOM document parses successfully, we know the document is well formed, a nice sanity check. If we don't get a valid XML document from the server, we might have a server error message in the response or a bug in server-side XML document generation. We can now move to the meat of the test, XML validation. We create a schema factory for the kind of grammar to use, in our case, XML Schema ❷, and load the XSD schema file in a Schema instance ❸. Finally, we can create an XML Validator for our schema and validate the DOM document ❹. At this point, we know that our document is valid *and* well formed.

The next step would be to check that the application data is as expected. The DOM document API can be painful to use, so at this point you have several options. The JDOM[19] API is a friendlier interface to XML than DOM. You can use Java's XPath[20] support to check the contents of a document. You can also use Sun's JAXB[21] framework, although it's not trivial, to transform XML into POJOs.

Next, let's consider JSON as the data format.

13.7.3 *Validating a JSON response*

JSON[22] (JavaScript Object Notation) is a data-interchange language based on a subset of the JavaScript Programming Language, Standard ECMA-262 3rd Edition, December 1999.[23] Applications use JSON instead of XML as their data format because it's text based and easy for people and machines to read and understand. In this first example in listing 13.12, we show a simple check of a JSON document.

Listing 13.12 A JSON service test

```
private static final String URL_FIXTURE =
    "http://localhost/ch13personal/glossary.json";

@Test
public void testGetJsonBasicCheck() throws IOException {
    HttpClient httpClient = new HttpClient();
    GetMethod get = new GetMethod(URL_FIXTURE);
    String responseString;
    try {
        httpClient.executeMethod(get);
        InputStream input = get.getResponseBodyAsStream();
        responseString = IOUtils.toString(input, "UTF-8");       <--❶
    } finally {
        get.releaseConnection();
    }
    String responseNoWs =
        StringUtils.deleteWhitespace(responseString);
    String response1Line = "{ \"glossary\": { \"title\":
➥\"example glossary\", \"GlossDiv\": { \"title\": \"S\",
➥\"GlossList\": { \"GlossEntry\": { \"ID\": \"SGML\", \"SortAs\":
➥\"SGML\", \"GlossTerm\": \"Standard Generalized Markup Language\",
➥\"Acronym\": \"SGML\", \"Abbrev\": \"ISO 8879:1986\", \"GlossDef\": {
➥\"para\": \"A meta-markup language, used to create markup languages
```

[19] http://www.jdom.org/
[20] http://java.sun.com/j2se/1.5.0/docs/api/javax/xml/xpath/package-summary.html
[21] https://jaxb.dev.java.net/
[22] http://www.json.org/
[23] http://www.ecma-international.org/publications/files/ecma-st/ECMA-262.pdf

```
➡such as DocBook.\", \"GlossSeeAlso\": [\"GML\", \"XML\"] },
➡\"GlossSee\": \"markup\" } } } } }";
    String response1LineNoWs =
        StringUtils.deleteWhitespace(response1Line);
    Assert.assertTrue(responseString,
        responseNoWs.equals(response1LineNoWs));
}
```

❷

In this test, we perform the same steps as our first XML example: we create an `Http-Client`, an HTTP `GET` method that we execute, and then read the results from the server into a `String` ❶. Unlike XML, JSON has no APIs to support checks for well-formed and valid documents. We strip whitespaces from our JSON document fixture, the server response, and compare the two ❷. Although this check is brute force, we use it to provide a simple check that's free of formatting issues. The Apache Commons Lang API `StringUtils.deleteWhitespace` performs the whitespace removal.

The next-best thing we can do is implement a well-formed check by parsing the document. Although www.json.org lists many libraries, including Java libraries to parse JSON, we use the JSLint wrapper jslint4java[24] to go beyond a simple well-formed check. As you saw earlier in the RhinoUnit section, JSLint provides lint-style reporting for JavaScript. In listing 13.13, we call JSLint through jslint4java and check its results.

Listing 13.13   A JSON service test with JSLint

```
@Test
public void testGetJsonAndValidate() throws IOException,
    ParserConfigurationException, SAXException {
    HttpClient httpClient = new HttpClient();
    GetMethod get = new GetMethod(URL_FIXTURE);
    String responseString;
    try {
        httpClient.executeMethod(get);
        InputStream input = get.getResponseBodyAsStream();
        responseString = IOUtils.toString(input, "UTF-8");
    } finally {
        get.releaseConnection();
    }
    JSLint JSLint = new JSLint();                                        ❶
    List<Issue> issues = JSLint.lint(URL_FIXTURE, responseString);     ❷
    StringBuilder builder = new StringBuilder();
    String eol = System.getProperty("line.separator");
    for (Issue issue : issues) {                                        ❸
        builder.append(issue.toString());
        builder.append(eol);
    }
    Assert.assertEquals(builder.toString(), 0, issues.size());          ❹
}
```

Our test starts as usual, and we check for results using a `JSLint` object ❶. We don't provide options in this example, but the `JSLint` class provides an `addOption` method

---

[24] jslint4java site: http://code.google.com/p/jslint4java/

to support the underlying JSLint options. The test calls the lint method by specifying two arguments: a String describing the source location and another String for the JavaScript code to check, in this case, a JSON document ❷. The test uses the lint results to create a message String ❸ used in the Assert call. If there's a problem, the test provides the assertEquals call ❹ with a full description of all issues JSLint found.

You'll notice that jslint4java is always behind JSLint in terms of features and fixes. This is because jslint4java embeds JSLint (fullJSLint.js) in its JAR file. If you need to use a newer or different version of JSLint in jslint4java, you'll need to download jslint4java, drop in the version of JSLint (fullJSLint.js) you need on top of the existing one, and rebuild jslint4java.

In this section, you've seen how to validate server-side services that participate in an Ajax application independently of the pages and code using them. We've used Apache Commons HttpClient as our HTTP communication library, Java's XML APIs, and JSLint through jslint4java. We've separated our tests along the boundary of the Ajax architecture.

We've now tested the full Ajax application stack. Let's now consider a different way to build, run, and test an Ajax application with the Google Web Toolkit.

13.8   Testing Google Web Toolkit applications

The Google Web Toolkit (GWT)[25] is a free, open source framework used to create JavaScript frontends to web applications. GWT application development has a twist, though: you write your applications in Java. To this end, Google provides the Google Plug-in for Eclipse; you develop and test in Java, and when your application is ready for deployment, GWT translates your Java into JavaScript. GWT allows you to run and test your application in *hosted mode*, which runs in Java, and in *web mode*, where you application is translated to JavaScript and then is run in a browser.

13.8.1   Choosing a testing framework for a GWT application

GWT supports JUnit with the GWTTestCase and GWTTestSuite classes, which both extend the JUnit TestCase class. GWT normally integrates with JUnit 3.8.2 and works with 4.6. GWT includes junitCreator, a program used to generate empty GWT test cases for a given GWT module. As a bonus, GWT can also benchmark your application. Because Java and JavaScript aren't the same, you should test in both hosted and web modes.

It's important to understand that GWTTestCase doesn't account for testing the user interface of an application. You use GWTTestCase to test the asynchronous portions of the application normally triggered by user actions. This means that you must factor your application and test cases with this element in mind. You can think of GWT tests as integration tests. The tests can't rely on any user interface element driving the application. Testing the GUI requires using the techniques presented in this and the previous chapters; you can create functional GUI tests with Selenium or HtmlUnit.

---

[25] http://code.google.com/webtoolkit/

> **GWTTestCase tip**
>
> You use the `GWTTestCase` class to test the application logic of the web client, not the user interface. Although seemingly an obstacle, this forces you to factor your GWT application cleanly between code for user interaction and application logic. This is a design best practice that you should follow.

Let's first look at how to create a `GWTTestCase` manually before we show how to use junitCreator. The example we use in this section is adapted from the GWT Stock-Watcher example[26] and extended with an RPC. Figure 13.5 shows what the application looks like running in hosted mode.

Our example tests the StockWatcher remote procedure call (RPC) to get stock price information for an array of stock symbols. We focus on RPC, because it's the heart of GWT JUnit testing.

**Figure 13.5
Running StockWatcher in
hosted mode**

---

[26] http://code.google.com/webtoolkit/

13.8.2 Creating a GWTTestCase manually

We start our asynchronous GWT RPC example test in familiar GWT territory with listing 13.14, where the refreshWatchList method performs a standard GWT RPC call.

Listing 13.14   The asynchronous RPC call

```
void refreshWatchList() {
    // Initialize the service proxy.
    if (this.stockPriceSvc == null) {
        this.stockPriceSvc = GWT.create(StockPriceService.class);      ←❶
    }

    // Set up the callback object.
    AsyncCallback<StockPrice[]> callback =
        new AsyncCallback<StockPrice[]>() {
        public void onFailure(Throwable caught) {
            StockWatcher.this.setLastRefreshThrowable(caught);         ←❷
        }

        public void onSuccess(StockPrice[] result) {
            StockWatcher.this.updateTable(result);                     ←❸
        }
    };

    // Make the call to the stock price service.
    this.stockPriceSvc.getPrices(                                      ❹
        this.getStocks().toArray(new String[0]), callback);
}
```

The implementation of refreshWatchList follows the standard pattern for GWT RPC; the method creates a new StockPriceService instance ❶ and defines the service callback. The callback defines two methods; in onFailure ❷ we save the given exception, and in onSuccess ❸, which is typed for our application model (StockPrice[]), we update the application. Next, we call service's getPrices method ❹ with input data and our callback. The key point to remember is that the call to the getPrices method is asynchronous, so the call to refreshWatchList is also asynchronous. Next, we test this method with a unit test.

To create a GWT test case, you start by creating a subclass of GWTTestCase, along the lines of listing 13.15.

Listing 13.15   StockWatcherTest.java—testing GWT RPC

```
[...]
public class StockWatcherTest extends GWTTestCase {                    ←❶

@Override
public String getModuleName() {
    return "com.google.gwt.sample.stockwatcher.StockWatcher";          ❷
}

public void testStockPrices() {
    final StockWatcher stockWatcher = new StockWatcher();
    final ArrayList<String> stocks = stockWatcher.getStocks();
```

```
        stocks.add("S1");
        stocks.add("S2");                                            ③
        stocks.add("S3");
        stockWatcher.refreshWatchList();                          ◄─④
        Timer timer = new Timer() {                                  ◄─
            private void assertStockPrice(FlexTable stocksFlexTable,
                int row, String price, String change) {             ⑤
                assertEquals(price, stocksFlexTable.getText(row, 1));
                assertEquals(change, stocksFlexTable.getText(row, 2));
            }

            @Override
            public void run() {
                Throwable lastRefreshThrowable =
                    stockWatcher.getLastRefreshThrowable();
                if (lastRefreshThrowable != null) {                 ⑥
                    this.throwUnchekedException(lastRefreshThrowable);
                }
                FlexTable stocksFlexTable = stockWatcher.getStocksFlexTable();
                assertEquals("Symbol", stocksFlexTable.getText(0, 0));
                assertEquals("Price", stocksFlexTable.getText(0, 1));   ⑦
                assertEquals("Change", stocksFlexTable.getText(0, 2));
                this.assertStockPrice(stocksFlexTable, 1,
                        "101.00", "+0.01 (+0.01%)");
                this.assertStockPrice(stocksFlexTable, 2,              ⑧
                        "102.00", "+0.02 (+0.02%)");
                this.assertStockPrice(stocksFlexTable, 3,
                        "103.00", "+0.03 (+0.03%)");
                StockWatcherTest.this.finishTest();                 ◄─
            }                                                         ⑨

            private void throwUnchekedException(
                Throwable lastRefreshThrowable) {
                String msg = lastRefreshThrowable.toString();
                if (lastRefreshThrowable instanceof StatusCodeException) {
                    msg = "HTTP status code " + ((StatusCodeException)
                        lastRefreshThrowable).getStatusCode() + ": " + msg;
                }
                throw new IllegalStateException(msg, lastRefreshThrowable);
            }
        };
        this.delayTestFinish(5000);                                 ◄─⑩
        timer.schedule(100);                                        ◄─
    }                                                                 ⑪
}
```

A GWT test case must extend the GWT class GWTTestCase ❶ and implement a method
with the signature public String getModuleName() to return the name of the module
being tested ❷. We start the test method by instantiating the model class and initializing it with input data ❸, the three stock symbols "S1", "S2", and "S3". Next, we call
the refreshWatchList method in listing 13.14, which performs the asynchronous
RPC ❹.

We need to allow the test method to complete while allowing assertions to run. To
do so, we use a GWT Timer ❺ to schedule our assertions. Our Timer's run method

starts by checking that the stock watcher RPC was able to run in the first place. We do this by checking to see whether the asynchronous callback caught an exception ❻. This arrangement is helpful in determining an incorrect test setup, in particular as it relates to the classpath and module file (see the tip in the section on running tests). If no exception is present, the validity checks on the StockWatcher object can proceed. We check that table headers are still there ❼ and then check the contents of the table ❽ for values we expect to be returned from the service. In this test, we changed the stock GWT example to return predictable values instead of randomly generated values. If the test calls the GWTTestCase finishTest ❾ method before the delay period expires, then the test succeeds.

Now that the Timer object is in place, we call delayTestFinish to tell GWT to run this test in asynchronous mode ❿. You give the method a delay period in milliseconds much longer than what is expected to run the test setup, do the RPC, and perform the assertions. When the test method exits normally, GWT doesn't mark the test as finished; instead, the delay period starts. During the delay period, GWT checks for the following:

1 If the test calls the GWTTestCase finishTest method before the delay period expires, then the test succeeds.
2 If an exception propagates to GWT, then the test fails with that exception.
3 If the delay period expires and neither of the previous conditions is true, then the test fails with a TimeoutException.
4 The last task in the test is to get the job off and running with a call to the Timer's schedule method ⓫. The argument is a delay in milliseconds, after which control returns to the caller.

We just examined asynchronous testing in GWT; next, we show how to use junit-Creator to create starter tests and how to run the tests.

13.8.3 Creating a GWTTestCase with junitCreator

The junitCreator utility allows you to create a GWTTestCase based on a module to which you then add your own test methods. junitCreator is a good place to get started on your first GWT test. For subsequent tests, you may prefer to clone a template class or write test case classes from scratch. junitCreator also creates Eclipse launch configurations and command-line scripts for hosted and web modes. To get your command processor to find junitCreator and other GWT programs, remember to add GWT to your path. Here's a sample invocation for our example:

```
junitCreator -junit /java/junit4.6/junit-4.6.jar -module
com.google.gwt.sample.stockwatcher.StockWatcher -eclipse ch13-gwt-
StockWatcher com.google.gwt.sample.stockwatcher.client.StockWatcherTest
```

The (abbreviated) console output is as follows:

```
Created file
    test\com\google\gwt\sample\stockwatcher\client\StockWatcherTest.java
```

```
Created file StockWatcherTest-hosted.launch
Created file StockWatcherTest-web.launch
Created file StockWatcherTest-hosted.cmd
Created file StockWatcherTest-web.cmd
```

The .launch files are Eclipse launch configurations and the .cmd files are command-line scripts. Use these files to invoke the generated test case in web or hosted mode. You may need to adapt the scripts for your location of the JUnit and GWT .jar files.

13.8.4   *Running test cases*

Using Eclipse, running a test is easy. You right-click a test case class and choose Run As or Debug As and then choose GWT JUnit Test to run the test in hosted mode or GWT JUnit Test (Web Mode) to run the test in web mode, as shown in figure 13.6.

Figure 13.6   Running a test

To use Ant, you need to make sure your build file points to the GWT SDK. Using a GWT example build file as a template, edit the gwt.sdk property to point to the GWT directory.

13.8.5   *Setup and teardown*

A GWTTestCase subclass can override the JUnit methods setUp and tearDown with the following restrictions:

- You can't call GWT JavaScript Native Interface (JSNI) methods.
- You can't call code that depends on deferred binding, which includes most of the UI library.

GWT 1.5 remedies these issues by the addition of two methods available for overriding:

- gwtSetUp runs before each test case method.
- gwtTearDown runs after each test case method.

13.8.6   *Creating a test suite*

The benefit of using a test suite with GWT goes beyond grouping related tests together. A performance gain is possible by using a GWT test suite. GWT sorts test cases in a suite by module name as returned by getModuleName. This causes all tests with the same module name to run one after the other.

To create a test suite, you can start with the Eclipse JUnit Test Suite Wizard. For example, to create a test suite that includes all test cases in a package, go to the Packages view, right-click a package, and choose New and then Other. In the New dialog box, open the JUnit node and choose JUnit Test Suite. Listing 13.16 shows the generated code with two changes we explain next.

Listing 13.16 A GWT test suite

```
public class AllTests extends GWTTestSuite {

    public static Test suite() {
        TestSuite suite = new TestSuite(
            "com.google.gwt.sample.stockwatcher.client.AllTests");
        // $JUnit-BEGIN$
        suite.addTestSuite(StockPriceTest.class);
        suite.addTestSuite(StockWatcherTest.class);
        // $JUnit-END$
        return suite;
    }

}
```

We made the class extend GWTTestSuite ❶ to make this suite a GWT test suite. We also replaced the String in the TestSuite constructor with the class name of the generated class ❷. This allows us to double-click the class name in the JUnit view and jump to an editor for that test suite. The rest is standard JUnit code; we call addTest-Suite with a class object to add a test case to the suite.

13.8.7 *Running a test suite*

In addition to the requirements for running a GWT test case, you must configure a GWT test suite with more memory than the default settings allocate. Configure the Java VM running the tests with at least 256 megabytes of RAM. With the Sun JVM, use the following option: -Xmx256M. You must also add to the classpath the source directories for application and test code.

To wrap up GWT testing, recall that GWT test cases verify the asynchronous aspects of your application, not the user interface. To test the GUI, use functional tests with Selenium or HtmlUnit.

Although we've finished our brief tour of GWT testing, it's worth noting that GWT includes the Speed Tracer tool to help you identify and fix performance problems by visualizing instrumentation data taken from the browser.

13.9 *Summary*

In this chapter, we built on what you learned in chapter 12 about testing the presentation layer of applications, specifically as it relates to Ajax applications.

We showed that Ajax applications use many technologies layered in broad tiers: HTML and JavaScript are used on the client; HTTP, XML, and JSON provide communication and data services; and the server side is viewed as a black box implementing services accessed over the internet with HTTP.

We divided our testing strategies along similar patterns. We used functional tests for the whole application stack as it appears to a user by driving and testing the application with HtmlUnit and Selenium. We isolated JavaScript into libraries and tested those independently with RhinoUnit and JsUnit. We validated server-side XML and JSON services using Apache Commons HttpClient, JSLint, and jslint4java.

You use RhinoUnit when your application is independent of operating system features and browser-specific implementations of JavaScript, DOM, CSS, and the like. You use JsUnit when you require validation of specific browsers and operating systems, especially if the application takes advantage of or depends on a browser's specific implementation of JavaScript, DOM, CSS, and so on.

Finally, we looked at the unique challenge posed by GWT, a framework that translates your Java code to JavaScript.

This chapter concludes our survey of user interface testing, and we now move to the server side and testing with Cactus.

14

Server-side Java
testing with Cactus

Good design at good times.
Make it run, make it run right.

—Kent Beck,
Test Driven Development:
By Example

This chapter covers

- Drawbacks of mock objects
- Testing inside the container with Cactus
- How Cactus works
- Integrating Cactus with other projects, including Ant and Maven

In the second part of the book we explained what mock objects are and how to benefit from using them. We also described different techniques for unit testing your server-side code, and we even compared these techniques against each other. The one thing that you should be aware of now is that there is no absolute truth—the best techniques to use depend on the situation you're currently in. For example, in most cases you might find server-side testing with mocks and stubs sufficient, but as you saw, this technique suffers some significant drawbacks. That's why we cover the in-container testing approach deeper in the book. Furthermore, this chapter focuses on the in-container testing methodologies by means of one of the most popular in-container testing frameworks: Cactus. We start by introducing the Cactus framework and then show you some real-world examples of how to use Cactus.

We begin by explaining what's so special about Cactus and the order of execution of Cactus tests. We then build a sample application that uses some components from the Java EE spec, and we write the tests for those components with the help of Cactus. The next step is to execute those tests; we show a sample integration between Cactus and some of the most popular build tools (Ant and Maven). But we go a bit further than that: we demonstrate the tight integration between Cactus and other projects, such as Cargo and Jetty. So let's start!

14.1   What is Cactus?

Cactus is an open source framework (http://jakarta.apache.org/cactus/) for in-container testing server-side Java code (mostly Java EE components in the current version of Cactus). It's an extension of JUnit that was created by Vincent Massol in 1998.

Before we go any further, I'd like to clarify the definitions just mentioned. When we say Cactus is a *framework*, we mean that it provides an API that you have to extend in order to use it.

Also, *in-container* means that (as you'll see later in the chapter) the tests get executed inside the virtual machine of the container. And finally, Cactus is an *extension* of JUnit for two reasons: First, it extends JUnit by empowering it with new functionality (Cactus makes JUnit tests get executed inside the container, something which otherwise wouldn't be possible). And second, Cactus's API extends JUnit's API; in low-level software engineering terms, it extends some of JUnit's classes and overrides some of JUnit's methods.

Let's see Cactus in action. In later sections, we explain in more detail how it works.

14.2   Testing with Cactus

This section is somewhat theoretical. You need this knowledge before you experiment with a sample application, because Cactus is different from the normal unit testing frameworks. Cactus executes the tests inside the container, which on its own raises a lot of questions, so we try to answer all of them here.

14.2.1 Java components that you can test with Cactus

As we mentioned in the previous section, the Cactus project is used for testing the core Java EE components (JSPs, tag libraries, servlets, filters, and EJBs). What's worth mentioning is that this is the only focus of the Cactus project. It doesn't test any specific framework (look at the next chapter if your application is framework specific), because it isn't intended to do so. A lot of the emails that come from the Cactus mailing list ask if people can use Cactus for testing an application based on a specific framework (like Struts, JSF, or Spring). There are quite a few tools dedicated to such testing, and we cover some of them later in the book. Most of those tools are based on Cactus and require Cactus in their classpath, but again Cactus is designed for in-container testing of the components from the Java EE spec.

14.2.2 *General principles*

Because Cactus is an extension of JUnit, every Cactus test is a JUnit test by itself. The reverse isn't true; most of the JUnit tests are Cactus tests. So what distinguishes the Cactus tests from the JUnit tests? You need to stick to a couple of rules in order to use Cactus.

We already discussed in chapter 8 what in-container testing means. Back then, we had a web application that uses servlets. We want to unit test the isAuthenticated method in listing 14.1 from a SampleServlet servlet.

Listing 14.1   Sample of a servlet method to unit test

```
[...]
import javax.servlet.http.HttpServlet;
import javax.servlet.http.HttpServletRequest;
import javax.servlet.http.HttpSession;

public class SampleServlet extends HttpServlet {
    public boolean isAuthenticated(HttpServletRequest request) {
        HttpSession session = request.getSession(false);
        if (session == null) {
            return false;
        }
        String authenticationAttribute =
                (String) session.getAttribute("authenticated");

        return Boolean.valueOf(authenticationAttribute).booleanValue();
    }
}
```

In order to be able to test this method, we need to get hold of a valid HttpServlet-Request object. Unfortunately, it isn't possible to call new HttpServletRequest to create a usable request. The lifecycle of HttpServletRequest is managed by the container. JUnit alone isn't enough to write a test for the isAuthenticated method.

So what must we do in order to obtain a valid HttpServletRequest? Wouldn't it be perfect if we had an HttpServletRequest object already instantiated in our test cases? And how can we achieve this? What if we always had to extend a certain class that takes care of providing us the server-side objects that are otherwise managed by the container (such as HttpServletRequest)? Listing 14.2 shows a corresponding Cactus test that tests the given servlet.

Listing 14.2   Using Cactus to unit test `SampleServlet`

```
[...]
import org.apache.cactus.ServletTestCase;
import org.apache.cactus.WebRequest;

public class TestSampleServletIntegration extends ServletTestCase {
    private SampleServlet servlet;

    protected void setUp() {
        servlet = new SampleServlet();
    }

    public void testIsAuthenticatedAuthenticated() {
        session.setAttribute("authenticated", "true");          ←❶
        assertTrue(servlet.isAuthenticated(request));
    }

    public void testIsAuthenticatedNotAuthenticated() {
        assertFalse(servlet.isAuthenticated(request));
    }

    public void beginIsAuthenticatedNoSession(WebRequest request) {
        request.setAutomaticSession(false);                      ←❷
    }

    public void testIsAuthenticatedNoSession() {
        assertFalse(servlet.isAuthenticated(request));
    }
}
```

Now you're probably asking, "At what place do the session ❶ and request ❷ objects get declared and initialized?" The answer is straightforward—they come from the base class, ServletTestCase, which is part of the Cactus API.

As you can see, the Cactus test case meets all of our requirements. It gives us access to the container objects, inside our JUnit test cases. As you can see from the previous listing, writing a Cactus test case involves several key points:

- The Cactus test case must extend one of the following, depending on what type of component you're testing: ServletTestCase, JSPTestCase, or FilterTest-Case. This is a rule: because Cactus extends the 3.8.x version of JUnit, your test cases always have to extend one of the latter classes.

- The Cactus framework exposes the container objects (in this case the Http-ServletRequest and HttpSession objects) to your tests, making it easy and quick to write unit tests.

- You get a chance to implement two new methods: begin*XXX* and end*XXX*. These two new methods are executed on the client side, and you can use them to place certain values in the request object or to get certain values from the response object.

- In order for Cactus to expose the container objects, Cactus needs to get them from the JVM they live in, and because the container is the only one managing the life-cycle of these objects, Cactus tests need to interact directly with the container. This leads us to the conclusion that Cactus tests must be deployed inside the container.

The last of these points tells us that Cactus tests live in the container JVM. This brings us to the next issue: if Cactus tests live in the container JVM, how are they executed? Also, how do we see the result from their execution?

14.2.3 *How Cactus works*

Before we rush into the details, you need to understand a bit more about how Cactus works. The lifecycle of a Cactus test is shown in figure 14.1.

Let's look at the steps in using the `TestSampleServletIntegration` Cactus test from listing 14.2. Say, now we have a sample servlet that we want to test and also a test written for that particular servlet. What we need to do now is package the servlet and the test, along with the necessary Cactus libraries, and deploy the package in the server. Once we start the server, we have the test and the servlet in both: deployed in the container and in our workspace on the client side. You can submit the client-side Cactus test to a JUnit test runner, and the runner starts the tests.

EXECUTING CLIENT-SIDE AND SERVER-SIDE STEPS
The lifecycle comprises steps that are executed on the client side and others that are executed on the server side (inside the container JVM). *Client side* refers to the JVM in which you started the JUnit test runner.

On the client side, the Cactus logic is implemented in the `YYYTestCase` classes that your tests extend (where `YYY` can be `Servlet`, `Jsp`, or `Filter`). More specifically, `YYYTestCase` overrides JUnit `TestCase.runBare`, which is the method called by the JUnit test runner to execute one test. By overriding `runBare`, Cactus can implement its own test logic, as described later.

On the server side, the Cactus logic is implemented in *a proxy redirector* (or *redirector* for short).

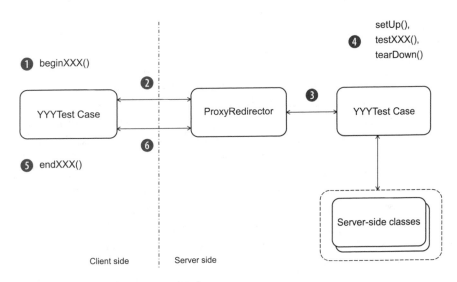

Figure 14.1 Lifecycle of a Cactus test

For each test (test*XXX* methods in the *YYY*TestCase classes), the six steps shown in figure 14.2 take place. Let's step through them.

1 *Execute beginXXX.* If there is a begin*XXX* method, Cactus executes it. The begin*XXX* method lets you pass information to the redirector. The TestSampleServletIntegration example extends ServletTestCase and connects to the Cactus servlet redirector. The servlet redirector is implemented as a servlet; this is the entry point in the container. The Cactus client side calls the servlet redirector by opening an HTTP connection to it. The begin*XXX* method sets up HTTP-related parameters that are set in the HTTP request received by the servlet redirector. This method can be used to define HTTP POST/GET parameters, HTTP cookies, HTTP headers, and so forth.

Here's an example:

```
public void beginXXX(WebRequest request) {
    request.addParameter("param1", "value1");
    request.addCookie("cookie1", "value1");
    [...]
}
```

In the TestSampleServletIntegration class, we've used the begin*XXX* method to tell the redirector not to create an HTTP session (the default behavior creates one):

```
public void beginIsAuthenticatedNoSession(WebRequest request) {
    request.setAutomaticSession(false);
}
```

2 *Open the redirector connection.* The *YYY*TestCase opens a connection to its redirector. In this case, the ServletTestCase code opens an HTTP connection to the servlet redirector (which is a servlet).

3 *Create the server-side TestCase instance.* The redirector creates an instance of the *YYY*TestCase class. Note that this is the second instance created by Cactus; the first one was created on the client side (by the JUnit TestRunner). Then the redirector retrieves container objects and assigns them in the *YYY*TestCase instance by setting class variables.

In the servlet example, the servlet redirector creates an instance of TestSampleServletIntegration and sets the following objects as class variables in it: HttpServletRequest, HttpServletResponse, HttpSession, and others. The servlet redirector is able to do this because it's a servlet. When it's called by the Cactus client side, it has received a valid HttpServletRequest, HttpServletResponse, HttpSession, and other objects from the container and is passing them to the *YYY*TestCase instance. It acts as a proxy/redirector (hence its name).

The redirector then starts the test (see step 4). Upon returning from the test, it stores the test result in the ServletConfig servlet object along with any exception that might have been raised during the test, so the test result can later be retrieved. The redirector needs a place to temporarily store the test result because the full Cactus test is complete only when the end*XXX* method has finished executing (see step 5).

4   *Call setUp, testXXX, and tearDown on the server.*   The redirector calls the JUnit setUp method of *YYY*TestCase, if there is one. Then it calls the test*XXX* method. The test*XXX* method calls the class/methods under test, and finally the redirector calls the JUnit tearDown method of the TestCase, if there is one.

5   *Execute endXXX on the client.*   Once the client side has received the response from its connection to the redirector, it calls an end*XXX* method (if it exists). This method is used so that your tests can assert additional results from the code under test. For example, if you're using a ServletTestCase, FilterTest-Case, or JspTestCase class, you can assert HTTP cookies, HTTP headers, or the content of the HTTP response:

```
public void endXXX(WebResponse response) {
    assertEquals("value", response.getCookie("cookiename").getValue());
    assertEquals("...", response.getText());
    [...]
}
```

6   *Gather the test result.*   In step 3, the redirector saves the test result in a variable stored with the ServletConfig object. The Cactus client side now needs to retrieve the test result and tell the JUnit test runner whether the test was successful, so the result can be displayed in the test runner GUI or console. To do this, the *YYY*TestCase opens a second connection to the redirector and asks it for the test result.

This process may look complex at first glance, but this is what it takes to be able to get inside the container and execute the test from there. Fortunately, as users, we're shielded from this complexity by the Cactus framework. You can use the provided Cactus frontends to start and set up the tests.

Now that you've seen what Cactus tests are and how they work, let's take a closer look at more component-specific tests.

14.3   *Testing servlets and filters*

As you already saw, Cactus is designed for testing the core components from the Java EE spec. This testing, however, has some component-specific characteristics. In this section we explore these characteristics.

When you unit test servlet and filter code, you must test not only these objects but also any Java class calling the Servlet/Filter API, the JNDI API, or any backend services. Starting from this section, we build a real-life sample application that will help demonstrate how to unit test each of the different kinds of components that make up a full-blown web application. This section focuses on unit testing the servlet and filter parts of that application. Later subsections test the other common components (JSPs and EJBs).

14.3.1 *Presenting the Administration application*

The goal of this sample Administration application is to let administrators perform database queries on a relational database. Suppose the application it administers already exists. Administrators can perform queries such as listing all the transactions that took place during a given time interval, listing the transactions that were out of service level agreement (SLA), and so forth. We set up a typical web application architecture (see figure 14.2) to demonstrate how to unit test each type of component (filter, servlet, JSP, and EJB).

The application first receives from the user an HTTP request containing the SQL query to execute. The request is caught by a security filter that checks whether the SQL query is a SELECT query (to prevent modifying the database). If not, the user is redirected to an error page. If the query is a SELECT, the AdminServlet servlet is called. The servlet performs the requested database query and forwards the results to a JSP page, which displays the results. The page uses JSP tags to iterate over the returned results and to display them in HTML tables. JSP tags are used for all the presentation logic code. The JSPs contain only layout/style tags (no Java code in scriptlets). We start by unit testing the AdminServlet servlet. Then, in the following subsections, we test the other components of the Administration application.

14.3.2 *Writing servlet tests with Cactus*

In this section, we focus on using Cactus to unit test the AdminServlet servlet (see figure 14.2) from the Administration application.

Let's test AdminServlet by writing the tests before we write the servlet code. This strategy is called test-driven development, or test first, and it's efficient for designing extensible and flexible code and making sure the unit test suite is as complete as possible. (See chapter 4 for an introduction to TDD.)

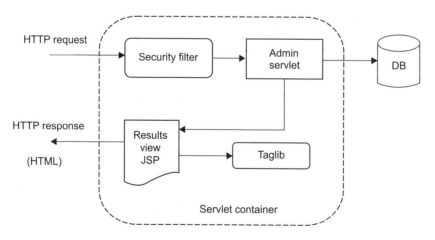

Figure 14.2   The sample Administration application. We use it as a base sample in this chapter to see how to unit test servlets, filters, JSPs, taglibs, and database applications.

Before we begin coding the test, let's review the requirement for AdminServlet. The servlet should extract the needed parameter containing the command to execute from the HTTP request (in this case, the SQL command to run). Then it should fetch the data using the extracted command. Finally, it should pass the control to the JSP page for display, passing the fetched data. Let's call the methods corresponding to these actions getCommand, executeCommand, and callView, respectively.

DESIGNING THE FIRST TEST

Listing 14.3 shows the unit tests for the getCommand method. Remember that we haven't yet written the code under test. The AdminServlet class doesn't exist, and our code doesn't compile (yet).

Listing 14.3   Designing and testing the getCommand method

```
[...]
import javax.servlet.ServletException;
import org.apache.cactus.ServletTestCase;
import org.apache.cactus.WebRequest;

public class TestAdminServlet extends ServletTestCase {      ←❶

    public void beginGetCommandOk(WebRequest request) {
        request.addParameter("command", "SELECT...");         ←❷
    }

    public void testGetCommandOk() throws Exception {
        AdminServlet servlet = new AdminServlet();
        String command = servlet.getCommand(request);
        assertEquals("SELECT...", command);                   ←❸
    }

    public void testGetCommandNotDefined {
        AdminServlet servlet = new AdminServlet();
        try {
            servlet.getCommand(request);
            fail("Command should not have existed");
        } catch (ServletException expected) {
            assertTrue(true);
        }
    }
}
```

This is a typical Cactus test case. We extended the ServletTestCase ❶, because the component that we want to test is a servlet. We also set a request parameter in the begin*XXX* method ❷ that we assert to be present in the test*XXX* method ❸.

Once we've written the test case, we can go on and implement the bare minimum of code that will allow us to compile the project. We need to implement a sample servlet with a getCommand method. Listing 14.4 shows the code.

Listing 14.4   Minimum code to make the `TestAdminServlet` compile

```
[...]
public class AdminServlet extends HttpServlet {

    public String getCommand(HttpServletRequest request)
                throws ServletException {
        return null;
    }
}
```

This is the minimum code that allows the `TestAdminServlet` to compile successfully.

The code compiles okay, but there's one more thing that we have to think about. What you probably notice at this point is that if this test gets executed it will fail, because of the `null` object that we return. Tests are used to prevent us from making mistakes. That said, we always have to ensure that tests fail if we provide corrupt data, as in the previous example. At this point, we need to ensure that the error is reported successfully. And after that, when we implement the code under test, the tests should succeed, and we'll know we've accomplished something. It's a good practice to ensure that the tests fail when the code fails.

> **JUnit best practice: always verify that the test fails when it should fail**
>
> It's a good practice to always verify that the tests you're writing work. Be sure a test fails when you expect it to fail. If you're using the test-driven development methodology, this failure happens as a matter of course. After you write the test, write a skeleton for the class under test (a class with methods that return `null` or throw runtime exceptions). If you try to run your test against a skeleton class, it should fail. If it doesn't, fix the test (ironically enough) so that it does fail! Even after the case is fleshed out, you can vet a test by changing an assertion to look for an invalid value that should cause it to fail.

But let's get back to the test. Listing 14.5 shows the code for `getCommand`. It's a minimal implementation that passes the tests.

Listing 14.5   Implementation of `getCommand` that makes the tests pass

```
[...]
public String getCommand(HttpServletRequest request)
                throws ServletException {

    String command = request.getParameter(COMMAND_PARAM);

    if (command == null) {
        throw new ServletException("Missing parameter ["
                + COMMAND_PARAM + "]");
    }
    return command;
}
[...]
```

The code in this listing is a simple implementation, but it's enough for our needs. We want our code not only to compile but also to pass the tests.

JUnit best practice: use TDD to implement The Simplest Thing That Could Possibly Work

The Simplest Thing That Could Possibly Work is an Extreme Programming (XP) principle that says overdesign should be avoided, because you never know what will be used effectively. XP recommends designing and implementing the minimal working solution and then *refactoring* mercilessly. This is in contrast to the *monumental methodologies*, which advocate fully designing the solution before starting development. When you're developing using the TDD approach, the tests are written first—you only have to implement the bare minimum to make the test pass in order to achieve a fully functional piece of code. The requirements have been fully expressed as test cases, and you can let yourself be led by the tests when you're writing the functional code.

FINISHING THE CACTUS SERVLET TESTS

At the beginning of the previous subsection, we mentioned that we need to write three methods: getCommand, executeCommand, and callView. We implemented getCommand in listing 14.5. The executeCommand method is responsible for obtaining data from the database. We defer this implementation until section 14.5, "Testing EJBs."

That leaves the callView method, along with the servlet's doGet method, which ties everything together by calling our different methods. One way of designing the application is to store the result of the executeCommand method in the HTTP servlet request. The request is passed to the JSP by the callView method (via servlet forward). The JSP can then access the data to display by getting it from the request (possibly using a useBean tag). This is a typical MVC Model 2 pattern used by many applications and frameworks.

We still need to define what objects executeCommand will return. The BeanUtils package in the Apache Commons (http://commons.apache.org/beanutils/) includes a DynaBean class that can expose public properties, like a regular JavaBean, but we don't need to hardcode getters and setters. In a Java class, we access one of the dyna properties using a map-like accessor:

```
DynaBean employee = ...
String firstName = (String) employee.get("firstName");
employee.set("firstName", "Petar");
```

The BeanUtils framework is nice for the current use case because we retrieve arbitrary data from the database. We can construct dynamic JavaBeans (or DynaBeans) that we use to hold database data. The mapping of a database to DynaBeans is covered in the last section.

TESTING THE CALLVIEW METHOD

We have enough in place now that we can write the tests for `callView`, as shown in listing 14.6.

To make the test easier to read, we create a `createCommandResult` private method. This utility method creates arbitrary DynaBean objects, like those that will be returned by `executeCommand`. In `testCallView`, we place the DynaBeans in the HTTP request where the JSP can find them.

Listing 14.6   Unit tests for `callView`

```
[...]
public class TestAdminServlet extends ServletTestCase {
[...]
    private Collection createCommandResult() throws Exception {
        List results = new ArrayList();

        DynaProperty[] props = new DynaProperty[] {
            new DynaProperty("id", String.class),
            new DynaProperty("responsetime", Long.class)
        };
        BasicDynaClass dynaClass = new BasicDynaClass("requesttime",
                                                       null, props);

        DynaBean request1 = dynaClass.newInstance();
        request1.set("id", "12345");
        request1.set("responsetime", new Long(500));
        results.add(request1);
        DynaBean request2 = dynaClass.newInstance();
        request1.set("id", "56789");
        request1.set("responsetime", new Long(430));
        results.add(request2);

        return results;
    }

    public void testCallView() throws Exception {
        AdminServlet servlet = new AdminServlet();
        // Set the result of the execution of the command in the
        // HTTP request so that the JSP page can get the data to
        // display
        request.setAttribute("result", createCommandResult());
        servlet.callView(request);
    }
}
```

There's nothing we can verify in `testCallView`, so we don't perform any asserts there. The call to `callView` forwards to a JSP. But Cactus supports asserting the result of the execution of a JSP page. We can use Cactus to verify that the JSP will be able to display the data that we created in `createCommandResult`. Because this would be JSP testing, we show how it works in section 14.4 ("Testing JSPs").

Listing 14.7 shows the `callView` method that we use to forward the execution to the JSP in order to display the results.

Listing 14.7 Implementation of `callView` that makes the test pass

```
[...]
public class AdminServlet extends HttpServlet {
[...]
    public void callView(HttpServletRequest request) {
        request.getRequestDispatcher("/results.jsp")
                                    .forward(request, response);
    }
}
```

We don't have a test yet for the returned result, so not returning anything is enough. That will change once we test the JSP.

TESTING THE DOGET METHOD

Let's design the unit test for the `AdminServlet` doGet method. To begin, we need to verify that the test results are put in the servlet request as an attribute. Here's how to do that:

```
Collection results = (Collection) request.getAttribute("result");
assertNotNull("Failed to get execution results from the request",
results);
assertEquals(2, results.size());
```

This code leads to storing the command execution result in doGet. But where do we get the result? Ultimately, from the execution of `executeCommand`—but it isn't implemented yet. The typical solution to this kind of deadlock is to have an `execute-Command` that does nothing in `AdminServlet`. Then, in our test, we can implement executeCommand to return whatever we want:

```
AdminServlet servlet = new AdminServlet() {
    public Collection executeCommand(String command) throws Exception {
        return createCommandResult();
    }
};
```

We can now store the result of the test execution in doGet:

```
public void doGet(HttpServletRequest request,
                  HttpServletResponse response) throws ServletException {
    try {
        Collection results = executeCommand(getCommand(request));
        request.setAttribute("result", results);
    } catch (Exception e) {
        throw new ServletException("Failed to execute command", e);
    }
}
```

Notice that we need the `catch` block because the servlet specification says doGet must throw a `ServletException`. Because `executeCommand` can throw an exception, we need to wrap it into a `ServletException`.

If you run this code, you'll find that you've forgotten to set the command to execute in the HTTP request as a parameter. You need a `beginDoGet` method to do that, such as this:

```
public void beginDoGet(WebRequest request) {
    request.addParameter("command", "SELECT...");
}
```

With this method we're ready to complete the test.

The `doGet` code is shown in listing 14.8.

Listing 14.8 Implementation of doGet that makes the tests pass

```
[...]
public class AdminServlet extends HttpServlet {
[...]
    public Collection executeCommand(String command) throws Exception {
        throw new RuntimeException("not implemented");                    ◁—❶
    }

    public void doGet(HttpServletRequest request,
                      HttpServletResponse response) throws ServletException {
        try {
            Collection results = executeCommand(getCommand(request));
            request.setAttribute("result", results);

        } catch (Exception e) {
            throw new ServletException("Failed to execute command", e);
        }
    }
}
```

There are two points to note. First, the call to `callView` isn't present in `doGet`; the tests don't yet mandate it. (They will, but not until we write the unit tests for our JSP.)

Second, we throw a `RuntimeException` object if `executeCommand` is called ❶. We could return `null`, but throwing an exception is a better practice. An exception clearly states that we haven't implemented the method. If the method is called by mistake, there won't be any surprises.

JUnit best practice: throw an exception for methods that aren't implemented

When you're writing code, there are often times when you want to execute the code without having finished implementing all the methods. For example, if you're writing a mock object for an interface and the code you're testing uses only one method, you don't need to mock all methods. A good practice is to throw an exception instead of returning `null` values (or not returning anything for methods with no return value). There are two good reasons: doing this states clearly to anyone reading the code that the method isn't implemented, and it ensures that if the method is called, it will behave in such a way that you can't mistake skeletal behavior for real behavior.

So far, we've discussed the Administrator application and shown how to test one part of it, the servlet part. Now it's time to move on and concentrate on probably the most difficult-to-test part of the application, the frontend.

14.4 Testing JSPs

In this section, we continue with the Administration application we introduced in the previous section. Here, we concentrate on testing the view components—namely the JavaServer Pages (JSPs).

14.4.1 *Revisiting the Administration application*

We call the application by sending an HTTP request (from our browser) to the Admin-Servlet (figure 14.2). We pass a SQL query to run as an HTTP parameter, which is retrieved by the AdminServlet. The security filter intercepts the HTTP request and verifies that the SQL query is harmless (it's a SELECT query). Then, the servlet executes the query on the database, stores the resulting objects in the HTTP Request object, and calls the Results View page. The JSP takes the results from the Request and displays them, nicely formatted, using custom JSP tags from our tag library.

14.4.2 *What is JSP unit testing?*

First, let's remove any doubt: what we call *unit testing a JSP* isn't about unit testing the servlet that's generated by the compilation of the JSP. We also assume that the JSP is well designed, which means there's no Java code in it. If the page must handle any presentation logic, the logic is encapsulated in a JavaBean or in a taglib. We can perform two kinds of tests to unit test a JSP: test the JSP page itself in isolation and/or test the JSP's taglibs.

We can isolate the JSP from the backend by simulating the JavaBeans it uses and then verifying that the returned page contains the expected data. We use Cactus to demonstrate this type of test. Because mock objects (see chapter 7) operate only on Java code, we can't use a pure mock objects solution to unit test our JSP in isolation. We could also write functional tests for the JSP using a framework such as HttpUnit. But doing so means going all the way to the backend of the application, possibly to the database. With a combination of Cactus and mock objects, we can prevent calling the backend and keep our focus on unit testing the JSPs themselves. We can also unit test the custom tags used in the JSP.

14.4.3 *Unit testing a JSP in isolation with Cactus*

The strategy for unit testing JSPs in isolation with Cactus is defined in figure 14.3.

Here's what happens. The Cactus test case class must extend ServletTestCase (or JspTestCase):

   1 In the test*XXX* method (called by Cactus from inside the container), we create the mock objects that will be used by the JSP. The JSP gets its dynamic

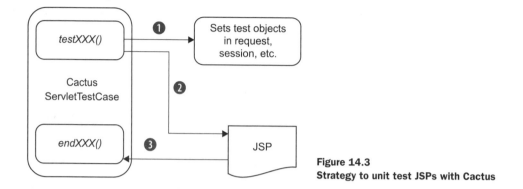

Figure 14.3
Strategy to unit test JSPs with Cactus

information either from the container-implicit object (`HttpServletRequest`, `HttpServletResponse`, or `ServletConfig`) or from a taglib.

2 Still in test*XXX*, we perform a `forward` to call the JSP under test. The JSP then executes, getting the mock data set up in step 1.

3 Cactus calls end*XXX*, passing to it the output from the JSP. This allows us to assert the content of the output and verify that the data we set up found its way to the JSP output, in the correct location on the page.

14.4.4 *Executing a JSP with SQL results data*

Let's see some action on the Administration application. In the servlet section ("Testing servlets and filters"), we defined that the results of executing the SQL query would be passed to the JSP by storing them as a collection of `DynaBean` objects in the `HttpServletRequest` object. Thanks to the dynamic nature of DynaBeans, we can easily write a generic JSP that will display any data contained in the DynaBeans. DynaBeans provide metadata about the data they contain. We can create a generic table with columns corresponding to the fields of the DynaBeans, as shown in listing 14.9.

> **Listing 14.9   Results View JSP (results.jsp)**

```
<%@ page contentType="text/html;charset=UTF-8" language="java" %>
<%@ taglib prefix="c" uri="http://jakarta.apache.org/taglibs/core" %>
<%@ taglib prefix="d" uri="/dynabeans" %>

<html>
   <head>
     <title>Results Page</title>
   </head>
   <body bgcolor="white">
     <table border="1">
        <d:properties var="properties"
           item="${requestScope.results[0]}"/>

        <tr>
           <c:forEach var="property" items="${properties}">
```

```
            <th><c:out value="${property.name}"/></th>
        </c:forEach>
    </tr>

    <c:forEach var="result" items="${requestScope.results}">
        <tr>
            <c:forEach var="property" items="${properties}">
                <td><d:getProperty name="${property.name}"
                                    item="${result}"/></td>
            </c:forEach>
        </tr>
    </c:forEach>
</table>
</body>
</html>
```

We use both JSTL tags and custom taglibs to write the JSP. The JSTL tag library is a standard set of useful and generic tags. It's divided into several categories (core, XML, formatting, and SQL). The category used here is the core, which provides output, management of variables, conditional logic, loops, text imports, and URL manipulation.

We also write two custom tags, <d:properties> and <d:getProperty>, which are used to extract information from the DynaBeans. <d:properties> extracts the name of all properties of a DynaBean, and <d:getProperty> extracts the value of a given DynaBean property.

There are two reasons for writing these custom tags. The primary reason is that it isn't possible to extract DynaBean information without (*ouch!*) embedding Java code in the JSP (at least not with the current implementation of the JSTL tags and the DynaBean package). The second reason is that it gives us a chance to write and unit test custom taglibs of our own.

WRITING THE CACTUS TEST

Now let's write a Cactus ServletTestCase for the JSP. The callView method from the AdminServlet forwards control to the Results View JSP, as shown in listing 14.10.

Listing 14.10 shows a unit test for callView that sets up the DynaBean objects in the Request, calls callView, and then verifies that the JSP output is what we expect.

Listing 14.10 TestAdminServlet.java: unit tests for results.jsp

```
[...]
public class TestAdminServlet extends ServletTestCase {
    private Collection createCommandResult() throws Exception {      ◄──❶
        List results = new ArrayList();

        DynaProperty[] props = new DynaProperty[] {
            new DynaProperty("id", String.class),
            new DynaProperty("responsetime", Long.class)
        };
        BasicDynaClass dynaClass = new
                            BasicDynaClass("requesttime",null,props);
```

```
        DynaBean request1 = dynaClass.newInstance();
        request1.set("id", "12345");
        request1.set("responsetime", new Long(500));
        results.add(request1);

        DynaBean request2 = dynaClass.newInstance();
        request2.set("id", "56789");
        request2.set("responsetime", new Long(430));
        results.add(request2);

        return results;
    }

    public void testCallView() throws Exception {
        AdminServlet servlet = new AdminServlet();
        request.setAttribute("results", createCommandResult());
        servlet.callView(request, response);
    }
    public void endCallView(com.meterware.httpunit.WebResponse response)
                                                throws Exception {
        assertTrue(response.isHTML());
[...]
        assertEquals("12345",
            response.getTables()[0].getCellAsText(1, 0));
        assertEquals("500",
            response.getTables()[0].getCellAsText(1, 1));
        assertEquals("56789",
            response.getTables()[0].getCellAsText(2, 0));
        assertEquals("430",
            response.getTables()[0].getCellAsText(2, 1));
    }
}
```

We start by defining the `createCommand` method ❶, which puts several DynaBeans in the request ❷. Then in the `testCallView` ❸ method (remember that it's executed on the server side) we instantiate the servlet to test ❹, set the DynaBeans in the request ❹, and call the JSP ❺ to display the result. The `endCallView` ❻, which is executed on the client side, has a `com.meterware.httpunit.WebResponse` parameter, holding the response from the server. In ❼ we assert different statements against the response of the server, in order to verify that the JSP displays the results properly.

We use the Cactus HttpUnit integration in the `endCallView` method to assert the returned HTML page. When Cactus needs to execute the `endXXX` method, first it looks for an `endXXX (org.apache.cactus.WebResponse)` signature. If this signature is found, Cactus calls it; if it isn't, Cactus looks for an `endXXX (com.meterware.httpunit.WebResponse)` signature, and if it's available, calls it. Using the `org.apache.cactus.WebResponse` object, we can perform asserts on the content of the HTTP response, such as verifying the returned cookies, the returned HTTP headers, or the content. The Cactus `org.apache.cactus.WebResponse` object supports a simple API. The HttpUnit web response API (`com.meterware.httpunit.WebResponse`) is much more comprehensive. With HttpUnit, we can view the returned XML or HTML pages as DOM objects. In listing 14.10, we use the provided HTML DOM to verify that the returned web page contains the expected HTML table.

In this section we described how to test the frontend of the Administrator application. What we're still missing is a few pages that will reveal to us how to unit test the `AdministratorBean` EJB, which executes our queries on the database. The secrets of EJB testing are covered in the next section.

14.5 Testing EJBs

Testing EJBs has a reputation of being a difficult task. One of the main reasons is that EJBs are components that run inside a container. You need to either abstract out the container services used by your code or perform in-container unit testing. In this section, we demonstrate different techniques that can help you write EJB unit tests. We also continue developing our Administrator application, showing you the module that executes the SQL queries.

The architecture of the Administrator application goes like this: The command to be executed gets through the filter, which determines whether it's a `SELECT` query. After that, the `AdminServlet` eventually receives the command/query.

The execution flow starts in the `AdminServlet` `doGet` method. It receives the HTTP requests and calls the `getCommand` method to extract the SQL query from it. It then calls `executeCommand` to execute the database call (using the extracted SQL query) and return the results as a `Collection`. The results are then put in the HTTP request (as a request attribute) and, at last, `doGet` calls `callView` to invoke the JSP page that presents the results to the user. So far, we've given no implementation of the `execute-Command` method. The idea behind it would be to call a given EJB, which would execute the query on a given database. One simple implementation of the `executeCommand` method would be as follows:

```
public Collection executeCommand(String command) throws Exception {
    Context context = new InitialContext();
    IAdministratorLocal administrator = (IAdministratorLocal)
                                    context.lookup("AdministratorBean");
    return administrator.execute(command);
}
```

The EJB itself is shown in listing 14.11.

Listing 14.11 AdministratorEJB

```
[...]

@Stateless
public class AdministratorBean implements IAdministratorLocal {

    public Collection execute(String sql) throws Exception {
        Connection connection = getConnection();
        // For simplicity, we'll assume the SQL is a SELECT query
        ResultSet resultSet =
                connection.createStatement().executeQuery(sql);    ❶  ❷
        RowSetDynaClass rsdc = new RowSetDynaClass(resultSet);
```

```
            resultSet.close();
            connection.close();
            return rsdc.getRows();                                    ◄─┐
    }                                                                   │
                                                                        ❸
    private Connection getConnection()
                        throws NamingException, SQLException {
        //RETURN SOME DATABASE CONNECTION
    }
}
```

We call the execute method from the servlet with the given query; there we try to
obtain a valid connection and execute the query ❶. After that we create a RowSet-
DynaClass object from the ResultSet ❷, and we return its rows ❸.

In order to test the EJB with Cactus, we have to instantiate it and then assert against
the result of the execution. We can use, again, mock objects to simulate the JNDI
lookup, but this approach is unnecessarily complicated, so we won't list it here. Let's
look at the test case for the EJB in listing 14.12, and then we'll go through it and discuss it.

Listing 14.12   Test case for `AdministratorEJB`

```
[...]
public class TestAdministratorEJB extends ServletTestCase {

    private IAdministratorLocal administrator;

    public void setUp() throws Exception {
        Properties properties = new Properties();                     ◄─❶
        properties.put("java.naming.factory.initial",
            "org.jnp.interfaces.NamingContextFactory");
        properties.put("java.naming.factory.url.pkgs",
            "org.jboss.naming rg.jnp.interfaces");

        InitialContext ctx = new InitialContext(properties);

        administrator = (IAdministratorLocal) ctx.lookup(
                "ch14-cactus-ear-cactified/"
                +AdministratorBean.class.getSimpleName()
                +"/local");                                           ◄─❷
    }

    public void testExecute() throws Exception {
        String sql = "SELECT * FROM CUSTOMER";
        Collection result = administrator.execute(sql);

        Iterator beans = result.iterator();
        assertTrue(beans.hasNext());                                  ◄─┐
        DynaBean bean1 = (DynaBean) beans.next();                       │
        assertEquals(bean1.get("Id"), new Integer(1));                  ❸
        assertEquals(bean1.get("name"), "John Doe");                    │
        assertTrue(!beans.hasNext());                                 ──┘
    }
}
```

At ❶ we start by initializing the context in the setUp method (remember that this method is called before each test method), and we get hold of a valid IAdministrator-BeanLocal instance from the JNDI ❷. Then in each test method we invoke the methods on the EJB with different parameters and assert the validity of the result ❸.

So far, we've covered what you need in order to write Cactus test cases. Before we rush into the section that deals with execution of our Cactus tests, it's essential that you get familiar with a project called Cargo. The tight integration between Cargo and Cactus is one of the new features that facilitate running your tests.

14.6 *What is Cargo?*

What we've seen so far is pretty much the bulk of how to write Cactus tests cases. At the beginning of the chapter, we mentioned that Cactus test cases are executed inside the container. In this section and in the ones that follow we focus on how to integrate execution of Cactus tests in your build lifecycle. In order to keep the Extreme Programming principles, you need to execute the tests every time you make a build. This requires a tight integration between Cactus and the build system—Ant or Maven. But before we jump into that integration, you need to become familiar with a project they both rely on: Cargo.

Cargo (http://cargo.codehaus.org/) is an open source project started, again, by Vincent Massol in 2004. The aim of the project is to automate container management in a generic way so that we could use the same mechanism to start and deploy a WAR file with Tomcat as we could with WebLogic or almost any other application server. It provides an API around most of the existent Java EE containers for managing those containers (starting, stopping, and deploying). But Cargo is a bit more than just an API, and that's where its strength comes from; it provides Ant tasks and Maven (1.x and 2.x) plug-ins for facilitating the management of those containers.

After this brief introduction to the secrets of Cargo you're probably asking yourself, what's the connection between Cargo and Cactus? The Cactus team realizes that the idea behind the project is great, but it seems as though there's too much of a burden regarding the process of executing the tests. Once written, the tests need to be packaged in a WAR or EAR archive; then the application descriptors need to be patched with the appropriate redirectors. After that, before the execution gets started, the archive needs to be *deployed* in a *container* that's already *started*. You've probably already noticed the three italicized words in the previous sentence. And you've probably already guessed that the main idea of the Cactus development team was to hide all the complexity regarding the management of the container by means of Cargo.

This gives us full automation. If we use Cargo's Ant tasks (or Maven plug-ins) to start the container, then deploy the WAR/EAR in it, and then stop the container we have achieved the Extreme Programming principles of *continuous integration*. Our build is fully automated, isn't it? That's all true, but deploying the archive with the tests by itself doesn't do anything magical—we still need to figure out a way to trigger the execution of the tests when the archive is deployed. We also need a way to prepare the archive for deployment. This is all part of the tight integration between Cactus and the various build systems. We deal with this integration in subsequent chapters.

14.7   *Executing Cactus tests with Ant*

The first way to fire up Cactus tests that we're going to show seems to be the most common one. Using Ant is easy and straightforward. If you're new to Ant, we'd like to recommend to you *Ant in Action*, by Steve Loughran and Erik Hatcher—a marvelous book. Also, before you read this section, please make sure you've already read chapter 8.

14.7.1   *Cactus tasks to prepare the archive*

Cactus comes bundled with two kinds of Ant tasks: the first one will facilitate you in preparing the archive (WAR or EAR) to hold the test cases, and the second will invoke the tests. We go through these tasks one after the other and show you how to use them.

The process of preparing the archive for executing the tests is called *cactification*. This term was introduced by the Cactus team. Imagine you have at some point an archive (a WAR or EAR file), which is the application that you want to deploy. The cactification process includes adding the required JARs into the lib folder of the archive and also patching the web.xml to include desired Cactus redirectors.

According to the type of archive that you want to cactify, there are two different tasks that you may want to use: cactifywar and cactifyear. Before we rush into describing these tasks, let's first take a minute to focus on the build.xml skeleton that we use for our presentation purposes (see listing 14.13).

Listing 14.13   Build.xml skeleton to execute the Cactus tests

```
<project name="Cactus sample tests" basedir="."
                         xmlns:ivy="antlib:org.apache.ivy.ant">

<target name="init" depends="">
    [...]
        <property name="target.dir" location="${basedir}/target"/>      ❶
        <property name="classes.dir" location="${target.dir}/classes"/>
        [...]

        <ivy:configure file="ivysettings.xml" />                        ❷
        <ivy:retrieve  file="ivy.xml" sync="true"/>

            <path id="compile.cp">
                <fileset dir="${lib.dir}">
                    <include name="*.*"/>                        ⬅❸
                </fileset>
            </path>
        </target>
```

```
<target name="prepare" depends="init">
    <mkdir dir="${target.dir}"/>
    [...]                                                    ⟵┐
    <mkdir dir="${lib.dir}"/>                                 ④
</target>                                                    ⟵┘

<target name="load.tasks" depends="init, prepare">
    <taskdef resource="cactus.tasks" classpathref="compile.cp"/>    ⟵❺
</target>

<target name="compile" depends="init,prepare">
    <javac srcdir="${src.dir}" destdir="${classes.dir}"
                         classpathref="compile.cp"/>         ⟵❻
</target>

<target name="prepareJar" depends="init,prepare">
    <jar jarfile="${target.dir}/ch14.ejb3">                  ⟵❼
        <fileset dir="${classes.dir}"/>
    </jar>
</target>

<target name="prepareWar" depends="init,prepare">
    <war destfile="${target.dir}/ch14.war"
                webxml="${basedir}/src/webapp/WEB-INF/web.xml">    ⟵❽
        <classes dir="${classes.dir}"/>
    </war>
</target>

<target name="packageEar" depends="init,compile, prepareJar,
prepareWar">
    <ear destfile="${target.dir}/ch14.ear"
                        appxml="${app.dir}/application.xml">    ⟵❾
        <fileset dir="${target.dir}" includes="*.jar,*.war"/>
    </ear>
</target>
[...]
</project>
```

This Ant descriptor is pretty simple. As you can see, one of the first things to do is declare some properties in the `init` target ❶. We use these properties later in the script. In this target we also resolve the additional dependencies with Ivy ❷ and construct a classpath `refid` ❸. The `prepare` target prepares the folder structure for the build ❹, and after that we use the `taskdef` task ❺ to define the external tasks (remember that `cactifyXXX` and `cargo` tasks are external tasks that come with Cactus/Cargo; they aren't part of the official Ant tasks). Then we compile our code ❻ and produce either a JAR file containing the EJBs ❼ or a WAR file ❽ containing the servlets (depending on what part of the code we test). We might use also a separate target to produce the EAR file ❾ that we will need.

Now that you're familiar with the structure of the build.xml, it's time to focus on the first set of tasks that Cactus provides.

THE CACTIFYWAR TASK

This task is used when your application is a WAR file and you want to cactify it. The `cactifywar` task extends the built-in `war` Ant task so it also supports all attributes and nested elements that the war task supports. Nothing explains better than an example, so let's start the test cases from this chapter using Ant. We walk through the build.xml in listing 14.14 and then discuss it.

Listing 14.14   Build.xml to present `cactifywar` task

```
<target name="cactifywar" depends="init,load.tasks, prepareWar">
    <cactifywar srcfile="${target.dir}/ch14.war"
                destfile="${target.dir}/ch14-cactified.war"/>
</target>
```

In the cactifywar target we call the cactifywar task, which we imported in the first steps (in the load.tasks target). As you can see, the cactifywar task takes the following parameters: srcfile, destfile, and a list of redirectors we want to define. There's a bunch of other, nonrequired parameters, all of which are perfectly documented on the Cactus website (http://jakarta.apache.org/cactus), where you can find additional help. Also, once again, because the cactifywar task extends the war task, you can pass all the parameters for the war task to it—they're all valid.

In the srcfile attribute you specify the archive file of the application that you want to cactify. The important thing to notice here is that you may need to specify not only the name of the file but also the destination path to it. In the destfile parameter, you specify the name of the cactified file to produce.

You also may want to describe a list of redirectors in the cactifywar task. This list of redirectors describes URL patterns to map the Cactus test redirectors to the nested elements filterredirector, jspredirector, and servletredirector. If you don't specify those elements, the test redirectors will be mapped to the default URL pattern.

After executing the target with

```
ant cactifywar
```

we should get the desired cactified archive, which we can examine.

THE CACTIFYEAR TASK

The cactifyear task is the analogue of the cactifywar task, but instead it's used to cactify EAR applications. It's a bit different from cactifywar, because in most cases EAR applications contain a WAR archive that needs to be cactified. The cactifyear task is, again, an external task that comes from the Cactus team and extends the Ant ear task. This way it accepts all of the parameters that are valid for the ear task.

Let's now execute our tests from an EAR archive (listing 14.15), and then we'll walk through the example application and discuss the different aspects.

Listing 14.15   Build.xml to present `cactifyear` task

```
<cactifyear srcfile="${target.dir}/ch14.ear"
            destfile="${target.dir}/ch14-cactified.ear">      ←─①
    <cactuswar srcfile="${target.dir}/ch14.war"
               mergewebxml="${src.webapp.dir}/WEB-INF/web.xml"
               context="/">
```

```
            <classes dir="${classes.dir}">
                <include name="Test*.class"/>
            </classes>
            <fileset dir="${src.webapp.dir}">
                <include name="*.jsp"/>
            </fileset>
            <lib dir="${lib.dir}">
                <include name="commons-beanutils*.jar"/>      ◁─❷
            </lib>
        </cactuswar>
    </cactifyear>
```

Once again, we use the build.xml skeleton from listing 14.13, and here we list the target that's responsible for the cactification of the already packaged EAR file.

As you can see, the `cactifyear` task accepts the `srcfile` and `destfile` parameters again ❶. Their meaning here is exactly the same as for the `cactifywar` task. The new component here is a `cactuswar` nested element. This element has all the parameters of the `cactifywar` task except the `destfile` parameter. The web application will always be named cactus.war and placed in the root of the EAR. We also add the commons-beanutils.jar file to the web application ❷, because our servlet and filter test cases need it.

Once we execute with

```
ant cactifyear
```

we get the cactified archive, which we can examine.

THE CACTUS TASK

Because the other Cactus-related tasks are external Ant tasks that extend some of the internal Ant tasks, this concept is also valid for the `cactus` task. The `cactus` task is used to execute the Cactus tests, and because every Cactus test is a pure JUnit test, you've probably already figured out what task the `cactus` task extends. That's right—the `cactus` task extends the `junit` task. This way, all the parameters that the `junit` task accepts are also valid for the `cactus` task.

Listing 14.16 extends listing 14.13 with the `cactus` task that executes the tests from the EAR archive.

Listing 14.16 The test target to demonstrate the `cactus` task

```
[...]
    <target name="test" depends="init,cactifyear">
        <cactus earfile="${target.dir}/ch14-cactified.ear"         ◁─❶
            printsummary="yes">
            <classpath>
                <path refid="compile.cp"/>
                <pathelement location="${classes.dir}"/>
                <pathelement location="${test.classes.dir}"/>
            </classpath>                                            ❷
            <containerset>                                     ◁──┘
                <cargo containerId="${jboss.container.id}"         ◁─❸
```

```
                    output="${logs.dir}/output.log"
                    log="${logs.dir}/cargo.log" home="${jboss.home}">
                <configuration>
                    <property name="cargo.servlet.port" value="8080"/>
                    <property name="cargo.logging" value="low"/>
                    <deployable type="ear" file="${target.dir}/ch14-
cactified.ear"/>
                </configuration>
            </cargo>
        </containerset>

        <formatter type="plain"/>
        <batchtest todir="${reports.dir}">
            <fileset dir="${src.dir}/cactus/">
                <include name="**/Test*.java"/>
            </fileset>
        </batchtest>
    </cactus>
  </target>
[...]
```

As you can see, the cactus task is used in connection with the cargo tasks (this is why we introduced Cargo a while ago). With the one declaration in the listing, we've defined all the necessary information to start and execute tests and stop the container.

The warfile/earfile parameter ❶ is used to specify the name of an archive file that we're going to deploy. This has to be the name of our cactified WAR/EAR file that holds our test cases as well as the classes that we want to test (it's the result of the corresponding cactify task). It's also obligatory to add a containerset nested element ❷. In this nested element we specify a number of cargo tasks ❸, which will define the containers in which to execute our tests. When we say that we specify cargo tasks, we mean it—these are pure cargo tasks, and they can take any parameter that a normal cargo task can take: proxy, timeout, server port, and so on.

In the given cargo tasks we have to specify the ID of the containers, the configuration of the containers, and the deployable (the cactified archive that contains our test cases). Cargo tasks can work with installed local or remote instances of a container; you need only specify the home directory of that container. But there's more; these tasks also let you specify the so-called ZipURLInstaller. In this installer you specify a URL to a given container archive, and Cargo will download the given container from there, extract the container from the archive, start the container, and deploy the given deployable. Then Cactus will execute the tests inside the container, and Cargo will stop the container. That's a fully automated cycle, and the Cactus project comes with several sample applications that use this automation.

Our application is done; not only this, but it's also well tested using Cactus. You already saw how to execute your tests with Ant, so it's time to show one final way to execute the given tests, this time using another build tool: Maven.

14.8   Executing Cactus tests with Maven2x

Another common approach for executing your Cactus tests is including them in your Maven[1] build.

Many people use Maven as their build system, and until version 1.8.1 of Cactus, the only way of executing Cactus tests with Maven was calling the Ant plug-in for Maven and executing the tests via Ant. The latest version of Cactus, however, contains a cactus-maven2 plug-in that significantly facilitates the cactification process. The Cactus Maven plug-in consists of two MOJOs (Maven POJOs, or plain old Java objects) you can use for cactification of a WAR or EAR.

Let's walk through the examples and see how to use them.

14.8.1   Maven2 cactifywar MOJO

Listing 14.17 shows a common pom.xml file that we enhance later.

Listing 14.17   Sample pom.xml for running the Cactus tests

```
<project>
    <modelVersion>4.0.0</modelVersion>
    <groupId>com.manning.junitbook2</groupId>
    <artifactId>ch14-cactus</artifactId>
    <packaging>jar</packaging>
    <version>2.0-SNAPSHOT</version>
</project>
```

This is a basic pom.xml, and we can use it for all our purposes: compile our source code and package our application in a WAR archive. There's nothing fancy here; we're just using the corresponding plug-ins of Maven. After executing the build with

```
mvn package
```

we should see the resulting archive and can examine its accuracy. Now we can add the Cactus plug-ins to prepare the archive for deployment.

The Cactus plug-in is nothing more than a declaration of several other plug-ins, in the correct order. We now show how to declare these plug-ins. The next three listings (14.18, 14.19, and 14.20) should be considered one big listing, but for the sake of readability, we've split them into three.

Listing 14.18   Build section of the pom.xml to enable Cactus tests execution

```
<build>
    <plugins>
      <plugin>
        <groupId>org.apache.cactus</groupId>
        <artifactId>ca        ctus.integration.maven2</artifactId>
        <version>1.8.1</version>
```
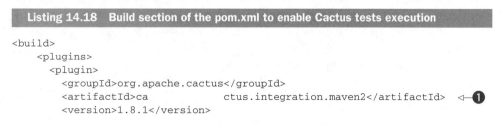

---

[1]   From now on, whenever we discuss the term *Maven*, we mean the Maven2 project, because the authors of this book consider Maven1 a dead technology.

```
    <configuration>
      <srcFile>${project.build.directory}/${pom.artifactId}-
                          ${pom.version}.war</srcFile>          ◁┐
      <destFile>${project.build.directory}/${pom.artifactId}-   ②
                          cactified.war</destFile>             ◁┘
      <testClasses>
        <directory>target/test-classes</directory>            ◁┐
        <includes>                                             ③
          <include>**/**Test*.class</include>                 ◁┘
        </includes>
      </testClasses>
      <libDependencies>
        <dependency>
            <groupId>commons-beanutils</groupId>              ④
            <artifactId>commons-beanutils</artifactId>
        </dependency>
      </libDependencies>
    </configuration>
    <executions>
      <execution>
        <id>cactus-cactifywar</id>
        <phase>pre-integration-test</phase>           ◁─⑤
        <goals>
          <goal>cactifywar</goal>
        </goals>
      </execution>
    </executions>
  </plugin>
<!-- Continue with listing 14.19 here -->
```

As we mentioned already, all we do is define three plug-ins, one after another in the correct order. The first one is the `cactus.integration.maven2` plug-in ①. We use it for cactification of the WAR file we got from the previous listing. Again, as in the `cactifywar` task, we specify `srcfile` and `destfile` parameters ②. We also specify which test classes to include ③ and which libraries to include in the WEB-INF/lib folder ④. In this case, we want only the commons-beanutils, because our tests use it.

It's important to specify the execution order of the plug-ins. In Maven we specify the execution order by attaching every plug-in goal to a single phase. For instance, in the listing we attached our plug-in's `cactifywar` goal to the pre-integration-test phase ⑤. This phase, as its name implies, is executed by Maven just before the integration-test phase (in which we're going to execute our tests). This is perfect, because we want our package cactified before we execute our tests.

Listing 14.19 displays the second plug-in.

Listing 14.19   Continuation of the plug-in declarations from listing 14.18

```
<!--We continue from listing 14.18 -->
  <plugin>
    <groupId>org.codehaus.cargo</groupId>
    <artifactId>cargo-maven2-plugin</artifactId>          ◁─⑥
```

```
        <version>1.0-beta-2</version>
        <executions>
          <execution>
            <id>start-container</id>
            <phase>pre-integration-test</phase>                    ←—❼
            <goals>
              <goal>start</goal>
            </goals>
          </execution>
          <execution>
            <id>stop-container</id>
            <phase>post-integration-test</phase>                   ←—❽
            <goals>
              <goal>stop</goal>
            </goals>
          </execution>
        </executions>
        <configuration>
          <wait>false</wait>
          <timeout>20000</timeout>
          <container>
            <containerId>tomcat5x</containerId>
            <zipUrlInstaller>
              <url>http://apache.speedbone.de/tomcat/
                  tomcat-5/v5.5.25/bin/apache-tomcat-5.5.27.zip</url>
              <installDir>${basedir}/install</installDir>
            </zipUrlInstaller>
          </container>
          <configuration>
            <deployables>
            <deployable>
              <location>cactifiedByMaven2.war</location>
              <pingURL>http://localhost:8080/test/</pingURL>
              <properties>
                 <context>/test</context>
              </properties>
            </deployable>
            </deployables>
          </configuration>
        </configuration>
      </plugin>
      <!--Continue with listing 14.20 here -->
```

The next plug-in declaration is for the `cargo-maven2-plugin`, which we use to declare the containers to execute our tests in ❻. As you can see, we attach its `start` goal to the pre-integration-test phase to start the container before we execute the tests ❼. But wait a second; didn't we attach the `cactifywar` goal to the same phase? What will be the execution order here? In this case, we need two different goals attached to the same phase, because we have more than one thing to do before the integration phase of Maven. In this situation, the `cactus` plug-in will execute first, because it's declared right before the `cargo` plug-in. And here you can see why we insisted that the *order* of declaration of the plug-ins in the <build> section is so important. This way we first prepare the cactified archive for deployment, and then we start the container with this archive as a deployable. We also attach this plug-in's stop goal with the post-integration-test phase ❽. This is normal; we need to stop the container once the tests are executed.

Listing 14.20 displays the third plug-in: the `maven-surefire-plugin`.

Listing 14.20   Continuation of the plug-in declarations from listing 14.19

```
<!—We continue from listing 14.19-->
<plugin>
  <groupId>org.apache.maven.plugins</groupId>
  <artifactId>maven-surefire-plugin</artifactId>          ◁─❾
  <configuration>
    <skip>true</skip>                                      ◁─❿
  </configuration>
  <executions>
    <execution>
      <id>surefire-it</id>
      <phase>integration-test</phase>                     ◁─⓫
      <goals>
        <goal>test</goal>
      </goals>
      <configuration>
        <skip>false</skip>                                 ◁─⓬
        <systemProperties>
          <property>
            <name>cactus.contextURL</name>                ◁─⓭
            <value>http://localhost:8080/test/</value>
          </property>
        </systemProperties>
      </configuration>
    </execution>
  </executions>
</plugin>
</plugins>
</build>
```

The last plug-in declaration is for the `maven-surefire-plugin` ❾. As you already saw in chapter 10, this Maven plug-in is responsible for executing JUnit tests. Because every Cactus test is also a JUnit test, we can use this plug-in to execute our Cactus tests. There are a couple of things to notice in its declaration. As you can see, we declare the `skip` parameter with `true` ❿. That's because the Surefire plug-in is by default attached to the test phase. We surely don't want it attached to this phase, so we declare the `skip` parameter to `true`, which will cause the plug-in to skip the execution. Further in the declaration we attach the test goal with the integration-test phase ⓫ (where we want it to be), and we declare the `skip` parameter with `false` ⓬. This will cause the plug-in to execute the tests in the integration-test phase, just as we want it to happen. There's also one thing to remember: whenever you execute Cactus tests, you always have to specify `cactus.contextURL` ⓭. The Cactus Ant task does it for you, but the Surefire plug-in doesn't, so that's what we do in the last part.

14.8.2 *Maven2 cactifyear MOJO*

To execute Cactus tests from an EAR file, we have to follow the same procedure as for the WAR file, except for the cactification of the archive. That's why we cover the `cactifyear` Cactus plug-in in this section. Listing 14.21 cactifies our example EAR package.

Listing 14.21 `cactifyear` Cactus plug-in declaration

```
<plugin>
        <groupId>org.apache.cactus</groupId>
        <artifactId>cactus.integration.maven2</artifactId>
        <version>1.8.1</version>
        <configuration>
          <srcFile>target/${pom.artifactId}-${pom.version}.ear</srcFile>      ◁┐
          <destFile>${project.build.directory}/${pom.artifactId}-                ①
                          cactified.ear</destFile>                             ◁┘

          <cactusWar>                                                      ◁─②
             <context>/</context>                                         ◁┐
             <testClasses>                                                 │
                <directory>target/test-classes</directory>               ③
                <includes>
                   <include>**/*Test*.*</include>                         ◁─④
                </includes>
             </testClasses>
             <version>2.3</version>                                        ◁─⑤
          </cactusWar>
        </configuration>
        <executions>
          <execution>
             <id>cactus-cactifyear</id>
             <phase>pre-integration-test</phase>                           ◁─⑥
             <goals>
                <goal>cactifyear</goal>
             </goals>
          </execution>
        </executions>
</plugin>
```

This declaration seems simple enough. All we have to do here is provide the `srcfile` and `destfile` parameters ①. In the `<cactusWar>` section ②, we describe parameters related to the WAR application inside our EAR file, such as the context of the application ③, which test classes to include ④, and which version of the web.xml will be used ⑤. In ⑥ we attach the plug-in to the pre-integration phase of Maven. The rest of the pom.xml is the same as the one in the previous section, so we won't discuss it further.

Now we move on and show you one other way of executing your Cactus tests. This time we use Jetty as an embedded container. Jetty is not only a servlet container, but it also provides you with an API for manipulating the container. This API is used by Cactus to fire up the container for you, execute the tests, and then stop the container—all with a single command.

14.9   *Executing Cactus tests from the browser*

We know several different ways to execute JUnit tests. We looked at executions through JUnit's own test runner, with the Ant and Maven test runners, and also through Jetty. As you already know, Cactus tests are also JUnit tests, so the question, "What is the analogue of the JUnit text test runner for Cactus?" seems valid and reasonable. JUnit's test runner communicates directly with the JVM in which the execution takes place and gets the result from there. Cactus tests are executed in the server JVM, so we need to find a way to communicate with the server (tell it to invoke the tests and get the results).

The easiest way to communicate with the server is via a browser. In order to do this, we need to take care of a couple of things.

First, we need to declare the `ServletTestRunner` servlet in the application's web.xml. The declaration is shown in listing 14.22.

Listing 14.22   `ServletTestRunner` declaration

```
[...]
<servlet>
    <servlet-name>ServletTestRunner</servlet-name>
    <servlet-class>
        org.apache.cactus.server.runner.ServletTestRunner
    </servlet-class>
</servlet>
[...]
<servlet-mapping>
    <servlet-name>ServletTestRunner</servlet-name>
    <url-pattern>/ServletTestRunner</url-pattern>
</servlet-mapping>
[...]
```

Once it's declared, we're going to use this servlet in our URL in the browser to tell the server to invoke the tests. We need to call the server with the following request in the browser:

```
http://server:port/mywebapp/ServletTestRunner?suite=mytestcase
```

Here you need to replace `server`, `port`, `mywebapp`, and `mytestcase` with the correct values of your server address, port number, context, and the fully qualified name (that is, with packages) of your `TestCase` class containing a `suite()` method.

After executing the given URL in the browser, the server should respond with the result shown in figure 14.4.

If you see a blank page, click the View Source option of your browser. It means your browser doesn't know how to display XML data. Okay, that's nice, but what if you want HTML instead of XML? Don't worry; there's a solution. Grab the XSLT stylesheet that comes with Cactus (cactus-report.xsl, based on the stylesheet used by

```
<?xml version="1.0" encoding="UTF-8" ?>
- <testsuites>
  - <testsuite name="org.apache.cactus.sample.TestSampleServlet" tests="13" failures="0" errors="0" time="0.871">
      <testcase name="testReadServletOutputStream" time="0.16" />
      <testcase name="testPostMethod" time="0.03" />
      <testcase name="testGetMethod" time="0.02" />
      <testcase name="testSetAttribute" time="0.04" />
      <testcase name="testSetRequestAttribute" time="0.03" />
      <testcase name="testSendParams" time="0.03" />
      <testcase name="testSendHeader" time="0.03" />
      <testcase name="testSendCookie" time="0.231" />
      <testcase name="testSendMultipleCookies" time="0.02" />
      <testcase name="testReceiveHeader" time="0.02" />
      <testcase name="testReceiveCookie" time="0.05" />
      <testcase name="testRequestDispatcherForward" time="0.13" />
      <testcase name="testRequestDispatcherInclude" time="0.02" />
    </testsuite>
  </testsuites>
```

Figure 14.4   XML result in the browser from Cactus tests

the `<junitreport>` Ant task), and drop it in your web app (in the root directory, for example). Then, open a browser and type

```
http://server:port/mywebapp/ServletTestRunner?suite=
➡mytestcase&xsl=cactus-report.xsl.
```

The .xsl stylesheet will generate the HTML report you're familiar with, so you can view it from within your browser.

14.10 Summary

When it comes to unit testing container applications, pure JUnit unit tests come up short. A mock objects approach (see chapter 7) works fine and should be used. But it misses a certain number of tests—specifically integration tests, which verify that components can talk to each other, that the components work when run inside the container, and that the components interact properly with the container. In order to perform these tests, an in-container testing strategy is required.

In the realm of Java EE components, the de facto standard framework for in-container unit testing is Jakarta Cactus. In this chapter, we ran through some simple tests using Cactus, in order to get a feel for how it's done. We also discussed how Cactus works, so we're now ready to in-container test our Java EE applications.

Testing the components from the Java EE spec is nice, but it isn't the whole picture. Most of our applications are heavily framework based. In the next chapters, we explore one of the most widely used MVC frameworks, JSF. We also introduce the JSFUnit project, which will let you test your JSF application inside the container.

Testing JSF applications

The first 90% of the code accounts for the first 10% of the development time. The remaining 10% of the code accounts for the other 90% of the development time.

—Tom Cargill

This chapter covers

- The problems of testing JSF applications
- Mock solution of the problems
- JSF unit/integration testing using JSFUnit
- JSF performance testing with JSFUnit

The Cactus framework we introduced in chapter 14 is great for testing most of the Java EE specifications. On a daily basis, the majority of Java developers write Java EE applications, all of which are based on the Java EE spec.

In this chapter we take a closer look at the newest member of the Java EE spec—the JavaServer Faces (JSF) technology. It's a standard specification developed through the Java Community Process (JCP) for building Java web-based user interfaces. We start the chapter by explaining what JSF is, the problems of testing JSF applications, and how to use the JSFUnit project to solve them. We then implement a sample `MusicStore` application and demonstrate the power of JSFUnit.

15.1 Introducing JSF

Apart from the specification we mentioned, people refer to JSF[1] as the implementation of this specification: a server-side, user-interface, component framework for Java technology–based applications. This means that different organizations can implement the specification and produce different frameworks, all compatible with the specification. Some of the most popular implementations are Apache MyFaces (http://myfaces.apache.org/) and Sun's Mojarra JSF reference implementation.

In this book, we use the Apache MyFaces implementation because we consider it the most robust.

Figure 15.1 shows an architectural overview of a sample JSF application. The JSF framework was intended to simplify development of web application. For this reason it's designed to get developers to think in terms of components, managed beans, page navigations, and so on, and not in terms of technical details such as request, response, session, and the like.

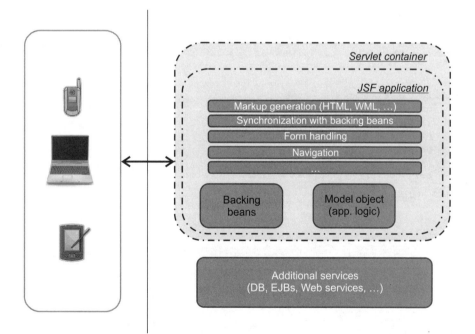

Figure 15.1   Architectural overview of a JSF application

---

[1] If you're new to the JavaServer Faces technology, we highly recommend *JavaServer Faces in Action*, by Kito Mann.

JSF handles most of the complexity that you might encounter during development of a web application. JSF also handles the user clicking a web browser button and sending a request to the server. This request needs to be translated in a way that your application can understand. The JSF framework is also responsible for translating and visualizing responses from the application in a way that the browser can display. The framework provides a large number of tag libraries that developers can use to visualize absolutely anything.

Next, we introduce a sample JSF application. In the course of the implementation we explain the different parts of the application, and further in the chapter we test our sample application.

15.2   *Introducing the sample application*

In the previous section we described the parts of a typical JSF application. We now introduce a real application, the `MusicStore` application, which we refine and test throughout this chapter.

The `MusicStore` is a simple JSF application that presents different kinds of music albums, which the user can navigate through and purchase. We start the implementation with a simple POJO (plain old Java object) representing an `Album`. The implementation is shown in listing 15.1.

Listing 15.1   Album.java POJO object

```
[...]

public class Album {                                  ←①
    private String name = null;
    private String author = null;
    private double price = 0;
    private int year = 0;
    private String style = null;
    private String imageURL = null;

        public Album(String name,                     ←②
                String author,
                double price,
                int year,
                String style,
                String imageURL) {
        this.name = name;
        this.author = author;
        this.price = price;
        this.year = year;
        this.style = style;
        this.imageURL = imageURL;
    }

//Getters and setter go here...
}
```

As you can see, the implementation is simple. The Album is a simple POJO that contains several properties ❶: the name of the album, author of the album, and so on. We have also added getters and setters for those properties and a constructor ❷ to instantiate different albums.

Listing 15.2 shows a manager class used to manipulate the albums.

Listing 15.2   The `AlbumManager` performs different operations on `Albums`

```
[...]
public class AlbumManager {
    final static List<Album> albums = new ArrayList<Album>();
    static {
        albums.add( new Album( ... ) );
        albums.add( new Album( ... ) );                     ❶
        albums.add( new Album( ... ) );
        albums.add( new Album( ... ) );
        albums.add( new Album( ... ) );
    }

    public static List<Album> getAvailableAlbums() {        ◁─❷
        return albums;
    }

    public static Album getAlbumByTitle(String title) {     ◁─❸
        for (Album album : albums) {
            if (album.getName().equals(title)) {
                return album;
            }
        }
        return null;
    }
}
```

The MusicStore application focuses only on JSF. We avoid additional layers such as interacting with a database. That's why we start the implementation with a declaration and initialization of a list of five hardcoded Albums ❶. Normally we'd invoke a database layer to get these albums, but for the sake of simplicity, we use hardcoded values. To keep the code listing simple and readable, we removed the Album declarations. Next, we implement a number of methods: one for retrieving all the available albums ❷ and another for finding an album by title ❸.

Listing 15.3 implements the bean that communicates with the frontend.

Listing 15.3   `ListAvailableAlbumsBean` implementation

```
[...]
public class ListAvailableAlbumsBean {

    private List<Album> albums = new ArrayList<Album>();     ◁─❶

    public List<Album> getAlbums() {                         ◁─❷
        this.albums = AlbumManager.getAvailableAlbums();

        return albums;
    }
```

```
    public void setAlbums( List<Album> albums ) {           ◁─❸
        this.albums = albums;
    }
}
```

Listing 15.4 describes the bean for our application. For every attribute we want to display in the frontend, we specify a corresponding property of the bean ❶. Depending on whether you only read or also write in your property, every property needs to have a getter method ❷ and a setter method ❸. JSPs interact with this bean, and the bean itself interacts with the AlbumManager. Before this bean can expose itself to the JSPs, we need to configure the bean in a configuration file called faces-config.xml.

Listing 15.4   faces-config.xml to configure our beans

```
<faces-config>
[...]
    <application>                                           ◁─❶
        <view-handler>
                com.sun.facelets.FaceletViewHandler
            </view-handler>
    </application>
    <managed-bean>                                          ◁─❷
        <managed-bean-name>
            listAlbumsBean                                  ◁─❸
        </managed-bean-name>
        <managed-bean-class>
            com.manning.junitbook.ch15.beans.ListAvailableAlbumsBean
        </managed-bean-class>
        <managed-bean-scope>request</managed-bean-scope>
    </managed-bean>
[...]
</faces-config>
```

We start with an application declaration ❶, which contains some information that's global for the whole application (like the view handlers, the locale parameters, and so on). The managed-bean declaration ❷ is used to expose our beans to the JSPs. Notice the managed-bean-name declaration ❸; this name will be used in the JSP to reference the bean with a class defined in the managed-bean-class declaration.

The only thing that we're missing to have the full picture of the MusicStore application is the page to display all the albums available. We show this in listing 15.5.

Listing 15.5   The JSP to display all the available albums

```
<html xmlns="http://www.w3.org/1999/xhtml"
    xmlns:h="http://java.sun.com/jsf/html"                 ❶
    xmlns:f="http://java.sun.com/jsf/core"
    xmlns:c="http://java.sun.com/jstl/core">
    <body>
        <h:form id="list_albums">

        [...]
```

```
      <table border='1'>
        <th>Name</th>
        <th>Author</th>
        <th>Year</th>
        <th>Price</th>
          <c:forEach var="album" items="#{listAlbumsBean.albums}">
          <tr>
            <td>
              <h:commandLink
                action="#{albumDetailsBean.showAlbumDetails}">

                <h:outputText value="${album.name}" />
                <f:param name="albumName" value="#{album.name}" />
            </h:commandLink></td>
            <td>${album.author}</td>
            <td>${album.year}</td>
            <td>$ ${album.price}</td>
          </tr>
        </c:forEach>
      </table>
    </h:form>
  </body>
</html>
```

We need to import the tag libraries that we want to use in this JSP ❶. All that our JSP is doing is iterating over all the albums ❷ and displaying the information for every album that we want. We use the standard JSTL tag libraries ❷ as well core JSF tag libraries ❸.

The JSP contains a link that to a managed bean we haven't defined yet:

```
<h:commandLink action="#{albumDetailsBean.showAlbumDetails}">
    [...]
</h:commandLink>
```

We want to implement the following: the list_albums.jsp presents all the albums to the user, and on clicking the name of an album you're redirected to a page that displays the album details. The new page then allows you to purchase the album or navigate back to the listing page.

Listing 15.6 gives the code for the bean that displays the details for the selected album.

Listing 15.6   AlbumDetailsBean implementation

```
[...]
public class AlbumDetailsBean {

    private String status = null;

    private HttpServletRequest request = null;          ❶

    private Album album = null;                         ❷

    public String showAlbumDetails() {                  ❸
        HttpServletRequest request = getRequest();
```

```
        String name = request.getParameter( "albumName" );        ⊲—④

        if ( name == null ) {
            return "";
        }

        setAlbum( AlbumManager.getAlbumByTitle( name ) );          ⊲—⑤

        return "showAlbumDetails";
    }

    protected HttpServletRequest getRequest() {
        if ( this.request == null ) {
            return (HttpServletRequest)                             ⑥
                    FacesContext.getCurrentInstance()
                        .getExternalContext().getRequest();
        } else {
            return this.request;
        }
    }

    public String cancel() {
        return "cancel";
    }

    public void purchase() throws InterruptedException  {           ⑦
        Thread.sleep( 1500 );                                      ⊲—┘
        // empty implementation
        System.out.println( "Here we must implement the purchase logic." );
    }

    //Additional getters and setters follow.
}
```

The bean tracks the request ❶ and the album that the user has selected ❷. The method that's called when the user clicks the name of a given album is showAlbum-Details ❸. In this method, we get the request and extract a parameter with the name "albumName" ❹. Then we use the AlbumManager to extract the Album object ❺. Pay attention to the way we extract the request ❻; if the attribute of the bean is null, we get it from the FacesContext object. In the next section, we mock the request object and set it as an attribute to the bean. The last method is the purchase method ❼; we call this method when a user wants to purchase a given album. For simplicity, we provide an empty implementation. Notice that we stop the execution exactly for a second and a half because we want to simulate that this method is time consuming, which we address when we write performance tests in the last section of this chapter.

Now let's move on to the JSP that provides the details for the bean (shown in listing 15.7).

Listing 15.7   album_details.jsp presenting the details for a given product

```
<html xmlns="http://www.w3.org/1999/xhtml"
    xmlns:h="http://java.sun.com/jsf/html"
    xmlns:f="http://java.sun.com/jsf/core"
    xmlns:rich="http://RichFaces.org/rich"
```

```
        xmlns:a4j="http://RichFaces.org/a4j"
        xmlns:c="http://java.sun.com/jstl/core">
<head>
<title>Album details</title>
</head>
<body>
<h:form id="view_details">
    <b>Details for album '#{albumDetailsBean.album.name}':</b>
    <table border='1'>
        <tr><td>
            <table>
                <tr><td>Title: #{albumDetailsBean.album.name}</td></tr>
                <tr><td>Year: #{albumDetailsBean.album.year}</td></tr>
                <tr><td>Style: #{albumDetailsBean.album.style}</td></tr>      ❶
                <tr><td>Author: #{albumDetailsBean.album.author}</td></tr>
                <tr><td>Price: $ #{albumDetailsBean.album.price}</td></tr>
                <tr><td>
                    <rich:panel bodyClass="rich-laguna-panel-no-header">
                        <a4j:commandButton id="PurchaseButton"
                            value="Purchase" reRender="rep"
                            action="#{albumDetailsBean.purchase}">

                            <a4j:actionparam id="status" name="status"     ❷
                              value="Successfully purchased:
                                #{albumDetailsBean.album.name}"
                                assignTo="#{albumDetailsBean.status}"/>
                        </a4j:commandButton>
                        <rich:spacer width="20" />
                        <a4j:commandButton value="Cancel" reRender="rep"   ❸
                                       action="#{albumDetailsBean.cancel}"/>
                    </rich:panel>
                    <rich:spacer height="1" />
                    <rich:panel bodyClass="rich-laguna-panel-no-header">
                        <h:outputText id="rep" name="rep"
                            value="#{albumDetailsBean.status}" />        ⟵ ❹
                    </rich:panel>
                </td></tr>
            </table>
        </td>
        <td><img src="#{albumDetailsBean.album.imageURL}"/></td></tr>
    </table>
</h:form>
</body>
</html>
```

This JSP is implemented using the RichFaces tag libraries. This JSP lists all details
for the selected album ❶. We have two button declarations: the Purchase button
❷ and the Cancel button ❸. We use RichFaces components to declare these buttons and to implement Ajax behavior. Notice the reRender attribute in the definition: this attribute holds the ID of another component that needs to be rerendered
when we get the response from the server. In our case, the rerendered component
is a text component that displays the status of the purchase ❹.

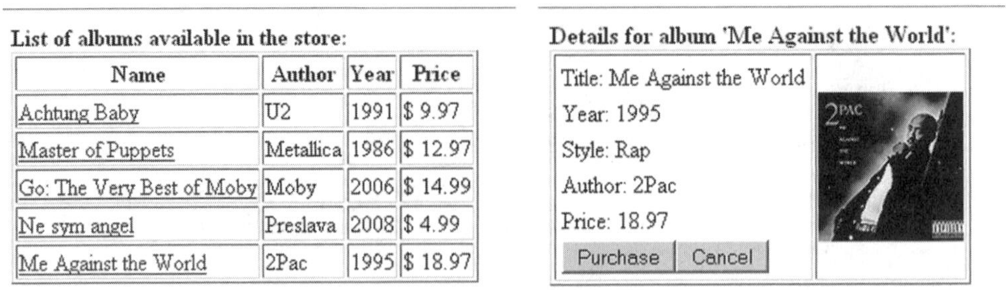

List of albums available in the store:				Details for album 'Me Against the World':

List of albums available in the store:

Name	Author	Year	Price
Achtung Baby	U2	1991	$ 9.97
Master of Puppets	Metallica	1986	$ 12.97
Go: The Very Best of Moby	Moby	2006	$ 14.99
Ne sym angel	Preslava	2008	$ 4.99
Me Against the World	2Pac	1995	$ 18.97

Details for album 'Me Against the World':

Title: Me Against the World
Year: 1995
Style: Rap
Author: 2Pac
Price: 18.97

Purchase   Cancel

Figure 15.2   The two screens of the `MusicStore` application

We're finished; the `MusicStore` application is now complete. In order to see it in action, you have to get the book source code online. We've provided a Maven script with a configured Jetty plug-in; all you have to do is go to the command line, navigate to the folder that contains the pom.xml file for the project, and invoke the Jetty plug-in:

```
> mvn jetty:run –Pjetty
```

The Jetty servlet container will start, and if you navigate to http://localhost:8080/ch15-jsfunit/, you should be able to see the application in action (figure 15.2).

The first image displays all the available albums, and if you click any given album, you should see the second part of the figure, where you can see the details for the album and purchase it.

Moving on, in the next sections we describe how to test the various parts of this application.

15.3   *Typical problems when testing JSF applications*

As you've seen so far, JSF applications typically consist of POJOs (called managed beans) and some frontend JSPs. Here, our managed beans are simple and therefore easy to unit test. So why are JSF applications hard to test?

Indeed, the managed beans are easy to unit test, but the hard part comes when you want to include interaction with a container in your tests. Normally tests give you the security you need to mercilessly refactor your application. They provide you with confidence that you haven't introduced a new bug into the system.

What could possibly break in a normal JSF application? Here's list of typical problems that might occur in a JSF application:

- Managed bean problems
- Managed bean method problems
- Faces-config.xml typos
- Improper interface implementation
- Missing getter/setter methods

- Duplicate managed bean declarations
- Various JSF tag problems
- Wrong-navigation problems

JSFUnit static analysis can solve all of these problems, as demonstrated in listing 15.8.

Listing 15.8   Static analysis for your faces-config.xml

```
[...]
public class FacesConfigTestCase extends AbstractFacesConfigTestCase {    <--❶

    private static Set<String> paths = new HashSet<String>()              <--❷
    {
        {
            add( "src/main/webapp/WEB-INF/faces-config.xml" );
        }
    };

    public FacesConfigTestCase()
    {
        super( paths );                      <--❸
    }
}
```

First, we extend the JSFUnit class `AbstractFacesConfigTestCase` ❶, and then we create a `Set` of `Strings` to hold the paths to our faces-config.xml files ❷ and call the constructor of the base class with the `Set` ❸. JSFUnit will parse the config files we've specified, and it will check the following:

- That all of our session and application scope beans are serializable
- That all of our managed beans are in a valid scope
- Whether we have missing managed beans
- Whether we're using the right `faces.config` class inheritance
- For missing setter methods and for duplicate managed beans

Next, we create tests.

15.4   Strategies for testing JSF applications

The problems that might occur when developing JSF applications have different approaches for solving them. Let's try to categorize the various ways to test a JSF application.

15.4.1   Black box approach

This is probably the most straightforward approach.[2] With JSF applications, a form of black box testing would be to open a web browser and start clicking pages to verify that everything works as expected. One way to automate black box testing would be to

---

[2] We highly recommend you read chapter 5 before continuing with this section.

use tools such as Selenium, HttpUnit, or HtmlUnit (see chapters 12 and 13). The point is that in most cases using plain Selenium or HtmlUnit to test your JSF application falls short in several ways. It's hard to validate expected HTML (which can be complicated by the use of Ajax), and in case you succeed, your tests may fail on minor HTML changes.

15.4.2 Mock objects to the rescue

Another approach you might take in order to test the `MusicStore` application is the white box approach. In this case you test only the server-side classes using mocks,[3] without running the whole application in a container.

The managed beans are so simple that to test them you don't need any kind of mocking. The problems appear when you want to involve objects like `FacesContext`, which you normally don't have access to. You can mock those objects, as well as `HttpServletRequest`, `HttpServletResponse`, and some other objects, using the techniques described in chapter 7.

For example, let's test the `showAlbumDetails` method of the `AlbumDetailsBean` from listing 15.6 using the JMock library. This method extracts a parameter from the request, so we need to mock the request and pass different values for the parameter, as shown in listing 15.9.

Listing 15.9   Testing the `AlbumDetailsBean` using JMock

```
[...]
public class TestAlbumDetailsBeanMock {

    private Mockery context = new JUnit4Mockery();                    ←①

    private HttpServletRequest mockRequest;                           ←②

    @Before
    public void setUp() {
        mockRequest = context.mock( HttpServletRequest.class );       ←③
    }

    @Test
    public void testShowAlbumDetailsRealAlbum() {
        context.checking( new Expectations() {
            {
                oneOf( mockRequest ).getParameter( "albumName" );
                will( returnValue( "Achtung Baby" ) );                 ④
            }
        } );

        AlbumDetailsBean albumDetailsBean = new AlbumDetailsBean();   ←⑤
        albumDetailsBean.setRequest( mockRequest );                   ←⑥

        String forwardString = albumDetailsBean.showAlbumDetails();   ←⑦
```

---

[3] You can learn more about mocks in chapter 7.

```
            assertEquals( "The return string must match 'showAlbumDetails'",
                              forwardString, "showAlbumDetails" );

            assertNotNull( "The album must not be null",
                                        albumDetailsBean.getAlbum() );
            assertEquals( "The author must be U2",
                        albumDetailsBean.getAlbum().getAuthor(), "U2" );
            assertEquals( "The year of the album must be 1991",
                        albumDetailsBean.getAlbum().getYear(), 1991 );
    }

    @Test
    public void testShowAlbumDetailsNoParameterAlbum() {
        context.checking( new Expectations() {
            {
                oneOf( mockRequest ).getParameter( "albumName" );
                will( returnValue( null ) );
            }
        } );

        AlbumDetailsBean albumDetailsBean = new AlbumDetailsBean();
        albumDetailsBean.setRequest( mockRequest );

        String forwardString = albumDetailsBean.showAlbumDetails();
        assertEquals( forwardString, "" );
        assertNull( "The album must be null",
                                    albumDetailsBean.getAlbum() );
    }

    @Test
    public void testShowAlbumDetailsNoRealAlbum() {
        context.checking( new Expectations() {
            {
                oneOf( mockRequest ).getParameter( "albumName" );
                will( returnValue( "No-real-album" ) );
            }
        } );

        AlbumDetailsBean albumDetailsBean = new AlbumDetailsBean();
        albumDetailsBean.setRequest( mockRequest );

        String forwardString = albumDetailsBean.showAlbumDetails();
        assertEquals( "The return string must match 'showAlbumDetails'",
                                    forwardString, "showAlbumDetails" );
        assertNull( "The album must be null", albumDetailsBean.getAlbum() );
    }
}
```

This test should be simple if you've already read chapter 7. We start by defining the Mockery context ❶ and the object that we want to mock ❷. After that, in the @Before method we initialize the request object to be ready for usage ❸. The next step defines several test methods, each of which will test the showAlbumDetails method by specifying a different parameter in the request. For each of those methods we define the expectations ❹, initialize AlbumDetailsBean ❺, set the mock request to the bean ❻, and execute the method under test ❼. The final test is to perform the assertions that we want ❽.

Although this kind of testing is easy, the drawback is that only the server-side logic is tested. These tests don't test the interaction with the HTML pages. Next we look at a non-trivial case, when you want to execute your tests inside the container and test all layers.

15.5   *Testing the sample application with JSFUnit*

The JSFUnit framework builds on Cactus,[4] which we discussed in the previous chapter, so the lifecycle of a sample test is the same. JSFUnit provides an API to gain access to all of the JSF-related objects in your tests.

Let's start with simple a JSFUnit test-case example, shown in listing 15.10.

Listing 15.10   First JSFUnit test

```
public class TestListAvailableAlbumsBean
    extends org.apache.cactus.ServletTestCase {        ←❶

    public void testInitialPage()
            throws IOException, SAXException {          ←❷
        JSFSession jsfSession = new JSFSession( "/" );          ←❸

        JSFServerSession server = jsfSession.getJSFServerSession();    ←❹

        assertEquals( "/list_albums.jsp", server.getCurrentViewID() );  ←❺

        UIComponent label = server.findComponent( "list_albums_label" );
        assertEquals( label.getParent().getId(), "list_albums" );

        assertEquals( 5, ((List<Album>)
                        server.getManagedBeanValue(
                        "#{listAlbumsBean.albums}" )).size());    ←❻
    }
}
```

As with Cactus, we create a test case by extending the Cactus `ServletTestCase` class ❶. Because Cactus extends JUnit 3, our test-case class needs to contain one or more `test`X (where X is user defined) methods ❷. In these test methods we perform the testing, using the JSFUnit API. In the example, we create a `JSFSession` object ❸, which points to the root of our application. From the `JSFSession` object, we get two important objects: `JSFServerSession` ❹ and `JSFClientSession`. We use the `JSFClientSession` to emulate the browser and test the HTML; the `JSFServerSession` is used to gain access to the JSF state and invoke operations on the managed beans. We check that the `viewID` is correct ❺ and that the managed bean always returns a list of `Albums` of size 5 ❻.

Testing JSF with JSFUnit looks much like testing with Cactus, but calls the API for testing the JSF components. Because JSFUnit is built on Cactus, we have the same features as we have with Cactus (including the `begin`X and `end`X methods we already covered in chapter 14). JSFUnit tests are executed the same way as Cactus tests. JSFUnit requires JDK 1.5+ and one of the following JSF implementations: MyFaces (1.1.x or 1.2.x) or Sun JSF RI (2.0.0-PR, 1.2.x, or 1.1.x).

---

[4] We strongly encourage you to go back and read chapter 14 if you skipped it and then come back to this chapter.

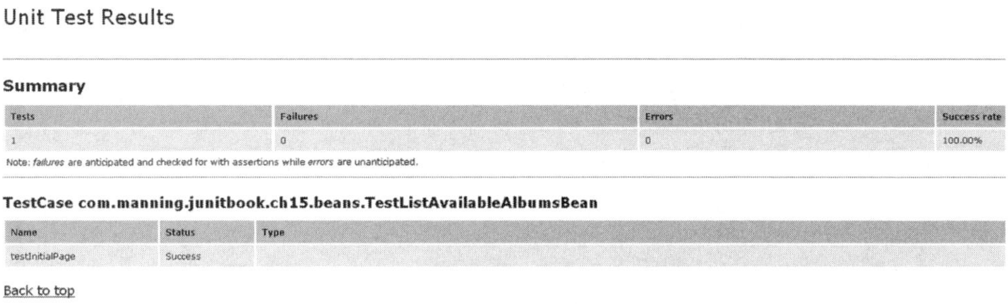

Unit Test Results

Summary

Tests	Failures	Errors	Success rate
1	0	0	100.00%

Note: *failures* are anticipated and checked for with assertions while *errors* are unanticipated.

TestCase com.manning.junitbook.ch15.beans.TestListAvailableAlbumsBean

Name	Status	Type
testInitialPage	Success	

Back to top

Figure 15.3   Results from the execution of our JSFUnit tests in a browser

To execute the tests you can use Ant or Maven (see chapter 14), or you can execute your tests from a browser.

15.5.1 *Executing a JSFUnit test from a browser*

To execute tests from a browser, place the cactus-report.xsl file that comes with the Cactus distribution in the root of your web application. After you package the application, deploy it to a servlet container and use a URL like the following:

> http://localhost:8080/ch15-jfsfunit/ServletTestRunner?suite=com.manning.
> junitbook.ch15.beans.TestListAvailableAlbumsBean&xsl=cactus-report.xsl

You'll see the results of the test execution, as shown in figure 15.3.

Now let's talk a little about Ajax.

15.5.2 *Testing Ajax using JSFUnit*

The Ajax elements of an application are scary for most developers to test. But as you saw in chapter 13, it isn't that hard to test Ajax. In this section we focus on testing the Ajax layer of our application, this time using JSFUnit.

Listing 15.11 shows the album_details.jsp page of our MusicStore application, which will allow us to purchase a given album.

Listing 15.11 album_details.jsp

```
...
<td>                                                                        ❶
    <rich:panel bodyClass="rich-laguna-panel-no-header">                    ⬅❶
        <a4j:commandButton id="PurchaseButton"                              ⬅❷
                    value="Purchase" reRender="rep"
                    action="#{albumDetailsBean.purchase}">
            <a4j:actionparam id="status" name="status"                      ⬅❸
                    value="Successfully purchased:
                            #{albumDetailsBean.album.name}"
                    assignTo="#{albumDetailsBean.status}"/>
        </a4j:commandButton>
        <rich:spacer width="20" />
```

```
            <a4j:commandButton value="Cancel" reRender="rep"
                              action="#{albumDetailsBean.cancel}"/>
        </rich:panel>
        <rich:spacer height="1" />
        <rich:panel bodyClass="rich-laguna-panel-no-header">          ← 4
            <h:outputText id="rep" name="rep"
                              value="#{albumDetailsBean.status}" />    ← 5
        </rich:panel>
    </td>
    ...
```

Although we already covered this page in listing 15.7, let's review it briefly. In our JSP, we use the RichFaces and Ajax4jsf tag libraries to implement the desired Ajax behavior. We start by defining two `rich:panel` components ❶ and ❹ to hold the rest of our components. In the first panel, we put a `commandButton` to submit the form to the bean specified in the `action` parameter ❷. The command button also submits a `status` parameter to the bean ❸. Notice the `reRender` parameter of the `commandButton`. This attribute specifies an ID of another component that needs to be rerendered. In our case, we specify an `outputText` ❺. You can see the screen for this JSP in figure 15.2.

Now let's implement some tests for this Ajax scenario. JSFUnit relies heavily on the HtmlUnit headless browser. You can use the `JSFClientSession` and click anything, regardless of the fact that the request to the bean will be submitted via JavaScript. The code for these tests is shown in listing 15.12.

Listing 15.12   Testing the Ajax components from the album_details.jsp

```
[...]
public class TestPurchaseAlbum extends ServletTestCase {          ← 1
    public static Test suite() {
        return new TestSuite( TestPurchaseAlbum.class );
    }
                                                                      2
    public void testCommandButton() throws IOException, SAXException {  ←┐
        JSFSession jsfSession = new JSFSession( "/album_details.jsp" );  ←┐

        JSFServerSession server = jsfSession.getJSFServerSession();      3
        JSFClientSession client = jsfSession.getJSFClientSession();    ─┘

        client.click( "PurchaseButton" );                             ← 4

        Object userBeanValue = server.getManagedBeanValue(
                                   "#{albumDetailsBean.status}");      ← 5

        assertEquals( "Successfully purchased: ", userBeanValue );     ← 6

        String spanContent =((HtmlPage) client.getContentPage())       ← 7
          .getElementsByTagName( "span" ).item( 0 ).getTextContent();

        assertEquals(spanContent, "Successfully purchased:");          ← 8
    }
}
```

As usual, we start the implementation by declaring a test case by extending the `Servlet-TestCase` ❶. In the test method ❷ we obtain a `JSFServerSession` object and extract the `JSFServerSession`/`JSFClientSession` ❸. Then we click the `"PurchaseButton"`

RichFaces button ❹. At ❺ we extract the value of the status parameter of the managed bean and assert its value ❻. On the client side, we also get the value of the span element on the page ❼ and assert its content ❽.

The JSFUnit project provides tight integration with the RichFaces project; if you find this treatment brief, you can use the RichFacesClient JSFUnit class. RichFaces-Client provides methods for testing drag-and-drop behavior, sliders, calendars, and other JSF widgets.

15.6 *Using HtmlUnit with JSFUnit*

In this section, we show how JSFUnit and HtmlUnit can work together.

Chapter 12 shows how to get to an HtmlUnit HtmlPage to start testing a page, for example:

```
WebClient webClient = new WebClient();
    webClient.setThrowExceptionOnScriptError(false);
    HtmlPage searchPage = (HtmlPage)
webClient.getPage("http://www.google.com");
```

Listing 15.13 shows how to use HtmlUnit in a JSFUnit test:

Listing 15.13 Using HtmlUnit in a JSFUnit test

```
[...]
public class TestListAvailableAlbumsWithHTMLUnit
                                    extends ServletTestCase {        ←❶

    public void testIntialPage() throws IOException {        ←❷
        JSFSession jsfSession = new JSFSession("/");
        JSFClientSession client = jsfSession.getJSFClientSession();        ❸

        HtmlPage page = (HtmlPage)client.getContentPage();
        HtmlTable table = (HtmlTable)
                        page.getFirstByXPath("/html/body/form/table");  ←
        assertNotNull("table should not be null",table);                    ❹
        assertEquals( 6, table.getRowCount() );

        HtmlAnchor link = table.getRow(1).getCell(0)
                                        .getFirstByXPath( "a" );  ←❺

        assertNotNull("link should not be null", link);        ←❻

        HtmlPage newPage = link.click();        ←❼

        assertEquals(newPage.getTitleText(), "Album details");  ←❽
    }
}
```

We start our test case again by extending the Cactus ServletTestCase class ❶. In our test ❷, we create a new JSFSession object with the request URL that we want to invoke. From the jsfSession object, we get a JSFClientSession ❸. From the client object, we get an HtmlTable using an XPath expression reflecting the DOM tree structure of our document ❹. We assert that the table isn't null and that the number of rows is six (we have five rows for the hardcoded albums and one for the header). From the table we retrieve the second row, the first cell out of it, and an HTMLAnchor out of the cell ❺. Again, we assert that the link isn't null ❻, and we click it ❼. The last assertion ❽ compares the title of the page that we got from clicking the link object; we want to make sure that we're taken to the new page.

15.7   *Performance testing for your JSF application*

JSFUnit provides the option to test the performance of an application. Going back to our MusicStore application, we'd like to ensure that the purchase method of our AlbumDetailsBeam is always executed in less than a second and a half. Although JUnit 4.5 provides the @Test annotation timeout parameter, when it comes to testing web applications this parameter isn't sufficient. In most cases, we want to time different phases of the application. JSFUnit provides the JSFTimer class to time the execution of a given phase of an application, as demonstrated in listings 15.14 and 15.15.

Listing 15.14   Enabling the JSFTimer for our application

```
//web.xml
<context-param>
  <param-name>javax.faces.CONFIG_FILES</param-name>
  <param-value>/WEB-INF/timer-config.xml</param-value>
</context-param>

//timer-config.xml
<?xml version='1.0' encoding='UTF-8'?>
<!DOCTYPE faces-config PUBLIC
  "-//Sun Microsystems, Inc.//DTD JavaServer Faces Config 1.1//EN"
  "http://java.sun.com/dtd/web-facesconfig_1_1.dtd">

<faces-config>
  <lifecycle>
    <phase-listener>
      org.jboss.jsfunit.framework.JSFTimerPhaseListener
    </phase-listener>
  </lifecycle>
</faces-config>
```

We declare a new context parameter with a value pointing to the timer-config.xml file, which holds the declaration for the timer.

Listing 15.15 shows how to use the timer.

Listing 15.15   Performance test for purchasing an album

```
[...]
public class TestPerformanceOfPurchaseBean extends ServletTestCase {        ◁─❶

    public void testPerformance() throws IOException {                      ◁─❷
        JSFSession jsfSession = new JSFSession( "/album_details.jsp" );     ◁─❸

        JSFClientSession client = jsfSession.getJSFClientSession();          ◁─❹

        client.click( "PurchaseButton" );                                    ◁─❺
```

```
JSFTimer timer = JSFTimer.getTimer();                      ◄─⑥
assertTrue( "Total time to get the response should not be  ◄─⑦
            more than 1600 ms.", timer.getTotalTime() < 1600 );

PhaseId appPhase = PhaseId.INVOKE_APPLICATION;                ⑧
assertTrue( "Execution should not be more than 1600 ms.",
                    timer.getPhaseTime( appPhase ) < 1600 );
    }
}
```

We start by creating a new test case ❶ and a test method ❷. We get a valid JSFSession ❸ and get its JSFClientSession ❹. Next, we click the PurchaseButton to initiate a request to the managed bean ❺. We create a JSFTimer to measure the execution time ❻, and we assert that the totalTime of the execution is less than 1600 milliseconds ❼.

We can also measure the execution time against some specific Phase ❽. The JSFUnit API provides for timing the execution interval upon any of the standard JSF phases:

- RESTORE_VIEW
- APPLY_REQUEST_VALUES
- PROCESS_VALIDATIONS
- UPDATE_MODEL_VALUES
- INVOKE_APPLICATION
- RENDER_RESPONSE

As we explained in chapters 3 and 4, the main benefit from the test cases is that they serve as a shield. Once you have your test cases written, you can proceed and refactor your application mercilessly, and you're assured that as long as the tests pass and the bar is green, everything is okay. In this sense, performance testing is important. You can write your tests and assert that the execution of a given method always takes less than a given time barrier. Now you're free to improve the logic behind that method, and you'll always be sure that the invocation of the given URL will take no more time than the time barrier allows.

15.8 *Summary*

Testing JSF applications requires preparation. Black box testing is brittle, limited, and hard to perform. The white box approach (mocking approach) also has its disadvantages; mock tests are always fine grained, which means that the interaction among the different components isn't tested well. Also, once written, the tests need to be rewritten in case of small cosmetic changes to the application.

JSFUnit, on the other hand, builds on the Cactus project and uses the in-container testing strategy. JSFUnit provides static and performance analysis mechanisms to fully inspect our applications. In this chapter we also showed how to test RichFaces Ajax components.

Starting with chapter 12, we discussed the challenges encountered when testing the frontend layer of a sample Java EE application. In the next chapter, we talk about one of the most recent booms in the Java world, OSGi, and the modularity that it provides.

Testing OSGi components

*Theory is when you know something, but it doesn't
work. Practice is when something works, but you
don't know why. Programmers combine theory and
practice: Nothing works and they don't know why.*

—Anonymous

This chapter covers

- The OSGi dynamic module system
- Mock testing of your modules
- In-container testing of your modules

So far, we've been testing everything from the Java EE spec. All the Java EE components that we've dealt with (JSPs, tag libraries, servlets, filters, EJBs, and so on) have been available for a long time. In this chapter we discuss a technology that became popular relatively recently and is getting more popular every day: OSGi.

We start the chapter by introducing OSGi[1] We then walk through the basic OSGi concepts and provide easy-to-grasp examples by means of the calculator application

---

[1] OSGi is a registered trademark of the OSGi Alliance.

from chapter 1. In the second part of the chapter, we show how to test our OSGi calculator bundle by introducing the JUnit4OSGi framework.

16.1 Introducing OSGi

The term *OSGi*[2] usually refers to two things: the OSGi alliance (http://osgi.org/) and the OSGi service platform.

The OSGi alliance is an organization of companies started in late March 1999. The initial companies involved in the alliance included Sun Microsystems, Ericsson, IBM, and others. The idea was to create a standards organization for defining specifications for a Java-based service platform, which could also be remotely managed. This platform consists of multiple bundles (aka modules) that can be installed, started, stopped, updated, and uninstalled remotely and dynamically. These operations can be performed at runtime without an application restart.

The specification this alliance deals with is the OSGi service platform, which defines a component and service model. All implementations of the OSGi framework need to provide an environment for the applications to run in. Applications comprise smaller components called bundles. A bundle is the smallest organization unit in OSGi—a collection of classes, resources, and configuration files, in which the bundle declares its dependencies. The key mission of a bundle is to declare and use services. The OSGi service platform provides a context where all the running services are registered. This bundle context is injected into every bundle during its startup.

The lifecycle of a given OSGi service is shown in figure 16.1.

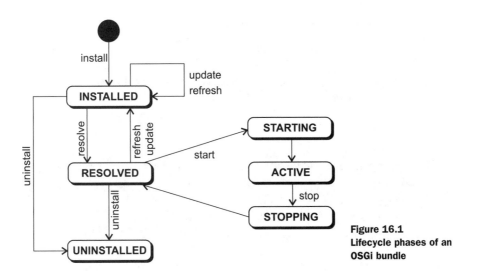

**Figure 16.1
Lifecycle phases of an
OSGi bundle**

---

[2] For a complete reference to OSGi we recommend *OSGi in Action*, by Richard S. Hall, Karl Pauls, Stuart McCulloch, and David Savage (Manning Publications, 2010).

As we mentioned, a bundle can be in different states. The lifecycle layer defines the following six states:

- INSTALLED: The bundle has been installed in the OSGi container.
- RESOLVED: All package requirements are fulfilled and the bundle is ready to be started.
- STARTING: The bundle is in the process of starting.
- ACTIVE: The bundle has started.
- STOPPING: The bundle is in the process of stopping. After this, the bundle will be in the RESOLVED state.
- UNINSTALLED: OSGi has removed the bundle from the container.

It may seem a bit confusing now, but the example we provide will clear things up, so let's move on and implement our first OSGi service.

16.2 Our first OSGi service

In the first chapter of the book, we implemented a simple calculator application. That application was simple enough to demonstrate the basic concepts of unit testing. We take the same approach in this chapter. We implement the calculator application as an OSGi service. We also implement a sample client for that service and a test bundle for the client. Finally, we install the three bundles in the Apache Felix environment.

Apache Felix—open source implementation of the service platform

The OSGi alliance defines a number of specifications for the OSGi service platform. The implementation of these specifications can be done by anyone. In this chapter, we use the Apache Software Foundation implementation Apache Felix (http://felix.apache.org/). The installation of the Felix project is easy. Start by downloading the latest distribution. Extract the archive and create an environment variable called FELIX_HOME pointing to the Felix folder. The Felix folder should contain the following:

- bin—This folder contains only one JAR file, called felix.jar. This JAR is used to instantiate the Felix console to remotely operate the different services.
- bundle—This folder contains the various Felix bundles.
- conf—This folder contains the Felix configuration file.
- doc—This folder contains the documentation.

The implementation of our calculator service starts with the interface in listing 16.1. Every OSGi service is defined by an interface.

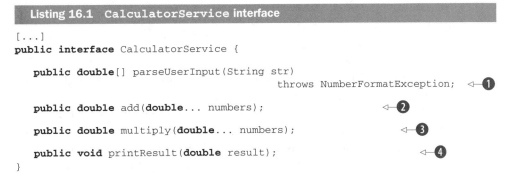

Listing 16.1 **CalculatorService** interface

```
[...]
public interface CalculatorService {

    public double[] parseUserInput(String str)
                                   throws NumberFormatException;   ⟵❶

    public double add(double... numbers);                    ⟵❷

    public double multiply(double... numbers);               ⟵❸

    public void printResult(double result);                  ⟵❹
}
```

The interface defines the four methods we want to implement in our service. The first one ❶ parses a line of user input. The user is supposed to input several numbers separated by spaces, and this method parses the input as numbers. The add method ❷ sums all the given numbers and returns the result. There is also a multiply method ❸, which multiplies numbers and returns the result. The printResult method ❹ prints a given result number.

As we already discussed, every OSGi service exposes a certain interface to other services. Your services *must* provide an interface and implement it.

Listing 16.2 contains the implementation of the interface in listing 16.1.

Listing 16.2 Implementation of **CalculatorService** interface

```
[...]
public class CalculatorImpl implements CalculatorService {

public double add(double... numbers) {
    double result = 0;
    for (double number:numbers)
       result+=number;
    return result;
}

public double multiply(double... numbers) {
    double result = 1;
    for (double number:numbers)
        result*=number;
    return result;
}

public double[] parseUserInput(String str)
                                  throws NumberFormatException {
    String[] numbers = str.split(" ");
    double[] result = new double[numbers.length];
    for (int i=0;i<numbers.length;i++) {
       result[i] = Double.parseDouble(numbers[i]);
    }
    return result;
}
```

```
public void printResult(double result) {
    System.out.println("The result is: " + result);
}

}
```

This listing declares a class that implements the interface in listing 16.1. The details of the implementation aren't relevant to OSGi, so we'll skip it.

There's no big difference between testing OSGi services and POJOs. You can reuse the test from chapter 1 and include it in a build, as we show in part 3 of this book. This chapter doesn't cover unit testing alone; it covers integration testing of OSGi services. Before we continue discussing the integration testing of the service that we just implemented, we create a bundle to hold our service and install the service with Apache Felix, an open source implementation of the OSGi R4 Service Platform.

To create the bundle we need an implementation of the BundleActivator interface to register and unregister the service, as shown in listing 16.3.

Listing 16.3 CalculatorBundleActivator

```
[...]
import org.osgi.framework.BundleActivator;          ❶
import org.osgi.framework.BundleContext;

public class CalculatorBundleActivator implements BundleActivator {    ◁─❷

    public void start(BundleContext bundleContext) throws Exception {   ◁─❸
        System.out.println("Starting calculator service ...");
        bundleContext.registerService(                                    ❹
            CalculatorService.class.getName(), new CalculatorImpl(), null);
    }

    public void stop(BundleContext bundleContext) throws Exception {    ◁─❺
        System.out.println("Stopping calculator service ...");

    }
}
```

We start by importing the required classes ❶ from felix.jar in the FELIX_HOME bin/ directory. Next, we declare our class to implement the BundleActivator interface ❷. In ❸ and ❺, we implement the required start and stop methods, which define how the bundle will behave once it's started or stopped. In the start method, we register the CalculatorService interface with the given BundleContext ❹. By doing so we notify the framework of our service, and our next step is to expose the interface to other services.

Our stop method ❺ doesn't need to do anything because Felix automatically unregisters the service when it stops.

To expose our calculator service so that it can be used by other services, we need to include it in a bundle: a JAR file containing all of our classes and the MANIFEST.MF file shown in listing 16.4.

Listing 16.4 Manifest file for the calculator bundle

```
Bundle-Name: Calculator
Bundle-Description: A sample calculator bundle that registers the
calculator service
Bundle-Vendor: Apache Felix
Bundle-Version: 1.0.0
Bundle-Activator: com.manning.junitbook.ch16.CalculatorBundleActivator
Export-Package: com.manning.junitbook.ch16.service
Import-Package: org.osgi.framework
```

❶ ❷ ❸ ❹

Every OSGi bundle is a JAR file, and what distinguishes the JAR as an OSGi bundle is the MANIFEST.MF file. In the MANIFEST.MF file, we specify different kinds of metadata for our bundle. The first few lines provide the name, description, vendor, and version of the bundle ❶. The `Bundle-Activator` ❷ specifies the full name of the `Activator` class (the one that implements `BundleActivator`). As we already mentioned, a bundle can export services. Which package is exported is specified in the `Export-Package` clause ❸. A bundle can also use and demand services; we specify which services we use with the last clause. There we define the packages that are needed by our service ❹. You can specify multiple values separated by commas.

The final step is to compile the source code and produce the bundle (the JAR file). Open a shell, navigate to the ch16-osgi\calculator-service folder, and type in the command to use Maven

```
mvn clean install
```

or the command to use Ant

```
ant
```

The result should be the same: a JAR file containing the classes and the MANIFEST.MF file in a META-INF folder.

Now that we have the bundle JAR that contains our service, we use the Felix console and install the bundle. Navigate to the FELIX_HOME directory and execute the following command:

```
java -jar bin/felix.jar
```

You'll see the following:

```
Welcome to Felix.
==================

->
```

The Felix console is up and running, and you can now manage your services. The first thing you can do from here is list all the services that are installed. Type in the command

```
-> ps
```

For a complete list of all the commands you can use, type in the `help` command:

```
-> help
```

We now install our `calculator-service` bundle. We first copy the JAR file to the FELIX_HOME/bundle folder. Next, we use the `install` command:

```
-> install file:bundle/calculator-service.jar
```

A `BundleID` will be assigned to our bundle. We use that `BundleID` to manage our bundle.
Start the service with the following command

```
-> start [BundleID]
```

where `[BundleID]` is a placeholder for your bundle ID.

We've installed the bundle and started it. The bundle is now running and exports the service as an API. Next, we create a sample client application for our `CalculatorService`.

16.2.1 *The sample application*

The idea behind the client application is to demonstrate how to make another bundle that uses the first one, the `CalculatorService`. We start by implementing the `Bundle-Activator` to override the behavior on start and stop. See listing 16.5.

Listing 16.5 `ClientBundleActivator` implementation

```
[...]
import com.manning.junitbook.ch16.service.CalculatorService;            ←— ❶

public class ClientBundleActivator implements BundleActivator {         ←— ❷

    public void start(BundleContext context) throws Exception {         ←— ❸

        ServiceReference reference = context.getServiceReference(
                            CalculatorService.class.getName());         ←— ❹

        if ( reference != null ) {

            CalculatorService calculator = (CalculatorService)
                            context.getService(reference);              ←— ❺

            BufferedReader in = new BufferedReader(
                        new InputStreamReader(System.in));

            System.out.println("Enter operation (add or multiply):");
            String operation = in.readLine();                              ❻

            System.out.println("Enter several numbers
                                separated with a space:");
            String line = in.readLine();

            double[] numbers = calculator.parseUserInput(line);         ←— ❼

            if (operation.equals("add")) {
                calculator.printResult(calculator.add(numbers));        ←— ❽
            } else if (operation.equals("multiply")) {
                calculator.printResult(calculator.multiply(numbers));   ←— ❾
            } else {
```

```
        throw new UnsupportedOperationException(
                            "Unknown command: " + operation);    ◁─❿
      }
      context.ungetService(reference);                           ◁─⓫
    }
    else {
      System.out.println("Calculator service is
                            not installed or not started ...");
    }
  }

  public void stop( BundleContext context ) {}                   ◁─⓬
}
```

This client reads several lines of user input. The first line must contain the operation the user wants to perform, and the next line should be in the form of several numbers separated by spaces. The client first invokes the parseUserInput method and with the result calls the corresponding add/multiply and print methods of the service we already installed and prints the result on the screen.

The client then imports the necessary classes ❶. Notice that this time we also import the service from the previous listings. Keep that in mind when it comes to describing services in the MANIFEST file. At ❷ we implement the BundleActivator interface and its two methods at ❸ and ⓬. At ❹ we get a ServiceReference from the context using our service's class name. If this reference isn't null, we get the CalculatorService interface from the context at ❺, by providing the reference to the service we already have. At ❻ we read two lines of user input from the command line. The first line contains the operation we want to perform (add or multiply), and the second line contains a set of numbers separated by spaces. At ❼ we call the parseUserInput method, and depending on the operation we call either the add method ❽ or the multiply method ❾, or we throw an UnsupportedOperation-Exception if the command is unknown ❿. The last step is to "unget" the service, at ⓫.

Let's see this client application in action. We need to package it in a bundle with a corresponding manifest file. Listing 16.6 contains the MANIFEST.MF file for the client application.

> ### Listing 16.6 MANIFEST.MF for the client application

```
Bundle-Name: Calculator client
Bundle-Description: A bundle that uses the calculator service if it finds
it at startup
Bundle-Vendor: Apache Felix
Bundle-Version: 1.0.0
Bundle-Activator: com.manning.junitbook.ch16.client.ClientBundleActivator
Import-Package: junit.framework, org.osgi.framework,
com.manning.junitbook.ch16.service
```

The only things different from the previous manifest file are the name of the bundle and the activator class. Notice that we also specify in the Import-Package directive a few more packages:

- junit.framework—We need this package because we have some tests to execute in the Felix service platform. More on this later in the chapter.

- com.manning.junitbook.ch16.service—We use the service that's already installed, so we need to specify its package here.

The one thing that's left is to navigate on the command line to the ch16-osgi/calculator-client folder from the source code of the book and invoke the appropriate Ant or Maven script. You do this the exact same way we already showed—no matter what script you use, the result should be identical.

Get the JAR file that's generated from the build and copy it to the FELIX_HOME/bundle folder. Go to the Felix command-line tool and invoke the two commands for installing and starting the bundle:

```
-> install file:bundle/calculator-client.jar

-> start [BundleID]
```

Again, you need to remember the assigned `BundleID` for this bundle and specify it when starting the bundle. If you don't remember it, use the `ps` command to find it.

Once the bundle is started, you will be asked to enter an operation and numbers separated by spaces.

Our client application implementation is so simple that we skipped data validation and exception handling. What happens if we were to enter a blank line or a random string? An exception would be raised, something we don't want to happen.

How do we test that the client application behaves in the expected way? We need to have some kind of integration tests that we execute *inside* the service platform (just like in chapter 14 where we executed Cactus tests inside the servlet container). That's exactly what we do next. In the next section, we introduce an OSGi testing framework called JUnit4OSGi; we also write some tests with that framework and include them in a separate test bundle.

16.3   *Testing OSGi services*

When it comes to testing OSGi services, we can apply the same categorization that we made in the second part of the book. The normal JUnit tests that you already know how to write would exercise each of your services on its own. Our attention is mainly focused on the integration tests that test the interaction between the different services. So for implementing integration tests there are different approaches that you might take; we already covered those different approaches in the second part of the book, and they include black box testing, using mock objects, and in-container testing.

As for black box testing, there isn't much you can do. A form of black box testing would be to get an OSGi container, install your services there, and hand it to someone to start playing around and test it "in the black."

We take a closer look at the other two approaches in the next sections.

16.3.1 *Mock objects*

Now that we have our services written, let's examine them. The calculator service exposes an API used by the `CalculatorClient` service to compute some sums or multiplications. The `CalculatorClient` service, on the other hand, reads some data input from the command line. This means that if we write a test for this service and invoke it, we have to enter some data on the command line, and because there's no restriction on the data that we can enter, there's no way to specify our assertions. There's also no way to automate those tests, because we always have to have someone entering data on the command line when the tests are executed. The solution for this problem is simple: refactoring.

We need to refactor the `ClientBundleActivator` in such a way that it allows it to be easily testable. Listing 16.7 shows the refactored class, where the changed lines are marked in bold.

Listing 16.7 Refactored `ClientBundleActivator` to enable testability

```
[...]
public class ClientBundleActivator implements BundleActivator {

    private String operation = null;                                    ❶
    private String userNumberInput = null;
    private double result = 0;                                       ← ❷

    public void start(BundleContext context) throws Exception {
        if (operation==null || userNumberInput==null) {              ❸
            initUserInput();
        }

        ServiceReference reference = context.getServiceReference(
                            CalculatorService.class.getName());

        if (reference != null) {

            CalculatorService calculator = (CalculatorService)
                                context.getService(reference);

            double[] numbers = calculator.parseUserInput(
                                        getUserNumberInput());    ← ❹

            if (getOperation().equals("add")) {
                result = calculator.add(numbers);
            } else if (getOperation().equals("multiply")) {          ❺
                result = calculator.multiply(numbers);
            } else {
                throw new UnsupportedOperationException(
                        "Unknown command: " + getOperation());
            }

            calculator.printResult(result);
            context.ungetService(reference);
        } else {
            System.out.println("Calculator service
                            is not installed or not started ...");
        }
    }
}
```

```
public void initUserInput() {                          ←─6
    BufferedReader in = null;

    try {
        in = new BufferedReader(new InputStreamReader(System.in));    7
        System.out.println("Enter operation (add or multiply):");
        operation = in.readLine();

        System.out.println("Enter several                            8
                            numbers separated with a space:");
        userNumberInput = in.readLine();
    } catch (IOException ex) {
        System.err.println("Error reading from the reader.");
        ex.printStackTrace();
    }
    finally
    {
        try {
            in.close();
        } catch (IOException e) {
            System.err.println("Error closing the reader.");
            e.printStackTrace();
        }
    }
}
// Getters and setters...
}
```

We start by extracting all the data the user normally enters on the command line (the operation and the numbers separated by spaces) as instance variables to the class ❶. We extract the result from the computation as a local variable ❷, and we provide getters and setters for both ❶ and ❷. This gives us the opportunity to set those parameters before we start the ClientBundleActivator as well as to assert the expected result. Next, in the start method we add a check to see if the user data has been set up ❸, and in case it hasn't we call the initUserInput method ❻. As you can see in ❹, everywhere in our code that we want to use the user data, we use the getter methods of the class. At this point we're sure that this data will be set up, either by the setter methods or by the initUserInput method, which reads the data from the command line. In ❺ we check the command we want to issue and call the corresponding method in the CalculatorService accordingly. Notice that the result is this time kept in a local variable, to which we have access through the getter methods.

The initUserInput method ❻ is called when we have no user data defined through the setter methods. This method has the responsibility for reading the operation we want to issue ❼ as well as the numbers on which we want to issue the command ❽.

Now that we've refactored the ClientBundleActivator class, we can test it. The class contains one entry-point method called start, which we want to unit test. In order to do this we must obtain a valid BundleContext object, because the method defines it as a parameter. BundleContext itself is an interface, so we have no way to instantiate.

Chapter 7 introduced mock objects, and we saw mock objects frameworks that can produce fake instances of interfaces that we can use in tests. That's exactly what we're going to do in listing 16.8.

Listing 16.8 Mock test for the `CalculatorService`

```
[...]
public class TestClientCalculatorServiceMock {                          ←─①

    private Mockery context = new JUnit4Mockery();                      ←─②

    private BundleContext mockBundleContext;
                                                                           ③
    private ServiceReference mockServiceReference;

    @Before
    public void setUp() {
        mockBundleContext = context.mock( BundleContext.class );        ④
        mockServiceReference = context.mock( ServiceReference.class );
        final CalculatorImpl service = new CalculatorImpl();

        context.checking( new Expectations()
        {
            {
                oneOf(mockBundleContext).getServiceReference(
                                    CalculatorService.class.getName());
                will(returnValue(mockServiceReference));                    ⑤

                oneOf(mockBundleContext).getService(mockServiceReference);
                will(returnValue(service));

                oneOf(mockBundleContext).ungetService(mockServiceReference);
            }
        } );
    }

    @Test                                                               ⑥     ⑦
    public void testAddMethod() throws Exception {                      ←─┐  ←─┐
        ClientBundleActivator activator = new ClientBundleActivator();       ⑧
        activator.setOperation( "add" );
        activator.setUserNumberInput( "1 2 3 4 5 6 7 8 9" );
        activator.start( mockBundleContext );                               ←─┐
        assertEquals( "The result is not the same as expected",             ⑨
                                activator.getResult(), 45, 0 );          ←─┘
    }

    @Test
    public void testMultiplyMethod() throws Exception {                 ←─⑩
        ClientBundleActivator activator = new ClientBundleActivator();
        activator.setOperation( "multiply" );

        activator.setUserNumberInput( "1 2 3 4 5 6 7 8 9" );
        activator.start( mockBundleContext );
        assertEquals( "The result is not the same as expected",
                                activator.getResult(), 362880, 0 );
    }
}
```

We start by creating a new JUnit test case **❶** that will exercise our CalculatorService. Just as we did in chapter 6, we define the Mockery context **❷** and the objects that we want to mock **❸**. The @Before method executes before every test method, so that's where we create the mock objects **❹**. At **❺**, we define the expectation for the mock objects. We got lucky—these expectations turn out to be the same for both tests, which is why we can extract them to the @Before method. We first call the get-ServiceReference on the mockBundleContext, and after that we call the getService on the same object, passing the ServiceReference we already have. Finally, we call the ungetService method on the mockBundleContext.

We have two tests: one to test the add method of the service **❻** and another to test the multiply method **❿**. Those tests have the same structure: We first get a new instance of the ClientBundleActivator class **❼** and then set the parameters using the setter methods on the class **❽**. The last step is to invoke the start method with our fake object **❾** and assert that the expected results are good.

As you can see, using mock objects to test our service requires quite a bit of preparation. We need to take care of the proper instantiation and configuration of the mock objects.

The next section introduces the JUnit4OSGi project, which implements an in-container strategy for testing the CalculatorClient service.

16.4   *Introducing JUnit4OSGi*

The JUnit4OSGi framework is a simple OSGi testing framework that comes from the iPOJO subcomponent of the Apache Felix project. You can download the JARs from the website of the project, or if you're using Maven, you can declare them as dependencies in your Maven project.

To use the framework you'll need several JAR files. The bare minimum you need is this:

- org.apache.felix.ipojo-1.4.0.jar
- org.apache.felix.ipojo.handler.extender-1.4.0.jar
- org.apache.felix.ipojo.junit4osgi-1.0.0.jar
- org.apache.felix.ipojo.junit4osgi.felix-command-1.0.0.jar

Place these files in the sample folder FELIX_HOME/bundles/junit4osgi. Then install them one by one with the Felix command-line tool. Once they're installed and started, you'll get the chance to use one extra command on the command line:

```
-> junit [BundleID]
```

This command will invoke all the JUnit and JUnit4OSGi tests that are present in the bundle with the given [BundleID] and are listed in the manifest descriptor.

Let's start implementing our first test cases. Listing 16.9 shows the JUnit4OSGi test case that tests the CalculatorService application.

Listing 16.9 JUnit4OSGi test for our `CalculatorService` application

```
[...]
import org.apache.felix.ipojo.junit4osgi.OSGiTestCase;       ❶
import org.osgi.framework.ServiceReference;
import com.manning.junitbook.ch16.service.CalculatorService;

public class TestClientActivator extends OSGiTestCase {       ❷  ❸

    public void testServiceAvailability() {                    ❹
        ServiceReference ref =
          context.getServiceReference(CalculatorService.class.getName());
        assertNotNull("Assert Service Availability", ref);     ❺
    }

    public void testParseUserCorrectInput() {
        ServiceReference ref =
          context.getServiceReference(CalculatorService.class.getName());
        assertNotNull("Assert Availability", ref);
        CalculatorService cs = (CalculatorService)             ❻
                                      context.getService(ref);
        double[] result = cs.parseUserInput("11.5 12.2 13.7"); ❼
        assertNotNull("Result must not be null", result);
        assertEquals("Result must be 11.5", 11.5, result[0]);  ❽
        assertEquals("Result must be 12.2", 12.2, result[1]);
        assertEquals("Result must be 13.7", 13.7, result[2]);
    }

    public void testParseUserIncorrectInput() {
        ServiceReference ref =
          context.getServiceReference(CalculatorService.class.getName());
        assertNotNull("Assert Availability", ref);
        CalculatorService cs = (CalculatorService)
                                      context.getService(ref);

        try {
          double[] result = cs.parseUserInput("THIS IS A RANDOM STRING TO
                                     TEST EXCEPTION HANDLING");  ❾
          fail("A NumberFormatException was
                              supposed to be thrown but was not");
        } catch (NumberFormatException nex) {
            assertTrue(true); //this is the normal execution flow  ❿
        }
    }

    public void testAddMethod() {
        assertTrue("Check availability of the service",
                   isServiceAvailable(CalculatorService.class.getName()));
        CalculatorService cs = (CalculatorService)
                getServiceObject(CalculatorService.class.getName(), null);
        double[] numbers = cs.parseUserInput("1.2 2.4");
        assertNotNull("Result from parseUserInput must not be null",
                       numbers);
        double result = cs.add(numbers);
        assertNotNull("Result from add must not be null", result);
        assertEquals("Result must be 3.6", 3.6, result);
    }
}
```

The listing starts by importing the necessary classes ❶. Remember that every external package you use needs to be declared in the MANIFEST.MF file of the bundle. Every JUnit4OSGi test case needs to extend from the `OSGiTestCase` class ❷. The JUnit4OSGi framework is a JUnit 3.x extension, so you need to follow the JUnit 3.x rules for writing test cases.

We start our first `test` method at ❸ and get a `ServiceReference` of the service we wrote and deployed ❹. We get the `ServiceReference` from the `context` object that JUnit4OSGi provides us. The framework gives us the access to the `Bundle-Context` to check the status of the given service, something that we do in ❺. By asserting the `ServiceReference` isn't `null`, we make sure that the service is installed and started correctly.

The following `test` methods test the `service` methods; by having the service reference we can get hold of the service itself (at ❻) and invoke different methods (at ❼) to see that it behaves the expected way ❽. We also test the exceptional case to provide a random string (at ❾), and we catch the `NumberFormatException` that we expect to be raised ❿.

It's a best practice to separate all your `junit-osgi` tests in a separate bundle, and that's what we're going to do. Go to the calculator-test folder of the source code of the book, and use Maven or Ant to package the bundle that contains the test from the previous listing. After you've done this, copy the resultant JAR file and paste it in the FELIX_HOME/bundle folder so that it's easy to install. The next step is to install and start the service in the bundle the way we described at the beginning of the chapter.

Our final step is to call the test inside the container

```
-> junit [BundleId]
```

replacing the `BundleId` with the number assigned to your module. If you're using the source code for the book and there are no errors, the result should be the same as this:

```
Executing [Client activator tests]
....1
Time: 0

OK (4 tests)
```

As we already mentioned, the `junit` command is currently available only for the Apache Felix implementation of OSGi. So how can we run our tests if we use any of the other implementations of OSGi? In that case we have to use the GUI runner that comes with the JUnit4OSGi project.

To use the GUI runner, you need to install and start the org.apache.felix.ipojo. junit4osgi.swing-gui.jar bundle. After the bundle is started, you'll see a Java pop-up that lets you select the bundles that contain JUnit tests. You can select as many as you want, and after clicking the Execute button you should see the result: a green bar for passing tests and a red bar for failing tests (see figure 16.2).

This example of executing unit tests through the GUI runner concludes our look at JUnit4OSGi and this chapter on OSGi.

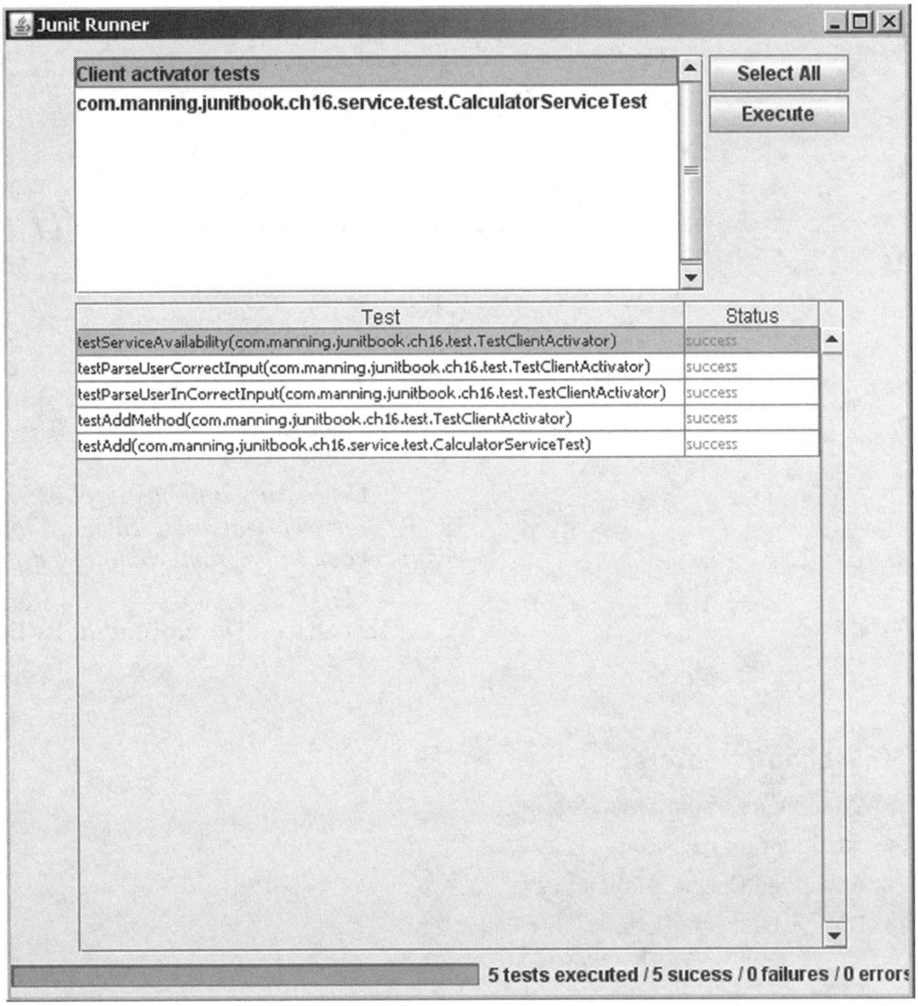

Figure 16.2 Executing the JUnit tests with the GUI runner

16.5 *Summary*

In this chapter, we discussed testing OSGi bundles, a technology that is getting more and more popular. We introduced the technology and its key concepts, the bundle and service. You should also be able to test all your OSGi bundles using JUnit4OSGi and to apply different techniques for testing your bundles, like testing with mock objects, integration testing, and so on.

In the following chapters, we begin to study the backend layer of applications. The remaining chapters are concerned with database interactions. We show you different techniques for testing Hibernate and JPA as well as integration testing of your data access layer.

Testing database access

17

Dependency is the key problem in software development at all scales.... Eliminating duplication in programs eliminates dependency.

—Kent Beck,
Test-Driven Development: By Example

This chapter covers

- Challenges of database testing
- Introduction to DbUnit
- Advanced DbUnit techniques
- DbUnit best practices

The persistence layer (or, roughly speaking, the database access code) is undoubtedly one of the most important parts of any enterprise project. Despite its importance, the persistence layer is hard to unit test, mainly because of the following issues:

- Unit tests must exercise code in isolation; the persistence layer requires interaction with an external entity, the database.
- Unit tests must be easy to write and run; code that accesses the database can be cumbersome.
- Unit tests must be fast to run; database access is relatively slow.

We call these issues the database unit testing impedance mismatch, in reference to the object-relational impedance mismatch (which describes the difficulties of using a relational database to persist data when an application is written using an object-oriented language).

The database-testing mismatch can be minimized using specialized tools, one of them being DbUnit. In this chapter, we show how DbUnit can be used to test database code, and we not only describe its basic concepts but also present techniques that make its usage more productive and the resulting code easier to maintain.

17.1   The database unit testing impedance mismatch

Let's take a deeper look at the three issues that compose the database unit testing impedance mismatch.

17.1.1   Unit tests must exercise code in isolation

From a purist point of view, tests that exercise database access code can't be considered unit tests because they depend on an external entity, the almighty database. What should they be called then? Integration tests? Functional tests? Non-unit unit tests?

Well, the answer is, there is no secret formula! In other words, database tests can fit into many categories, depending on the context.

Pragmatically speaking, though, database access code can be exercised by both unit and integration tests:

- Unit tests are used to test classes that interact directly with the database (like DAOs). Such tests guarantee that these classes execute the proper SQL statements, assemble the right objects, and so on. Although these tests depend on external entities (such as the database and/or persistence frameworks), they exercise classes that are building blocks in a bigger application (and hence are units).

- Similarly, unit tests can be written to test the upper layers (like façades), without the need to access the database. In these tests, the persistence layer can be emulated by mocks or stubs.

- Even with both layers (persistence and upper) unit tested aside, it's still necessary to write integration tests that access the database, because some situations can arise only in end-to-end scenarios (like the dreaded lazy-initialization exception that frequently haunts JPA applications).[1]

Despite the theoretical part of the issue, there's still a practical question: can't the data present in the database get in the way of the tests?

---

[1] If you don't have a clue as to what we're talking about, don't panic! JPA testing and its issues will be explained in detail in the next chapter.

Yes, it can, so before you run the tests, you must assure that the database is in a known state. Fortunately, there are plenty of tools that can handle this task, and in this chapter we analyze one of them, DbUnit.

17.1.2 Unit tests must be easy to write and run

It doesn't matter how much a company, project manager, or technical leader praises unit tests; if they're not easy to write and run, developers will resist writing them. Moreover, writing code that accesses the database isn't the sexiest of tasks. One would have to write SQL statements, mix many levels of try-catch-finally code, convert SQL types to and from Java, and so on.

Therefore, in order for database unit tests to thrive, it's necessary to alleviate the database burden on developers. Luckily again, there are tools that provide such alleviation, and DbUnit is one of them.

17.1.3 Unit tests must be fast to run

Let's say you've overcome the first two issues and have a nice environment, with hundreds of unit tests exercising the objects that access the database, and where a developer can easily add new ones. All seems nice, but when a developer runs the build (and they should do that many times a day, at least after updating their workspace and before submitting changes to the source control system), it takes 10 minutes for the build to complete, 9 of them spent in the database tests. What should you do then?

This is the hardest issue, because it can't always be solved. Typically, the delay is caused by the database access per se, because the database is probably a remote server, accessed by dozens of users. A possible solution is to move the database closer to the developer, by either using an embedded database (if the application uses standard SQL that enables a database switch) or locally installing lighter versions of the database.

> **DEFINITION**   *Embedded database*—An embedded database is a database that's bundled within an application instead of being managed by external servers (which is the typical scenario). A broad range of embedded databases is available for Java applications, most of them based on open source projects, such as HSQLDB (http://hsqldb.org), H2 (http://h2database.com), Derby (http://db.apache.org/derby), and Java DB (http://developers.sun.com/javadb). Notice that the fundamental characteristic of an embedded database is that it's managed by the application and not the language it's written in. For instance, both HSQLDB and Derby support client/server mode (besides the embedded option), although SQLite (which is a C-based product) could also be embedded in a Java application.

In the following sections, we show how DbUnit (and, to a lesser degree, embedded databases) can be used to solve the database unit testing impedance mismatch.

17.2 Introducing DbUnit

DbUnit (http://www.dbunit.org) is a JUnit[2] extension created by Manuel LaFlamme in 2002, when Java Unit testing was still in its infancy and there was no framework focused on database testing. At about the same time, Richard Dallaway wrote an online article titled "Unit testing database code" (http://dallaway.com/acad/dbunit.html), which inspired the creation of DbUnit.

Since then, DbUnit has became the de facto Java framework for database testing, and its development has had its up and downs. After a period of high activity, when most of its codebase was created, it faced a long drought. Fortunately, though, new developers jumped in and, during the time this book was written, several new versions have been cut, providing many improvements and bug fixes.

Although DbUnit comprises hundreds of classes and interfaces, DbUnit usage roughly consists of moving data to and from the database, and that data is represented by datasets (more specifically, classes that implement the `IDataSet` interface).

In the following subsections, we examine the basic usage of datasets and some other DbUnit artifacts.

17.2.1 The sample application

Throughout this chapter, we use DbUnit to unit test the persistence layer of a Java application. In order to simplify, this layer consists of only the interface defined in listing 17.1.

Listing 17.1 DAO interface used in the examples

```
public interface UserDao {
  long addUser(User user) throws SQLException;
  User getUserById(long id) throws SQLException;
}
```

The DAO implementation (using plain JDBC) isn't shown here but is available for download at the book's website. The `User` object is a simple POJO,[3] described in listing 17.2.

Listing 17.2 Domain model used in the examples

```
public class User {
  private long id;
  private String username;
  private String firstName;
  private String lastName;
  // getters and setters omitted
}
```

The `User` object will be mapped in the database by the users table, which can be created using the SQL statement shown in listing 17.3.

---

[2] Although it can be used without JUnit.
[3] Plain old Java object.

Listing 17.3   SQL script that creates the users table

```
CREATE TABLE users (
  id INTEGER GENERATED BY DEFAULT AS IDENTITY(START WITH 1),
  username VARCHAR(10),
  first_name VARCHAR(10),
  last_name VARCHAR(10) )
```

Finally, the examples will use HSQLDB as the database, because it's Java based and doesn't require any further configuration. HSQLDB is also flexible: it can be run as client/server or embedded, using disk or memory. The simplest—and fastest—mode is as an in-memory embedded database, and that's the mode used in the examples.

17.2.2 *Setting up DbUnit and running the sample application*

DbUnit itself comprises just one JAR (dbunit.jar), and the only required external dependency is the logging framework, SLF4J (Simple Logging Façade for Java). SLF4J requires two JARs: slf4j-api.jar (which contains only the framework interfaces) and an implementation, such as slf4j-nop.jar (which doesn't log anything; we talk more about logging later on). Of course, because DbUnit will connect to a database, it's also necessary to add the JDBC driver to the classpath; in the sample application, it's hsqldb.jar.

The sample application is available in two flavors: Maven and Ant. To run the tests on Maven, type `'mvn clean test'`. Similarly, to use Ant instead, type `'ant clean test'`. The application is also available as two Eclipse projects, one with the required libraries (under the lib directory) and another with the project itself.

17.3   *Using datasets to populate the database*

Let's start by writing a unit test for the `getUserById()` method.

First, we need to analyze what the method does: it fetches data from the relational database, creates a Java object, populates that object with the fetched data, and then returns the object.

Consequently, our test case must prepare the database with the proper data, run the code being tested, and verify that the object returned contains the expected data. The latter two steps can be done with trivial Java code, whereas the former needs interaction with a database—that's where DbUnit is handy.

Data in DbUnit is represented by a dataset (interface `org.dbunit.dataset. IDataSet`), and DbUnit provides dozens of different `IDataSet` implementations, the most common ones being `XmlDataSet` and `FlatXmlDataset`. In our example, we need to insert a row in the table users with the values id=1, username=ElDuderino, firstName=Jeffrey, and lastName=Lebowsky. Let's see how this data could be represented on these two different dataset implementations, first in the `XmlDataSet` format (listing 17.4).

Listing 17.4 `XmlDataSet` representation of users table

```
<?xml version="1.0"?>
<!DOCTYPE dataset SYSTEM "dataset.dtd">
<dataset>
  <table name="users">
    <column>id</column>
    <column>username</column>
    <column>first_name</column>
    <column>last_name</column>
    <row>
      <value>1</value>
      <value>ElDuderino</value>
      <value>Jeffrey</value>
      <value>Lebowsky</value>
    </row>
  </table>
</dataset>
```

The `XmlDataSet` format is self-described, but it has two problems. First, it's verbose. As you can see in the previous example, a simple row in a table required 16 lines of XML code. The advantage of this format is that it follows a well-defined DTD (available inside DbUnit's JAR), which could avoid problems caused by bad XML syntax. But that brings up the second issue: DbUnit doesn't validate the DTD (that `DOCTYPE` line could be removed or even changed to any garbage, and the result would be the same).

Although the lack of XML validation is a DbUnit bug, the verboseness of the format is a design option. A much simpler option is to use `FlatXmlDataSet`, where each line describes a row in the database. Listing 17.5 shows the same dataset using the flat XML format.

Listing 17.5 `FlatXmlDataSet` representation of users table (user.xml)

```
<?xml version="1.0"?>
<dataset>
  <users id="1" username="ElDuderino"
                first_name="Jeffrey" last_name="Lebowsky" />
</dataset>
```

The `FlatXmlDataSet` format is much clearer and easier to maintain,[4] so we use it in our examples. Listing 17.6 shows our first test case.

Listing 17.6 Initial test case for UserDaoJdbcImpl (UserDaoJdbcImplTest)

```
[...]
public class UserDaoJdbcImplTest {                              ←-❶

    private static UserDaoJdbcImpl dao = new UserDaoJdbcImpl();
    private static Connection connection;
    private static HsqldbConnection dbunitConnection;
```

---

[4] This format has its issues as well, which we will cover later in the chapter.

```
@BeforeClass                                                  ←—❷
public static void setupDatabase() throws Exception {
  Class.forName("org.hsqldb.jdbcDriver");
  connection = DriverManager.getConnection(
    "jdbc:hsqldb:mem:my-project-test;shutdown=true");
  dbunitConnection = new HsqldbConnection(connection,null);   ←—❸
  dao.setConnection(connection);
  dao.createTables();
}

@AfterClass                                                   ←—❹
public static void closeDatabase() throws Exception {
  if ( connection != null ) {
    connection.close();
    connection = null;
  }
  if ( dbunitConnection != null ) {
    dbunitConnection.close();
    dbunitConnection = null;
  }
}

protected IDataSet getDataSet(String name) throws Exception {    ←—❺
  InputStream inputStream = getClass().getResourceAsStream(name);
  assertNotNull("file"+name+" not found in classpath", inputStream);  ←—❻
  Reader reader = new InputStreamReader(inputStream);
  FlatXmlDataSet dataset = new FlatXmlDataSet(reader);
  return dataset;
}

@Test
public void testGetUserById() throws Exception {
  IDataSet setupDataSet = getDataSet("/user.xml");
  DatabaseOperation.CLEAN_INSERT.execute(dbunitConnection,
    setupDataSet);                                              ←—❼
  User user = dao.getUserById(1);
  assertNotNull(user);
  assertEquals("Jeffrey", user.getFirstName());
  assertEquals("Lebowsky", user.getLastName());
  assertEquals("ElDuderino", user.getUsername());
}

}
```

Our test case ❶ doesn't need to extend any DbUnit or JUnit class. Although it doesn't sound like a big deal in this example, being forced to extend a superclass could be a big limitation in real life, especially if you use different testing frameworks such as TestNG.[5]

Remember that test methods (such as ❷ and ❹) are still code, and hence "real code" best practices should be applied to them as well. In particular, because opening a database connection can be an expensive operation (in terms of time and number

---

[5] Such testing framework independence is a DbUnit 2.2+ feature; before that release, all classes had to extend `DatabaseTestCase`, which would make it hard to use DbUnit with TestNG.

of concurrent connections), it's a good practice to open it at the beginning of the tests and close it at the end. Alternatively, if a connection pool was used instead, these methods could be defined at @Before/@After, respectively.

At ❸, connection is a just a regular JDBC connection (java.sql.Connection), but dbunitConnection is a DbUnit IDatabaseConnection instance. DbUnit uses IDatabaseConnection to encapsulate access to the database, and it provides implementations for the most common databases. The advantage of using a specialized IDatabaseConnection implementation (HsqldbDatabaseConnection in this case) rather than the generic one (DatabaseConnection) is that it can handle nuances specific to that database, like conversion between nonstandard SQL types and Java classes.

Notice that in this example, both connection and dbunitConnection were created using hardcoded values; in real projects, a better practice would be to define these settings externally, such as in a property file. That would allow the same tests to be run in different environments, such as using alternate databases or getting the connection from a pooled data source. Getting an IDataSet from an XML file is so common that it deserves its proper method ❺. It's also a good practice to load these XML files as resources in the classpath, instead of physical files in the operating system. And if the file isn't found in the classpath (which is a common scenario when you're writing the test cases—you might have forgotten to create the file or misspelled its name), get-ResourcesAsStream() returns null (instead of throwing a resource-not-found exception), which in turn would cause a NullPointerException in the caller method. Because an NPE is a sure bet to cause a lot of headaches, adding an assertNotNull() ❻ with a meaningful message is a one-liner that can save you time troubleshooting.

Finally, ❼ the DbUnit job is effectively performed. We have a dataset (setupData-Set) with the data we want to insert and a connection to the database (dbunit-Connection). All that's left is the class responsible to do the dirty work, and that's DatabaseOperation or, more precisely, one of its subclasses. In this case, we use CLEAN_INSERT, which first deletes all rows from all tables defined in dataset and then inserts the new ones. See the next section for more details about DatabaseOperation and its implementations.

A final note about transactions: in order to keep this example simple, we aren't dealing with transactions at all, and every database operation is done in one transaction (using JDBC's autocommit feature). Although this simplification is fine here, usually the test cases must be aware of the transaction semantics. For instance, a transaction could be started before the test (using a @Before method) and committed afterwards (using @After), the test cases could explicitly set the autocommit property (particularly if the connections were obtained from a pool), and so on. The exact approach depends on many factors, like the type of test (unit or integration) being written and the underlying technologies used in the code tested (like pure JDBC or ORM frameworks).[6]

---

[6] Chapter 18 offers more detailed insight on transactions in JPA-based test cases.

Best practice: define a superclass for your database tests

The UserDaoJdbcImplTest class in listing 17.6 defines four methods, but only one is effectively a test case—the other three are helpers used in the testing infrastructure. As you add more test cases, the proportion tends to revert, although it's common to add more helper methods as well. These helpers can typically be reused by other test classes.

Consequently, it's good practice to create a superclass that defines only these infrastructure methods and then make the real test classes extend this superclass. This best practice applies not only to DbUnit-based tests but also to testing in general.

The class in the listing 17.6 example could be refactored into two classes, an AbstractDbUnitTestCase superclass (with methods setupDatabase(), close-Database(), and getDataSet()) and the UserDaoJdbcImplTest properly speaking (which for now contains only testGetUserById()). The next example will use this technique.

Now let's look at DatabaseOperation in detail.

17.3.1 *DatabaseOperation dissected*

DatabaseOperation is the class used to send datasets to the database. Although DbUnit makes good use of interfaces and implementations, DatabaseOperation is one of the few concepts that isn't defined by an interface. Instead, it's defined as an abstract class with an abstract method (execute(), which takes as parameters a dataset and a database connection). The reason for such different design is to facilitate its use, because the abstract class also defines constants for its implementations (DbUnit was created on Java 1.3/1.4 when there was no native enum), so the operations can be executed with just one line of code, as we saw in the first example.

The implementations provided by DatabaseOperation as static fields are as follows:

- UPDATE—Update the database with the dataset content. It assumes the rows in the dataset already exist in the database (that is, the database contains rows with the same primary keys as the rows in the dataset); if they don't exist, DbUnit will throw an exception.

- INSERT—Insert the dataset rows in the database. Similarly to UPDATE, DbUnit will throw an exception if any row already exists. Because rows are inserted in the order in which they appear in the dataset, care must be taken when tables have foreign keys: rows must be defined in the dataset using the right insertion order.

- REFRESH—This is a mix of INSERT and UPDATE: rows that exist in the dataset but not in the database are inserted, but rows that exist in both are updated.

- DELETE—Delete from the database only the rows present in the dataset, in the reverse order in which they appear in the dataset.

- `DELETE_ALL`—Delete from the database all rows from each table present in the dataset. Although it's an aggressive approach in many cases (such as when the database is shared by many developers or it contains data that shouldn't be deleted), it's the simplest way to guarantee the state of the database (because sometimes the database might contain data that isn't deleted by `DELETE` and hence can interfere in the test results).

- `TRUNCATE`—Same purpose as `DELETE_ALL`, but faster, because it uses the SQL's `TRUNCATE TABLE`. The only drawback is that not all databases support such SQL operation.

- `CLEAN_INSERT`—Composite operation, first calls `DELETE_ALL`, then `INSERT`, using the same dataset.

- `TRANSACTION(operation)`—Not exactly a field but a method. It creates a `DatabaseOperation` that will wrap another operation inside a database transaction. It's particularly useful in cases where tables have circular dependency and rows can't be inserted outside a transaction with deferred constraints.

- `CLOSE_CONNECTION(operation)`—Another wrapper, it executes the operation and then automatically closes the connection. This can be useful in teardown methods.

- `NONE`—An empty operation that does nothing.

That's it; we wrote our first DbUnit test case and set the foundation for most of the tests to come.

17.4 Asserting database state with datasets

Another common use of datasets is to assert that the database has the right data after an insert or update. Back to our DAO example: we need a test case for the `addUser()` method, and the workflow for this test is the opposite from `getUserById()`'s test. Here we first create a `User` object, ask our DAO to persist it, then use a DbUnit dataset to assert that the data was properly inserted. The code snippet in listing 17.7 is our first attempt at such a test case.

Listing 17.7 Test case for `addUser()` method

```
[...]
import org.dbunit.Assertion;
[...]
public class UserDaoJdbcImplTest extends AbstractDbUnitTestCase {    <-①
  [...]
  @Test
  public void testAddUser() throws Exception {
    User user = new User();
    user.setFirstName("Jeffrey");
    user.setLastName("Lebowsky");
    user.setUsername("ElDuderino");                                  <-②
    long id = dao.addUser(user);
    assertTrue(id>0);                                                <-③
```

```
      assertEquals(id, user.getId());
      IDataSet expectedDataSet = getDataSet("/user.xml");
      IDataSet actualDataSet = dbunitConnection.createDataSet();
      Assertion.assertEquals( expectedDataSet, actualDataSet );
   }
}
```

We start by extending the DbUnit class `AbstractDbUnitTestCase` **1**. The `@Test` method `testAddUser()` first creates and populates a `User` object **2**.

Next, we ask DAO to persist the `User` object and check that it generates a valid ID **3** (a positive value, in this case) and that the returned ID matches the object. Such checking is important in situations where the caller needs to use the new ID (for instance, in a web page that generates a link to edit the newly created object). It may sound trivial and redundant in this case, but you'd be surprised by how often the ID isn't set correctly in more complex combinations (like multilayered applications with Spring managing transactions and Hibernate being used as the persistence layer).

At **4** we use the same dataset (user.xml) and same method (`getDataSet()`) as the previous example—it's always a good practice to reuse code and testing artifacts. At **5** `IDatabaseConnection.createDataSet()` returns a dataset containing all tables (with all rows) in the database. Finally, at **6** `Assertion.assertEquals()` compares both datasets, and if a discrepancy is found, it fails with the proper message. Notice that we did not statically import this method. Because both JUnit's `Assert` and DbUnit's `Assertion` have `assertEquals()` methods, if you static import both, chances are a call to `assertEquals()` will reference the wrong one.

Best practice: use a helper class to create and assert object instances

In the previous example, `testGetUserById()` fetched an object from the database and asserted its attributes, but `testAddUser()` did the opposite (instantiated a new object, filled its attributes, and then inserted it in the database). As your test cases grow, more and more tests will need to do the same. To avoid the DRY (don't repeat yourself) syndrome, it's better to create a helper class containing methods and constants for these tasks. Doing so improves reuse in the Java classes and facilitates maintenance of dataset files. If you use Java 5 and static imports, accessing members in this helper class is simple. Listing 17.8 shows a revised version of `testAddUser()` using this practice.

Listing 17.8   Revised version of `testAddUser()`, using a helper class

```
[...]
import static EntitiesHelper.*;
[...]
public class UserDaoJdbcImplTest extends AbstractDbUnitTestCase {
   [...]
```

```
@Test
public void testAddUser() throws Exception {
  User user = newUser();                              ←②
  long id = dao.addUser(user);
  [...]
}
}
[...]
public final class EntitiesHelper {                   ←③

  public static final String USER_FIRST_NAME = "Jeffrey";   ←④
  public static final String USER_LAST_NAME = "Lebowsky";
  public static final String USER_USERNAME = "ElDuderino";

  public static User newUser() {                      ←⑤
    User user = new User();
    user.setFirstName(USER_FIRST_NAME);
    user.setLastName(USER_LAST_NAME);
    user.setUsername(USER_USERNAME);
    return user;
  }
  public static void assertUser(User user) {          ←⑥
    assertNotNull(user);
    assertEquals(USER_FIRST_NAME, user.getFirstName());
    assertEquals(USER_LAST_NAME, user.getLastName());
    assertEquals(USER_USERNAME, user.getUsername());
  }
}
```

The newUser() method is statically imported ❶ and called ❷ in the helper class ❺. The helper class itself ❸ provides an assertUser() method ❻ (used by testGet-UserById()); it uses constants ❹ to define the User attributes.

17.4.1 *Filtering data sets*

The method IDatatabaseConnection.createDataSet() returns a dataset representing the whole database. This is fine in our example, where the database has only one table and the database access is fast (because it's an embedded database). In most other cases, though, it would be overkill—either the test would fail because it would return tables that we're not interested in or it would be slow to run.

The simplest way to narrow the field is by filtering the tables returned by create-DataSet(), by passing an array containing the name of the tables that should be returned. Applying that change to the previous example, we have the following:

```
IDataSet actualDataSet = dbunitConnection.createDataSet(
  new String[] { "users" } );
```

A similar approach is to use a FilteredDataSet to wrap the dataset containing the full database:

```
IDataSet actualDataSet = dbunitConnection.createDataSet();
FilteredDataSet filteredDataSet = new FilteredDataSet(
  new String[] {"users"}, actualDataSet );
```

A `FilteredDataSet` decorates a given dataset using an `ITableFilter`, which in turn is a DbUnit interface that defines which tables belongs to a dataset and in what order they should be retrieved. In the previous example, the constructor implicitly creates a `SequenceTableFilter`, which returns the tables in the order defined by the array passed as a parameter.

Finally, a third option is to use a `QueryDataSet`, where you explicitly indicate which table should be present in the dataset. The next example returns a dataset that has the exact same contents as the previous example:

```
QueryDataSet actualDataSet = new QueryDataSet(dbunitConnection);
actualDataSet.addTable("users");
```

Comparing the three options, the overloaded `createDataSet()` is obviously simpler in this case. But the other options have their usefulness in different scenarios:

- `QueryDataSet` is more flexible, because you can also provide the query that will be used to populate the dataset (if you don't provide one, it assumes `SELECT * FROM table_name`). Using a query, you can narrow the field even more, by selecting only the rows the test case is interested in, which is useful when the database contains a lot of data, for example:

  ```
  QueryDataSet actualDataSet = new QueryDataSet(dbunitConnection);
  actualDataSet.addTable("users",
    "select * from users where id = " + id);
  ```

- `FilteredDataSet` can be used with any `ITableFilter`, such as a filter that returns tables in the right foreign-key dependency order (as will be shown in section 17.6).

17.4.2 *Ignoring columns*

If you run the previous test method alone, it will pass. But if you append it to the existing `UserDaoJdbcImplTest` class and run the whole class, it will fail:

```
junit.framework.AssertionFailedError: row count (table=users) expected:<1>
➥but was:<2>
    at junit.framework.Assert.fail(Assert.java:47)
```

This is a common problem when using DbUnit—and one of the most annoying. A test case passes when it's run alone but fails when run as part of a suite. In this particular case, our user.xml dataset has only one row, and this is what we assume the database should contain after we insert the `User` object. When many tests are run, it fails because the database contains something else. Where does the extra row come from? From the previous test (`testGetUserById()`) execution, because that method also inserted a row. We could say the culprit is the previous test, which did not clean itself up.[7] It's the test case's responsibility to make sure the database is in a

---

[7] The DbUnit documentation states: "Good setup don't need cleanup" and you "should not be afraid to leave your trace after a test." This isn't always true, though, as you'll see in section 17.8.

known state before the test is run. This is achieved by using the same dataset and a DELETE_ALL operation:

```
IDataSet setupDataSet = getDataSet("/user.xml");
DatabaseOperation.DELETE_ALL.execute(dbunitConnection, setupDataSet);
```

If we add this code and run the whole test again, the test fails:

```
junit.framework.AssertionFailedError: value (table=users, row=0, col=id):
expected:<1> but was:<2>
    at junit.framework.Assert.fail(Assert.java:47)
    at org.dbunit.Assertion.assertEquals(Assertion.java:147)
    at org.dbunit.Assertion.assertEquals(Assertion.java:80)
```

Now the number of rows is correct (because we deleted all rows from the users table before running the test), but the ID of the inserted row doesn't match what we expect. This is another common problem, and it happens frequently when the database generates the ID. Although we cleaned up the rows, we didn't reset the primary key generation, so the next row inserted has an ID of 2 and not 1 as we expected.

There are many solutions for this issue, ranging from simple (like ignoring the ID column in the comparison) to sophisticated (like taking control of how IDs are generated—we show this approach in the next chapter). For now, let's just ignore the ID column, using the method Assertion.assertEqualsIgnoreCols() instead of Assertion.assertEquals():

```
Assertion.assertEqualsIgnoreCols( expectedDataSet, actualDataSet, "users",
  new String[] { "id" } );
```

Listing 17.9 shows the full method for our new test case.

Listing 17.9 Second approach for testAddUser()

```
[...]
public class UserDaoJdbcImplTest extends AbstractDbUnitTestCase {
  @Test
  public void testAddUserIgnoringIds() throws Exception {
    IDataSet setupDataSet = getDataSet("/user.xml");
    DatabaseOperation.DELETE_ALL.execute(dbunitConnection, setupDataSet);
    User user = newUser();
    long id = dao.addUser(user);
    assertTrue(id>0);
    IDataSet expectedDataSet = getDataSet("/user.xml");
    IDataSet actualDataSet = dbunitConnection.createDataSet();
    Assertion.assertEqualsIgnoreCols( expectedDataSet, actualDataSet,
      "users", new String[] { "id" } );
  }
}
```

Although ignoring the column is the simplest approach to the problem (in the sense that it doesn't require any advanced technique), it introduces a maintenance bug: now it's necessary to keep both the dataset file (user.xml) and the Java class (which has references to both the users table and the ID column) in sync. In the next section we examine a better (although not yet optimal) approach, where the database information (table and column names) is contained just in the dataset file.

17.5   *Transforming data using ReplacementDataSet*

DbUnit provides a simple yet powerful IDataSet implementation called Replacement-DataSet. In the following sections, we explore how it can be used to solve some common problems.

17.5.1   *Using ReplacementDataSet to handle the different IDs issue*

Let's try a different approach for the "same dataset, different IDs" issue. Instead of ignoring the ID column, couldn't we dynamically change a dataset value before the test case uses it?

   Changing the data inside a dataset would be quite complicated. Fortunately, though, DbUnit provides the ReplacementDataSet class, which decorates an existing dataset to dynamically replace tokens, according to your needs.

   Back to our problem: first we need to change the dataset XML file, by replacing the hardcoded IDs by a token (we used [ID] in this case, but it could anything, as long as that string doesn't occur somewhere else in the dataset). Listing 17.10 shows the new XML.

Listing 17.10   user-token.xml, a dataset that uses a token for IDs

```
<?xml version="1.0"?>
<dataset>
  <users id="[ID]" username="ElDuderino"
                 first_name="Jeffrey" last_name="Lebowsky" />
</dataset>
```

Next, we change the test case class, with the changed (and new) methods shown in listing 17.11.

Listing 17.11   Changes on `UserDaoJdbcImplTest` to handle dynamic IDs

```
[...]
public class AbstractDbUnitTestCase {
[...]
  protected IDataSet getReplacedDataSet(IDataSet originalDataSet, int id)
    throws Exception {
    ReplacementDataSet replacementDataSet =
      new ReplacementDataSet(originalDataSet);
    replacementDataSet.addReplacementObject("[ID]", id);
    return replacementDataSet;
  }

  protected IDataSet getReplacedDataSet(String name, int id)
    throws Exception{
    IDataSet originalDataSet = getDataSet(name);
```

❶

❷

❸

```
      return getReplacedDataSet(originalDataSet, id);                    ←④
   }
}
[...]
public class UserDaoJdbcImplTest extends AbstractDbUnitTestCase {
   [...]
   @Test
   public void testGetUserByIdReplacingIds() throws Exception {        ⑤
      long id = 42;                                                      ←┐
      IDataSet setupDataset = getReplacedDataSet("/user-token.xml", id);←┤
      DatabaseOperation.INSERT.execute(dbunitConnection, setupDataset); │
      User user = dao.getUserById(id);                                  ⑥
      assertUser(user);
   }
   @Test
   public void testAddUserReplacingIds() throws Exception {
      IDataSet setupDataSet = getDataSet("/user-token.xml");
      DatabaseOperation.DELETE_ALL.execute(dbunitConnection,
         setupDataSet);                                                 ←⑦
      User user = newUser();
      long id = dao.addUser(user);
      assertTrue(id>0);
      IDataSet expectedDataSet = getReplacedDataSet(setupDataSet, id);  ←⑧
      IDataSet actualDataSet = dbunitConnection.createDataSet();
      Assertion.assertEquals(expectedDataSet, actualDataSet);
   }
}
```

In the first getReplacedDataSet() utility method, the ReplacementDataSet constructor ❶ takes as a parameter the dataset it's decorating. Notice that the original dataset remains intact, and the method returns a new dataset. Next, we define what must be replaced ❷, using addReplacementObject() (the API also provides an addReplacementSubstring() method, but addReplacementObject() is the most common option). The second getReplacedDataSet() utility method gets a dataset ❸ and calls the first getReplacedDataSet() method we defined ❹.

In the first test, the value of the ID ❺ doesn't matter, as long as the same value is used in both places (getReplacedDataSet() and getUserById()). Next, we call ❻ the new method, which reads the original XML file and returns a dataset with the [ID] dynamically replaced.

In the second test, we use DELETE_ALL ❼ to clean up the database; note that the IDs are irrelevant. But if we used another DatabaseOperation (like DELETE), we'd need to use a decorated dataset here as well. For the next part of the test ❽, we need to use a decorated dataset in the assertion; we use the ID returned by the DAO itself. If the test still fails because of a wrong ID, then something is wrong with the DAO class.

Next, let's look at how DbUnit handles NULL values.

Best practice: don't hardcode values

This example uses hard coded 1s in method calls:

```
IDataSet setupDataset =
  getReplacedDataSet("/user-token.xml", 1);
DatabaseOperation.INSERT.execute(dbunitConnection,
  setupDataset);
User user = dao.getUserById(1);
```

If you didn't write that code (or even if you wrote it a long time ago), the following questions might pop up in your mind: What does the 1 in the first line stands for? Is that method replacing just one line? Does it sound like that 1 is directly related to the 1 in the third line? Now take a look back at the `testGetUserById()` method from the previous listing. Would you have the same doubts? This example illustrates how a subtle change (which costs just a few seconds of a developer's time) makes code much more understandable (and consequently easier to maintain). Create variables or constants whenever appropriate, even if the variable will be used only once.

17.5.2 *Handling NULL values*

Another situation where a `ReplacementDataSet` is useful is to represent NULL values (SQL's NULL, not Java's null) in a dataset. The way DbUnit handles NULL in `FlatXml-DataSet` files is tricky and deserves clarification:

1 *If* a column exists in the database but is missing in an XML line, then the value of that column (for that row in the dataset) is assumed to be NULL.

2 *But* that applies only if the column was present in the first line of XML. DbUnit uses the first line to define which columns a table is made of.

3 This is true *unless* the database columns are defined in a DTD!

It's frustrating to spend hours trying to figure out why your test case is failing, just to realize you were caught by a DbUnit idiosyncrasy.[8] Let's try to make it clearer with a naive example, where we have two XML files with the exact same lines but in different order (as shown by listings 17.12 and 17.13).

Listing 17.12   user-ok.xml, where the first line has all columns

```
<?xml version="1.0"?>
<dataset>
  <users id="1" username="ElDuderino"
                first_name="Jeffrey" last_name="Lebowsky" />
  <users id="2" username="TheStranger"/>
</dataset>
```

---

[8] This situation has improved in more recent versions of DbUnit. Although the idiosyncrasy still exists, at least now DbUnit is aware of the problems it can cause and logs a warning message whenever it finds a line in the XML file with different columns than the first one.

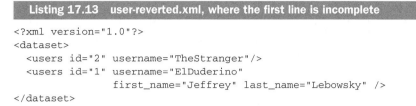

Listing 17.13 user-reverted.xml, where the first line is incomplete

```xml
<?xml version="1.0"?>
<dataset>
  <users id="2" username="TheStranger"/>
  <users id="1" username="ElDuderino"
                first_name="Jeffrey" last_name="Lebowsky" />
</dataset>
```

Now let's write a test case (listing 17.14) that does the following:

1 It uses the first dataset (user-ok.xml) to populate the database. Because the second line doesn't have the first_name and last_name attributes, DbUnit inserts NULL in the equivalent database columns.

2 Then it compares the database contents with the contents of both datasets (user-ok.xml and user-reverted.xml).

Because both datasets contain the same lines (but in different order), both tests should pass, but the user-reverted.xml assertion fails, complaining that the dataset expected two columns but the database contained four:

```
junit.framework.ComparisonFailure: column count
(table=users, expectedColCount=2, actualColCount=4) expected:
<[[id, username]]> but was:<[[FIRST_NAME, ID, LAST_NAME, USERNAME]]>
    at org.dbunit.Assertion.assertEquals(Assertion.java:244)
    at org.dbunit.Assertion.assertEquals(Assertion.java:204)
    at org.dbunit.Assertion.assertEquals(Assertion.java:186)
```

The reason for such failure is item 2: DbUnit uses the content of the first line to define how many columns it is expecting thereafter.

Listing 17.14 Test case that demonstrates the missing column issue

```java
[...]
public class NULLTest extends AbstractDbUnitTestCase {
  @Test
  public void testNULL() throws Exception {
    IDataSet okDataset = getDataSet("/user-ok.xml");
    DatabaseOperation.CLEAN_INSERT.execute(dbunitConnection, okDataset);
    IDataSet actualDataSet = dbunitConnection.createDataSet();
    assertEquals(okDataset, actualDataSet);
    IDataSet revertedDataSet = getDataSet("/user-reverted.xml");
    Assertion.assertEquals(revertedDataSet, actualDataSet);
  }
}
```

There are many ways to resolve this issue. The two most common ones are

- Using a ReplacementDataSet
- Using a DTD

Let's look at both in detail.

USING A REPLACEMENTDATASET

We already used a `ReplacementDataSet` to replace the `[ID]` token; we could reuse the same dataset to also replace `NULL` values. All we need is to define a new token (say, `[NULL]`) and add another replacement role:

```
replacementDataSet.addReplacementObject("[NULL]", null);
```

Listing 17.15 shows all relevant changes, with comments.

Listing 17.15 `ReplacementDataSet` **approach to the missing column issue**

```
[...]
public class AbstractDbUnitTestCase {
[...]
  protected IDataSet getReplacedDataSet(IDataSet originalDataSet, long id)
    throws Exception {
  ReplacementDataSet replacementDataSet = new
    ReplacementDataSet(originalDataSet);
  replacementDataSet.addReplacementObject("[ID]", id);
  replacementDataSet.addReplacementObject("[NULL]", null);          <--1
  return replacementDataSet;
 }
}

[...]
public class NULLTest extends AbstractDbUnitTestCase {
  @Test
  public void testNULLReplacementDataset() throws Exception {
    IDataSet okDataSet = getDataSet("/user-ok.xml");
    DatabaseOperation.CLEAN_INSERT.execute(dbunitConnection, okDataSet);
    IDataSet actualDataSet = dbunitConnection.createDataSet();
    Assertion.assertEquals(okDataSet, actualDataSet);
    IDataSet revertedDataSet = getReplacedDataSet("/user-replacement.xml",
      -1);                                                          <--2
    IDataSet sortedDataSet = new SortedDataSet(revertedDataSet);   <--3
    Assertion.assertEquals(sortedDataSet, actualDataSet);          <--4
  }
}
```

This is the same method we used before; we just added a new replacement role here **1**.

In **2**, in order to simplify, we're using the method that expects an ID and passing a bogus value (-1), because it won't be replaced anyway (as the dataset doesn't have any `[ID]` token). Ideally, though, `getReplacedDataSet()` should be overloaded to handle the situation where the ID isn't necessary. Better yet, the tokens to be replaced shouldn't be passed as parameters (we look at how to do that later, in section 17.7.3).

If in **4** we compared `actualDataSet` against `revertedDataSet` (which is the original XML file with the proper `[NULL]` tokens replaced), the assertion would still fail. Although this time the number of columns is correct, the order would be reverted; the database query would return rows 1 and 2, whereas the dataset defines the order as 2 and 1. In order to solve this issue without changing the order in the dataset (whose wrong order is the whole purpose of the example), we wrapped the dataset in a `SortedDataSet` ❸, which returns a new dataset with the tables sorted by the order in which its columns were defined in the database. In this example, it would sort first by ID, which is the first column in the `CREATE TABLE` statement. If any two or more lines had the same ID (which isn't the case here, because ID is the primary key), then it would sort them by username (the second column), first_name (third column), and so on.

USING A DTD

You can explicitly define the database structure (instead of letting DbUnit implicitly "guess" it when it reads the XML first line) in a DTD and add that DTD to the dataset header, as shown in listings 17.16 and 17.17.

Listing 17.16   New version of user-reverted.xml, with DTD declaration

```xml
<?xml version="1.0"?>
<!DOCTYPE dataset SYSTEM "target/test-classes/user.dtd">
<dataset>
  <users id="2" username="TheStranger"/>
  <users id="1" username="ElDuderino"
             first_name="Jeffrey" last_name="Lebowsky" />
</dataset>
```

Listing 17.17   user.dtd

```
<!ELEMENT dataset (users*)>
<!ATTLIST users
    id CDATA #REQUIRED
    username CDATA #REQUIRED
    first_name CDATA #REQUIRED
    last_name CDATA #REQUIRED
>
```

Notice the odd location (target/test-classes/) of the user.dtd file; that's the relative directory where our test artifacts are compiled. Unfortunately, DbUnit supports only physical locations, so the DTD path must be relative to the project's root directory or an absolute path in the filesystem. Ideally, DbUnit should support looking up the DTDs in the classpath.

Once user-reverted.xml is changed, the method `testNULL()` can be run again (without any change) and will succeed.

Both approaches have their advantages and disadvantages. Using a DTD adds more validation to the datasets (which can prevent other errors), at the cost of a more complicated initial setup (creating the DTD, making sure it's in the right place, and so on). On the other hand, using [NULL] makes the datasets clearer, because its presence explicitly indicates that a value is NULL. It also has a setup cost, but if you're already using a `ReplacementDataSet`, that cost is minimal (just one more line of code). Hence, the decision depends more on the project context and personal preferences than on the technical merits of the approach per se.

LOGGING

Earlier on we said that DbUnit would warn us about the missing column in the XML issue, but if you run the testNULL() method, it fails without any warning. If that happens, it means DbUnit logging is somehow disabled.

There's no API or DbUnit configuration file to explicitly enable logging. Instead, you must configure SLF4J in your project. It isn't the intent of this book to explain how SLF4J works or why the DbUnit chose this tool (until release 2.2, DbUnit used no logging framework at all). Briefly, you need to add to the project's classpath a JAR containing a real SL4J implementation. In our cases we didn't see any log because the project's Ant script is explicitly using sl4j-nop.jar, which doesn't log anything (this is also the default implementation included in your Maven project if you just add DbUnit as a project dependency).

If your project already uses a logging framework (like log4j or Java's java.util. logging), chances are there's an SLF4J provider for that framework, so you can just include its JAR (such as sl4j-log4j12.jar) in the classpath. If you don't use any logging framework, the easiest solution (the one that requires no extra configuration) is to add sl4j-simple.jar. This provider sends info messages to System.out, sends warnings and errors to System.err, and ignores all other logging levels (like debug and trace).

Adding sl4j-simple.jar to the classpath and running the test case again, we get the aforementioned warning:

```
474 [main] WARN org.dbunit.dataset.xml.FlatXmlProducer - Extra columns on
➥line 2.  Those columns will be ignored.
474 [main] WARN org.dbunit.dataset.xml.FlatXmlProducer - Please add the
➥extra columns to line 1, or use a DTD to make sure the value of those
➥columns are populated or specify 'columnSensing=true' for your
➥FlatXmlProducer.
474 [main] WARN org.dbunit.dataset.xml.FlatXmlProducer - See FAQ for more
➥details.
```

Whenever you're facing problems that sound like a DbUnit bug or usage issue, try enabling the lower logging levels[9] like debug or trace. DbUnit will output a lot of debugging information, which will hopefully help you resolve the issue.

17.6   *Creating datasets from existing database data*

So far in the examples, we created dataset XML files from scratch, in a bottom-up approach. This is the ideal situation when you're doing pure TDD, but often you need to create these files from the data already in the database.

For instance, you might be working on a big project, where the database development is done by a separate team of DBAs and a QA team maintains a database instance full of testing data. Typically in these situations, your Java code (and test cases) will have to deal with complex scenarios, like tables with dozens of columns and many foreign key relationships. It would be unpractical and error prone to create the datasets

---

[9]   Notice that you'll need a better SL4J implementation than sl4j-simple in this case.

from scratch, so you can leverage the existing data to create the initial files and then prune the data your test cases don't need.

Even if your project is simpler and you can create the XML files from scratch in your typical development cycle, you may face bugs that are hard to reproduce in a test case. For instance, the user accesses a web application, executes a couple of inserts and updates, and then a page displays a table with incorrect data. In this case, instead of trying to reproduce all steps through code in your test case, you could just manually reproduce the steps, then export the relevant database contents to a dataset, and reproduce only the buggy method call in the test case.

In its simplest form, exporting a dataset is a straightforward task: all you need to do is create a dataset object containing the data you want to export (for instance, using `DatabaseConnection.createDataset()` to export the whole database or a `Query-DataSet` to narrow the data) and then call a static method from the dataset format class (like `FlatXmlDataSet`):

```
IDataSet fullDataSet = dbunitConnection.createDataSet();
FileOutputStream xmlStream = new FileOutputStream("full-database.xml");
FlatXmlDataSet.write(fullDataSet, xmlStream);
```

Similarly, you could also generate the dataset's DTD:

```
FileOutputStream dtdStream = new FileOutputStream("full-database.dtd");
FlatDtdDataSet.write(fullDataSet, dtdStream);
```

This simple approach works fine most of the time, but it has a drawback: the tables in the dataset are created in no particular order. Therefore, if one table has a foreign key constraint with another table, and they're generated in the wrong order, attempts to insert the dataset into the database will mostly likely fail (because of constraint violations).

Fortunately, the solution for this problem is also simple; all it takes is to wrap the dataset in a `FilteredDataSet` that uses a `DatabaseSequenceFilter`, which in turn will return the tables in the right order:

```
IDataSet fullDataSet = dbunitConnection.createDataSet();
ITableFilter filter = new DatabaseSequenceFilter(dbunitConnection);
FilteredDataSet filteredDatSet = new FilteredDataSet(filter, fullDataSet);
FileOutputStream xmlStream = new FileOutputStream("full-database.xml")
FlatXmlDataSet.write(fullDataSet, xmlStream);
```

17.7 *Advanced techniques*

In this section, we analyze techniques that make DbUnit usage easier to understand and maintain. These techniques don't employ any particular DbUnit feature, just advanced Java and JUnit APIs.

17.7.1 *DbUnit and the Template Design Pattern*

If you look at the previous examples from a higher level, you might realize they all follow the same workflow:

1 Prepare the database, using a dataset XML file.

2 Develop some Java code for the test.

3 (Optionally) Compare the state of the database with another dataset file.

Going further, only step 2 is specific for each test; steps 1 and 3 are the same (except for the XML file locations) for all tests. In the examples so far, we achieved a level of reuse by delegating part of step 1 to helper methods (like `getDataSet()` and `get-ReplacedDataSet()`), but we can improve reuse even more if we use the Template Design Pattern.

Design patterns in action: Template Method

The Template (or Template Method) is a behavioral design pattern described in the classic GoF[10] book. In this pattern, a superclass defines the overall skeleton of an algorithm (that is, the template) but leaves some details to be filled in by subclasses.

Back to our example: the template is the workflow we just described, where a superclass defines the skeleton and takes care of steps 1 and 3, and the subclasses are responsible for step 2.

The most common—and simpler—way to implement the template pattern in Java is through an abstract superclass that implements the template and defines abstract methods for the steps the subclasses must implement. This isn't a good approach in our case, because it would allow each subclass to have only one test method, which in turn would require dozens or even hundreds of test classes in a typical project.

A second approach is to create an interface that defines the steps the template method isn't responsible for and receive an implementation (which is typically an anonymous class) of that interface as parameter. This is the approach the Spring Framework uses in its templates (like JdbcTemplate and HibernateTemplate), and it's the approach used in listing 17.18.

Listing 17.18 `UserDaoJdbcImplTest` using the Template Design Pattern

```
[...]
public class UserDaoJdbcImplTemplatePatternTest extends
    AbstractDbUnitTestCase {
  protected interface TemplateWorker {                      ◁─①
    long getId();
    void doIt() throws Exception;
    String getSetupDataSet();
    String getAssertDataSet();
  }
```

---

[10] See *Design Patterns: Elements of Reusable Object-Oriented Software,* by Eric Gamma et al (the Gang of Four).

```
protected void runTemplateTest(TemplateWorker worker)
                                            throws Exception {          ◁───┐
  IDataSet setupDataSet = getReplacedDataSet(worker.getSetupDataSet(),       ❷
    worker.getId() );
  DatabaseOperation.CLEAN_INSERT
                          .execute(dbunitConnection, setupDataSet);   ◁───
  worker.doIt();                                                      ◁───❸
  String comparisonDataSetName = worker.getAssertDataSet();                ❹
  if ( comparisonDataSetName != null ) {                              ◁───
    IDataSet expectedDataSet = getReplacedDataSet(comparisonDataSetName,
      worker.getId());                                                     ❺
    IDataSet actualDataSet = dbunitConnection.createDataSet();
    Assertion.assertEquals( expectedDataSet, actualDataSet );
  }
}

@Test
public void testGetUserById() throws Exception {
  final long id = 42; // value here does not matter
  TemplateWorker worker = new TemplateWorker() {
    public void doIt() throws Exception {
      User user = dao.getUserById(id);
      assertUser( user );
    }
    public String getSetupDataSet() { return "/user-token.xml"; }
    public String getAssertDataSet() { return null; }              ◁─❻
    public long getId() { return id; }
  };
  runTemplateTest(worker);
}

@Test
public void testAddUser() throws Exception {
  TemplateWorker worker = new TemplateWorker() {
    private long id = -1;
    public void doIt() throws Exception {
      User user = newUser();
      id = dao.addUser(user);
      assertTrue(id>0);
    }
    public String getSetupDataSet() { return "/empty.xml"; }        ◁─❼
    public String getAssertDataSet() { return "/user-token.xml"; }
    public long getId() { return id; }
  };
  runTemplateTest(worker);
}
}
```

We start by defining the interface TemplateWorker ❶, which will be implemented as
an inner class by the test cases that use the template method. In the template method
runTemplateTest ❷, notice that ❸, ❹, and ❺ match the three workflow steps
described previously.

In the first test method, testGetUserById(), it isn't necessary to check the database state after this test case is run, so null is returned ❻.

In the second test method `testAddUser()`, we use `CLEAN_INSERT` to prepare the database; in this test case we opted for a total cleanup with `"/empty.xml"` **❼**, a dataset that contains all tables used by the test cases (its content is shown in listing 17.19).

Listing 17.19   empty.xml, dataset used to clean up the database

```xml
<?xml version="1.0"?>
<dataset>
  <users/>
</dataset>
```

The problem with this approach is that it's too verbose and unnatural, because we have to create an inner class on each test method and do the work inside that class (instead of inside the method). In the next section we show a much cleaner approach.

17.7.2 *Improving reuse through custom annotations*

Since their introduction to the Java language, annotations have grown in popularity and are used by many development tools, such as JUnit itself (we've been using JUnit annotations, such as `@Test`, throughout this book). What most developers don't realize, though, is that they don't need to limit themselves to using third-party annotations; they can create their own project-specific annotations. Although Joshua Bloch preaches the opposite in *Effective Java Second Edition*,[11] we believe that custom annotations can boost a project's productivity, particularly in the test-cases arena.

That being said, let's use custom annotations as a third approach to the template pattern implementation. The idea is to clear the noise out of the test method and let it focus on step 2. We use annotations to pass the information necessary to complete steps 1 and 3. Listing 17.20 shows the custom annotation, and listing 17.21 shows the new test methods.

Listing 17.20   Custom annotation `@DataSets`

```java
@Retention(RetentionPolicy.RUNTIME)
@Target(ElementType.METHOD)
public @interface DataSets {

  String setUpDataSet() default "/empty.xml";        ◁──┘ ❶
  String assertDataSet() default "";                       ❷
}                                                     ◁──┘
```

This listing defines an annotation called `DataSets`. The annotation attribute `setUpDataSet` **❶** defines the dataset used to prepare the database. If not specified, the default value is `"/empty.xml"`, which will clean up the entire database.

Similarly, `assertDataSet()` defines the dataset that will be used to check the database state after the test is executed. Because not all test cases must check that (typically, test cases for methods that load data don't), the default is `""` **❷**, which in our case means no dataset. (Notice that the meaning of an annotation value is relevant to

---

[11] Item 35, page 175: "Most programmers will have no need to define annotation types."

the classes that will use the annotation. Because it isn't possible to use `null`, we use the empty string to indicate no dataset.)

Listing 17.21 `UserDaoJdbcImplTest` using custom annotations

```
[...]
public class UserDaoJdbcImplAnnotationTest extends
  AbstractDbUnitTemplateTestCase {
  @Test
  @DataSets(setUpDataSet="/user-token.xml")
  public void testGetUserById() throws Exception {
    User user = dao.getUserById(id);
    assertUser(user);
  }
  @Test
  @DataSets(assertDataSet="/user-token.xml")
  public void testAddUser() throws Exception {
    User user = newUser();
    id = dao.addUser(user);
    assertTrue(id>0);
  }
}
```

Compare this new test class with the previous example (listing 17.19). You barely notice the template pattern being used.

The magic is done by the `AbstractDbUnitTemplateTestCase`, which extends `AbstractDbUnitTestCase` and uses a custom `TestRunner`; this `TestRunner` intercepts the test methods[12] and plays the template role. Listing 17.22 shows this new superclass.

Listing 17.22 New superclass, `AbstractDbUnitTemplateTestCase`

```
[...]
@RunWith(AbstractDbUnitTemplateTestCase.DataSetsTemplateRunner.class)   ←❶
public abstract class AbstractDbUnitTemplateTestCase extends
    AbstractDbUnitTestCase {

  protected static long id;                                              ←❷

  public static class DataSetsTemplateRunner extends JUnit4ClassRunner {

    public DataSetsTemplateRunner(Class<?> klass) throws
                                               InitializationError {
      super(klass);
    }

    @Override
    protected void invokeTestMethod(Method method,
                                RunNotifier notifier) {                  ←❸
      setupDataSet(method);
      super.invokeTestMethod(method, notifier);
      assertDataSet(method);
    }
```

---

[12] This technique is explained in more detail in appendix B.

```
private void setupDataSet(Method method) {
  DataSets dataSetAnnotation = method.getAnnotation(DataSets.class);
  if ( dataSetAnnotation == null ) {
    return;
  }
  String dataSetName = dataSetAnnotation.setUpDataSet();
  if ( ! dataSetName.equals("") ) {
    try {
      IDataSet dataSet = getReplacedDataSet(dataSetName, id);
      DatabaseOperation.CLEAN_INSERT.execute(dbunitConnection,
        dataSet);
    } catch (Exception e) {
      throw new RuntimeException( "exception inserting dataset " +
        dataSetName, e );
    }
  }
}

private void assertDataSet(Method method) {
  DataSets dataSetAnnotation =
    method.getAnnotation(DataSets.class);
  if ( dataSetAnnotation == null ) {
    return;
  }
  String dataSetName = dataSetAnnotation.assertDataSet();
  if ( ! dataSetName.equals("") ) {
    try {
      IDataSet expectedDataSet = getReplacedDataSet(dataSetName, id );
      IDataSet actualDataSet = dbunitConnection.createDataSet();
      Assertion.assertEquals( expectedDataSet, actualDataSet );
    } catch (Exception e) {
      throw new RuntimeException( "exception asserting dataset " +
        dataSetName, e );
    }
  }
}
```

The dirty work is done by DataSetsTemplateRunner ❶, a static inner class. Abstract-DbUnitTemplateTestCase itself does almost nothing other than using @RunWith to drive the test.

The variable id ❷ can't be passed around in annotations, because it can have dynamic values (like in testAddUser()), and annotations can receive only literals (because they're defined at compile time), so it must be shared among test cases. Such an approach might annoy purists, but keeping state in tests is not only acceptable in some cases but often is the best approach for a given problem. The state (id) in this case is passed around only to solve an issue caused by the way the tests are executed.

The template method invokeTestMethod() ❸ defines the three steps of the workflow described earlier. First, the annotation is read ❹ and the dataset is used only if the annotation value isn't an empty string ❺.

17.7.3 *Using Expression Language in datasets*

Our `getReplacedDataSet()` method has two issues: it requires passing the tokens to be replaced (like id) as parameters and then explicitly calls `addReplacementObject()` for each token.

If later on we create a test case where it's necessary to replace two ids, and we know they will be generated in sequence, the method is

```
IDataSet dataSet = getReplacedDataSet(dataSetName, id, id+1);
```

The method changes to

```
public static IDataSet getReplacedDataSet(IDataSet originalDataSet,
                                          long id, long id2) {
  [...]
  replacementDataSet.addReplacementObject("[ID2]", id2);
  [...]
}
```

And the dataset XML would have both [ID] and [ID2]:

```
<dataset>
  <users id="[ID]" ... />
  <users id="[ID2]" ... />
</dataset>
```

That looks like an ugly hack, not to mention the changes to `DataSetsTemplate-Runner`. A much cleaner approach would be to figure out the tokens dynamically, where the following apply:

- Values to be replaced aren't passed by parameter but added to a context.
- Tokens are evaluated so that values in the context are replaced dynamically. It's better yet if the syntax allows basic operations, like [ID+1].

Fortunately, there's a standard Java technology that fits perfectly in this description, the Expression Language (EL).

EL has been around in Java for many years and has made steady progress toward being an integral part of the platform: first as part of JSP tag attributes on JSTL 1.0 and JSF 1.0, then available anywhere inside a JSP 2.0 page, and finally as a standalone Java API (`javax.el`). Besides the standard Java EL, many open source projects offer alternative EL libraries, like OGNL (http://ognl.org) and Marmalade (http://marmalade.codehaus.org).

Using EL, the same dataset would be expressed as

```
<dataset>
  <users id="${id}" ... />
  <users id="${id+1}" ... />
  </dataset>
```

And the `getReplacedDataSet ()` would not require id parameters anymore; instead, the id would be bound to the EL context:

```
getContext().bind( "id", id );
IDataSet dataSet = getReplacedDataSet(dataSetName);
```

Listing 17.23 shows the changes necessary to support EL. Notice that, despite EL being a standard API, it's still necessary to create an ELContext implementation (ELContext-Impl, in our example), and that isn't a trivial task (because of lack of documentation). It's out of the scope of this book to explain how that class was implemented (although the code is available for download), but a quick explanation can be found at the author's blog (http://weblogs.java.net/blog/felipeal/).

Listing 17.23 New `AbstractDbUnitELTemplateTestCase` that supports EL

```
[...]
public abstract class AbstractDbUnitELTemplateTestCase [...] {
[...]
  private static ELContextImpl context;
  @Override
  protected void invokeTestMethod(Method method, RunNotifier notifier) {    ❶
    context = new ELContextImpl();
    context.bind("id", id);                                                  ❷
    setupDataSet(method);
    super.invokeTestMethod(method, notifier);
    context.bind("id", id);                                                  ❸
    assertDataSet(method);
  }
  protected static ELContextImpl getContext() {                              ❹
    return context;
  }
  public static IDataSet getReplacedDataSet(String name) throws Exception {
    [...]
    final FlatXmlDataSet dataSet = new ELAwareFlatXmlDataSet( reader );      ❺
    [...]
  }

  private static class ELAwareFlatXmlDataSet extends FlatXmlDataSet {
    [...]
    @Override
    public void row(Object[] values) throws DataSetException {              ❻
      final ELContextImpl context = getContext();
      if ( context != null ) {                                              ❼
        ExpressionFactory factory = context.getFactory();
        int i = 0;
        for ( Object value : values ) {
          String stringValue = ""+value;
          Object newValue;
          if ( stringValue.startsWith("${") &&                             ❽
               stringValue.endsWith("}") ) {
            ValueExpression converted = factory.createValueExpression(
                              context, stringValue, Object.class );         ❾
            newValue = converted.getValue(context);
          } else {
            newValue = value;
          }
```

```
        values[i++] = newValue;
      }
    } else {
      throw new IllegalStateException( "No context on thread" );
    }
    super.row(values);
  }
}
```

We start by creating a new EL context object ❶ before each test and making it available through the method getContext() ❹, so the test cases could bind more objects to the context as needed. Using the EL context, the id is bound ❷ before the setup dataset is read and bound again ❸ before the assert dataset is read. This is necessary because the test case might have changed the id (like on testAddUser()), and the id is represented by a primitive type (if it was a mutable object, this second bind would not be necessary).

In the method getReplacedDataSet() ❺, the only relevant change (aside from the absence of the id parameter) is that it now uses a custom dataset (ELAware-FlatXmlDataSet).

In the class ELAwareFlatXmlDataSet ❻, we override the method row(), such that it passes each dataset value to the EL engine for evaluation. The code at ❼ shows a subtle trick: instead of passing the EL context as a parameter to ELAwareFlatXmlData-Set constructor, it's accessed with a call to getContext(). This is necessary because row() is used during XML parsing, and FlatXmlDataSet parses the XML in the constructor. This is a bad practice on DbUnit's part—a constructor shouldn't call methods that can be overridden by subclasses.

We note the optimization at ❽: if the value isn't enclosed in ${}, there's no need to evaluate it.

Finally, we get to where the EL engine does its job of evaluating the expression ❾, according to the values bound in the context.

Listing 17.24 shows the new test case. Notice that the only differences from the previous version (listing 17.20) are the superclass and the dataset being used (which is shown in listing 17.25).

Listing 17.24 `UserDaoJdbcImplELTest` using custom annotations

```
[...]
public class UserDaoJdbcImplAnnotationTest extends
    AbstractDbUnitELTemplateTestCase {
  @Test
  @DataSets(setUpDataSet="/user-EL.xml")
  public void testGetUserById() throws Exception {
    User user = dao.getUserById(id);
    assertUser(user);
  }
  @Test
  @DataSets(assertDataSet="/user-EL.xml")
```

```
public void testAddUser() throws Exception {
  User user = newUser();
  id = dao.addUser(user);
  assertTrue(id>0);
  }
}
```

Listing 17.25   user-EL.xml, dataset that uses EL syntax for tokens

```
<?xml version="1.0"?>
<dataset>
  <users id="${id}" username="ElDuderino"
                  first_name="Jeffrey" last_name="Lebowsky" />
</dataset>
```

Now that we've covered some of the advanced techniques you can use with DbUnit, we look next at best practices that are specific to database access testing.

17.8   *Database access testing best practices*

Throughout this chapter, we described in detail best practices that apply to our examples. In this final section, we present additional best practices.

17.8.1 *Use one database per developer*

When you run a database test case, the test can leave the database in an unknown state. Furthermore, the actions of other users can affect the test results. One solution to this problem is to have each developer and build machine use their own database.

If you're fortunate enough to be developing an application that can be run in different database products (for instance, if it uses only standard SQL statements or if the SQL is managed by an ORM tool), then the best approach is to use an embedded database. Not only would each developer would have their own instance, but the database access would be fast.

If the embedded database approach isn't possible, then you should try to install a matching database in each developer's machine (many database vendors, such as Oracle, provide a light version of their product, a good option for this approach).

If neither the embedded nor the light database is possible, then try to allocate one database instance for each developer in the database server. In the worst case, if not even that is possible (too many instances could be costly in resources or in license fees), allocate a few instances to be used for test cases and a few others for regular development.

17.8.2 *Make sure the target database is tested*

If you can implement the embedded database approach, but the final application will be deployed in another database product, make sure the application is tested against the target database. A reasonable approach is to let the developers use the embedded database but have a daily or continuous build use the target database.

Don't make the mistake of assuming databases can be substituted at will; there are always incompatibilities, even if you use an ORM tool. The sooner you catch these issues, the better.

17.8.3 Create complementary tests for loading and storing data

As the old sayings goes, "everything that goes up must come down." If you write a test case that verifies an object is correctly stored in the database, chances are you should write the test that asserts it's loaded correctly. And if you keep that in mind when you write one of them, it makes it easy to write the other one; you could reuse the same dataset or even write special infrastructure to handle both.

17.8.4 When writing load test cases, cover all the basic scenarios

All versions of `testGetUserById()` used in this chapter covered just one scenario: the database contained a row with the tested ID and only that row. That was enough for the purpose of describing the techniques, but in a real project you should test other scenarios, such as testing an ID that doesn't exist in the database, testing an empty database, testing when more than one row is available, and testing joins when multiple rows are available.

The last scenario deserves special attention, because it's a common issue when you use an ORM tool and you're testing a method that uses a complex query where one or more tables are selected using a join. Let's say a `User` object has a `List<Telephone>` relationship, the `Telephone` class is mapped to a telephones table with a foreign key to the users table, you're using JPA in the persistence layer, and the `getUserById()` must do a join fetch to get all telephones in just one query (if you aren't familiar with these concepts, don't worry; we explain them better in chapter 18). You write just one test case, where the dataset contains only one row in both users and telephone rows, and you implement the JPA query as something like `"from User user left join fetch user.telephones where user.id = ?"`. Your test case passes, so you commit your code. Then once the application is in production, and a user happens to have more than one telephone, your code returns two users for the query. After half a day of debugging, you figure out the fix would be to change the query to `"select distinct(user) from User user left join fetch user.telephones where user.id = ?"`. Had your initial test case covered more than the canonical scenario, you wouldn't have had this bug. This particular issue is common.

17.8.5 Plan your dataset usage

As your application grows and you write more database test cases, your datasets become hard to manage. If you have 20 dataset XML files containing a particular table, and that table changes, then you have to change 20 XML files. This is probably the biggest DbUnit drawback, and unfortunately it's a problem without a clear solution.

The best "practice" here is to be aware of this problem and plan in advance. With this in mind, the following techniques can mitigate the problem:

- Use the same dataset for loading/storing an object.
- Keep datasets small, restricting the tables and columns compared.
- If you always use the same values for the same objects (as described in "Best practice: use a helper class to create and assert object instances"), at least you can apply the changes with just one search-and-replace command. Or, in a more sophisticated approach, you could keep smaller XML files for groups of objects and then use XML `include` or `CompositeDataSet` to join them. Keep in mind, though, that any of these approaches brings more complexity to the test cases, and you might end up with something that's harder to maintain than a good, old search and replace.

17.8.6 *Test cleanup*

In all examples so far, the test cases set up the database but didn't bother to clean it up after they did their job. This is *typically* a good practice and is indeed one of the best practices endorsed by DbUnit.

Notice our emphasis on the *typically*, though. The problem of not cleaning up the database after the test is done is that a test case could make another test's life miserable if it inserts data that's hard to be cleaned, like rows with foreign keys. Back to the users/telephones tables example, let's say a test case adds one row to each table, with the telephones row having a foreign key to users, and this test case doesn't clean up these rows after it's run. Then a second test case is going to use the same users row, but it doesn't care about the telephones table. If this test tries to remove the users row at setup, it will fail because of a foreign key violation.

So, long story short, although typically a good setup doesn't need cleanup, it doesn't hurt to clean up, especially when the test case inserts rows with foreign key constraints.

17.9 *Summary*

The persistence layer is undoubtedly one of the most important parts of any enterprise application, although testing it can be a challenge: test cases must be agile, but database characteristics make them bureaucratic. Although JUnit itself doesn't have an answer to this problem, many tools do. In this chapter, we used DbUnit to validate an application's database access.

DbUnit is a stable and mature project, comprising a few dozen interfaces, implementations, and helpers. Despite this high number of classes, DbUnit usage is relatively simple, because it consists of setting up the database before a test is run and comparing its state afterwards.

Although DbUnit is a great tool, it's a low-level library, which provides the basic blocks for database testing. To use it efficiently, it's necessary to define infrastructure classes and methods that at the same time leverage DbUnit strengths and provide reuse throughout the project. With creativity, experience, and planning, it's possible to write DbUnit tests in an efficient and enjoyable way.

In this chapter, we demonstrated through progressive examples how to use DbUnit to populate the database before tests, assert the database contents after the tests, create datasets from existing databases, and use advanced APIs to make tests easier to write and maintain. In the next chapter, we show how to extend these techniques to JPA-based applications, and in chapter 19 we cover tools that enhance JUnit, including Unitils, which provides some of this chapter's techniques out of the box.

Testing JPA-based applications

Unfortunately we need to deal with the object relational (O/R) impedance mismatch, and to do so you need to understand two things: the process of mapping objects to relational databases and how to implement those mappings.

—Scott W. Amber, *Mapping Objects to Relational Databases: O/R Mapping In Detail*

This chapter covers

- Multilayered application testing
- Using DbUnit to test JPA applications
- JPA mapping tests
- Testing JPA-based DAOs
- Verifying JPA-generated schema

Most Java applications need to store data in persistent storage, and typically this storage is a relational database. There are many approaches to persisting the data, from executing low-level SQL statements directly to more sophisticated modules that delegate the task to third-party tools.

Although discussing the different approaches is almost a religious matter, we assume it's a good practice to abstract data persistence to specialized classes, such as DAOs. The DAOs themselves can be implemented in many different ways:

- Writing brute-force SQL statements (such as the `UserDaoJdbcImpl` example in chapter 17)
- Using third-party tools (like Apache iBATIS or Spring JDBC templates) that facilitate JDBC programming
- Delegating the whole database access to tools that map objects to SQL (and vice-versa)

Over the last few years, the third approach has become widely adopted, through the use of ORM (object-relational mapping) tools such as Hibernate and Oracle TopLink. ORM became so popular that JCP (Java Community Process, the organization responsible for defining Java standards) created a specification[1] to address it, the JPA (Java Persistence API). JPA, as the name states, is just an API; in order to use it, you need an implementation. Fortunately, most existing tools adhere to the standard, so if you already use an ORM tool (such as Hibernate), you could use it in JPA mode, that is, using the Java Persistence APIs instead of proprietary ones.

This chapter consists of two parts. First, we show how to test layers that use DAOs in a multilayered application. Then we explain how to test the JPA-based DAO (data access object) implementation, using DbUnit.[2]

And although this chapter focuses on JPA and Hibernate, the ideas presented here apply to other ORM tools as well.

18.1 Testing multilayered applications

By *multilayered* (or multitiered) application we mean an application whose structure has been divided in layers, with each layer responsible for one aspect of the application. A typical example is a three-tiered web application comprising of presentation, business, and persistence layers.

Ideally, all of these layers should be tested, both in isolation (through unit tests) and together (through integration tests). In this section, we show how to unit test the business layer without depending on its lower tier, the persistence layer. But first, let's look at the sample application.

18.1.1 The sample application

The examples in this chapter test the business and persistence layers (presentation layer testing was covered in chapter 11) of an enterprise application. The persistence layer comprises a `User` object and an `UserDao` interface, similar to those defined in

---

[1] Some people may argue that two standards already existed before JPA: EJB entities and JDO. Well, EJB entities were too complicated, and JDO never took off.

[2] And in this aspect, this chapter is an extension of chapter 17; if you aren't familiar with DbUnit, we recommend you read that chapter first.

chapter 17, but with a few differences: a new method (`removeUser()`)on UserDao, the User object now has a one-to-many relationship with a `Telephone` object, and both of these classes are marked with JPA annotations, as shown in listing 18.1.

Listing 18.1   User and Telephone class definitions

```
@Entity
@Table(name="users")
public class User {

  @Id @GeneratedValue(strategy=GenerationType.AUTO)
  private long id;

  private String username;

  @Column(name="first_name")
  private String firstName;

  @Column(name="last_name")
  private String lastName;

  @OneToMany(cascade=CascadeType.ALL)
  @JoinColumn(name="user_id")
  @ForeignKey(name="fk_telephones_users")
  private List<Telephone> telephones = new ArrayList<Telephone>();

  // getters and setters omitted
}

@Entity
@Table(name="phones")
public class Telephone {

  public static enum Type {
    HOME, OFFICE, MOBILE;
  }

  @Id @GeneratedValue(strategy=GenerationType.AUTO)
  private long id;
  private String number;
  private Type type;
  // getters and setters omitted

}
```

This chapter's sample application also has a business layer interface (UserFacade, defined in listing 18.2), which in turn deals with DTOs (data transfer objects), not the persistent objects directly. Therefore, we need a UserDto class (also defined in listing 18.2).

Listing 18.2   Business layer interface (UserFacade) and transfer object (UserDto)

```
public interface UserFacade {
  UserDto getUserById(long id);
}
```

```
public class UserDto {
  private long id;
  private String username;
  private String firstName;
  private String lastName;
  // getters and setters omitted
}
```

Finally, because the persistence layer will be developed using JPA, a new implementation (UserDaoJpaImpl) is necessary, and its initial version is shown in listing 18.3.[3]

Listing 18.3   Initial implementation of UserDao using JPA

```
public class UserDaoJpaImpl implements UserDao {

  private EntityManager entityManager; // getters and setters omitted

  public void addUser(User user) {
    entityManager.persist(user);
  }

  public User getUserById(long id) {
    return entityManager.find(User.class, id);
  }

  public void deleteUser(long id) {
    String jql = "delete User where id = ?";
    Query query = entityManager.createQuery(jql);
    query.setParameter(1, id);
    query.executeUpdate();
  }

}
```

The sample application is available in two flavors, Maven and Ant. To run the tests on Maven, type 'mvn clean test'. Similarly, to use Ant instead, type 'ant clean test'. The application is also available as two Eclipse projects, one with the required libraries (under the lib directory) and another with the project itself.

18.1.2 *Multiple layers, multiple testing strategies*

Because each application layer has different characteristics and dependencies, the layers require different testing strategies. If your application has been designed to use interfaces and implementations, it's possible to test each layer in isolation, using mocks or stubs to implement other layers' interfaces.

In our example, the business layer façade (listing 18.4) will be tested using Easy-Mock as the implementation of the DAO interfaces, as shown in listing 18.5.

---

[3] The astute reader might be wondering why we listed UserDaoJpaImpl in this chapter but omitted UserDaoJdbcImpl in chapter 17. The reason is that the JPA implementation is much simpler, just a few lines of nonplumbing code.

Listing 18.4 Façade implementation (`UserFacadeImpl`)

```
[...]
public class UserFacadeImpl implements UserFacade {

  private static final String TELEPHONE_STRING_FORMAT = "%s (%s)";
  private UserDao userDao; // getters and setters omitted

  public UserDto getUserById(long id) {
    User user = userDao.getUserById(id);
    UserDto dto = new UserDto();
    dto.setFirstName(user.getFirstName());
    dto.setLastName(user.getLastName());
    dto.setUsername(user.getUsername());
    List<String> telephoneDtos = dto.getTelephones();
    for ( Telephone telephone : user.getTelephones() ) {
      String telephoneDto =
        String.format(TELEPHONE_STRING_FORMAT,
          telephone.getNumber(), telephone.getType());
      telephoneDtos.add(telephoneDto);
    }
    return dto;
  }

}
```

Listing 18.5 Unit test for `UserFacadeImpl`

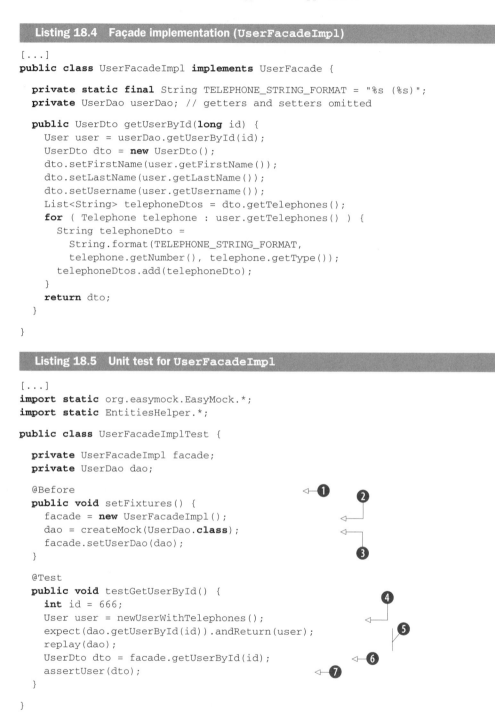

```
[...]
import static org.easymock.EasyMock.*;
import static EntitiesHelper.*;

public class UserFacadeImplTest {

  private UserFacadeImpl facade;
  private UserDao dao;

  @Before
  public void setFixtures() {                          ◄─❶  ❷
    facade = new UserFacadeImpl();                     ◄──┘
    dao = createMock(UserDao.class);                   ◄──┐
    facade.setUserDao(dao);                            ◄──┘
  }                                                         ❸

  @Test
  public void testGetUserById() {                               ❹
    int id = 666;
    User user = newUserWithTelephones();               ◄──┐
    expect(dao.getUserById(id)).andReturn(user);       ◄──┘❺
    replay(dao);                                          │
    UserDto dto = facade.getUserById(id);              ◄─❻◄─┘
    assertUser(dto);                                   ◄─❼
  }

}
```

Before the test is run, we prepare the fixtures ❶ that will be used in the test methods, the object being tested ❷, and a mock ❸. Even if you have only one test method (as is the case in this example), eventually more will be added, so it's worth having such a setup method from the beginning.

Then, on the test case we create a User object ❹ and set the mock expectation ❺ to return it when requested (see more about mock expectations in chapter 6). Notice that newUser() belongs to EntitiesHelper, which provides methods to create new entities (like User) and assert the properties of existing ones (EntitiesHelper was introduced in chapter 17, and new methods are added in this chapter; the full code isn't listed here but is available for download).

Finally, on ❻ the method being tested is called, and the result is checked on ❼ (which is another method defined in EntitiesHelper).

This test case seems pretty much complete, and it almost is, except that it exercises only the best-case scenario. But what if the DAO didn't find the request user? To be complete, the test cases must also exercise negative scenarios. Let's try to add a new test case that simulates the DAO method returning null:[4]

```
@Test
public void testGetUserByIdUnknownId() {
  int id = 666;
  expect(dao.getUserById(id)).andReturn(null);
  replay(dao);
  UserDto dto = facade.getUserById(id);
  assertNull(dto);
}
```

Running this test, we get the dreaded NPE (NullPointerException):

```
java.lang.NullPointerException
    at com.manning.junitbook.ch18.business.UserFacadeImpl.getUserById
    ➥(UserFacade Impl.java:49)
    at com.manning.junitbook.ch18.business.UserFacadeImplTest.testGetUserById
    ➥UnkownId(UserFacadeImplTest.java:51)
```

This makes sense, because the Facade method isn't checking to see if the object return by the DAO is null. It could be fixed by adding the following lines after the user is retrieved from the DAO:

```
if ( user == null ) {
  return null;
}
```

Once this test case is added and the method fixed, our Facade is complete and fully tested, without needing a DAO implementation.

Such separation of functionalities in interfaces and implementations greatly facilitates the development of multilayered applications, because each layer can be

---

[4] How do we know the DAO returns null in this case? And who defined what the Facade should return? What happens in these exceptional cases should be documented in the DAO and Facade methods' Javadoc, and the test cases should follow that contract. In our example, we don't document that on purpose, to show how serious that lack of documentation can be. Anyway, we're returning null in both cases, but another approach could be throwing an ObjectNotFoundException.

developed in parallel, by different teams. Using this approach, the whole business layer could be developed and unit tested without depending on the persistence layer, which would free the business developers from database worries. It's still necessary to test everything together though, but that could be achieved through integration tests. A good compromise is to write many small (and fast) unit tests that extensively exercise individual components and then a few (and slower) integration tests that cover the most important scenarios.

Similarly, we could test the persistence layer using mocks for the JPA interfaces. But this approach isn't recommended, because mocks only emulate API calls, and that wouldn't be enough, for a few reasons. First, the API is part of JPA-based development; it's still necessary to annotate classes and provide configuration files. Second, even if the JPA part is correctly configured, there are still third parties involved: the JPA vendor (like Hibernate), the vendor's driver (such as `HibernateDialect` implementations) for the database being used, not to the mention the database itself. Many things could go wrong (like vendor or drivers bugs, the use of table names that are illegal for a given database, transaction issues, and the like) at runtime that wouldn't be detected by using mocks for testing.

Who let the transactions out?

In a JPA-based application, it's paramount to start and commit transactions, and the methods that use an `EntityManager` have two options: either they handle the transactions themselves, or they rely on the upper layers for this dirty job. Typically, the latter option is more appropriate, because it gives the caller the option to invoke more than one DAO method in the same transaction. Looking at our examples, `UserDaoJpaImpl` follows this approach, because it doesn't deal with transaction management. But if you look at its caller, `UserFacadeImpl`, it doesn't handle transactions either! So, in our application example, who is responsible for transaction management?

The answer is the container. In our examples, we're showing pieces of an application. But in a real project, these pieces would be assembled by a container, like a Java EE application server or Spring, and this container would be responsible for wrapping the `Facade` methods inside a JPA transaction and propagating it to the DAO object. In our DAO test cases, we play the role of the container and explicitly manage the transactions.

For the persistence layer, it's important to test real access to the database, as we demonstrate in the next section.

18.2   Aspects of JPA testing

When you use JPA (or any other ORM software) in your application, you're delegating the task of persisting objects to and from the database to an external tool. But in the end, the results are the same as if you wrote the persistence code yourself. So, in its essence, JPA testing isn't much different than testing regular database access code, and hence most of the techniques explained in chapter 17 apply here. A few differences and caveats are worth mentioning though, and we cover them in the next subsections. But first, let's consider some aspects of JPA testing.

WHAT SHOULD BE TESTED?

JPA programming could be divided in two parts: entities mapping and API calls. Initially, you need to define how your objects will be mapped to the database tables, typically through the use of Java annotations. Then you use an `EntityManager` object to send these objects to or from the database: you can create objects, delete them, fetch them using JPA queries, and so on.

Consequently, it's a good practice to test these two aspects separately. For each persistent object, you write a few test cases that verify that they're correctly mapped (there are many caveats on JPA mapping, particularly when dealing with collections). Then you write separate unit tests for the persistence code itself (such as DAO objects). We present practical examples for both tests in the next subsections.

THE EMBEDDED DATABASE ADVANTAGE

As we mentioned in section 17.1.3, unit tests must be fast to run, and database access is typically slow. A way to improve the access time is to use an in-memory embedded database, but the drawback is that this database might not be totally compatible with the database the application uses.

But when you use JPA, database compatibility isn't an issue—quite the opposite. The JPA vendor is responsible for SQL code generation,[5] and vendors typically support all but the rarest databases. It's perfectly fine to use a fast embedded database (like HSQLDB or its successor, H2) for unit tests. Better yet, the project should be set in such a way that the embedded database is used by default, but databases could be easily switched. That would take advantage of the best of both worlds: developers would use the fast mode, whereas official builds (like nightly and release builds) would switch to the production database (guaranteeing the application works in the real scenario).

COMMITMENT LEVEL

JPA operations should happen inside a transaction, which typically also translates to a vendor-specific session. A lot of JPA features and performance depends on the transaction/session lifecycle management: objects are cached, new SQL commands are issued on demand to fetch lazy relationships, update commands are flushed to the database, and so on.

On the other hand, committing a transaction is not only an expensive operation, but it also makes the database changes permanent. Because of that, there's a tendency

---

[5] This is the ideal scenario; some applications might still need to manually issue a few SQL commands because of JPA bugs or performance requirements. These cases are rare, though, and they could be handled separately in the test cases.

for test cases to roll back the transaction on teardown, and many frameworks (such as Spring TestContext) follow this approach.

So what is the better approach, to commit or not? Again, there's no secret ingredient, and each approach has its advantages. We, in particular, prefer the commit option, because of the following aspects:

- If you're using an embedded database, speed isn't an issue. You could even re-create the whole database before each test case.
- As we mention in section 18.8.5, test cases can do cleanup on teardown when necessary. And again, when using an embedded database, the cleanup is a cheap operation.
- If you roll back the transaction, the JPA vendor might not send the real SQL to the database (for instance, Hibernate issues the SQL only at commit or if `session.flush()` is explicitly called). There might be cases where your test case passes, but when the code is executed in real life, if fails.
- In some situations, you want to explicitly test how the persistent objects will behave once outside a JPA transaction/session.

For these reasons, the test cases in this chapter manually handle the transaction's lifecycle.

Now, without further ado, let's start testing it.

18.3   *Preparing the infrastructure*

Okay, we lied: before our first test, we need some more ado! More specifically, we need to define the infrastructure classes that our real test case classes will extend (remember section 17.3's best practice: define a superclass for your database tests). Figure 18.1 shows the class diagram for such infrastructure.

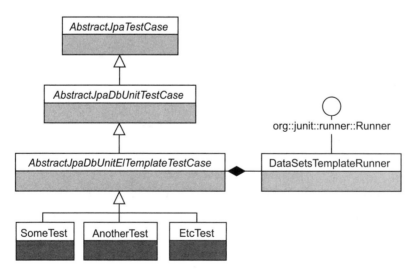

Figure 18.1   Class diagram of the testing infrastructure

The infrastructure class hierarchy depicted in figure 18.1 is quite similar to the one used in chapter 17. The only difference is the root class, AbstractJpaTestCase, which is shown in listing 18.6.

Listing 18.6   Root class of testing infrastructure, `AbstractJpaTestCase`

```
[ ... ]

public abstract class AbstractJpaTestCase {

  private static EntityManagerFactory entityManagerFactory;
  protected static Connection connection;
  protected EntityManager em;

  @BeforeClass
  public static void setupDatabase() throws Exception {          ❶
    entityManagerFactory =
      Persistence.createEntityManagerFactory("chapter-18");      ⟵
    connection = getConnection(entityManagerFactory);            ⟵
  }                                                              ❷

  @AfterClass
  public static void closeDatabase() throws Exception {    ⟵❸
    if ( connection != null ) {
      connection.close();
      connection = null;
    }
    if ( entityManagerFactory != null ) {
      entityManagerFactory.close();
    }
  }
                                                      ❹
  @Before
  public void setEntityManager() {                    ⟵
    em = entityManagerFactory.createEntityManager();
  }

  @After
  public void closeEntityManager() {          ⟵❺
    em.close();
  }

  public static Connection getConnection(Object object) throws Exception {
    Connection connection = null;
    if ( object instanceof EntityManagerFactoryImpl ) {                     ⟵
      EntityManagerFactoryImpl impl = (EntityManagerFactoryImpl) object;
      SessionFactory sessionFactory = impl.getSessionFactory();            ❻
      if ( sessionFactory instanceof SessionFactoryImpl ) {
        SessionFactoryImpl sfi = (SessionFactoryImpl) sessionFactory;
        Settings settings = sfi.getSettings();
        ConnectionProvider provider = settings.getConnectionProvider();
        connection = provider.getConnection();
      }
    }
    return connection;
  }
```

```
  protected void beginTransaction() {                    ◄─●7

    em.getTransaction().begin();
  }

  protected void commitTransaction() {                   ◄─●8
    em.getTransaction().commit();
  }

  protected void commitTransaction(boolean clearContext) {    ◄─●9
    commitTransaction();
    if ( clearContext ) {
      em.clear();
    }
  }
}
```

●1 The first step is to create an `EntityManagerFactory`, and as this is an expensive operation, it's done only once, using the `@Before` annotation. Notice that this initialization doesn't contain any information about the JPA provider (Hibernate) or database (HSQLDB) used in the test case. That information is defined in the persistence.xml and hibernate.properties files (shown in listings 18.7 and 18.8, respectively).

●2 Although when you use JPA you don't need to deal with low-level JDBC interfaces directly, DbUnit needs a database connection. You could define the JDBC settings for this connection in a properties file, but that would be redundant; it's better to extract the JDBC connection from JPA's entity manager. Also notice that such reuse is the reason why this chapter's `AbstractJpaDbUnitTestCase` (which isn't shown here either, but is the same as chapter's 17 `AbstractDbUnitTestCase`) extends `AbstractJpaTestCase`, and not vice versa. If `@BeforeClass` methods didn't have to be static, such reversal of fortune wouldn't be necessary: `AbstractJpaDbUnitTest-Case` could define a protected `getConnection()` method, which in turn would be overridden by `AbstractJpaTestCase`.

●3 Don't forget to close at `@After` what you opened at `@Before`!

●4, ●5 The `EntityManager`, which is the object effectively used by the test cases, is created before each test method and closed thereafter. This is the way JPA is supposed to be used, and this object creation is cheap.

●6 Unfortunately, there's no standard way to extract the JDBC `Connection` from the JPA `EntityManagerFactory`, so it's necessary to use proprietary APIs from the chosen JPA vendors.

●7, ●8 Because our test cases will manually manage transactions, it's convenient to create helper methods for this task.

●9 Similarly, some test cases will test how objects behave outside the JPA context, so we define an overloaded `commitTransaction()`, which also clears the context.

The JPA configuration is quite simple: persistence.xml (listing 18.7) only defines a persistence-unit name, and the vendor-specific configuration is defined in hibernate.properties (listing 18.8). Such a split is a good practice, because if the test cases must change any configuration (as you'll see later on), we could create a new hibernate.properties file in the test directories, without interfering with the artifacts used by the production code. Notice also that we set the property `hibernate.hbm2ddl.auto` to `update`, so the test cases don't need to create the database tables (Hibernate will automatically create or update the database schema as needed).

Listing 18.7   JPA configuration (persistence.xml)

```
<persistence xmlns="http://java.sun.com/xml/ns/persistence"
    xmlns:xsi="http://www.w3.org/2001/XMLSchema-instance"
    xsi:schemaLocation=
        "http://java.sun.com/xml/ns/persistence persistence_1_0.xsd"
    version="1.0">
    <persistence-unit name="chapter-18">
      <!-- properties are loaded from a separate file, and classes are
           scanned through annotations -->
  </persistence-unit>

</persistence>
```

Listing 18.8   Hibernate-specific configuration (hibernate.properties)

```
hibernate.hbm2ddl.auto=update
hibernate.show_sql=false
hibernate.dialect=org.hibernate.dialect.HSQLDialect
hibernate.connection.driver_class=org.hsqldb.jdbcDriver
hibernate.connection.url=jdbc:hsqldb:mem:my-project-test;shutdown=true
```

As a final note, some frameworks—such as Spring and Unitils (which we cover in the next chapter)—already provide a similar setup. So even though this infrastructure is based on real projects (it was not created for the book samples), provides flexibility (and can be adapted to your project needs), and is simple enough (just a few classes), you might prefer—or it might be more suitable for your project—to use such frameworks instead.

Now that the infrastructure is set, let's move on to our tests, starting with the JPA entity mapping tests.

18.4   *Testing JPA entities mapping*

The first step in JPA development is mapping your objects to tables. Although JPA does a good job of providing default values for most mappings, it's still necessary to tune it up, typically through the use of Java annotations. And as you annotate the persistent classes, you want to be sure they're correctly mapped, so you write test cases that exercise the mapping alone (without worrying about how your final code is going to call the JPA API).

You might be wondering whether these tests are necessary. What could be wrong?

Unfortunately, despite the fact that JPA is a powerful and helpful tool, many things could be wrong in the mappings, and the sooner you figure it out, the better, for instance:

- Some table or column name (like user, role, or group) might be a reserved word in the chosen database.

- If you don't set the relationship annotations (like @OneToMany) correctly, JPA will create many weird mappings, sometimes even unnecessary tables.

- When dependent objects must be persisted automatically, it's important to verify that the proper cascade options have been set.

Not to mention the mother of all reasons why you write unit tests: you need to somehow verify that JPA is persisting/restoring your objects! Without the entity mapping tests, you'd have to either rely on your IDE or manually test it using the main() method of some hacky class.

In order to avoid these issues, it's a good practice to write a couple (at least two: one for loading, another for saving) of unit tests for each primary persistent entity in the system. You don't need to write tests for all of them, though. Some entities are too simple or can be indirectly tested (like the Telephone entity in our examples).

Also, because the load and save tests are orthogonal, they should use the same dataset whenever possible, to facilitate maintenance; listing 18.9 shows the dataset used in the user entity mapping tests (listing 18.10).

Listing 18.9   Dataset file for `User` and `Telephone` tests, user-with-telephone.xml

```
<?xml version="1.0"?>
<dataset>
  <users id="${id}" username="ElDuderino"
                  first_name="Jeffrey" last_name="Lebowsky" />
  <phones id="${phoneId}" user_id="${id}" type="0" number="481 516-2342"/>
  <phones id="${phoneId+1}" user_id="${id}" type="2"
                  number="108 555-6666"/>
</dataset>
```

Notice that the IDs are dynamically defined using EL expressions, so the test cases succeed regardless of the order in which they're executed.

Listing 18.10   Entity mapping unit tests for `User` and `Telephone` classes

```
[...]
public class EntitiesMappingTest extends AbstractJpaDbUnitELTemplateTestCase
    {

  @Test
  @DataSets(setUpDataSet="/user-with-telephone.xml")
  public void testLoadUserWithTelephone() {
    beginTransaction();                                        ❶
    User user = em.find(User.class, id);                       ❷
    commitTransaction();                                       ❸
    assertUserWithTelephone(user);                             ❹
    id++; phoneId+=2;                                          ❺
  }

  @Test
  @DataSets(assertDataSet="/user-with-telephone.xml")
```

```
public void testSaveUserWithTelephone() throws Exception {        ◁─❻
    User user = newUserWithTelephone();
    beginTransaction();
    em.persist(user);
    commitTransaction();
}
```

❶, ❸ As explained earlier, we opted for manual transaction control, so the test case explicitly starts and finishes the transaction.

❷ Because we're testing the entity mappings and not the real persistence layer code such as DAO implementations, we deal with the persistence manager directly.

❹ Once the object is read from the database, we assert that it has the expected values, using our old friend EntitiesHelper **❺**; id and phoneId (which are defined in the superclass and have the initial value of 1) are updated to reflect the objects that were loaded from the database. If they aren't updated, the next test case could fail (if it saves objects, which is the case in our example).

❻ The test case for saving an entity is pretty much orthogonal to the load entity test case; nothing new here.

Although these tests run fine and pass, the way the IDs (id and phoneId) are handled is far from elegant and presents many flaws. For instance, if a test case fails, the IDs aren't updated, and then other tests running after it will fail as well. Sure, a try/finally block would fix this particular issue, but that would make the test even uglier and more verbose. Another problem is that testSaveUserWithTelephone() doesn't update the IDs (because its dataset assertion would fail), so a third test case would probably fail.

What should we do to solve these ID issues? Well, don't throw the book away (yet)—a solution for this problem follows.

18.4.1 *Integrating test cases with JPA ID generators*

In JPA, every persistent entity needs an ID, which is the equivalent of a primary key. When a new entity is persisted, the JPA engine must set its ID, and how its value is determined depends on the mapping. For instance, our User class has the following mapping:

```
@Id @GeneratedValue(strategy=GenerationType.AUTO)
private long id;
```

The @Id annotation indicates this attribute represents the entity's primary key, and @GeneratedValue defines how its value is obtained when the entity is persisted. AUTO in this case means we left the decision to the JPA vendor, which will pick the best strategies depending on what the target database supports. Other values are IDENTITY (for databases that support autogenerated primary keys), SEQUENCE (uses database sequences, where supported), and TABLES (uses one or more tables only for the purpose of generating primary keys). A fifth option would be omitting @GeneratedValue, which means the user (and not the JPA engine) is responsible for setting the IDs. In most cases, AUTO is the best choice; it's the default option for the @GeneratedValue annotation.

Back to our test cases, the dataset files contain references to the ID columns (both as primary key in the users table and foreign key on telephones), and because we're using the same dataset for both load and save, the ID values must be defined dynamically at the time the test is run. If we used distinct datasets, the IDs wouldn't matter on the load test (because JPA wouldn't be persisting entities, only loading them), and for the save tests, we could ignore them. The problem with this option is that it makes it harder to write and maintain the test cases. It would require two datasets and also changes in the `DataSetsTemplateRunner.assertDataSet()` method in order to ignore the ID columns. Because our goal is always to facilitate long-term maintenance, we opted for using the same dataset, and hence we need a solution for the ID synchronization problem.

Listing 18.10 tried to solve the problem the simplest way, by letting the test case update the IDs, but that approach had many issues. A better approach is to integrate the dataset ID's maintenance with the JPA's entity ID's generation, and there are two ways to achieve such integration: taking control of ID generation or being notified of the generated IDs.

Generating IDs for persistent objects isn't a simple task, because there are many complex aspects to be taken into account, such as concurrent ID generation in different transactions. Besides, when you use this approach, your test cases won't be reflecting the real application scenario (and hence they could hide potential problems). For these reasons, we choose the second approach: being notified of the generated IDs.

Using pure JPA, it's possible to define a listener for entity lifecycle events (like object creation, update, and deletion). But this approach doesn't work well in our case, because these events don't provide a clear way to obtain the ID of the saved objects. A better solution is to use vendor-specific extensions.

Hibernate provides its own API for lifecycle events, with listeners for many pre and post events. In particular, it provides a `PostInsertEventListener` interface with an `onPostInsert(PostInsertEvent event)` method, and the event itself contains a reference to both the entity inserted and the generated ID.

The `PostInsertEventListener` API solves part of our problem: our test cases now can be notified of the IDs generated for each object. Good, but now what? Well, the answer relies on our good, old friend EL (Expression Language, introduced in chapter 17, section 17.7.3). So far, we've been using simple variable resolution (like `${id}`) on our datasets. But EL also supports function resolution, so we could have a function that returns an ID for a given class and then use a `PostInsertEventListener` to set the values returned by the function. Let's start with the new dataset, shown in listing 18.11.

> **Listing 18.11   New version of user-with-telephone.xml dataset, using EL functions**

```
<dataset>
  <users id="${db:id('User')}" username="ElDuderino"
                     first_name="Jeffrey" last_name="Lebowsky" />
```

```
<phones id="${db:id('Telephone')}" user_id="${db:id('User')}" type="0"
                                number="481 516-2342"/>
</dataset>
```

Instead of using hardcoded IDs for each class (like ${id} and ${phoneId}), this new version uses a generic ${db:id('ClassName')} function, which is much more flexible. The db:id() function then returns the respective ID for a given class, which is either the value defined by the Hibernate listener or 1 by default (which means no entity has been generated by JPA for that class. In this case the value doesn't matter, but using 1 makes it easier to debug in case of errors). To add support for this function, first we need to change ELContextImpl to support function mapping, as shown in listing 18.12.

Listing 18.12   Changes to `ELContextImpl` to support the `id` function

```
[...]
public final class ELContextImpl extends ELContext {
[...]
  private FunctionMapper functionMapper = new ELFunctionMapperImpl();
[...]
  @Override
  public FunctionMapper getFunctionMapper() {
    return functionMapper;
  }
[...]
}
```

The ID function itself is defined at ELFunctionMapperImpl, shown in listing 18.13.

Listing 18.13   Custom EL functions (`ELFunctionMapperImpl`)

```
[...]
public class ELFunctionMapperImpl extends FunctionMapper {
  private static final Map<String, Method> METHODS =
    new HashMap<String, Method>();
  private static final Map<String,Long> IDS = new HashMap<String, Long>();   ❶
  private static final int INITIAL_ID = 1;

  static {                                                                    ❷
    for ( Method method : ELFunctionMapperImpl.class.getDeclaredMethods() ) {
      int modifiers = method.getModifiers();
      String name = method.getName();
      if ( Modifier.isStatic(modifiers) && name.startsWith("db_")) {
        METHODS.put(name.replace('_', ':'), method);
      }
    }
  }

  @Override
  public Method resolveFunction(String prefix, String localName) {           ❸
    return METHODS.get(prefix+":"+localName);
  }
```

```
    public static long db_id(String className) {                    ← 4
        long id;
        if ( IDS.containsKey(className) ) {
            id = IDS.get(className);
        } else {
            id = INITIAL_ID;
        }
        return id;
    }

    public static void setId(String className, long newId) {        ← 5
        if ( ! IDS.containsKey(className) ) {
            IDS.put(className, newId);
        }
    }

    public static void resetIds() {                                 ← 6
        IDS.clear();
    }

    public static long getId(Class<?> clazz) {                      ← 7
        return db_id(clazz.getSimpleName());
    }

}
```

❶ This defines the value returned by the ID function when no ID was set for a given class.

❷ This initializes the map of static methods that define EL functions. To facilitate the mapping, these methods starts with db_.

❸ resolveFunction() is part of the EL API and is used to map an EL function (such as db:id) to a Java method (db_id(), in this case). It returns the method defined at ❷.

❹ This is the id function properly speaking, which returns either the initial ID or the value present in the ID's map.

❺ Our custom Hibernate listener calls this method every time a new entity is generated, but only the first value is saved in the ID's map; the other values are calculated by the dataset, using this base ID when necessary (such as ${db:id('Telephone')+1}, if the dataset has two telephone rows). Notice that this mechanism assumes IDs are generated in sequence, which is true most of the time, but not always. If that doesn't apply in your case (for instance, if you're using a generation strategy based on UUIDs), you'll need a different (and more complex) approach to represent multiple IDs, like using a sequence parameter in the id function: ${db:id('Telephone',1)} would return the first generated ID, ${db:id('Telephone',2)} would return the second, and so on. Then instead of keeping a single ID in the map, you'd keep a list of the generated IDs for each class.

❻ The ID map must be reset before each method, so load methods always start with id=1 (or whatever value is defined at ❶).

❼ This is the helper method used by test cases that need to know the base ID for a given class.

The next step is the Hibernate integration. But first we need a listener, as defined in listing 18.14.

```
import org.hibernate.event.PostInsertEvent;
import org.hibernate.event.PostInsertEventListener;

public class ELPostInsertEventListener implements PostInsertEventListener {

    public void onPostInsert(PostInsertEvent event) {
        String className = event.getEntity().getClass().getSimpleName();   ←❶
        Long id = (Long) event.getId();
        ELFunctionMapperImpl.setId(className, id);
    }

}
```

In order to simplify the datasets, only the simple name ❶ of the class is used, not the whole fully qualified name (otherwise, the datasets would need something like `${db:id('com.manning.jia.chapter18.model.User')}`). If your project has more than one class with the same name (but in different packages), then you'll need some workaround here, but keeping the simple class name should be enough most of the time (and having multiple classes with the same name isn't a good practice anyway).

Next, we change hibernate.properties to add the custom listener, by including the following property:

```
hibernate.ejb.event.post-insert=
    ➥org.hibernate.ejb.event.EJB3PostInsertEventListener,
    ➥com.manning.jia.chapter18.hibernate.ELPostInsertEventListener
```

Notice that when you set the listeners for a lifecycle event in the properties, you're defining all listeners, not just adding new ones. Therefore, it's recommended to keep the default Hibernate listeners. But Hibernate doesn't clearly document what these listeners are, so you need to figure that out by yourself, and one way of doing that is by changing the `setEntityManager()`, as shown in listing 18.15.

```
[...]
public abstract class AbstractJpaTestCase {
[...]
  @Before
  public void setEntityManager() {
    em = entityManagerFactory.createEntityManager();
    // change if statement below to true to figure out the Hibernate
    // listeners
    if ( false ) {
      Object delegate = em.getDelegate();
      SessionImpl session = (SessionImpl) delegate;
      EventListeners listeners = session.getListeners();
      PostInsertEventListener[] postInsertListeners =
        listeners.getPostInsertEventListeners();
```

```
for ( PostInsertEventListener listener : postInsertListeners ) {
    System.out.println("Listener: " + listener.getClass().getName() );
  }
}
}
}
```

Finally, it's necessary to change the test case classes: first the infrastructure classes (as shown in listing 18.16) and then the test methods themselves (listing 18.17).

Listing 18.16   Changes on `AbstractJpaDbUnitELTemplateTestCase`

```
[...]
public abstract class AbstractJpaDbUnitELTemplateTestCaseJUnit      ❶
  extends AbstractJpaDbUnitTestCase {

    @Override
    protected void invokeTestMethod(Method method, RunNotifier notifier) {
        context = new ELContextImpl();
        ELFunctionMapperImpl.resetIds();
        setupDataSet(method);                                        ❷
        super.invokeTestMethod(method, notifier);
        assertDataSet(method);
    }
}
```

❶ Although not shown here, superclass `AbstractJpaDbUnitTestCase` also changed; it doesn't need to keep track of the IDs anymore, so `id` and `phoneId` were removed.

❷ This method now is also simpler than before. Instead of binding the `id` variable to the EL context before and after invoking the test, it resets the ID's map before each test is run.

Listing 18.17   New version of `EntitiesMappingTest` using JPA ID's integration

```
[...]
public class EntitiesMappingTest extends
  AbstractJpaDbUnitELTemplateTestCase {

    @Test
    @DataSets(setUpDataSet="/user-with-telephone.xml")
    public void testLoadUserWithTelephone() {
        beginTransaction();
        long id = ELFunctionMapperImpl.getId(User.class);            ❶
        User user = em.find(User.class, id);
        commitTransaction();
        assertUser(user,true);
    }

    @Test
    @DataSets(assertDataSet="/user-with-telephone.xml")
    public void testSaveUserWithTelephone() throws Exception {        ❷
        User user = newUser(true);
        beginTransaction();
        em.persist(user);
```

```
      commitTransaction();
    }
  }
```

Because IDs aren't tracked by a superclass anymore, it's necessary to ask ELFunction-
MapperImpl ❶ to get the ID on testLoadUserWithTelephone(). Test case testSave-
UserWithTelephone() ❷, on the other hand, was not changed, because it doesn't use
the IDs directly (only in the dataset).

18.5   *Testing JPA-based DAOs*

Once you're assured the persistence entities are correctly mapped, it's time to test the
application code that effectively uses JPA, such as DAOs. The test cases for JPA-based
DAOs are similar to the entity mapping tests you saw in the previous section; the main
difference (besides the fact that you use DAO code instead of direct JPA calls) is that
you have to cover more scenarios, paying attention to some tricky issues.

Let's start with the simplest cases, the same cases for getUserById() and addUser()
we implemented in chapter 17 (where the DAOs were implemented using pure JDBC),
plus a test case for testRemoveUser(). The test cases are shown in listing 18.18, and the
initial DAO implementation was shown in listing 18.4.

> **Listing 18.18   Initial version of `UserDaoJpaImplTest`**

```
[...]
public class UserDaoJpaImplTest extends AbstractJpaDbUnitELTemplateTestCase {

  UserDaoJpaImpl dao;

  @Before
  public void prepareDao() {
    dao = new UserDaoJpaImpl();
    dao.setEntityManager(em);
  }

  @Test
  @DataSets(setUpDataSet="/user.xml")
  public void testGetUserById() throws Exception {
    beginTransaction();
    long id = ELFunctionMapperImpl.getId(User.class);
    User user = dao.getUserById(id);
    commitTransaction();
    assertUser(user);
  }

  @Test
  @DataSets(assertDataSet="/user.xml")
  public void testAddUser() throws Exception {
    beginTransaction();
    User user = newUser();
    dao.addUser(user);
    commitTransaction();
    long id = user.getId();
```

```
    assertTrue(id>0);
  }

  @Test
  @DataSets(setUpDataSet="/user.xml",assertDataSet="/empty.xml")
  public void testDeleteUser() throws Exception {
    beginTransaction();
    long id = ELFunctionMapperImpl.getId(User.class);
    dao.deleteUser(id);
    commitTransaction();
  }
}
```

Compare this test case with chapter 17's latest version (listing 17.24) of the equivalent test; they're almost the same, the only differences being the pretest method prepare-Dao() (which instantiates a DAO object and sets its EntityManager), the local variable representing the user's ID (because of the Hibernate ID generation integration we discussed in the previous section), and the transaction management calls.

But now the User object could also have a list of telephones; it's necessary, then, to add analogous test cases to handle this scenario, as shown in listing 18.19. Note that if the User/Telephone relationship was mandatory (and not optional), the new tests would replace the old ones (instead of being added to the test class).

Listing 18.19   New test cases on `UserDaoJpaImplTest` to handle user with telephone

```
[...]
public class UserDaoJpaImplTest extends AbstractJpaDbUnitELTemplateTestCase {
[...]
  @Test
  @DataSets(setUpDataSet="/user-with-telephone.xml")
  public void testGetUserByIdWithTelephone() throws Exception {
    beginTransaction();
    long id = ELFunctionMapperImpl.getId(User.class);
    User user = dao.getUserById(id);
    commitTransaction();
    assertUserWithTelephone(user);
  }

  @Test
  @DataSets(assertDataSet="/user-with-telephone.xml")
  public void testAddUserWithTelephone() throws Exception {
    beginTransaction();
    User user = newUserWithTelephone();
    dao.addUser(user);
    commitTransaction();
    long id = user.getId();
    assertTrue(id>0);
  }

  @Test
  @DataSets(setUpDataSet="/user-with-telephone.xml",
            assertDataSet="/empty.xml")
```

```
public void testDeleteUserWithTelephone() throws Exception {
  beginTransaction();
  long id = ELFunctionMapperImpl.getId(User.class);
  dao.deleteUser(id);
  commitTransaction();
}

}
```

Running these tests will expose the first bug in the DAO implementation, because testDeleteUserWithTelephone() fails with a constraint violation exception. Although the user row was deleted, its telephone wasn't. The reason? Cascade deletes are taken into account only when the EntityManager's remove() method is called, and our DAO used a JPA query to delete the user. The fix is shown in listing 18.21.

Regardless of this delete issue, the tests presented so far cover only the easy scenarios: saving, loading, and deleting a simple user, with or without a telephone. It's a good start but not enough; we need to test negative cases as well.

For the addUser() method, the only negative case is receiving a null reference. It's always a good practice to check for method arguments and throw an Illegal-AccessArgumentException if they don't comply. The getUserById() method has at least two negative cases: handling an ID that doesn't exist in the database and loading from an empty database. In our sample application, a null reference should be returned in these cases (but another valid option would be to throw an exception). Negative cases for removeUser() would be the same as for getUserById(), and in our example they don't need to be tested because nothing happens when the user doesn't exist (if an exception should be thrown, we should exercise these scenarios). Listing 18.20 adds these new tests.

Listing 18.20 New test cases for negative scenarios

```
[...]
public class UserDaoJpaImplTest extends AbstractJpaDbUnitELTemplateTestCase {
[...]
  @Test(expected=IllegalArgumentException.class)
  public void testAddNullUser() throws Exception {
    dao.addUser(null);
  }

  @Test
  public void testGetUserByIdOnNullDatabase() throws Exception {
    getUserReturnsNullTest(0);
  }

  @Test
  @DataSets(setUpDataSet="/user.xml")
  public void testGetUserByIdUnknownId() throws Exception {
    getUserReturnsNullTest(666);
  }

  private void getUserReturnsNullTest(int deltaId) {
    beginTransaction();
    long id = ELFunctionMapperImpl.getId(User.class)+deltaId;
```

```
    User user = dao.getUserById(id);
    commitTransaction(true);
    assertNull(user);
  }
}
```

Notice that the workflow for getUserById() negative cases is the same for both scenarios, so we used a private helper method (getUserReturnsNullTest()) on both.

Now we have a fully tested DAO implementation, right? Well, not really. Once you put this code into production (or hand it to the QA team for functional testing), a few bugs are bound to happen.

To start with, the first time someone calls UserFacade.getUserById() (which in turn calls the DAO method; see listing 18.4) on a user that has at least one telephone and tries to call user.getTelephones(), the following exception will occur:

```
org.hibernate.LazyInitializationException: failed to lazily initialize
  ➥a collection of role: com.manning.jia.chapter18.model.User.telephones,
  ➥no session or session was closed
  at org.hibernate.collection.AbstractPersistentCollection.throwLazy
  ➥InitializationException(AbstractPersistentCollection.java:358)
  at org.hibernate.collection.AbstractPersistentCollection.
  ➥throwLazyInitializ ationExceptionIfNotConnected
  ➥(AbstractPersistentCollection.java:350)
  at org.hibernate.collection.AbstractPersistentCollection.
  ➥readSize(Abstract PersistentCollection.java:97)
  at org.hibernate.collection.PersistentBag.size(PersistentBag.java:225)
  at com.manning.jia.chapter18.model.EntitiesHelper.
  ➥assertUserWithTelephones(EntitiesHelper.java:39)
  at com.manning.jia.chapter18.model.EntitiesHelper.assertUserWithTelephone
  ➥(EntitiesHelper.java:29)
  at com.manning.jia.chapter18.dao.UserDaoJpaImplTest.testGetUserByIdWith
  ➥Telephone(UserDaoJpaImplTest.java:62)
```

When that happens, you, the developer, are going to curse Hibernate, JPA, ORM, and (with a higher intensity) this book's authors: you followed our advice and created unit tests for both the Façade and DAO classes in isolation, but once one called the other in real life, a JPA exception arose! Unfortunately, situations like these are common. Just because you wrote test cases, it doesn't mean your code is bug free. But on the bright side, because you have a test case, it's much easier to reproduce and fix the issue. In this case, the exception is caused because the User/Telephone relationship is defined as lazy, which means the telephones were not fetched by the JPA queries and are loaded on demand when getTelephones() is called. But if that method is called outside the JPA context, an exception is thrown. So, to simulate the problem in the test case, we change testGetUserByIdWithTelephone() to clear the context after committing the transaction:

```
@Test
@DataSets(setUpDataSet="/user-with-telephone.xml")
public void testGetUserByIdWithTelephone() throws Exception {
  beginTransaction();
  long id = ELFunctionMapperImpl.getId(User.class);
```

```
        User user = dao.getUserById(id);
        commitTransaction(true);
        assertUserWithTelephone(user);
    }
```

Running the test case after this change fails because of the same exception our poor user faced in the real application. The solution then is to fix the JPA query to eagerly fetch the telephones, as shown here:

```
    public User getUserById(long id) {
        String jql = "select user from User user left join fetch " +
                     "user.telephones where id = ?";
    Query query = entityManager.createQuery(jql);
    query.setParameter(1, id);
    return (User) query.getSingleResult();
    }
```

Such a change allows `testGetUserByIdWithTelephone()` to pass, but now `testGet-UserByIdOnNullDatabase()` and `testGetUserByIdUnknownId()` fail:

```
javax.persistence.NoResultException: No entity found for query
    at org.hibernate.ejb.QueryImpl.getSingleResult(QueryImpl.java:83)
    at com.manning.jia.chapter18.dao.UserDaoJpaImpl.
    ➥getUserById(UserDaoJpaImpl.java:45)
```

Let's change the method again, using `getResultList()` instead of `getSingle-Result()`:

```
    public User getUserById(long id) {
        String jql = "select user from User user left join fetch " +
                     "user.telephones where id = ?";
    Query query = entityManager.createQuery(jql);
    query.setParameter(1, id);
    @SuppressWarnings("unchecked")
    List<User> users = query.getResultList();
    // sanity check
    assert users.size() <= 1 : "returned " + users.size() + " users";
    return users.isEmpty() ? null : (User) users.get(0);
    }
```

Although the change itself is simple, this issue illustrates the importance of negative tests. If we didn't have these tests, the lazy-initialization fix would have introduced a regression bug!

Once these two fixes are in place, the application will run fine for awhile, until a user has two or more telephones, which would cause the following exception:

```
java.lang.AssertionError: returned 2 users
    at com.manning.jia.chapter18.dao.UserDaoJpaImpl.getUserById
    ➥(UserDaoJpaImpl.java:49)
    at com.manning.jia.chapter18.dao.UserDaoJpaImplTest.
    ➥testGetUserByIdWithTelephones(UserDaoJpaImplTest.java:114)
```

What's happening now is that a query that was supposed to return one user is returning two—weird!

But again, because the testing infrastructure is already in place, it's easy to reproduce the problem. All we have to do is add a new `testGetUserByIdWithTelephones()` method:[6]

```
@Test
@DataSets(setUpDataSet="/user-with-telephones.xml")
public void testGetUserByIdWithTelephones() throws Exception {
    beginTransaction();
    long id = ELFunctionMapperImpl.getId(User.class);
    User user = dao.getUserById(id);
    commitTransaction(true);
    assertUserWithTelephones(user);
}
```

What about the issue itself? The solution is to use the `distinct` keyword in the query, as shown here:

```
jql = "select distinct(user) from User user left join fetch " +
      "user.telephones where id = ?";
```

Notice that having both `testGetUserByIdWithTelephone()` and `testGetUserByIdWithTelephones()` methods is redundant and would make the test cases harder to maintain. Once we add `testGetUserByIdWithTelephones()`, we can safely remove `testGetUserByIdWithTelephone()` and its companion helpers `newUserWithTelephone()` and `assertUserWithTelephone()`, which would be replaced by `newUserWithTelephones()` and `assertUserWithTelephones()`, respectively.

Listing 18.21 shows the final version of `UserDaoJpaImpl`, with all issues fixed.

Listing 18.21 Final (and improved) version of `UserDaoJpaImpl`

```
[...]
public class UserDaoJpaImpl implements UserDao {
  public void addUser(User user) {

    if ( user == null ) {
      throw new IllegalArgumentException("user cannot be null");
    }
    entityManager.persist(user);
  }
  public User getUserById(long id) {

    String jql = "select distinct(user) from User user left join fetch " +
                 "user.telephones where id = ?";
    Query query = entityManager.createQuery(jql);
    query.setParameter(1, id);
    @SuppressWarnings("unchecked")
    List<User> users = query.getResultList();
    // sanity check assertion
```

---

[6] We also need a new `assertUserWithTelephones()` method on `EntitiesHelper` and a new user-with-telephones.xml dataset, but because they're very similar to the existing method and dataset, they aren't shown here.

```
    assert users.size() <= 1 : "returned " + users.size() + " users";
    return users.isEmpty() ? null : (User) users.get(0);
  }

  public void deleteUser(long id) {
    User user = entityManager.find(User.class, id);
    entityManager.remove(user);
  }
}
```

18.6 Testing foreign key names

When the first version of testDeleteUserWithTelephone() failed, the error message was

```
Integrity constraint violation FKC50C70C5B99FE3B2 table:
➥PHONES in statement [delete from users where id=?]
```

Because we're just starting development, it's easy to realize that the violated constraint is the telephones foreign key on the users table. But imagine on down the road you face a bug report with a similar problem—would you know what constraint FKC50C70C5B99FE3B2 refers to?

By default, Hibernate doesn't generate useful names for constraints, so you get gibberish like FKC50C70C5B99FE3B2. Fortunately, you can use the @ForeignKey annotation to explicitly define the FK names, as we did in the User class (see listing 18.1). But as more entities are added to the application, it's easy for a developer to forget to use this annotation, and such a slip could stay undetected for months, until the application is hit by a foreign key violation bug (whose violated constraint would be a mystery).

As you can imagine, there's a solution for this problem: writing a test case that verifies that all generated foreign keys have meaningful names. The skeleton for this test is relatively simple: you ask Hibernate to generate the schema for your application as SQL statements and then check for invalid foreign key names. The tricky part is how to generate the SQL code in a string, using only the project JPA settings. We present a solution in the listing below, and although it isn't pretty, it gets the work done.[7] Anyway, let's look at the test case by itself first, in listing 18.22.

Listing 18.22   Test case for Hibernate-generated database schema (SchemaTest.java)

```
[...]
public class SchemaTest extends AbstractJpaTestCase {        ←❶

  @Test
  public void testForeignKeysNames() {                       ←❷
    SqlHandler handler = new SqlHandler() {
      public void handle(String sql) {
```

---

[7]   We could do further diligence and present a more elegant solution, because this is a book (and hence educational). But when you're writing unit tests in real life, many times you have to be pragmatic and use a quick-and-dirty solution for a given problem, so we decided to take this approach here as well.

```
        assertForeignKeysDoesNotHaveFunnyNames(sql);
      }
    };
    analyzeSchema(handler);
  }

  private static final String FK_LINE_REGEXP =
    "alter table (.*) add constraint (.*) foreign key .*";         ◁─❸
  private static final Pattern FK_LINE_PATTERN =
    Pattern.compile(FK_LINE_REGEXP);
  private static final Matcher FK_LINE_MATCHER =
    FK_LINE_PATTERN.matcher("");
  private static final String FK_REGEXP = "fk_[a-z]+_[a-z]+$";     ◁─❹
  private static final Pattern FK_PATTERN = Pattern.compile(FK_REGEXP);
  private static final Matcher FK_MATCHER = FK_PATTERN.matcher("");

  private void assertForeignKeysDoesNotHaveFunnyNames(String sql) {
    String[] lines = sql.split("\n");                              ◁─❺
    StringBuilder buffer = new StringBuilder();
    for ( String line : lines ) {
      FK_LINE_MATCHER.reset(line);
      if( FK_LINE_MATCHER.find() ) {
        String table = FK_LINE_MATCHER.group(1);
        String fk = FK_LINE_MATCHER.group(2);
        if ( ! isValidFk(fk) ) {
          buffer.append(table).append("(").append(fk).append(") ");  ◁─❻
        }
      }
    }
    String violations = buffer.toString();
    if ( violations.length() > 0 ) {                              ◁─❼
      fail( "One or more tables have weird FK names: " + violations );
    }
  }

  private boolean isValidFk(String fk) {                          ◁─❽
    FK_MATCHER.reset(fk);
    return FK_MATCHER.find();
  }

}
```

❶ Although we're testing only foreign key names, we could test other aspects of the generated schema, so we create a generic `SchemaTest` class.

❷ The test case method by itself is quite simple: it calls the superclass `analyzeSchema()` method (described shortly), passing as a parameter an inner class that will do the job.

❸ This regular expression is used to identify whether a line defines a foreign key.

❹ This regular expression is used to extract the foreign key name.

❺ The SQL representing the schema generation is parsed in two levels: first, `split()` is used to break the lines, and then a regular expression ❸ checks for lines that define a foreign key. We could use only one regular expression to handle both, but the result would be more complex.

6, **7** Once we find an invalid foreign key, we buffer it and fail later, with the failure message containing all violations. Although it would be simpler to fail right away, this approach is more helpful, because it requires just one run to spot all invalid names.

8 The meaning of a valid foreign key is up to the project. In our case, we define that it has to start with FK_ and have two names (which should represent the tables involved in the relationship) separated by an underscore (_).

This test case relies on a new infrastructure method, analyzeSchema(), which is defined in AbstractJpaTestCase; listing 18.23 shows all changes required to implement it.

Listing 18.23 Changes on `AbstractJpaTestCase` to support `analyzeSchema()`

```
[...]
public abstract class AbstractJpaTestCase {
[...]
  protected void analyzeSchema( SqlHandler handler ) {              ⟵ 1
    ConfigurationCreator cfgCreator = new ConfigurationCreator();
    Configuration cfg = cfgCreator.createConfiguration();
    SchemaExport export = new SchemaExport(cfg);                    ⟵ 2

    ByteArrayOutputStream outputStream = new ByteArrayOutputStream();
    PrintStream oldOut = System.out;
    PrintStream newOut = new PrintStream(outputStream);
    System.setOut(newOut);
    try {
      export.create(true, true);                                   ⟵ 3
      String sql = outputStream.toString();
      handler.handle(sql);
    } finally {
      System.setOut(oldOut);
      newOut.close();
    }
  }

  protected interface SqlHandler {
    void handle( String sql );
  }

  private class ConfigurationCreator extends JPAConfigurationTask {    ⟵ 4
    @Override
    protected Configuration createConfiguration() {
      return super.createConfiguration();
    }
  }
}
```

1 analyzeSchema() is based on the Template Design Pattern (see section 17.7.1). It knows how to create a Java string containing the database schema but doesn't know what to do with it, so it passes this string to a SqlHandler, which was passed as a parameter.

2 SchemaExport is the Hibernate class (part of the Hibernate Tools project) used to export the schema. It requires a Hibernate Properties object, which unfortunately can't be obtained from EntityManager or EntityManagerFactory, the objects our test case has references to. To overcome this limitation, we need our first hack: using an Ant task (JPAConfigurationTask), which is also part of Hibernate Tools.

❸ This is where the schema is effectively generated. The problem is, SchemaExport either exports it to the system output or to a file. Ideally, it should allow the schema to be exported to a Writer or OutputStream object, so we could pass a StringWriter as a parameter to this method. Because this isn't the case, we have to use a second hack: replace the System.out when this method is executed and then restore it afterwards. Yes, we know this is ugly, but we warned you.

❹ A final hack: because JPAConfigurationTask's createConfiguration() method is protected, our test case won't have access to it, so we create a subclass and override that method, making it accessible to classes in the same package.

18.7 *Summary*

Using ORM tools (such as Hibernate and JPA) greatly simplifies the development of database access code in Java applications. But regardless of how great the technology is or how much it automates the work, it's still necessary to write test cases for code that uses it.

A common practice among Java EE applications is to use Façades and DAOs in the business and persistence layers (respectively). In this chapter, we showed how to test these layers in isolation, using mocks as DAO implementation.

We also showed how to leverage DbUnit and advanced techniques to effectively test the JPA-based persistence layer, first testing the entity mappings and then the DAOs, properly speaking. We also demonstrated how to use JPA-generated IDs in your DbUnit datasets.

And although JPA testing is an extension of database testing (which was covered in chapter 17), it has its caveats, such as lazy initialization exceptions, duplicated objects returned in queries, cascade deletes, and generation of weird constraint names. The examples in this chapter demonstrated how to deal with such issues.

JUnit on steroids

*Make everything as simple as
possible, but not simpler.*

—Albert Einstein

This chapter covers

- Transparent mocks utilization
- Out-of-the-box DbUnit integration
- Extended assertion capabilities
- Bypassing encapsulation through
  reflection

Throughout this final part of the book, we've analyzed tools focused on testing specific technologies, such as AJAX applications and database access. In this final chapter, we evaluate tools that don't fit a particular niche but rather facilitate overall test development by providing helper methods and plumbing infrastructure. By using such tools, the developer can focus on the real functionality being tested, which can greatly improve productivity.

Functionally speaking, we analyze tools that automate mock usage, provide a wider number of assertion methods, use reflection to access private members of tested objects, and make DbUnit usage easier. Because these tools provide generic testing support, many of these features are provided by more than one tool. Such feature overlap might sound redundant (the classic NIH[1] syndrome), but this diversity allows you to choose the most appropriate tool for your needs.

19.1 Introduction

Let's take a brief look at the tools analyzed and how to run this chapter's examples. All of these tools are open source projects; some are active and mature, and others have been stalled in development for quite awhile.

19.1.1 Tools overview

Following are descriptions of all tools analyzed in this chapter.

UNITILS

Unitils (http://unitils.org) is a library that provides plumbing infrastructure for many types of testing needs, such as database access, mocks usage, and Spring integration. Although it's a relatively new framework (created at the end of 2006), it's a mature project and has been designed from the ground up with modern testing concepts in mind. It's framework agnostic (works with JUnit 3.x, JUnit 4.x, and TestNG), its features are offered as modules (which provides room for extensibility), and it makes heavy use of Java annotations.

JUNIT-ADDONS

Created in 2002, JUnit-addons is the oldest tool analyzed in this chapter. As the website (http://sourceforge.net/projects/junit-addons) states, "JUnit-addons is a collection of helper classes for JUnit." Sounds quite simple, and indeed it is. But despite its simplicity and the fact that its development has pretty much stalled (the last version was released in 2003!), it's still a useful tool, especially for projects based on JUnit 3.x, because many of the features it provides are already available on JUnit 4.x.

FEST

FEST (http://fest.easytesting.org) stands for Fixtures for Easy Software Testing, and as the name implies, it's another library providing a useful testing infrastructure. Similarly to Unitils, FEST also works with JUnit or TestNG[2] and is based on modules. Although most of the modules provide functionalities already offered by other tools, they do it in different ways, which might sound more natural for developers used to the JMock style of declarations, more specifically, to the fluent interface style, as defined at http://martinfowler.com/bliki/FluentInterface.html. But regardless of these overlapping features, it offers a module (`FEST Swing`) that's quite unique, because it provides support for GUI testing.

---

[1] Not Invented Here
[2] The project was initialized under the name TestNG-Abbot.

MYCILA TESTING FRAMEWORK

Mycila (http://code.google.com/p/mycila) is an umbrella for many subprojects, each one focused on particular needs, such as testing. It's the latest offspring of this new breed of general-purpose testing libraries (which also includes Unitils and FEST), and at the time this chapter was written it was still in its infancy. Although all of its features we analyze in this chapter are provided by other tools, this project also offers unique features, such as a module to test Guice[3]-based applications; if it fulfills its ambitious goal of providing "Powerful projects for everyday needs!" it could be another valuable asset in the toolbox.

19.1.2 Running the examples

The test cases for this sample application are available in two flavors: Maven and Ant. To run the tests on Maven, run `mvn clean test`. Similarly, to run them using Ant, type `ant clean test`. Some of these tools might require esoteric dependencies at runtime (for instance, Unitils database support uses Spring for transaction management), but all such dependencies are commented in the build.xml file. The application is also available as two Eclipse projects, one with the required libraries and another with the project itself.

Now that all introductions have been made, let's get down to business.

19.2 Transparent mock usage

When you use mocks in your test cases,[4] the test method is typically structured as follows:

1. Create an instance of the object being tested.
2. Create mock instances for dependent objects, and inject them into the tested object.
3. Set mock expectations.
4. Call the method being tested.
5. Optionally, verify mock expectations.

You could manually write these five steps in every test (that's the approach we've taken so far, in chapters 6 and 16), but as you learned in chapter 17 (section 17.7.1), such repetitive workflow is a strong candidate for refactoring through the Template Design Pattern. Only steps 3 and 4 are test specific; all other steps are pretty much the same for all tests.

In this section, we analyze three tools that provide infrastructure for transparent mock usage, and we refactor the existing `UserFacadeImplTest` (originally defined in listing 18.5) to use each of them.

---

[3] Guice (http://code.google.com/p/google-guice) is "a lightweight dependency injection framework for Java 5 and above, brought to you by Google." In other words, it's the simplified Google-based version of Spring.

[4] Mocks are explained in more detail in chapter 7.

19.2.1 *Unitils EasyMock support*

Before we dig into Unitils mock support, let's first see how Unitils works so we can configure it properly.

Unitils is configured through standard Java properties (those defined by a pair of strings in the form name=value), and these properties can be defined in three distinct files. The first file is called unitils-default.properties, and it's provided on Unitils' JAR.[5] As the name implies, it provides default values for most of the properties, so Unitils could be used out of the box without custom configuration. But default properties aren't always enough—if they were, there'd be no need for properties at all—so Unitils allows project-specific properties to be overridden in a unitils.properties file, which should be available either in the classpath or in the user's home directory.[6] Finally, Unitils also allows each developer to override the properties in a user-specific file called unitils-locals.properties,[7] which should also be present in the classpath or user's home directory.

This configuration mechanism allows a high degree of flexibility, which can be dangerous. If tests rely too heavily on the user-specific properties, they might be hard to reproduce. Ideally, the whole test suite should be runnable using only the project-specific properties, and the user-specific ones should be used only in some particular cases, like when each user has its own testing database.

That being said, each module has its own properties, and even which modules are available are defined by a property, unitils.modules, which by default includes all modules. For our mock example (listing 19.1), it isn't necessary to change any properties, although the mock configuration is quite extensive (two modules are involved, as you can see in the listing).

> **Listing 19.1 `UserFacadeImpl` test refactored to use Unitils mock support**

```
[...]
import static com.manning.junitbook.ch19.model.EntitiesHelper.*;
import static org.unitils.easymock.EasyMockUnitils.replay;        ❶
import static org.easymock.EasyMock.expect;

import org.junit.Test;
import org.junit.runner.RunWith;
import org.unitils.UnitilsJUnit4TestClassRunner;
import org.unitils.easymock.annotation.Mock;
import org.unitils.inject.annotation.InjectIntoByType;
import org.unitils.inject.annotation.TestedObject;

import com.manning.junitbook.ch19.dao.UserDao;
import com.manning.junitbook.ch19.model.User;
import com.manning.junitbook.ch19.model.UserDto;
```

---

[5] The contents of this file are also documented online, at http://unitils.org/unitils-default.properties.
[6] The home directory is defined by the Java system property user.home.
[7] The name of this file is defined itself by a property, so it could have any name, as long as the name property is changed in unitils.properties.

```
@RunWith(UnitilsJUnit4TestClassRunner.class)        ◁━❷
public class UserFacadeImplUnitilsTest {

    @TestedObject
    private UserFacadeImpl facade;              ◁━┐

    @Mock                                         ❸
    @InjectIntoByType
    private UserDao dao;                        ◁━┘

    @Test
    public void testGetUserById() {             ◁━❹
        int id = 666;
        User user = newUserWithTelephones();
        expect(dao.getUserById(id)).andReturn(user);
        replay();
        UserDto dto = facade.getUserById(id);
        assertUser(dto);
    // verify();
    }

}
```

In order to use Unitils, first the test class must either extend the superclass that provides support for the testing framework being used (like UnitilsJUnit4) or annotate it with the proper JUnit runner; in this example, we opted for the latter ❷. The next step is to declare fields representing the object being tested and the mocks; Unitils provides annotations for both, as shown in ❸. Notice that the @Mock annotation will create an EasyMock mock; although Unitils mock support is provided through modules, currently only EasyMock is available. Next comes the test method itself ❹, whose content is pretty much the same as before; the only differences are that it uses Unitils' replay() method instead of EasyMock's (that's why in ❶ we statically imported any methods explicitly, instead of using *) and it isn't necessary to call verify() (Unitils will automatically do that after the test is run, although such behavior could also be changed by modifying a property).

Compare this example with chapter 18's (shown in listing 18.5). Although the core of the class (the test method itself) is the same, this new example requires much less setup. It might not sound like a big difference in these two simple examples, but in a real project, with dozens or even hundreds of such test cases, such small local improvement results in a big gain in the global productivity.

Behind the scenes, Unitils uses two modules, inject and easymock. Because we didn't configure anything, Unitils loaded all modules. The default value for the modules property is

```
unitils.modules=database,dbunit,hibernate,mock,easymock,inject,spring,jpa
```

If this property isn't overridden, Unitils will load all modules, which means more implicit setup methods need to be called before and after each test. If you don't need all modules, set this property with just the necessary ones. In our example, it would be

```
unitils.modules=easymock,inject
```

If you forget to include a module, Unitils won't instantiate the attributes that use annotations from that module, and the test case will eventually throw an exception. For instance, if the `easymock` module was not included, the `dao` reference wouldn't be set, and the `expect(dao.getUserById(id))` statement would throw a `NullPointerException`.

Besides configuring which modules are used, you can also change some module behavior through module-specific properties. For instance, to disable calls to Easy-Mock's `verify()` after the test cases are run, you set `EasyMockModule.autoVerify-AfterTest.enabled` to `false`. It's also possible to set the mock behavior mode (lenient or strict), even if the order of calls should be taken into account.

Another interesting Unitils feature is the `@Dummy` concept. Attributes annotated with `@Dummy` behave similarly to those annotated with `@Mock`, except that you don't need to set expectations: all method calls will return default values (such as `0` for methods that return an int). These dummies are convenient for cases where your tested objects need a valid reference to another object, but the behavior of that object is irrelevant for the test case where it's used.

19.2.2 FEST-Mocks

Listing 19.2 shows the same example using FEST-Mocks.

Listing 19.2 `UserFacadeImpl` test refactored to use FEST-Mocks

```
[...]
import static org.easymock.EasyMock.*;
import org.fest.mocks.EasyMockTemplate;

import org.junit.Before;
import org.junit.Test;

import com.manning.junitbook.ch19.dao.UserDao;
import com.manning.junitbook.ch19.model.User;
import com.manning.junitbook.ch19.model.UserDto;

public class UserFacadeImplFESTTest {                    ←-❶

  private UserFacadeImpl facade;
  private UserDao dao;

  @Before
  public void setFixtures() {                            ←-❷
    facade = new UserFacadeImpl();
    dao = createMock(UserDao.class);
    facade.setUserDao(dao);
  }

  @Test
  public void testGetUserById() {
    final int id = 666;
    final User user = newUserWithTelephones();
    new EasyMockTemplate(dao) {                          ←-❸
      @Override
```

```
      protected void expectations() throws Throwable {
        expect(dao.getUserById(id)).andReturn(user);
      }
      @Override
      protected void codeToTest() throws Throwable {
        UserDto dto = facade.getUserById(id);
        assertUser(dto);
      }
    }.run();                          ◁─④
  }
```

FEST-Mocks doesn't require the test class ① to extend any class or to use any special runner; as a drawback, it's necessary to manually instantiate the mocks and objects being tested ②. All it does is provide an abstract template class that must be extended on each test case ③, which in turn must explicitly set the expectations and run the code to be tested. Then when the method run() is called ④, it executes a workflow similar to that described at the beginning of this section (the main difference is that the verify step isn't optional, and verify() is always called).

Overall, FEST-Mocks is a bit convoluted, because it explicitly uses the Template Design Pattern, but in a complex way. Its creators claim that separating the mock's expectation and code being tested makes the test case clear. Although we agree that the result is clear to read, it seems less natural and more verbose to develop.

19.2.3 *Mycila*

Mycila mock support is similar to Unitils in the way that you mark your mock attributes with annotations. Unlike Unitils, however, you still need to do some manual setup in a @Before method, such as creating the objects being tested and calling the Mycila initialization method. Listing 19.3 shows our example converted to Mycila.

> **Listing 19.3 `UserFacadeImpl` test refactored to use Mycila EasyMock plug-in**

```
[...]
import static com.manning.junitbook.ch19.model.EntitiesHelper.*;
import static org.easymock.EasyMock.*;

import org.junit.Before;
import org.junit.Test;

import com.manning.junitbook.ch19.dao.UserDao;
import com.manning.junitbook.ch19.model.User;
import com.manning.junitbook.ch19.model.UserDto;
import com.mycila.testing.core.TestSetup;
import com.mycila.testing.plugin.easymock.Mock;

public class UserFacadeImplMycilaEasyMockTest {          ◁─①

  private UserFacadeImpl facade;

  @Mock
  private UserDao dao;                          ◁─②
```

```
@Before
public void setFixtures() {
    facade = new UserFacadeImpl();
    TestSetup.setup(this);          ◁──❸
    facade.setUserDao(dao);                    ◁──❹
}

@Test
public void testGetUserById() {             ◁──❺
    int id = 666;
    User user = newUserWithTelephones();
    expect(dao.getUserById(id)).andReturn(user);
    replay(dao);
    UserDto dto = facade.getUserById(id);
    assertUser(dto);
    verify(dao);
}
}
```

As you can see on ❶, Mycila doesn't require any special inheritance or custom runner, which forces the test case to explicitly call its `TestSetup.setup()` in a `@Before` method ❸. That method then scans the test class looking for `@Mock` annotations and does the proper EasyMock setup when they're found, such as in ❷. Notice that each test case statement that requires a reference to these mocks (like the dependency injection defined in ❹) must be executed after `TestSetup.setup()` is called. Mock injection is the only mock support Mycila provides; the test method itself ❺ is responsible for calling `replay()` and `verify()` in the mocks.

Mycila also supports other mock frameworks, such as JMock (also analyzed in chapter 6) and Mockito (http://mockito.org). Listing 19.4 shows the same example using the JMock plug-in.

Listing 19.4 `UserFacadeImpl` **test refactored to use Mycila JMock plug-in**

```
[...]

import static com.manning.junitbook.ch19.model.EntitiesHelper.*;

import org.jmock.Expectations;
import org.jmock.Mockery;
import org.junit.Before;
import org.junit.Test;

import com.manning.junitbook.ch19.dao.UserDao;
import com.manning.junitbook.ch19.model.User;
import com.manning.junitbook.ch19.model.UserDto;
import com.mycila.testing.core.TestSetup;
import com.mycila.testing.plugin.jmock.Mock;              ◁──❶
import com.mycila.testing.plugin.jmock.MockContext;

public class UserFacadeImplMycilaJMockTest {

    private UserFacadeImpl facade;

    @MockContext                              ◁──❷
    private Mockery context;
```

```
@Mock                              ⟵ ❸
private UserDao dao;

@Before
public void setFixtures() {        ⟵ ❹
  facade = new UserFacadeImpl();
  TestSetup.setup(this);
  facade.setUserDao(dao);
}

@Test
public void testGetUserById() {
  final int id = 666;
  final User user = newUserWithTelephones();
  context.checking(new Expectations() {{    ⟵ ❺
    one(dao).getUserById(id);
    will(returnValue(user));
  }});
  UserDto dto = facade.getUserById(id);
  assertUser(dto);
  context.assertIsSatisfied();     ⟵ ❻
}

}
```

This new example is similar to the previous one; the test setup ❹ is even exactly the same. The only differences are the dao reference ❸ being marked with a @Mock annotation defined in another package ❶, the need for a Mockery object ❷, and the way expectations are set and verified (❺ and ❻ respectively).

So, given the mock support offered by these three tools, which one should you use in your project? If you're looking for transparent EasyMock usage, Unitils is clearly the best option, because it requires less effort in the test cases (no setup or calls to verify) and is highly configurable. But if you need to use JMock or prefer a clear separation between expectations and tested code, then Mycila or FEST, respectively, is the more suitable option.

19.3   DbUnit integration

In chapter 17 we presented an in-house framework that uses Java annotations to facilitate usage of DbUnit datasets in test cases. Wouldn't it be nice if such a framework was offered out of the box? Well, guess what? Unitils' dbunit module provides exactly that!

Unitils provides four modules related to database testing: database, dbunit, hibernate, and jpa. The database module is mainly responsible for providing a database connection that will be used by tests and managing transactions, although it offers other features, such as a database maintainer that can be used to synchronize the developer's databases. Then the dbunit module scans the test class for annotations that define which DbUnit datasets should be used on each test. Finally, the hibernate and jpa modules can be used to inject the necessary ORM classes (such as

Hibernate's `Session` or JPA's `EntityManager`) into the test cases, which can also be done through the use of annotations.

The `dbunit` module works similarly to the infrastructure provided in chapter 17: you mark the test methods with annotations (`@DataSet` and/or `@ExpectedDataSet`), and Unitils takes care of preparing the database or asserting its content with the dataset defined by these annotations. The main differences are where the datasets are located (relative to the class's package directory in the classpath) and also the fact that the annotations could be defined at class or method levels (class level is useful when many methods use the same dataset; individual methods could then override it by using the annotation again with different values).

In chapter 17 we used DbUnit to test a JDBC-based DAO, and in chapter 18 we used it to test a JPA-based DAO that used Hibernate as the JPA implementation. Let's rewrite these two test cases using Unitils, starting with the JDBC version in listing 19.5.

Listing 19.5 Refactored `UserDaoJdbcImplTest` using Unitils

```
[...]
import static com.manning.junitbook.ch19.model.EntitiesHelper.*;
import static org.junit.Assert.*;

import java.sql.Connection;
import java.sql.SQLException;

import javax.sql.DataSource;

import org.junit.Test;
import org.unitils.UnitilsJUnit4;
import org.unitils.database.annotations.TestDataSource;
import org.unitils.dbunit.annotation.DataSet;
import org.unitils.dbunit.annotation.ExpectedDataSet;

public class UserDaoJdbcImplTest extends UnitilsJUnit4 {          ◄──❶

  private UserDaoJdbcImpl dao = new UserDaoJdbcImpl();

  @TestDataSource
  void setDataSource(DataSource ds) throws SQLException {          ◄──❷
    Connection connection = ds.getConnection();
    dao.setConnection(connection);
    dao.createTables();
  }

  @Test
  @DataSet("user.xml")
  public void testGetUserById() throws Exception {
    long id = 1;
    User user = dao.getUserById(id);                              ❸
    assertUser(user);
  }

  @Test
  @DataSet("user.xml")
  public void testGetUserByIdUnknowId() throws Exception {
    long id = 2;
```

```
    User user = dao.getUserById(id);
    assertNull(user);
  }

  @Test                                                          ④
  @ExpectedDataSet("user.xml")
  public void testAddUser() throws Exception {
    User user = newUser();
    dao.addUser(user);
    long id = user.getId();
    assertTrue(id>0);
  }

}
```

In the mock example we used a custom runner to provide Unitils integration; this time we opt to extend in ❶ the proper Unitils superclass. The next step is to signal the database module that the test case needs a data source (which in turn will be used to configure the DAO); that's accomplished through the `@TestDataSource` annotation, which could be used in an attribute or a method. In our case, we use it in a method ❷, because it's necessary to pass the database connection to the DAO and call the DAO to create the database tables;[8] otherwise, the `dbunit` module will fail when it tries to load the datasets.

Then in ❸ we have tests that load data from the database, so we use the `@DataSet` annotation to define a dataset that will be used to prepare the database before the test. Notice that the name `"user.xml"` refers to a dataset file located in the classpath within the same directory structure as the test class package (in our example, com/manning/junitbook/ch19/dao/user.xml). The content of this file is the same as the one listed in chapter 17, listing 17.5. Finally, on ❹ we have a test case where data is inserted into the database and DbUnit is used to compare the results; we use `@ExpectedDataSet` in this case.

The JPA example is pretty much the same; the main difference is the code to set up the `EntityManager` and the DAO. Listing 19.6 shows the new test case, focusing on test setup and showing only one test method.

Listing 19.6   Relevant changes to `UserDaoJpaImplTest`

```
[...]

import static com.manning.junitbook.ch19.model.EntitiesHelper.*;
import static org.junit.Assert.*;

import java.sql.Connection;
import java.sql.SQLException;

import javax.sql.DataSource;
```

---

[8] If we weren't using an embedded database but rather a developer database with the tables already created, then we could use `@TestDataSource` in a `DataSource` attribute and use a `@Before` method to pass the connection to the DAO.

```
import org.junit.Test;
import org.unitils.UnitilsJUnit4;
import org.unitils.database.annotations.TestDataSource;
import org.unitils.dbunit.annotation.DataSet;
import org.unitils.dbunit.annotation.ExpectedDataSet;

import com.manning.junitbook.ch19.model.User;

public class UserDaoJpaImplTest extends UnitilsJUnit4 {

  @JpaEntityManagerFactory(persistenceUnit="chapter-19")          ◁──❶
  @PersistenceContext
  EntityManager em;

  private final UserDaoJpaImpl dao = new UserDaoJpaImpl();

  @Before
  public void prepareDao() {                                      ◁──❷
    dao.setEntityManager(em);
  }

  @Test
  @DataSet("user.xml")
  public void testGetUserById() throws Exception {                ◁──❸
    long id = 1;
    User user = dao.getUserById(id);
    assertUser(user);
  }
[...]
}
```

The only differences in this test case are that in ❶ two annotations are used to mark
the `EntityManager` (which will be injected by Unitils before the tests are run), and
then in ❷ the `EntityManager` is passed to our DAO. At ❸ we have the test method
itself; notice that it's identical to the same test method in listing 19.5 (even though the
DAO implementation is different) and similar to chapter's 18 test, except that in this
new example it isn't necessary to manage the transaction, because Unitils does that
automatically for us.[9]

Besides the test classes themselves, it's necessary to set the database connection on
unitils.properties, as shown in listing 19.7.

Listing 19.7   unitils.properties settings for the DbUnit examples

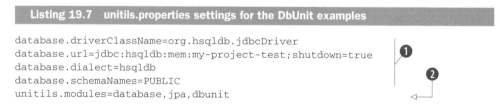

```
database.driverClassName=org.hsqldb.jdbcDriver
database.url=jdbc:hsqldb:mem:my-project-test;shutdown=true     ❶
database.dialect=hsqldb
database.schemaNames=PUBLIC                                     ❷
unitils.modules=database,jpa,dbunit
```

The database information is set on ❶, and ❷ lists the modules used in these tests.
Notice that ❷ could be omitted, because by default Unitils uses all modules.

---

[9] Unitils starts a transaction before each test and commits it afterward, although it could be configured to roll
back instead (through the `DatabaseModule.Transactional.value.default` property).

As shown in these examples, Unitils DbUnit support is similar to the framework developed in chapter 17, although each has its pros and cons. For instance, Unitils allows you to use merged datasets, whereas the in-house framework provides EL support. Another major difference is that Unitils automatically manages the transaction.

From the tools analyzed, Unitils is the only one currently supporting DbUnit, although Mycila seems to have plans to provide a DbUnit plug-in in the near future.

19.4 Assertions made easy

Having a powerful toolbox of assertion methods readily available is an important asset in test case development. Why? For two main reasons: productivity and clarity.

When you're writing a test case, your focus is on the test case logic; assertions are just an accessory. For example, if you need to assert that a variable is greater than a certain number, your first instinct is to write something like `assertTrue(x>42)`. Such assertions work fine when the condition holds true, but when it fails, all you get is a `junit.framework.AssertionFailedError: null` message, which is far from clear. A second approach would be to include a message in the assertion, such as `assert-True("X should be greater than 42, but it is "+x, x>42)`. Sure, the clarity is improved but at the cost of productivity: you now need to create a long string, which contains the name of the variable (`X`), the operand (`greater`), and the current value concatenated, which is not only boring but also error prone. A better approach would be to have an assertion method specialized in comparisons, which would make it as simple as `assertGreaterThan(x, 42)`.

JUnit provides a handful of assertions out of the box through the `org.junit.` `Assert` class, and although such features cover the basic needs, they come up short in some particular cases, such as comparing collections or properties in a JavaBean (not to mention the example in the previous paragraph). Fortunately, many third-party libraries provide complementary assertions, and in this section we analyze a few of them.

19.4.1 JUnit-addons assertions package

JUnit-addons provides a bunch of *XXX*Assert classes (such as `ListAssert` and `FileAssert`) in the `junitx.framework` package, and each of them provides static methods aimed to assert specific objects. Although some of the assertion features they offer are now present in JUnit 4.x,[10] some are still surprisingly missing. For instance, JUnit's `Assert` class provides `assertTrue()`, `assertFalse()`, and `assert-Equals()` methods, but there isn't an `assertNotEquals()` method, which is provided by JUnit-addons' `Assert`.

Let's start with our prologue example, comparing a variable to a number. For that purpose, JUnit-addons offers the `ComparableAssert` class, which provides methods to

---

[10] Such as the `AssertArray` class, whose methods provides the same functionality as `Assert.assert-ArrayEquals()`.

assert objects implementing `java.lang.Comparable` (numbers happen to be a subset of such objects). For instance, to assert that a variable *x* is greater than 42, we'd write

```
ComparableAssert.assertGreater(42, x);
```

And in the case of failure, the message would be

```
junit.framework.AssertionFailedError: expected greater than:<42> but was:<23>
```

The next interesting class is `ListAssertions`, which, as the name implies, provides methods to verify lists. More specifically, it has only two methods: `assert Equals (List, List)` and `assertContains(List, Object)`.[11] Before we see them in action, let's define a few `List` fixtures:

```
List<Integer> LIST1 = Arrays.asList(4, 8, 15, 16, 23, 42);
List<Integer> LIST2 = Arrays.asList(108);
List<Integer> LIST3 = Arrays.asList(4, 8, 15, 16, 42, 23);
List<Integer> LIST4 = Arrays.asList(4, 8, 15, 16, 108, 23);
```

The first list (`LIST1`) contains six random numbers and is the list that will be compared with a list with a different number of elements (`LIST2`), a list with the same elements but in a different order (`LIST3`), and a list with the same number of elements but some different ones (`LIST4`).

If you used JUnit's `assertEquals()` method to compare `LIST1` and `LIST4`, the message would be

```
java.lang.AssertionError: expected:<[4, 8, 15, 16, 23, 42]> but was:
⟹<[4, 8, 15, 16, 108, 23]>
```

Although the message contains a clear description of the list's content, it's not easy to realize why they aren't equal. The reason is that JUnit's `assertEquals()` method treats the list as any other object, delegating its message formatting to Java's `String` class.

If we used the JUnit-addons alternative (`ListAssert.assertEquals()`) instead, the result would be

```
junit.framework.AssertionFailedError: expecting <42> in
⟹<4, 8, 15, 16, 108, 23>
```

That's a better message, although it doesn't inform us as to where the lists are different, only that one element is missing. The way the method works, it would fail to detect that `LIST1` and `LIST3` are different, because they have the same elements but in different order. It sounds like a bug, but it's a design decision, as stated in the Javadoc: "Asserts that two lists are equal (the order is not relevant)."[12] If the lists have different sizes (like `LIST1` and `LIST2`), the message is even more confusing:

```
junit.framework.AssertionFailedError: expecting <4> in <108>
```

---

[11] Technically speaking, it provides four methods, because each assert method has an overloaded version that also takes a message.

[12] It's still a conceptual bug; such behavior would make more sense comparing sets.

So, long story short, `ListAssert.assertEquals()` isn't that much better than JUnit's cousin. You'll see better options for list comparison, but don't throw the JAR away yet, because it provides the useful `assertContains()` method. For instance, calling `ListAssert.assertContains(LIST1, 666)` would result in

```
junit.framework.AssertionFailedError: expecting <666>
in <4, 8, 15, 16, 23, 42>
```

JUnit-addons offers a couple more assertion classes, such as `FileAssert` (which provides methods to compare contents of text and even binary files), `NamingAssert` (for JNDI-related assertions), `StringAssert` (which contain assert methods for `String`'s own methods, such as `assertStartsWith()`), and even `ObjectAssert` (which contains methods such as `assertInstanceOf()`). These classes are pretty straightforward—simple, but quite useful for what they offer.

19.4.2 *Unitils' ReflectionAssert*

Unitils has only one class that provides extended assertions: `org.unitils.reflection-assert.ReflectionAssert`. That class is powerful, though, because it knows how to compare many types of objects, from simple JavaBeans to collections and Hibernate proxies, using reflection. More specifically, it uses reflection to compare the value of each field and offers options to harden or relax the comparison (for instance, comparing only fields when a value isn't `null` or ignoring dates).

ReflectionAssert contains literally dozens of methods, and their usage isn't trivial. Some methods are named similarly (like `assertLenEquals()` and `assertLenientEquals()`; the former is deprecated and calls the latter); many methods take as a parameter an array of `ReflectionComparatorMode` (which is an enum that defines the comparison behavior); and the array is a vararg (which means the method also works without that parameter!). That being said, let's start with the class's main method, `assertReflectionEquals()`.

The full signature[13] of this method is `assertReflectionEquals(Object expected, Object actual, ReflectionComparatorMode... modes)`. Because the `modes` parameter uses a vararg, it's optional, so if you don't pass a comparator mode, it does a strict comparison in all fields. For instance, having two `User` objects (as defined in listing 19.1), with the difference being that user1's username field is `null`, calling `assertReflectionEquals(user1, user2)` would result in the following:

```
junit.framework.AssertionFailedError: Found following differences:

username
    =>  null
    =>  "ElDuderino"
```

---

[13] Here, and throughout this whole chapter, we're ignoring the most complete version that also takes a message, because it isn't relevant to what's being explained.

```
--- Difference details ---
 =>  User<id=0, username=null, firstName="Jeffrey", lastName="Lebowsky",
     telephones=[]>
 =>  User<id=0, username="ElDuderino", firstName="Jeffrey",
     lastName="Lebowsky", telephones=[]>

username =>  null
username =>  "ElDuderino"
```

Not only did it find the difference, but it printed both brief and detailed messages of what went wrong (and all assertion methods from this class behave this way).

If you want to ignore the fields that are null, you need to pass the Reflection-ComparatorMode.IGNORE_DETAILS mode as a parameter, such as assertReflection-Equals(user1, user2, IGNORE_DETAILS). Be aware that the order is important here, because fields are ignored only when their value is null in the *expected* parameter. Calling assertReflectionEquals(user2, user1, IGNORE_DETAILS) with these same User instances would fail, whereas assertReflectionEquals(user1, user2, IGNORE_DETAILS) would pass.

The other two comparison modes are LENIENT_DATES, which ignores in the comparison any field that's a java.util.Date, and LENIENT_ORDER, which is relevant only when comparing collections. Because the lenient comparison is common, most of the ReflectionAssert assertReflection*XXX*() methods offer a counterpart called assertLenient*XXX*() that automatically includes IGNORE_DETAILS and LENIENT_ORDER, such as assertLenientEquals(Object expect, Object actual). The idea behind this behavior is that in many cases the functionality being tested doesn't fill every field of an object, and having to compare all of them would require a lot more work. That's particularly useful in database access tests, such as in a getLoginAndPassword() method where the user's table has dozens of fields but only two of them are filled and need to be compared.

These methods can also be used to compare collections. For instance, using the lists defined a few examples ago and calling assertReflectionEquals(LIST1, LIST4) results in the following:

```
junit.framework.AssertionFailedError: Found following differences:

 [4]
    =>  23
    =>  108
 [5]
    =>  42
    =>  23

--- Difference details ---

 =>  [4, 8, 15, 16, 23, 42]
 =>  [4, 8, 15, 16, 108, 23]

[4] =>  23
[4] =>  108
```

```
[5] => 42
[5] => 23
```

This message might look cryptic at first sight, but it's pretty straightforward: it says that elements on indexes 4 and 5 are different (23 instead of 108, and 42 instead of 23, respectively). If the order of the elements isn't important, you could pass LENIENT_ORDER as parameter or call assertLenientEquals() instead. The message in this case would be slightly different, though, as shown here:

```
junit.framework.AssertionFailedError: Found following differences:

  [5,4]
    => 42
    => 108

--- Difference details ---
 => [4, 8, 15, 16, 23, 42]
 => [4, 8, 15, 16, 108, 23]

[5,4] => 42
[5,4] => 108
```

Here it shows that these lists have only one element that's different, although they're different in distinct locations (indexes 5 and 4, respectively).

Overall, ReflectionAssert is a powerful class. Once you break the learning curve barrier, you get a valuable tool for your day-to-day assertions.

19.4.3 FEST Fluent Assertions Module

FEST Fluent Assertions Module (also called FEST-Assert) provides custom assertion for many types of objects, such as collections, strings, exceptions, files, Big-Decimals, and even BufferedImages. And not only does it supports a great variety of objects, but the assertions are expressed in a different syntax, similar to the Hamcrest syntax (described in chapter 3) but even more natural, because the assertion methods can be chained.

The entry point for the assertions is the method assertThat(actual) from the org.fest.assertions.Assertions class. That method is overloaded a dozen times, each with a different type for the actual parameter and returning the proper assertion class for that type. Sound confusing? It's quite clever and simple (once you get used to it), so let's use the x > 42 example to make it clear. Assuming a variable x of type int, that assertion would be

```
Assertions.assertThat(x).isGreaterThan(42);
```

And the result would be

```
java.lang.AssertionError: actual value:<23> should be greater than:<42>
```

Behind the scenes, all Assertions.assertThat() methods return a subclass of Assert, in this case an IntAssert (because x is an int), which has methods such as isGreaterThan(int). These methods, in turn, also return IntAsserts, allowing many calls to be chained, as follows:

```
Assertions.assertThat(x).isGreaterThan(42).isLessThan(108);
```

You can make this easier to read if you static import Assertions and split the methods one per line:

```
assertThat(x).isGreaterThan(42)
            .isLessThan(108) ;
```

All asserts have common methods, like as(String description), which can be used to describe the actual object. In the previous example, we could describe it as "X":

```
assertThat(x).as("X").isGreaterThan(42)
                    .isLessThan(108);
```

And the message would be

```
java.lang.AssertionError: [X] actual value:<23> should be greater than:<42>
```

Overall, FEST-Assert assertions are easy to use and straightforward, especially when using an IDE with autocompletion. But for comparison purposes, here are some examples of collection assertions, similar to the ones we looked at so far (using other tools).

- Comparing collections contents (assertThat(LIST1).isEqualTo(LIST4)):

  ```
  java.lang.AssertionError: expected:<[4, 8, 15, 16, 108, 23]>
  but was:
  <[4, 8, 15, 16, 23, 42]>
  ```

- Checking that a list has a given element (assertThat(LIST1).contains(666)):

  ```
  java.lang.AssertionError: collection:<[4, 8, 15, 16, 23, 42]>
  does not contain element(s):
  <[666]>
  ```

- Checking that a list has many given elements (assertThat(LIST1).contains(108, 666)):

  ```
  java.lang.AssertionError: collection:<[4, 8, 15, 16, 23, 42]>
  does not contain element(s):
  <[108, 666]>
  ```

- Asserting that a collection doesn't have duplicates (assertThat(Arrays.asList(42,42)).doesNotHaveDuplicates()):

  ```
  java.lang.AssertionError: collection:<[42,42]>
  contains duplicate(s):
  [42]>
  ```

19.4.4 *Mycila extend assertions*

Mycila also provides a module for assertions, which uses a Hamcrest-like style similar to FEST, as shown in the examples at the project's wiki page (http://code.google.com/p/mycila/wiki/ExtendedAssertions). Unfortunately though, this module was not widely available at the time the book was written, so we had to skip it. But it's a project that's worth watching.

As you can see in this section, custom assertions are provided by many tools. Whatever your assertion needs are, most likely one (or more) of these tools supports it. And by using them, you can easily increase the productivity and/or clarity of the failure messages. The gain might sound small, but every small improvement adds up when you write hundreds or even thousands of test cases.

19.5 *Using reflection to bypass encapsulation*

Ideally, test cases should not know anything about the internal state of the test objects. But the truth is, even in a perfect world where classes were designed with good encapsulation and testability in mind, sometimes it's still necessary to bypass encapsulation and access internal members. With the advent of dependency injection (DI) containers such as Spring and Java EE 5 application servers, it's common to have attributes defined as private without any getter or setter, only a Java annotation (like `@Resource` or `@Autowired`), which is the hint for the container to inject the dependency at runtime.

When fields of tested objects are private, most likely they will be accessed through reflection later on by some framework class. So, instead of complaining about privacy concerns, why don't you play by the same rules and use reflection to access these fields in the test cases?

For instance, the `UserFacadeImpl` object defined in listing 19.4 has a private reference to a `UserDao`, and so far this reference could be set only through a public `setUserDao()` method. But if that method isn't available, we could use reflection to access it instead. In this section we show how to do so, first using an in-house utility class and then analyzing two tools that provide such features for free.

19.5.1 *In-house alternative*

If you eventually need to set a private field in an object being tested, your first attempt might be using the reflection API directly in the test method. This isn't a good approach, though, because the API is cumbersome to use, and most likely such a need will arise in other test cases. In situations like this, it's better to add a new method to an existing utility class or create a new one if none exists yet. This particular method requires three parameters: a reference to the object whose field will be set, the name of the field, and its new value. And because you'll probably need to get the value of the field at some point, why not add a helper method for that as well? Listing 19.8 shows these two methods.

Listing 19.8   Initial implementation of `TestingHelper` using the reflection API directly

```
[...]

import java.lang.reflect.Field;

public class TestingHelper {

  public static void set( Object object, String fieldName,
                          Object newValue) {                          ◁─┐
    Field field = getField(object.getClass(), fieldName);          ◁─┐ │
    try {                                                             │ │
      field.set(object, newValue);                                 ◁┐│ │
    } catch (IllegalAccessException e) {                            ││││
      throw new RuntimeException(                           ❶       ││││
        "Could not set value of field '" + fieldName +      ❷       ││││
        "' on object "  + object + " to " + newValue, e );         ❸ ◁─┐
    }                                                                 │ │
  }                                                                   │ │

  public static <T> T get(Object object, String fieldName) {  ◁─────┘ │
    Field field = getField(object.getClass(), fieldName);          ◁─┘ ❹
    Object value;
    try {
      value = field.get(object);                                   ◁┐
    } catch (IllegalAccessException e) {                            │
      throw new RuntimeException( "Could not get value of field '" + │
        fieldName + "' from object "  + object, e );                ◁┘
    }
    @SuppressWarnings("unchecked")
    T castValue = (T) value;                         ◁─❺
    return castValue;
  }

  private static Field getField(Class<?> clazz, String fieldName) {    ◁─❻
    Class<?> tmpClass = clazz;
    do {
      for ( Field field : tmpClass.getDeclaredFields() ) {        ◁─❼
        String candidateName = field.getName();
        if ( ! candidateName.equals(fieldName) ) {
          continue;
        }
        field.setAccessible(true);                  ◁─❽
        return field;
      }
      tmpClass = tmpClass.getSuperclass();                         ❾
    } while ( clazz != null );
    throw new RuntimeException("Field '" + fieldName +
      "' not found on class "  + clazz);
  }
}
```

This class provides two helper methods ❶, set() and get(), whose implementation follows the same workflow: get a reference to a java.lang.reflect.Field ❷, do something with it ❸, and convert ❹ any reflection API exceptions to a RuntimeException so callers don't need to worry about checked exceptions. `get()` also runs the extra Java 5 mile and casts the result ❺ to the expected type, so callers don't need an explicit cast when assigning it to a variable.[14]

The dirtiest part is getting the `Field` reference ❻; this method has to scan all methods of the object's class ❼ and its superclass ❾, and once the method is found, it must be made accessible ❽.

Going back to our `UserFacadeImpl` example, once it doesn't offer a setter for `UserDao` and these new helper methods are available, we could rewrite the `facade.setUserDao(dao)` statement on `UserFacadeImplTest.setFixtures()` (defined in listing 19.5) as

```
TestingHelper.set(facade, "userDao", dao);
```

Bypassing encapsulation, or how I learned to stop worrying and love reflection

One of the first things you learn when studying object-oriented languages is that they're built on three pillars: encapsulation, inheritance, and polymorphism. And encapsulation best practice dictates that attributes should be defined as private and accessed only through getters and setters. As a good student and disciplined developer, you follow that practice and happily declare all your object fields as private, using a few hotkeys from your favorite IDE to generate those boring getters and setters. Then after a hard day at the office, you decide to read a few more pages of this book at home to relax, when you read something disturbing: those tightly encapsulated fields that you protected with so much care can be easily accessed throughout reflection! Your whole world falls apart, and your first instinct is to sell all your Java books and buy Y2K survival kits with the few bucks you get from the sale. Well, if that happens to you, please go back to the couch and relax again: you can only bypass encapsulation if you grant the permissions to the JVM to do so. More specifically, when you call methods such as `Field.set-Accessible(true)`, the JVM will first check with the `SecurityManager` to see if the calling method has permission to change the accessibility rules. You could argue that the permission is granted by default and hence the fields are wide open, but the truth is that such behavior is convenient most of the times, at least in the Java SE environment.

Anyway, the fact that such access is allowed or not by default is out of the scope of the book. Even if the JVM had a more strict default behavior, you could still configure the `SecurityManager` to lower the restrictions in your test case environment.

---

[14] This might sound like black magic, but what happens is that the compiler knows what type is expected and does the proper casting (because the method returns a parameterized type, `<T>`). That doesn't eliminate `ClassCastExceptions` at runtime, but it does make the code cleaner, which is particularly welcome in test cases (in fact, many tools analyzed in the book, such as EasyMock and FEST, use this trick).

19.5.2   *JUnit-addons*

Junit-addons' `PrivateAccessor` class provides methods similar to the ones we implemented from scratch in the previous section. The only differences are the name (`get-Field()` and `setField()`, instead of `get()` and `set()`); how they're implemented (although the logic is the same, they use `for` instead of `while`); and the fact that `get-Field()` doesn't return a parameterized value (because JUnit-addons predates Java 5).

Using `PrivateAccessor` directly, we'd rewrite our set DAO statement at `setFixtures()` as

```
PrivateAccessor.setField(facade, "userDao", dao);
```

Although using `PrivateAccessor` directly is fine, it has three drawbacks: `getField()` isn't parameterized (so you'd need to cast its returned value on each test case), the caller would have to check for `NoSuchFieldException`, and you'd have to add a direct dependency on a third-party tool on all test cases (which would make it harder to switch to another tool later on). A better approach would be to use `PrivateAccessor` indirectly in the `TestingHelper` methods, rather than in the test cases themselves, as shown in listing 19.9.

Listing 19.9   `TestingHelper` refactored to use JUnit-addons

```
[...]

import junitx.util.PrivateAccessor;

public class TestingHelperJUnitAddons {

  public static void set( Object object, String fieldName,
    Object newValue ) {
    try {
      PrivateAccessor.setField(object, fieldName, newValue);
    } catch (Exception e) {
      throw new RuntimeException( "Could not set value of field '" +
        fieldName + "' on object " + object + " to " + newValue, e );
    }
  }

  public static <T> T get(Object object, String fieldName) {
    try {
      Object value = PrivateAccessor.getField(object, fieldName);
      @SuppressWarnings("unchecked")
      T castValue = (T) value;
      return castValue;
    } catch (NoSuchFieldException e) {
      throw new RuntimeException( "Could not get value of field '" +
        fieldName + "' from object " + object, e );
    }
  }
}
```

`PrivateAccessor` also provides a few more methods, such as `invoke()` (to invoke any instance or static method), and overloaded versions of `getField()` and `setField()` to deal with static methods.

19.5.3 *FEST-Reflect*

FEST-Reflect offers helper classes to access all sorts of Java entities, such as fields, methods, constructors, and even inner classes. And as is the case with all other FEST modules, it follows the fluent interface approach, this time using `org.reflect.core.Reflection` as the entry point. For instance, to create an instance of a `User` object, you use the `constructor()` method:

```
User user = Reflection.constructor().in(User.class).newInstance();
```

Behind the scenes, `constructor()` returns a `TargetType` object, whose method `in()` returns an `Invoker`, which in turn creates the actual `User` instance through the `new-Instance()` method. All these methods use parameterized arguments and return values (similar to the `get()` method in listing 19.9), so the result can be used without an explicit cast. The only catch is that most of the time you must pass the expected class as a parameter somewhere in the chain; for instance, to use FEST to set our DAO, it would be necessary to explicitly indicate that the field is of type `UserDao`, as shown here:

```
Reflection.field("userDao").ofType(UserDao.class).in(facade).set(dao);
```

Because of such requirements, `TestingHelper` couldn't be rewritten using FEST without changing its signature to include the field class (as shown in listing 19.10), which would also require a change in the set DAO statement:

```
TestingHelperFESTReflect.set(facade, "userDao", UserDao.class, dao);
```

Listing 19.10 `TestingHelper` refactored to use FEST-Reflect

```
[...]

import org.fest.reflect.core.Reflection;

public class TestingHelperFESTReflect {

    public static <T> void set(Object object, String fieldName,
                               Class<T> fieldClass, T newValue) {
        Reflection.field(fieldName).ofType(fieldClass).in(object).set(newValue);
    }

    public static <T> T get(Object object, String fieldName,
                            Class<T> fieldClass) {
        return Reflection.field(fieldName).ofType(fieldClass).in(object).get();
    }
}
```

Given these two alternatives, the choice again depends on personal style: FEST-Reflect is more powerful and follows a more natural syntax than its JUnit-addons counterpart, at the cost of being more complex (its syntax is less natural for developers who are not used to it) and requiring one more piece of information (the type of the field being accessed).

19.6   *Summary*

In this chapter we analyzed a few tools that complement JUnit, provide additional features, or make some tasks more productive.

We learned three different ways to use mocks in our test cases in a more productive way, how to leverage DbUnit usage through third-party annotations, many custom assertions that cover a wide variety of object comparisons, and how to access private fields without dealing with the low-level reflection API directly.

Some of the features analyzed were offered by more than one tool, which might make it hard to decide which one to use. Although we described the pros and cons of each option, typically the best option depends on the project's needs and your personal style. What is most important, though, is to be aware that such tools exist, so you can evaluate them early in the project. The sooner such tools are used, the more time is saved because of productivity gains.

appendix A:
Differences between
JUnit 3 and JUnit 4

This appendix covers

- Changes between version 3.x and 4.x of JUnit
- API changes
- New features in JUnit 4.x

As you've probably seen, the new 4.x version of JUnit is a completely new framework. It's more of a totally new project than a bug-fixing improvement of the old one. But it still deals with unit testing your Java code. That said, we will try to define all the differences between the latest version of JUnit and the 3.x version.

A.1 Global changes

This section discusses the changes in the requirements for using JUnit.

A.1.1   JDK required

JUnit 4 uses a lot from Java 5 annotations, generics, and static import features. Although the JUnit 3.x version can work with JDK 1.2+, this usage requires that the new version of JUnit be used with Java 5 or higher.

A.1.2   Backward/forward compatibility

All of the JUnit 4.x test runners are able to execute JUnit 3.x tests with no modification whatsoever. But what about executing JUnit 4.x tests with the JUnit 3.x test runner? Now this is a trickier one, but it's absolutely necessary to support so that external tools such as Ant or Eclipse can work with JUnit without needing an update.

The key is to use the JUnit4TestAdapter and wrap all of your tests like the one shown in listing A.1.

Listing A.1   JUnit4TestAdapter to wrap your JUnit 4.x tests

```
[...]
import junit.framework.JUnit4TestAdapter;

public class TestJUnit4Tests extends TestCase {
    public static junit.framework.Test suite() {
        return new JUnit4TestAdapter(SampleTest.class);        ◁──❶
    }
}
```

It's that simple. At ❶ you need to pass your JUnit 4.x tests to the JUnit4TestAdapter, and they immediately get converted to JUnit 3.x tests so that they can be run with the JUnit 3.x runners.

A.2   Changes in the API

The changes listed here concern the inner structure of JUnit: all the new features added to the API that we need to know.

A.2.1   Package structure

The new version of JUnit is built on the idea of backward compatibility. The developers wanted to make sure that you, as a software developer, are able to execute any JUnit 3.x test case with the JUnit 4.x library in your classpath. That's why they included all the new features in a new package, org.junit. The old package, junit.framework, is also bundled in the distribution.

A.2.2   Constructors

If you're maintaining tests written prior to JUnit 3.8.1, your class needs a String constructor, for example:

```
public CalculatorTest(String name) { super(name); }
```

This is no longer required with JUnit 3.8.1 and later.

A.2.3 Extending TestCase

In the new version of JUnit, your test cases no longer need to extend the `junit.framework.TestCase` class. Instead, any `public` class with a zero-argument `public` constructor can act as a test class.

A.2.4 Test method names

In the new version of JUnit, test names no longer need to follow the `testXXX` pattern. Instead, any method that you want to be considered a test method should be annotated with the `@Test` annotation. For instance, the method shown in listing A.2 is a valid test method.

Listing A.2   Test method annotations in JUnit 4.x

```
@Test
public void substract () {
    assertEquals(2, 5-3);
}
```

A.3 Annotations and static imports added

JUnit 4.x is based on annotations, a concept introduced in JDK 1.5 along with static imports and some other features. This section lists those changes to the JUnit API.

A.3.1 @Before and @After annotations

If you remember, with JUnit 3.x we used to override the `setUp()` and `tearDown()` methods when we extended the `junit.framework.TestCase` class. These methods (or fixtures, as they're called) are executed right before/after each of the tests gets executed. Their purpose is to execute some common logic before or after each of the tests. As we already mentioned (several times, at least), in JUnit 4.x you no longer extend the `junit.framework.TestCase` class. So how can we execute some common logic before/after each of the tests?

The answer is again (guess what?) an annotation. You can annotate any of the methods you want to execute before your tests with the `@Before` annotation. And you can have as many annotated methods as you want. In the 3.x version of JUnit, you can have only one `setUp()` and only one `tearDown()` method (the method name restricts you). But in the 4.x version of the framework, the declaration shown in listing A.3 is pretty normal.

Listing A.3   @Before and @After annotations in action

```
public class CalculatorTest {
[...]

    @Before
    public void initializeMocks() { ... }
```

```
    @Before
    public void prepareFilesForReading() { ... }
[...]
}
```

WARNING Indeed, you can have as many @Before and @After annotated methods as you want, but be aware that nothing is specified about the order of execution of these methods. There is no guarantee, whatsoever, that any of the @Before methods will be executed before/after the other ones.

Also, there's one possible pitfall. If you have several test classes that extend from a common superclass, what will be the order of execution of the @Before and @After methods? The answer is that @Before methods in the superclass get executed earlier than the ones in the subclasses. The @After methods, on the contrary, have a mirrored execution; the @After methods in the subclass get executed first.

You need to remember that the @Before annotated methods must be public by signature and return void.

The same thing applies to the @After annotated methods.

A.3.2 *@BeforeClass and @AfterClass annotations*

One of the features that people wanted most from JUnit is the ability to execute some common logic before/after a whole set of tests. For instance, if your setUp() or tear-Down() methods consume a lot of resources (like opening a connection to a database or creating some file structure), you'll find it useful to have a way of executing the setUp() or tearDown() methods not *before every test* but instead *before a whole set of tests*.

JUnit 4.x offers such an option with the @BeforeClass and @AfterClass annotations. Just like the @Before and @After annotations that we already covered, you can annotate any of your methods with the @BeforeClass and @AfterClass annotations. In listing A.4 we show how to use these annotations in your tests.

Listing A.4   @BeforeClass and @AfterClass annotations in action

```
[...]
public class CalculatorTest {

    @BeforeClass
    public static void setupFileStructure() { ... }

    @AfterClass
    public static void cleanupFileStructure() { ... }
}
```

There are several things to notice here. First of all, you can add as many @BeforeClass and @AfterClass annotated methods as you want. Again, the same condition applies as with the @Before/@After annotated methods; no guarantee whatsoever is given for the order of execution. One more thing to notice is that the methods that are annotated with @BeforeClass and @AfterClass must not only be public and return void type but also be static.

A.3.3 Differences in ignoring a test

Sometimes, because of a system reconfiguration or a change of client requirements, you need to skip the execution of a certain test method. In the 3.x version of JUnit, the only way to do that is to comment the whole test method or rename the method. This way, if you start commenting your test methods, you get no detailed statistics of how many methods were skipped during test execution.

This is significantly improved in JUnit 4.x, by the introduction of the @Ignore annotation. You can use it to annotate any of your test methods, with the result that this method will be skipped at the time of test execution. The best part is that at the end of the execution you get detailed statistics of not only how many of your tests were successful or failed but also the number of the skipped tests.

One last thing—from version 4.3 on of JUnit, you can annotate not only test methods but also the whole class with @Ignore. As a result, all of the tests in that class will be skipped.

A.3.4 Static imports

As mentioned already, your test cases no longer need to extend the `junit.framework.TestCase` class, whereas in the previous versions of JUnit the assert methods would come from the `junit.framework.TestCase` class that you used to extend. The question that you'll ask now is, "How on earth do I get the assert methods in my class?"

The answer to this question is one of the new features of Java 5: static imports. With Java's static imports, you can write the code shown in listing A.5.

Listing A.5 Static imports in action

```
import static org.junit.Assert.assertEquals;          ←—❶
import org.junit.Test;

public class CalculatorTest {

    @Test
    public void add() {
        assertEquals(60, 50+10);          ←—❷
    }
}
```

At ❶ we use the static import feature to import one of the assert methods we need, and later on, at ❷, we call it.

A.3.5 Exception testing

One of the most important aspects of unit testing is the ability to test exceptional situations in your code. You need to make sure that whenever an exception is thrown, it's handled properly. In listing A.6 you can see how exception handling is done in the previous version of JUnit.

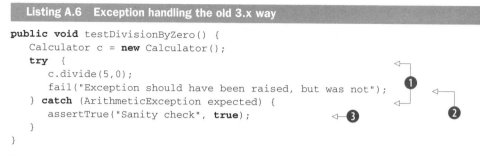

Listing A.6   Exception handling the old 3.x way

```
public void testDivisionByZero() {
    Calculator c = new Calculator();
    try {
        c.divide(5,0);
        fail("Exception should have been raised, but was not");
    } catch (ArithmeticException expected) {
        assertTrue("Sanity check", true);
    }
}
```

Basically, what you do is surround the troublesome code with a try-catch block ❶ and after that deliberately fail the test ❷ if the exception was not thrown. A good practice is also to place a dummy assert in the catch clause ❸ just to make sure you always pass through the catch clause.

In JUnit 4 we have a better solution for handling exceptional situations than we had in JUnit 3. Every time you want to make sure that an exception is thrown, you can use an expected parameter with the @Test annotation. Listing A.7 shows you how to ensure that an Arithmetic exception is thrown.

Listing A.7   Exception handling with the expected parameter of the @Test annotation

```
[...]
public class CalculatorTest {

    @Test(expected=ArithmeticException.class)          ⊲─❶
    public void testDivisionByZero() {
        Calculator c = new Calculator();
        c.divide( 5, 0 );
    }
}
```

As you can see in ❶, we've added the expected attribute to the @Test annotation to denote that this method is supposed to throw an exception of the provided type.

A.3.6   *Timeout testing*

Another parameter you can add to the @Test annotation is the timeout parameter. This feature was also missing in the "old" JUnit. With this parameter, you can specify a value in milliseconds that you expect to be the upper limit of the time you spend executing your test. What happens when the time runs out? An exception will be raised, and the test will marked as failed, telling you that the test couldn't finish execution in the given Test timeout parameter. Listing A.8 shows you how to use the timeout parameter of the @ annotation.

Listing A.8   Timeout parameter in the @Test annotation

```
public class CalculatorTest {

    @Test(timeout=5000)
    public void testSomethingTimeConsuming() {
        [...]
    }
}
```

A.4   New JUnit runners

This section briefly covers some of the new JUnit runners included in JUnit 4.x.

A.4.1   Test runners

The 3.x version of JUnit comes with Swing and AWT test runners that are no longer part of the JUnit distribution. The test runner façade that you can use to start your tests from the console is now called `org.junit.JUnitCore`.

With no GUI test runners included in the distribution, the only way to glimpse the old green bar is to use your favorite IDE; they all have JUnit 4.x support.

A.4.2   Test suites

The old way of constructing sets of your tests involved writing a `suite()` method and manually inserting all the tests that you want to be present in the suite. Because the new version of JUnit is annotation oriented, it seems somehow logical that the construction of suites is also done by means of annotation. Further, the suite construction is done not by one annotation but by two annotations: the `@RunWith` and `@Suite-Classes` annotations.

The first annotation lets you define test runners that you can use to run your tests. The `@RunWith` annotation accepts a parameter called `value`, where you need to specify the test runner to run your suite: `Suite.class`. This test runner is included with JUnit, along with some other runners. But in this annotation you can also specify a custom runner. You can find out how to implement your own JUnit runners in appendix B.

The second annotation declares all the tests that you want to include in the suite. You list the classes that hold your tests in the `value` parameter of the `@SuiteClasses` annotation.

Listing A.9 shows how to construct test suites in JUnit 4.x.

Listing A.9   Constructing test suites with JUnit 4.x

```
@RunWith(value=Suite.class)
@SuiteClasses(value={CalculatorTest.class, ComputerTest.class})
public class CalculatorTests {
    [...]
}
```

Some people find the way test suites are done in JUnit 4.x unnatural, and indeed, at first sight it is. But once you start writing tests, you'll see that there's nothing unnatural in the way things are done. Remember that you can include the @BeforeClass and @AfterClass annotated methods in the suite. This wasn't possible with the 3.x versions of JUnit.

A.4.3   *Parameterized tests*

As you saw, the @RunWith annotation lets you define a test runner to use. The Suite test runner that we already presented lets you run your test cases in a suite. Another test runner that's bundled with the JUnit distribution is the Parameterized test runner. This test runner lets you run the same tests with different input test data. We know that an example is worth several pages of explanation, so listing A.10 shows the example.

Listing A.10   Parameterized test runner in action

```
@RunWith(value=Parameterized.class)                    ◁─┐
public class SquareRootTest {                            ❶

    private int expected;
    private int actual;

    @Parameters                                        ◁─❷
    public static Collection data() {
        return Arrays.asList( new Object[][] {          ◁─❸
                            { 1, 1 },
                            { 2, 4 },
                            { 3, 9 },
                            { 4, 16 },
                            { 5, 25 },
                            });
    }

    public SquareRootTest(int expected, int actual) {
        this.expected = expected;
        this.actual = actual;
    }

    @Test                                              ◁─❹
    public void squareRoot() {
        Calculator calculator = new Calculator();
        assertEquals(expected, calculator.squareRoot(actual));   ◁─❺
    }
}
```

Imagine that we have a squareRoot method in our Calculator class that we want to test. This listing demonstrates how to test this method with different input test data. We start by declaring the use of the Parameterized test runner at ❶. Then, at ❷, we define the static data() method that we annotate with @Parameters, denoting that this method returns the actual test data for our test. This test data is made from a java.util.List, and each element of the List is a two-dimensional array, the elements of which will be used to make a new instance of the SquareRootTest. At ❸ we fill in the test data and return it. At ❹ we start the test method, and inside it we instantiate the `Calculator` object. After that, at ❺ we assert the correctness of the result of the `Calculator`'s `squareRoot()` method with all of the test data.

If you run this example, you'll get a result like what you'd see if you'd just run five distinct assertions like the following:

```
assertEquals( 1, calculator.squareRoot ( 1 ) );
assertEquals( 2, calculator.squareRoot ( 4 ) );
assertEquals( 3, calculator.squareRoot ( 9 ) );
assertEquals( 4, calculator.squareRoot ( 16 ) );
assertEquals( 5, calculator.squareRoot ( 25 ) );
```

A.5   New assertions and assumptions

This final section deals with the new assertion and assumption mechanisms introduced in JUnit 4.x. It also reveals the integration between JUnit and the Hamcrest matcher—something that allows you to write useful match statements to simplify your assertions.

A.5.1   Hamcrest assertions

In version 4.4 of JUnit, the Hamcrest assertion mechanism was incorporated. The Hamcrest assertion mechanism was introduced in JMock and provides a new, robust, fluent API for assertions. With Hamcrest assertions, you're able to write more readable and flexible test assertions like these in listing A.11.

> **Listing A.11   Hamcrest assertions in JUnit 4.4+**

```java
[...]
import org.junit.Test;
import static org.junit.Assert.*;
import static org.hamcrest.CoreMatchers.is;
import static org.hamcrest.CoreMatchers.not;

public class CalculatorTest {

    @Test
    public void squareRoot() {
        Calculator c = new Calculator();
        assertThat(2, is(c.squareRoot(4)));
        assertThat(3, is(not(c.squareRoot(4))));
    }
}
```

The `org.hamcrest.CoreMatchers` and `org.junit.matchers.JUnitMatchers` packages are distributed with JUnit and contain numerous matchers. The Hamcrest matchers that come with JUnit are the first third-party classes included in JUnit.

If you find them insufficient, you can always get the full Hamcrest project from the internet and use any of those matchers with JUnit.

A.5.2   *Assumptions*

As a developer, you always strive to execute your tests against various scenarios. But sometimes you have no control over the environment the tests are run in, as in the case when the test depends on the operating system path-separator character (in Windows it is \ and in UNIX it is /). This may mandate that your test cases run in Windows boxes and not in Linux boxes. It would be good if you could make an assumption as to what the character separator is and execute the tests only if your assumption is correct.

With the 4.4 release of JUnit, assumptions were introduced. `assumeThat` is the natural way in JUnit to run a given test against assumptions you make. You can assume that a given condition is set and then assert that the tests pass. Consider listing A.12.

Listing A.12   Assumptions in JUnit

```
[...]
import java.io.File;

import org.junit.Test;
import static org.junit.Assert.*;
import static org.junit.Assume.*;
import static org.hamcrest.CoreMatchers.is;

public class PathSeparatorTest {

    @Test
    public void pathSeparatorIsOK() {
        assumeThat(File.separatorChar, is('/'));                    ←❶
        assertThat((new FileManager()).getDBConfFile().getPath(),      ❷
                                    is("conf/db.cfg"));            ←┘
    }
}
```

As you can see, we use the `assumeThat` method to make sure the file separator is UNIX style ❶ and then assert that the database configuration file path is correct ❷. What happens if the assumption is wrong, and we're running the tests on a Windows box? Our tests are marked as passing, regardless of the assertions we make!

A.5.3   *New assertions*

The assert*XXX* methods in JUnit 3.x are thorough enough, but they lack any method to compare equality of arrays. Two methods with these signatures

```
assertEquals(Object[] expected, Object[] actual)
assertEquals(String message, Object[] expected, Object[] actual)
```

were added to the JUnit 4.0 framework to help with that task. These methods, given two arrays, start by checking the sizes of the arrays. If the sizes are the same, they will call the `equals()` method on each of the elements.

In version 4.3 these two methods were deprecated in the way they're used, and a whole new bunch of methods named `assertArrayEquals()` were introduced.

From version 4.6 on of the JUnit framework, you can use a convenient new method for testing the equality of two arrays of doubles:

```
assertArrayEquals(double[]first ,double[] second, double delta);
```

This compares every element of the first element with the corresponding element of the second array using the given delta.

A.5.4 *Assertion errors*

When you test with the 3.x version of JUnit, and any part of your assert is wrong, you get a `junit.framework.AssertionFailedError` message. With the new version of JUnit, that's no longer true, and in case of wrong assertions you see the `java.lang.AssertionError` message. The `java.lang.AssertionError` class was introduced in JDK 1.4.

appendix B:
Extending the JUnit
API with custom
runners and matchers

This appendix covers

- Introducing the Interceptor pattern
- Implementing custom runners for JUnit
- Implementing custom matchers for JUnit

As we already discussed in chapter 2, the backbone of JUnit consists of three classes—TestClass, Runner, and Suite—the latter one being a Runner itself. This means that once we understand how those classes operate, we can write whatever tests we need with JUnit. If you find JUnit insufficient for your testing needs, you can extend the JUnit API with custom classes. Since JUnit is open source you can rebuild or extend. There is no obvious benefit in extending the TestClass class.

On the other hand, the Runner class is especially designed to be easily extensible for our needs.

This appendix gives a brief introduction to how to extend the JUnit API with custom Runner objects. It also describes how to extend the Hamcrest API with custom matchers so that we eventually customize not only our runners but also our assert calls.

B.1   Introducing the Interceptor pattern

So far in the book, we've gotten to know a lot of design patterns: the Controller, the Façade, Inversion of Control, and so on. Now it's time to look at another one: the Interceptor pattern.

> ### Design patterns in action: Interceptor
> The Interceptor pattern can be described as a method that intercepts a business method invocation. The pattern usually consists of several objects. The first one is an Interceptor interface that defines one or more methods that your interceptors will implement. The next is a Delegate object that holds a list of interceptors. The Delegate object is called at the intercepting points of your application, and it invokes the interceptors one after another.
>
> Here are some interesting features of the Interceptor pattern:
>
> - It propagates extensibility and flexibility.
> - It enables separation of concerns.
> - It increases reusability.
> - If not used properly, security issues might occur.

Imagine you're designing an application for a group of developers. You want them to plug their code into your application as painlessly as possible, and at the same time you don't want them to change it. What can you do? You can provide some points in your application where the developers can intercept the invocation of the program and introduce their own logic. Others don't need to change your code; they can simply plug their code into your framework.

B.2   Implementing a custom runner

Let's start implementing our own custom runner. As you might have already guessed, we want to develop a custom runner that implements the Interceptor pattern we just discussed.

We want to define an Interceptor interface, which will be implemented by the various interceptors that we have. That's why we start with the Interceptor interface, shown in listing B.1.

Listing B.1 `Interceptor` interface defining the methods for any of our interceptors

```
[...]
public interface Interceptor {

    public void interceptBefore();

    public void interceptAfter();

}
```
❶

We use this generic interface to define the two methods ❶ in which we define our custom logic to plug into the program execution. Notice that our interceptor methods don't accept any parameters. The normal way of implementing the Interceptor pattern would be to call the interceptor methods with some kind of a context object, so that these methods could monitor and gain access to our application. This can also allow our application to get some feedback from the execution of the interceptor methods. But for our needs it's sufficient to implement the interceptor methods with no input parameters.

After release 4.5, tests in JUnit are executed in a block of statements. That block of statements contains all the features a test might have attached: @Before/@After methods, timeout seconds, ignore features, and the like. Based on these features, different kinds of actions are performed. The tricky part is that the @Before/@After methods are very near the border of the block, and the actual execution of the test is the core of the block of statements (see listing B.2).

Our idea is to wrap the block of statements in another statement that we implement (InterceptorStatement) and pass this statement to the custom runner we write. The custom runner invokes the block of statements, which reaches our statement at some point, and then our statement starts executing the interceptors we've defined. Then our statement invokes the wrapped block of statements in order to proceed with the execution in a normal manner. This way, we serve the Interceptor-Statement as the delegate object of the Interceptor pattern.

Moving on, listing B.2 presents the InterceptorStatement we use for our own runner.

Listing B.2 `InterceptorStatement` that wraps the original statement

```
[...]
import org.junit.runners.model.Statement;

    public class InterceptorStatement extends Statement {          ❶  ❷

    private final Statement invoker;
    private List<Interceptor> interceptors =
                                                                          ❸
                                    new ArrayList<Interceptor>();

    public InterceptorStatement(Statement invoker) {
        this.invoker = invoker;
    }                                                                     ❹
```

```java
    @Override
    public void evaluate() throws Throwable {
        for (Interceptor interceptor:interceptors) {
            interceptor.interceptBefore();
        }

        invoker.evaluate();

        for (Interceptor interceptor:interceptors) {
            interceptor.interceptAfter();
        }
    }

    public void addInterceptor(Interceptor interceptor) {
        interceptors.add(interceptor);
    }
}
```

As we already discussed, after JUnit 4.5 every test is executed by a block of statements.[1] Here we create our `InterceptorStatement` by extending the `Statement` object ❶, and we override the `evaluate` method ❺. Our statement holds a statement to invoke ❷ and a list of `Interceptor` implementations ❸ that were added to it ❾. In the constructor we initialize the `invoker` statement ❹ that we're wrapping. The `evaluate` method ❺ implements the entire logic of the statement; it iterates over all the interceptors and invokes their `interceptBefore` method ❻. Next we invoke the `evaluate` method of the wrapped statement object ❼ and again iterate over all the interceptors, this time to invoke the `interceptAfter` method ❽.

Now that we've prepared the `InterceptorStatement` object, it's time to move on and implement the real heart of the custom JUnit runner that we're making. We do this by extending the `BlockJUnit4ClassRunner` class, as shown in listing B.3, which was added in version 4.5 of the JUnit framework to help people create custom runners.

Listing B.3 Custom JUnit runner—`InterceptorRunner`

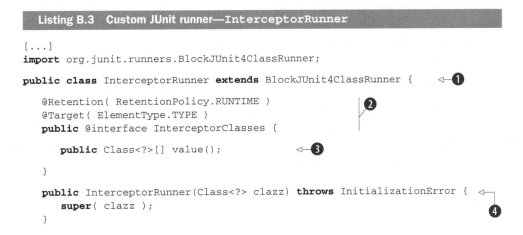

```java
[...]
import org.junit.runners.BlockJUnit4ClassRunner;

public class InterceptorRunner extends BlockJUnit4ClassRunner {

    @Retention( RetentionPolicy.RUNTIME )
    @Target( ElementType.TYPE )
    public @interface InterceptorClasses {

        public Class<?>[] value();

    }

    public InterceptorRunner(Class<?> clazz) throws InitializationError {
        super( clazz );
    }
```

---

[1] For more on this topic you can read an article by Kent Beck here: http://threeriversinstitute.org/TwoMoreImplementationPatterns.htm.

```
@Override                                                                   ❺
public Statement methodInvoker(FrameworkMethod method, Object test) {  ◁┘
    InterceptorStatement statement = new InterceptorStatement(
                          super.methodInvoker( method, test ));    ◁─❻
    InterceptorClasses annotation = test.getClass().getAnnotation(    ◁┐
                          InterceptorClasses.class);                      ❼
    Class<?>[] klasez = annotation.value();                    ◁─❽
    try {
        for (Class<?> klaz : klasez) {
            statement.addInterceptor((Interceptor) klaz.newInstance());  ◁┐
        }                                                                │
    }                                                                    ❾
    catch ( IllegalAccessException ilex ) {
        ilex.printStackTrace();
    }
    catch ( InstantiationException e ) {
        e.printStackTrace();
    }
    return statement;                        ◁─❿
    }
}
```

As we just said, in order to implement a custom JUnit runner we need to extend the BlockJUnit4ClassRunner ❶. In our custom runner we also declare an annotation called @InterceptorClasses at ❷, which we use to hold the implementations of the Interceptor interface that we want to plug into our execution. Our @Interceptor-Classes annotation defines a value() method, to return the classes that it holds at ❸. In ❹ we define the constructor that we must have, and in ❺ we override the methodInvokerStatement method. We start the method by creating an instance of our InterceptorStatement at ❻.

Notice that the InterceptorStatement we wrote in listing B.2 accepts a statement to wrap around. We create this statement by calling the super.methodInvoker method with parameters: our test method and the test class. This creates a Statement one level closer to the core of the statement block. And because the core of the statement block is the test itself, we wrap the test in our custom statement.

At ❼ we obtain the @InterceptorClasses annotation, which must be defined for the test class. Then, in ❽, we get all the classes that the annotation holds, iterate over the collection of classes, and add them to the InterceptorStatement object at ❾. The last step is to return our ready-made InterceptorStatement object ❿.

Our custom JUnit runner is finished! But in order to use it we need some sample implementations of the Interceptor interface. Here comes the real question: "What kind of events do we want to plug into the execution of the tests?"

One of the simplest implementations that could possibly come to mind is a logging implementation; we log a message before and after execution of every test. Listing B.4 contains the code for this interceptor.

```
[...]
public class SampleLoggingInterceptor implements Interceptor {          ◄─❶

    public void interceptBefore() {                              ◄─
        System.out.println( "Before-test" );
    }                                                               ❷      ❸

    public void interceptAfter() {                               ◄─
        System.out.println( "After-test" );
    }
}
```

This implementation is simple, but it's enough for what we currently need. The code implements the `Interceptor` interface ❶ (to make it a valid interceptor according to our terms) and gives body to the `interceptBefore` ❷ and `interceptAfter` methods ❸.

We use our interceptor in conjunction with our `InterceptorRunner`. And we use our JUnit runner just like we use any other JUnit runner. Let's examine it in listing B.5.

```
[...]

@RunWith( InterceptorRunner.class )                               ◄─❶
@InterceptorClasses( value = { SampleLoggingInterceptor.class } )   ◄─
public class TestCustomRunnerWithLoggingInterceptor {                   ❷
    @Before
    public void setUp() {
        System.out.println( "Real before" );
    }

    @Test                                                         ❸
    public void testDummy() {                                    ◄─
        assertTrue( true );
        System.out.println( "Some text for test purpose" );

    }

    @After
    public void tearDown() {
        System.out.println( "Real after" );
    }
}
```

The test case we provide starts with the `@RunWith` annotation. With this annotation we indicate which JUnit runner we want to execute our tests; in this case we want the `InterceptorRunner` that we just implemented ❶. We also provide an `@Interceptor-Classes` annotation to hold the interceptors we want to plug into our execution ❷. Then we start implementing our test case. In this scenario we have only one test method, defined just for testing purposes ❸.

The results from the execution are shown here:

```
Real before
Before-test
Some text for test purpose
After-test
Real after
```

What's obvious is that the `@Before` methods are executed before the `intercept-Before` method of the interceptor, and the `@After` methods are executed after the `interceptAfter` method. We'll use this feature shortly.

But let's move on and make another interceptor, this time more valuable than just logging some text to the screen. Listing B.6 shows a sample interceptor that's used for timing purposes.

Listing B.6   Second interceptor—`SampleTimingInterceptor`

```
[...]
public class SampleTimingInterceptor implements Interceptor {        ←── ❶
    Timer timer = new Timer();                                       ←──

    public void interceptBefore() {                                  ←──      ❷
        System.out.println("Interceptor started.");                  ❸
        timer.start();
    }
                                                                ❹
    public void interceptAfter() {                              ←──
        timer.stop();
        System.out.println("Interceptor ended."
                        + "The test executed for " + timer.time());
    }

    class Timer  {
        private long nanoStart = 1;
        private long nanoEnd = 0;

        void start() {
            nanoStart = System.nanoTime();
        }

        void stop() {
            nanoEnd = System.nanoTime();
        }

        long time() {
            return nanoEnd - nanoStart;
        }
    }
}
```

Again, for this interceptor to be a valid interceptor according to our terms, it needs to implement the `Interceptor` interface ❶. In ❷ we declare a local `timer` variable of type `Timer`, which we use to time the execution of the test method. The interceptBefore method starts the timer ❸, and the interceptAfter method stops it and prints the execution time on the screen ❹.

Now we need a test case for this interceptor. And here it comes—listing B.7.

Listing B.7   Test case for the timing interceptor

```
[...]
@RunWith( InterceptorRunner.class )                          ← ❶
@InterceptorClasses( SampleTimingInterceptor.class )          ← ❷
public class TestCustomRunnerWithTimingInterceptor {
    @Before
    public void longSetUp() throws InterruptedException {      ←┐
        Thread.sleep( 1000 );                                   │
    }                                                           │
                                                                │
    @Test                                                       │
    public void testDummy() throws InterruptedException {       │ ❸
        Thread.sleep( 2000 );                                   │
        assertTrue( true );                                     │
    }                                                           │
                                                                │
    @After                                                      │
    public void longTearDown() throws InterruptedException {   ←┘
        Thread.sleep( 1000 );
    }
}
```

We take the same approach as we used for the last interceptor test case: declare the runner we use with the @RunWith annotation ❶ and specify at ❷ which interceptor classes we use by means of the @InterceptorClasses annotation.

You might be wondering why we need these interceptors; they simply execute some common logic before/after the tests (the same way the @Before/@After methods do). The point is that sometimes it's hard to determine how much time is required for a test method to execute. In our case we have the longSetUp() and longTearDown() methods (at ❸), which also could take a lot of time, thus making it harder to determine the execution time of the testDummy() method itself. Because our timing interceptor keeps track of the execution time for the test methods only (the interceptBefore method is executed after the @Before methods, and intercept-After is executed before the @After methods), this makes it a perfect candidate to solve our problem.

Upon executing the test case, we should see something like the following in the console, despite the fact that the JUnit runner might show a different value (figure B.1).

```
Interceptor started.
Interceptor ended. The test executed for 2 sec.
```

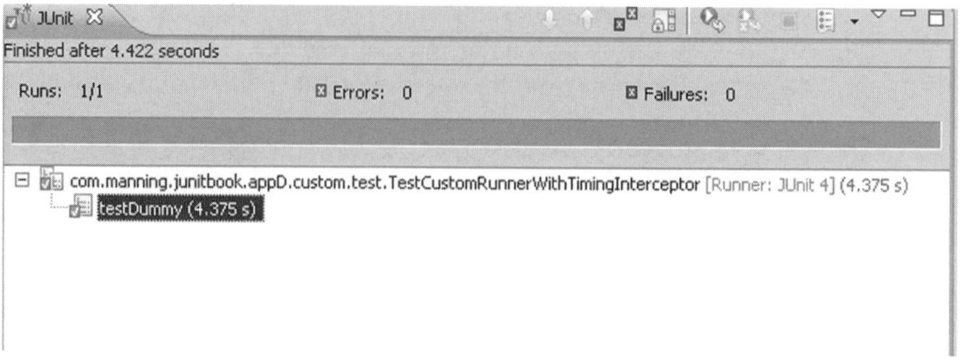

Figure B.1   The JUnit test runner shows that it takes 4.375 seconds to execute the whole test (with @Before and @After methods).

B.3   Implementing a custom matcher

As you write more and more tests, you'll see that sometimes it's difficult to read an assert statement at first glance. For instance, consider this one:

```
assertTrue( user.getContext().getPassword().size() >= 6
                && containsADigit(user.getContext().getPassword()) );
```

No matter how familiar you are with the code, you'll always need a few seconds to understand the assert statement. One way to simplify it is by introducing a new method (like the `containsADigit` method we added). Another way is to add Hamcrest matchers; that will greatly simplify the assert statement. But we might use this assert statement a lot in our tests, and it's very cumbersome to copy and paste the same long assert everywhere. Wouldn't it be great if there was a way to implement a custom Hamcrest matcher, so that the assert statement would be simplified?

Fortunately, there is a way, and that's exactly what we show next. We start by implementing a simple matcher that checks whether a given string is `null` or empty. Listing B.8 shows the code for the matcher.

Listing B.8   Our first Hamcrest matcher implementation

```
[...]
import org.hamcrest.BaseMatcher;
import org.hamcrest.Description;
import org.hamcrest.Factory;
import org.hamcrest.Matcher;

public class IsNotNullOrEmpty extends BaseMatcher<String> {      ←❶

    public boolean matches( Object string ) {                    ←❷
        String str = (String) string;
        return ( str != null ) && !str.equals( "" );
    }
}
```

```
public void describeTo( Description description ) {
    description.appendText("a string that is not null and not empty");
}

@Factory
public static <T> Matcher<String> isNotNullOrEmpty() {
    return new IsNotNullOrEmpty();
}

@Factory
public static <T> Matcher<String> notNullOrEmpty() {
    return new IsNotNullOrEmpty();
}

}
```

③

④

Basically, if we want to create a custom matcher, we need to extend one of the two classes BaseMatcher<T> or TypeSafeMatcher<T>. In this listing, we extend the first one **①**. Next, we override the matches method **②**, and we implement our logic on what occasion the matcher will match the conditions; our condition is matched successfully if the string parameter to which it is applied is not null and is different from an empty string.

Here comes the difference between BaseMatcher<T> and TypeSafeMatcher<T>. As you'll see later, if you extend TypeSafeMatcher<T>, then you'll have to override another method with the signature

```
protected boolean matchesSafely(T item);
```

This means that the method that has to implement our logic can never accept a null object. It will always accept a parameter of type T, which has already been checked for null value and can never be null. We want to implement this check, however, so we stick with the BaseMatcher<T> class.

In **③** we append a description for the matcher. This description is used in our test cases in case the matcher can't match the condition. In **④** we provide two factory methods (denoted by the @Factory annotation). We call these methods from our test cases to create an instance of our matcher. We provide two methods, only for readability purposes; sometimes it will be more readable to call one of them and sometimes the other.

Listing B.9 shows the corresponding test class that uses our test methods.

Listing B.9 Test class to demonstrate the `IsNotNullOrEmpty` matcher

```
[...]

import static com.manning.junitbook.appD.custom.matchers
                        .IsNotNullOrEmpty.isNotNullOrEmpty;
import static com.manning.junitbook.appD.custom.matchers
                        .IsNotNullOrEmpty.notNullOrEmpty;

public class TestStringIsNullUsingMatcher {

    @Test(expected=java.lang.AssertionError.class)
    public void testIsNotNullOrEmptyButIsNull() {
```

①

②

```
        String str = null;

        assertThat( str, isNotNullOrEmpty() );                    3
        assertThat( str, is( notNullOrEmpty() ) );
    }

    @Test(expected=java.lang.AssertionError.class)
    public void testIsNotNullOrEmptyButIsEmpty() {
        String str = "";

        assertThat( str, isNotNullOrEmpty() );
        assertThat( str, is( notNullOrEmpty() ) );
    }

    @Test
    public void testIsNotNullOrEmptyIsNotNull() {
        String str = "test";
        assertThat( str, isNotNullOrEmpty() );
        assertThat( str, is( notNullOrEmpty() ) );
    }
}
```

All we need to do is use the static import feature of Java 1.5 and import the matcher that we want to use ❶. After that, we implement three test methods using the custom matcher we just implemented. The first two deliberately test failing conditions, and we denote this with the `expected` parameter of the `@Test` annotation ❷. We also use the two factory methods ❸, the second one in conjunction with one of the core matchers of Hamcrest.

Now we demonstrate another example of making a custom matcher, this time by using `TypeSafeMatcher<T>`. For this case, we implement a custom Hamcrest matcher, which checks to see if a given password is valid. We consider the password to be valid if it's longer than six characters, contains a digit, and also contains a special symbol (any of the following: !, ", #, $, %, &, ', (,), *, +, -, ., /).

Listing B.10 shows our custom Hamcrest matcher.

Listing B.10 IsStrongPassword custom matcher

```
[...]
public class IsStrongPassword extends TypeSafeMatcher<String> {      ◁─❶
    @Override
    public boolean matchesSafely( String str ) {                     ◁─❷
        return containsSpecialSymbol( str )
                && containsDigit( str )
                && str.length() >= 6;
    }

    private boolean containsDigit( String str ) {                    ◁─❸
        for ( char ch : str.toCharArray() ) {
            if ( Character.isDigit( ch ) ) {
                return true;
            }
        }
        return false;
    }
```

```
    private boolean containsSpecialSymbol( String str ) {          ◀─❹
        for ( char ch : str.toCharArray() ) {
            if ( ( (int) ch ) <= 47 && ( (int) ch ) >= 33 ) {
                return true;
            }
        }
        return false;
    }                                                                ❺
    public void describeTo( Description description ) {          ◀─┘
        description.appendText( "string that contains"
            + "a digit, a special character and is at least 6 symbols" );
    }

    @Factory
    public static <T> Matcher<String> isStrongPassword() {       ◀─❻
        return new IsStrongPassword();
    }
                                                                    ❼
    @Factory
    public static <T> Matcher<String> strongPassword() {        ◀─┘
        return new IsStrongPassword();
    }
}
```

We start the implementation of our custom matcher by extending the TypeSafe-Matcher class ❶. This is the second way to create a matcher.

In ❷ we override the matchesSafely method and implement our code logic on what occasion the matcher should match the condition. In our case, the condition is that the password be longer than six characters and contain a digit and a special symbol. ❸ and ❹ are two helper methods that we use to validate the password.

The matchesSafely method will never accept a null value. If that occurs, the matcher will throw a java.lang.AssertionFailedError exception—something that we strive for (a password can never be null).

The describeTo method ❺ appends a description for our matcher to show in the log in case the condition does not match. Next, in ❻ and ❼ we provide two static factory methods that construct an instance of our matcher. We provide two methods instead of one because sometimes it's more readable to use one name rather than the other.

Let's see our matcher in action! It's time to create a test case and use the matcher. Listing B.11 shows the code. The results from the execution are shown in figure B.2.

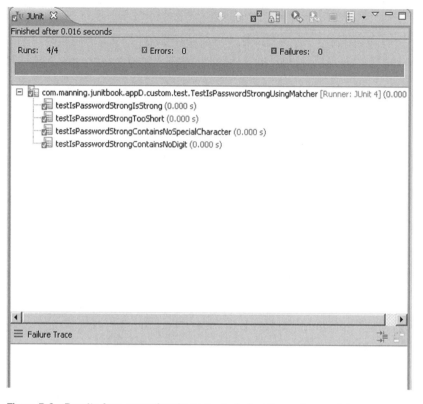

Figure B.2   Results from executing the tests, including the custom matcher

---

Listing B.11   Test case using our custom matcher

```
[...]
import static org.hamcrest.core.Is.is;
import static com.manning.junitbook.appD.custom.matchers.
                            IsStrongPassword.isStrongPassword;
import static com.manning.junitbook.appD.custom.matchers.
                            IsStrongPassword.strongPassword;

public class TestIsPasswordStrongUsingMatcher {

    @Test
    public void testIsPasswordStrongIsStrong() {
        final String pass = "!abcde0";

        assertThat( pass, isStrongPassword() );
        assertThat( pass, is( strongPassword() ) );
    }

    @Test( expected = java.lang.AssertionError.class )
    public void testIsPasswordStrongTooShort() {
        final String shortPass = "abcde";
```

① (annotation markers pointing to the import static lines)

② (annotation marker pointing to the assertThat lines)

```
        assertThat( shortPass, isStrongPassword() );
        assertThat( shortPass, is( strongPassword() ) );
    }

    @Test( expected = java.lang.AssertionError.class )
    public void testIsPasswordStrongContainsNoSpecialCharacter() {
        final String noSpecialCharacterPass = "abcdef0";

        assertThat( noSpecialCharacterPass, isStrongPassword() );
        assertThat( noSpecialCharacterPass, is( strongPassword() ) );
    }

    @Test( expected = java.lang.AssertionError.class )
    public void testIsPasswordStrongContainsNoDigit() {
        final String noDigitPass = "abcdef!";

        assertThat( noDigitPass, isStrongPassword() );
        assertThat( noDigitPass, is( strongPassword() ) );
    }

    @Test( expected = java.lang.AssertionError.class )
    public void testIsPasswordStrongIsNull() {
        final String nullPass = null;

        assertThat( nullPass, isStrongPassword() );
        assertThat( nullPass, is( strongPassword() ) );
    }

}
```

In ❶ we import the matchers that we want to use as static imports. Notice that we import our matchers the exact same way as we would any of the Hamcrest core matchers. Then we can use any of them, again as we would any Hamcrest matcher ❷.

The code is nice and clear now, isn't it?

appendix C:
The source code for
the book

This appendix covers

- Installing the book's source code
- Software versions required
- Directory structure conventions

This appendix gives an overview of the book's source code, where to find it, how to install it, and how to run it. When we were writing this book, we decided to donate all of the book's source code to the Apache Software Foundation, because we used many Apache frameworks in the making of this book. Therefore, we've made our source code available as open source on SourceForge at http://junitbook.sourceforge. net/junit2/.

We're also committed to maintaining this source code and fixing it if bugs are found, as a standard open source project. In addition, a Manning author forum has been set up for discussing the code at http://www.manning-sandbox.com/forum. jspa?forumID=502.

C.1   Getting the source code

There are two possibilities for getting the source code on your local machine:

- Download a released version from http://sourceforge.net/project/showfiles. php?group_id=68011 and unzip it somewhere on your hard drive.
- Use an SVN client and get the source from SVN HEAD. Getting the source from SVN is explained at http://sourceforge.net/svn/?group_id=68011. Either way, place the source code in a local directory named junitbook2/ (for example, C:\junitbook2 on Windows or /opt/junitbook2 on UNIX).

C.2   Source code overview

Once you put the source code in the junitbook2/ directory, you should have the directory structure shown in figure C.1. Each directory represents the source code for a chapter of the book (except the repository/ directory, which contains external JARs required by the chapter projects). The mapping between chapter names and directory names is listed in table C.1.

Each directory maps directly to a project. A project is a way to regroup Java sources, test sources, configuration files, and so on under a single location. A project

.svn	File Folder	2/15/2010 6:01 PM
appB-customAPI	File Folder	1/16/2010 5:34 PM
appC-sourceinfo	File Folder	1/16/2010 5:35 PM
ch01-jumpstart	File Folder	1/16/2010 5:43 PM
ch02-internals	File Folder	1/16/2010 5:35 PM
ch05-cobertura	File Folder	1/16/2010 5:34 PM
ch06-stubs	File Folder	1/16/2010 5:35 PM
ch07-mocks	File Folder	1/16/2010 5:42 PM
ch08-incontainer	File Folder	1/16/2010 5:42 PM
ch09-ant	File Folder	2/15/2010 6:01 PM
ch10-maven	File Folder	1/16/2010 6:34 PM
ch12-gui	File Folder	1/16/2010 5:29 PM
ch13-ajax	File Folder	1/16/2010 5:34 PM
ch14-cactus	File Folder	1/16/2010 5:34 PM
ch15-jsfunit	File Folder	1/16/2010 5:34 PM
ch16-osgi	File Folder	1/16/2010 5:36 PM
ch17-dbunit	File Folder	1/16/2010 5:35 PM
ch18-jpa	File Folder	1/16/2010 5:42 PM
ch19-steroids	File Folder	1/16/2010 5:35 PM
lib	File Folder	1/16/2010 5:42 PM
LICENSE.txt	1 KB Text Document	1/16/2010 5:42 PM
pom.xml	4 KB XML Document	1/16/2010 5:42 PM
README.INSTALL	1 KB INSTALL File	1/16/2010 5:42 PM

Figure C.1   Directory structure for the source code, shown here in Windows Explorer. (Note that the directory and file icons are decorated by the TortoiseSVN client.)

Table C.1   Mappings between chapter names and source directory names

Chapter name	Directory name
Chapter 1: JUnit jump-start	junitbook2/ch01-jumpstart/
Chapter 2: Exploring core JUnit	junitbook2/ch02-internals/
Chapter 3: Mastering JUnit	
Chapter 4: Software testing principles	
Chapter 5: Test coverage and development	junitbook2/ch05-coberturra/
Chapter 6: Coarse-grained testing with stubs	junitbook2/ch06-stubs/
Chapter 7: Testing with mock objects	junitbook2/ch07-mocks/
Chapter 8: In-container testing	junitbook2/ch08-incontainer/
Chapter 9: Running JUnit tests from Ant	junitbook2/ch09-ant/
Chapter 10: Running JUnit tests from Maven2	junitbook2/ch10-maven/
Chapter 11: Continuous integration tools	
Chapter 12: Presentation-layer testing	junitbook2/ch12-gui/
Chapter 13: Ajax testing	junitbook2/ch13-ajax/
Chapter 14: Server-side Java testing with Cactus	junitbook2/ch14-cactus/
Chapter 15: Testing JSF applications	junitbook2/ch15-jsfunit/
Chapter 16: Testing OSGi components	junitbook2/ch16-osgi/
Chapter 17: Testing database access	junitbook2/ch17-dbunit/
Chapter 18: Testing JPA-based applications	junitbook2/ch18-jpa/
Chapter 19: JUnit on steroids	junitbook2/ch19-steroids/

also has a build, which lets you perform various actions such as compiling the code, running the tests, and generating the Javadoc. We use various build tools (Ant and Maven) for the different projects, as explained in the chapter matching each project.

C.3   External libraries

You may have noticed a directory named repository/ in figure C.1. It contains the different external libraries (JARs) that all the other projects need in order to compile and run. As a convenience, we make them readily available to prevent you from having to fish for them all over the Net.

C.4   JAR versions

Table C.2 lists the versions of all external JARs and applications used in the projects. We recommend using these versions when you try the book examples.

Table C.2   External JAR/application versions (sorted in alphabetical order)

External project name	Version	Project URL
Ant	1.7.1	http://ant.apache.org/
Cactus	1.8.1	http://jakarta.apache.org/cactus
Commons BeanUtils		http://commons.apache.org/
Commons Collections		http://commons.apache.org/
Commons HttpClient		http://commons.apache.org/
Commons Logging		http://commons.apache.org/
DBUnit	1.5.5	http://dbunit.sourceforge.net/
EasyMock	1.0	http://easymock.org/
Eclipse	3.5.2	http://eclipse.org/
HttpUnit	1.5.3	http://httpunit.sourceforge.net/
Jakarta Taglibs/JSTL	1.0.2	http://jakarta.apache.org/taglibs/
JBoss	4.2.1	http://jboss.org/
Jetty	7.0.0.pre5	http://jetty.mortbay.org/
JUnit	4.6	http://junit.org/
Maven	2.0.10	http://maven.apache.org/
MockObjects	0.09	http://mockobjects.com/
ServletAPI	2.5	http://repo1.maven.org/maven2/javax/servlet/
Tomcat	6.0.14	http://tomcat.apache.org/

C.5   *Directory structure conventions*

For each project, we followed the directory conventions listed in table C.3.

Table C.3   Directory structure conventions

Directory name	Explanation
<project name>/src/main/java	Java runtime sources.
<project name>/src/test/java	Java test sources.
<project name>/src/main/webapp	Web app resources (JSPs, web.xml, taglibs, and so on).
<project name>/src/main/conf	Configuration files (if any).
<project name>/target	Directory created by the build process (Ant or Maven) to store generated files and temporary files. It can be safely deleted, because it's re-created by the build.

appendix D:

JUnit IDE integration

This appendix covers

- Installing Eclipse and NetBeans
- Setting up the book's source code in Eclipse and NetBeans
- Running JUnit tests in Eclipse and NetBeans

In this appendix, you'll get to know the two most popular Java IDEs: the Eclipse IDE and the NetBeans IDE. We cover installation procedures, configuration, and how to run the book's source code from within the IDEs.

D.1   JUnit integration with Eclipse

This section serves as a quick start to get you up and running with Eclipse and with the integrated JUnit.

D.1.1   *Installing Eclipse*

Installing Eclipse is very simple; the process consists of downloading Eclipse from http://eclipse.org/ and then unzipping it to somewhere on your hard drive. We recommend downloading Eclipse 3.2 or greater. In the remainder of this appendix, we assume Eclipse is installed in [ECLIPSE_HOME] (for example, C:\eclipse-3.2).

D.1.2   *Setting up Eclipse projects from the source*

It's extremely easy to set up an Eclipse project, because we provide the Eclipse project files with the book's source code distribution. Please refer to appendix C, "The source code for the book," for directory structure organization and project names.

The first Eclipse project to import corresponds to the ch01-jumpstart/ directory. This project contains the source code for the first chapter of the book. To import this project, select File > Import and then select Existing Project Into Workspace. Point the Project Content to the ch01-jumpstart/ directory on your hard disk.

Repeat the process for all the projects you wish to see in your Eclipse workspace. If you import all the projects, you should end up with the workspace shown in figure D.1.

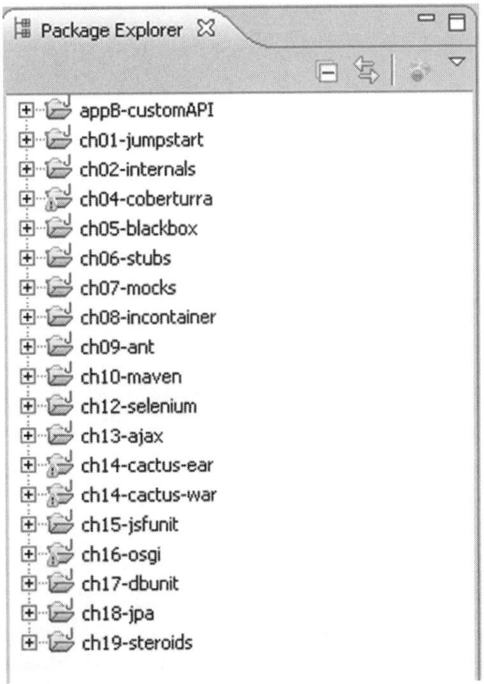

D.1.3   *Running JUnit tests from Eclipse*

To run a JUnit test in Eclipse, select the Java perspective ( ), click the test class to execute, click the Run As icon arrow ( ), and select JUnit Test. Figure D.2 shows what you get if you run the `TestWebClient1` test case found in the ch05-stubs Eclipse project from chapter 5.

For full details on how to run JUnit tests from Eclipse, please see the integrated Eclipse Help: Click Help > Help Contents. Then, in the Help browser, select the following topic: Java Development User Guide > Getting Started > Basic Tutorial > Writing And Running JUnit tests.

Figure D.1   Eclipse workspace when all the book projects have been imported

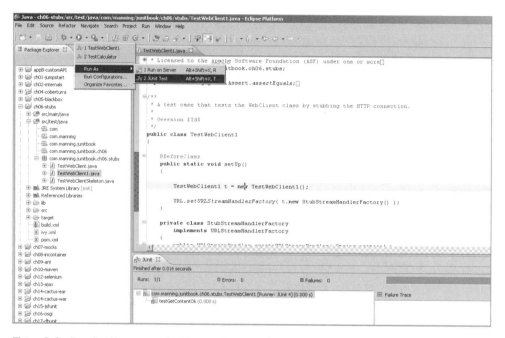

Figure D.2   Running the `TestWebClient1` test case in Eclipse using the built-in JUnit plug-in

D.1.4   *Running Ant scripts from Eclipse*

Before running Ant scripts, make sure you've added the Ivy ivy.jar library to your Ant classpath (it's needed by our Ant scripts). To do so, select Window > Preferences, choose Ant > Runtime in the Preferences dialog box, and add the JAR, as shown in figure D.3.

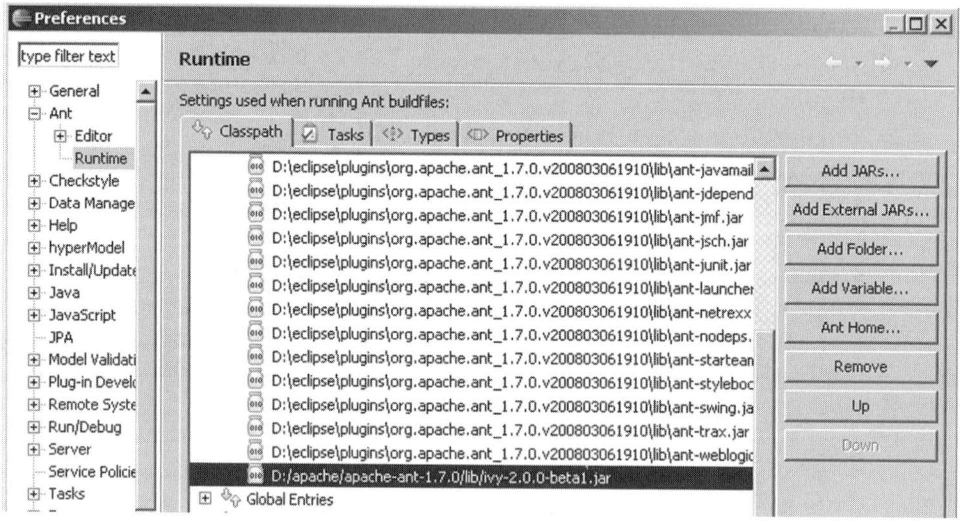

Figure D.3   Adding the JDK ivy-[version].jar to the Ant classpath in Eclipse

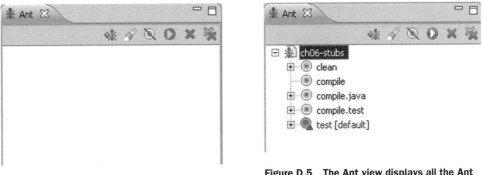

Figure D.4   Eclipse displays the Ant view.

Figure D.5   The Ant view displays all the Ant targets found in build.xml.

To execute a target from an Ant buildfile, first tell Eclipse to display the Ant view by clicking the Window > Show View menu item and selecting Ant. Figure D.4 shows the result.

Then, click the icon to add a buildfile to the Ant view. For example, add the build.xml file from the ch06-stubs project. The Ant view now lists all the Ant targets it has found in the build.xml file, highlighting the default target (see figure D.5).

To execute a target, select it and click the button. Figure D.6 shows the result of executing the compile target. Note that Eclipse captures the Ant output and displays it in the console view at the bottom right of the figure.

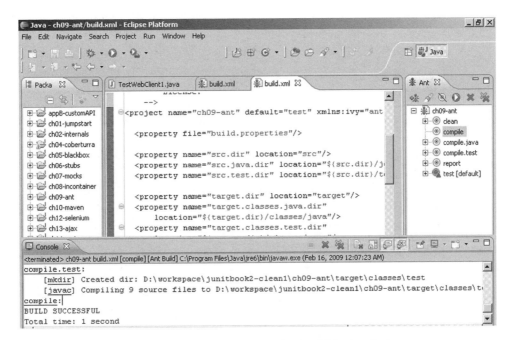

Figure D.6   Result of executing the compile Ant target for the ch09-ant project

For full details on how to run Ant scripts from Eclipse, please see the integrated Eclipse Help; click Help > Help Contents. Then, in the Help browser, select the following topic: Workbench User Guide > Getting Started > Ant & External Tools Tutorial > Eclipse Ant Basics.

D.2   *Introducing the JUnitMAX Eclipse plug-in*

Kent Beck, one of the creators of JUnit, started another Eclipse plug-in called JUnitMAX (http://www.threeriversinstitute.org/junitmax/subscribe-w-infinitest.html). JUnitMAX requires a \$2 monthly subscription, but it offers quite a few features that you might find interesting.

Let's take another look at the very first test case that we introduced in this book (listing D.1).

> **Listing D.1   The `CalculatorTest` case**

```
public class CalculatorTest {
    @Test
    public void add() {
        Calculator calculator = new Calculator();
        double result = calculator.add( 10, 50 );
        assertEquals( 60, result, 0 );
    }
}
```

D.2.1   *Integrated in your development cycle*

One of the main features of JUnitMAX is that it's tightly integrated in your development cycle. For instance, let's get an Eclipse with JUnitMAX installed and type in the code from listing D.1. Now let's deliberately introduce an error inside the test. After you press Ctrl+S to save your file, Eclipse will compile it, and JUnitMAX will run the test for you, showing you the error we just introduced (figure D.7).

The test errors and failures are shown as compilation problems. You can also see them on a project level in the package explorer; this way the risk of missing them and committing broken tests is almost zero.

Now it's time to fix the error and save the document. The result is shown in figure D.8.

You see that the plug-in ran our test again and flagged it with a blue icon to denote that it passed.

Figure D.7   Introducing an error in our test case causes JUnitMAX to execute the tests and report the error as a red marker at the beginning of the line.

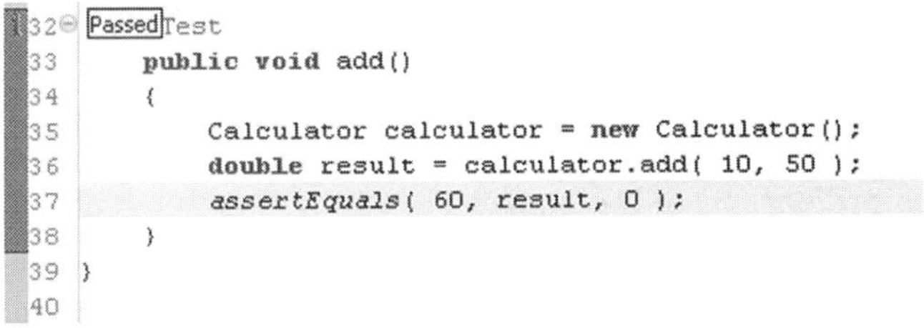

```
32  Passed Test
33      public void add()
34      {
35          Calculator calculator = new Calculator();
36          double result = calculator.add( 10, 50 );
37          assertEquals( 60, result, 0 );
38      }
39  }
40
```

Figure D.8
Our test passes when we fix
the error and save the file.

JUnitMAX runs your tests during development time, thus saving you the time required to explicitly run your tests through a separate interface—Ant, Maven, or some other graphic runner.

D.2.2 *Execution order*

Another neat feature of this JUnit plug-in is the special order in which different tests are executed.

Tests don't fail at random. Recently failed tests are more likely to fail again. When you execute your tests with the JUnitMAX plug-in, it will take note of this and will run your recently failed tests first. This way, you get valuable feedback on the status of your tests very early in the running phase. The plug-in also executes your short tests before longer ones, again giving you valuable information early.

D.2.3 *Reverting to last stable version*

One of the most annoying problems is someone committing code in the source repository that breaks existing functionality—obviously he forgot to run his set of tests. We can detect possible problems early by using a continuous integration system like the ones we explored in chapter 10. Obviously, we need some time to see why the things are breaking down. But how do we know what the last stable version of a test was? How do we easily revert to the last version of our test case in which all the tests passed?

One way is to check your version control logs. The JUnitMAX plug-in, however, offers an easier solution to this problem. You right-click your test in the package explorer of Eclipse and select the Revert To Last Green item. Nice, isn't it?

D.3 *JUnit integration with NetBeans*

This section serves as a reference guide to how to work with the NetBeans IDE and how to write, execute, and compose JUnit tests from within NetBeans.

D.3.1 *Installing NetBeans*

NetBeans installation requires several steps. First, you need to go to the download section of the NetBeans website (http://www.netbeans.org/downloads/index.html). You need to select from the upper-right corner of the page the platform on which you'll install the software as well as the type of installation you want. In this book we use the 6.5 version of the NetBeans project installed on Windows.

The second step consists of downloading the appropriate installer (for Windows machines it's an .exe wizard, and for UNIX it's an .sh script). The last step is to follow the wizard and actually install the software.

D.3.2   *Setting up NetBeans projects from the source*

Luckily enough, the NetBeans IDE recognizes the Eclipse configuration files, so you can easily import any Eclipse project into NetBeans and start working. We used the Eclipse IDE to develop the software that comes with the book, so if you want to import it, all you have to do is follow these steps:

1 Click File > Import Project > Eclipse Project.
2 In the wizard that appears, browse to the folder that contains the workspace with all the chapter projects.
3 Select the projects that you want to import (figure D.9).

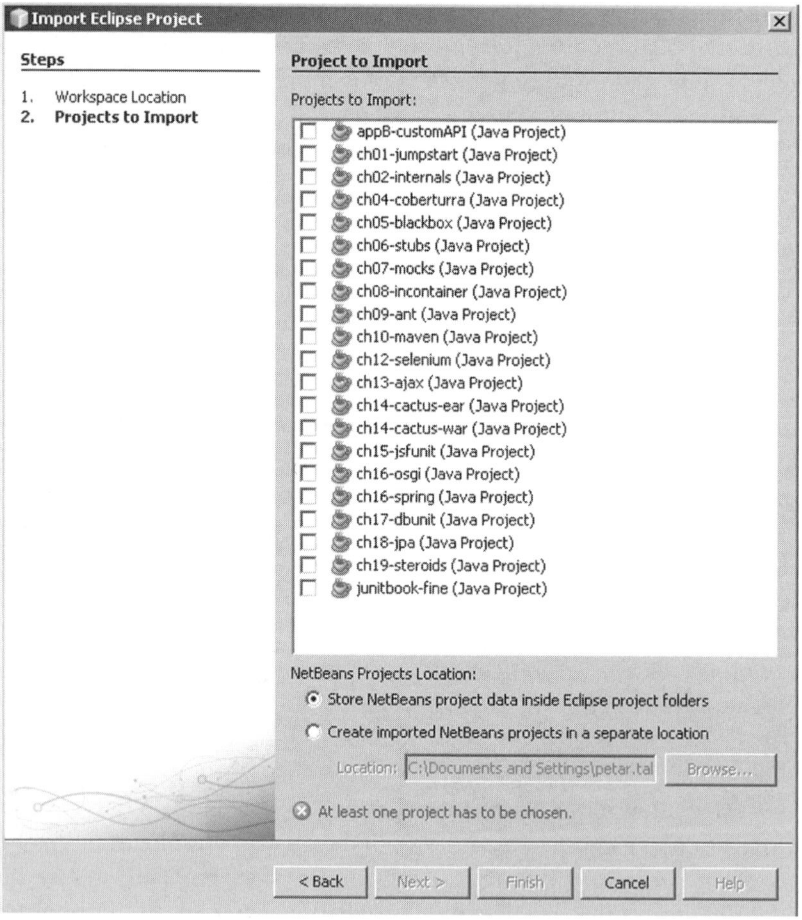

Figure D.9   Import Eclipse projects into NetBeans.

D.3.3   *Running JUnit tests from NetBeans*

Once you import the projects into your workspace, we can demonstrate how to run some of the tests there. Before we do that, there are several things to consider.

First, take a closer look at any of the projects. You'll see something like the tree shown in figure D.10.

These compilation problems are due to the fact that NetBeans, unlike Eclipse, explicitly keeps two separate directories: one for the source files and one for the test-source files. For each of these folders NetBeans keeps a different set of libraries to include in the classpath. As you see in the figure, NetBeans detects src\test\java as a source folder, and the source-folder classpath probably doesn't contain the JUnit JAR file. To see all the libraries that are included in the classpath, right-click your project, choose Properties, and in the box that appears choose the Libraries tag from the left tree. As you will see, the Compile Tests tab contains the JUnit JAR, so indeed the compilation problems were caused by the fact that NetBeans recognizes the folder as a source folder and not as a source-test folder.

To solve this problem, again right-click your project, choose Properties, and in the Sources tag remove your src\test\java folder from the Source Package Folders list and add it to the Test Package Folders list. The final setup should look like the one shown in figure D.11.

To execute a JUnit test from within NetBeans, you need to make sure the test resides in the correct folder (the test-source folder). Unlike Eclipse, NetBeans will never execute a JUnit test if it resides in the source folder (if your class resides in the source folder and you try to execute it, NetBeans will start looking for a main method instead of running the class as a test). Given that you already made sure all of your tests are located in the test-source folder, you have several options. Either right-click inside the class and choose Run File (Shift+F6), or right-click the file inside the Projects view and select Run File, or simply press Shift+F6. No matter what method you use, the result should be similar to the screen shown in figure D.12.

Figure D.10
Compilation problems with NetBeans

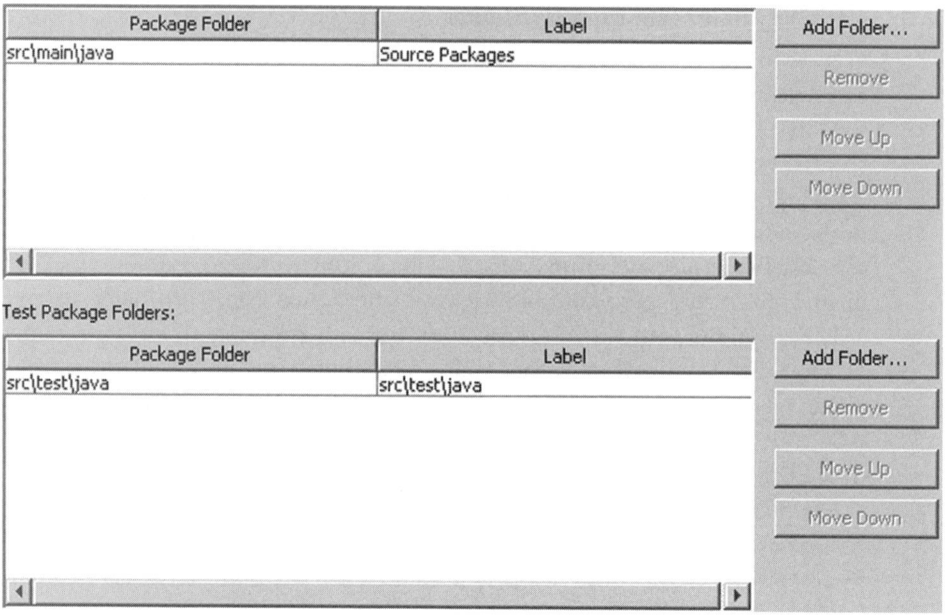

Figure D.11   Resolved source folders

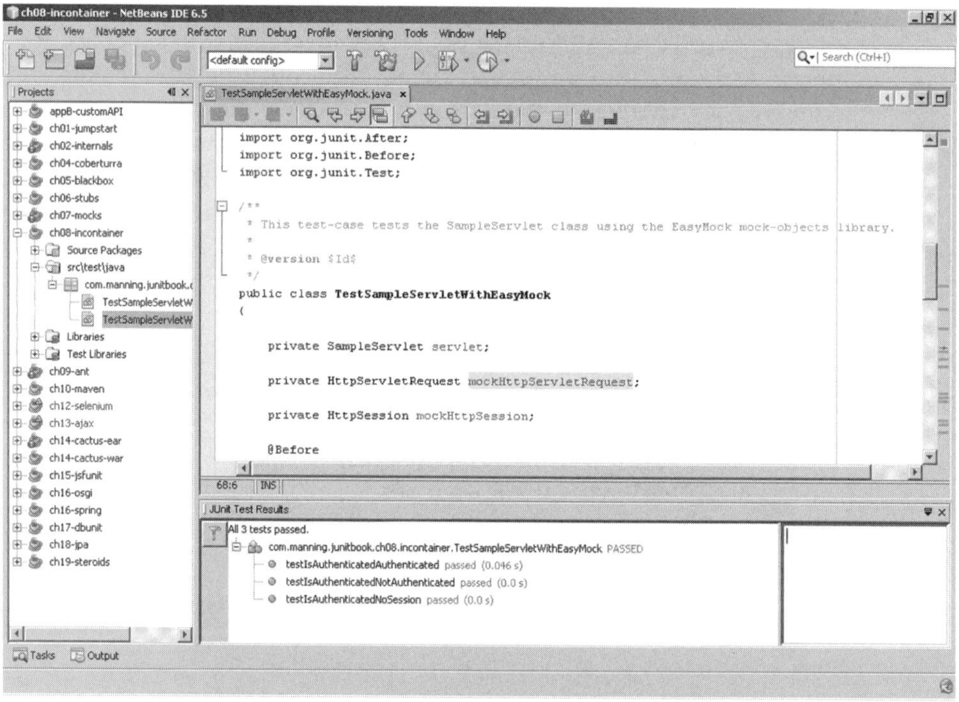

Figure D.12   Result from executing a sample JUnit test case

D.3.4   *Running Ant scripts from NetBeans*

To run an Ant script from NetBeans, first you need to open the Files perspective. You can do that by choosing the Window > Files menu. Then navigate to your project and right-click the build.xml. There should be Run Target item in the context menu. From there you can choose the targets that you want to execute. You can also specify which of the targets should be your default target.

If you want to add additional libraries to the Ant installation, it's good to know that NetBeans uses its own Ant installation. You can add your additional JAR files in the lib/ folder of the NetBeans Ant installation (normally this would be [NETBEANS_INSTALLATION]/java2/ant/lib).

Figure D.13 shows the output of the execution of an Ant build script in NetBeans.

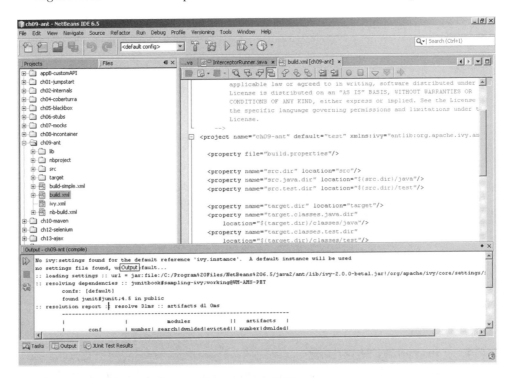

Figure D.13   Results from executing the Ant script in NetBeans

appendix E:
Installing software

E.1   Installing HtmlUnit

Download HtmlUnit from http://htmlunit.sourceforge.net/ and unzip it to your local drive. In our examples, we have unzipped it to C:\Java\htmlunit-2.7.

E.1.1   Standard configuration

Add all JAR files to the classpath except for the three XML libraries: XML-APIs, Xalan, and Xerces. Starting with version 1.4.2, Java ships with an XML parser and transformer (Apache Xalan). Because HtmlUnit ships with XML-APIs, Xalan, and Xerces, the version of these libraries must override the default Java versions through the Java-endorsed mechanism.[1, 2]

Move all XML libraries to a subdirectory of HTmlUnit-2.7/lib called *endorsed*. For example, the lib directory should contain the following files:

```
commons-codec-1.4.jar
commons-collections-3.2.1.jar
commons-httpclient-3.1.jar
commons-io-1.4.jar
commons-lang-2.4.jar
commons-logging-1.1.1.jar
cssparser-0.9.5.jar
htmlunit-2.7.jar
htmlunit-core-js-2.7.jar
nekohtml-1.9.14.jar
sac-1.3.jar
serializer-2.7.1.jar
```

The directory lib/endorsed should contain these files:

```
xalan-2.7.1.jar
xercesImpl-2.9.1.jar
xml-apis-1.3.04.jar
```

Your classpath must list all JAR files in lib. In addition, you must add the following to your Java VM invocation:

```
-Djava.endorsed.dirs=C:\Java\htmlunit-2.7\lib\endorsed
```

If you're lucky enough to develop on Java 6, your command line classpath doesn't need to list each HtmlUnit JAR file; instead, it can contain

```
C:\Java\htmlunit-2.7\lib\*
```

Starting with Java 6, at last you can use * to include all JAR files in a directory.

E.1.2 Eclipse configuration

In Eclipse, you must set up a JRE as shown in figure E.1.

The two key items in this JRE configuration are as follows:

- Default VM Arguments sets the endorsed path to our HtmlUnit lib/endorsed directory.
- JRE System Libraries lists the HtmlUnit lib/endorsed JAR files first.

Eclipse will automatically set up all other entries in the JRE System Libraries list.

---

[1] For Java 5, see http://java.sun.com/j2se/1.5.0/docs/guide/standards/index.html.
[2] For Java 6, see http://java.sun.com/javase/6/docs/technotes/guides/standards/.

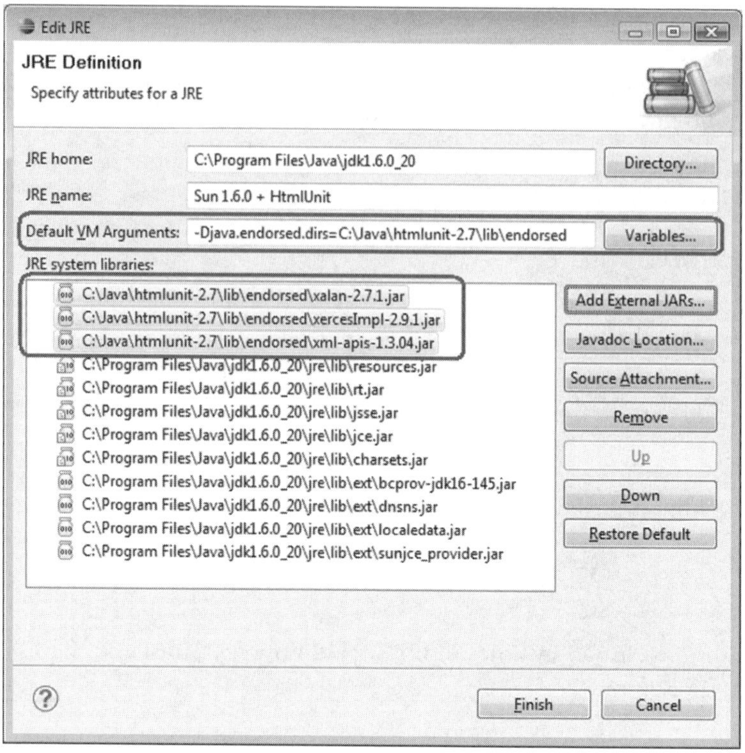

Figure E.1 Setting up a JRE in Eclipse for HtmlUnit

E.2   *Configuring Cactus with HtmlUnit*

HtmlUnit integration requires Cactus version 1.8 or greater and a container such as Tomcat or Jetty. Depending on which container you pick, and the version of Cactus and HtmlUnit, you might have to adjust your installation.

Because Cactus 1.8.1 ships with HtmlUnit 1.6, you may want to update Cactus to HtmlUnit 2.7 by copying the HtmlUnit JAR files over the ones provided by Cactus and deleting htmlunit-1.6.jar. The HtmlUnit 2.7 HTML parser depends on the Xerces and Xalan classes, so make sure you also make these JAR files available to your web application or container.

Chapter 12 introduces writing HtmlUnit tests in the Cactus framework and chapter 14 dives into the details. For the details regarding the installation and management of applications and tests within particular containers, we refer you to the Cactus documentation. We wrote the examples in this chapter with Tomcat 6.0.18 and Cactus 1.8.1, and setup is per the Cactus installation guide.[3]

---

[3] For Cactus and Tomcat setup, see http://jakarta.apache.org/cactus/integration/howto_tomcat.html.

E.3 *Installing Selenium*

Download Selenium Remote Control (Selenium RC) from http://seleniumhq.org/ download/, unzip it to your local drive, and add the Selenium Java client driver to your classpath. As of this writing, the current Selenium version is 1.0 Beta 2, and the client JAR file is selenium-remote-control-1.0-beta-2\selenium-java-client-driver-1.0-beta-2\selenium-java-client-driver.jar.

E.4 *Installing RhinoUnit*

RhinoUnit is a library of scripts used to run JavaScript unit tests from Ant, tested here with Ant 1.7.1. If you're running Java 6 or later, you don't need any additional setup because Java 6 includes the Java Scripting Framework (http://jakarta.apache.org/bsf/) and the Mozilla Rhino JavaScript engine. So, for Java 5 and earlier, use the following steps.

The Ant script task is an optional task package with the core tasks. It requires Apache BSF, which you can download from http://jakarta.apache.org/site/downloads/downloads_bsf.cgi. Unzip the download and copy the file bsf-2.4.0\lib\bsf.jar to one of the Ant locations used for optional tasks as documented in Ant (http://ant.apache.org/manual/install.html#optionalTasks), for example, in ANT_HOME/lib to make the JAR file available to all Ant users and builds.

Next, get the Mozilla Rhino JavaScript (http://www.mozilla.org/rhino/) engine from http://www.mozilla.org/rhino/download.html. For Java 5, copy the file js.jar; for Java 1.4.2, copy the file js-1.4.jar to an Ant location used for optional tasks.

Apache BSF uses Apache Commons Logging, which has been included with Ant since version 1.6. If you must use a version of Ant older than 1.6.x, you can download Apache Commons Logging from http://commons.apache.org/logging/ and copy commons-logging-1.1.1.jar to an Ant location used for optional tasks.

E.5 *Installing JsUnit*

You can find JsUnit at http://jsunit.net/. We've included in the source for chapter 13 the build for version 2.2. This build is located in the jsunit directory in the chapter 13 source.

index

RELATED MANNING TITLES

Spring in Action, Third Edition
by Craig Walls

ISBN: 978-1935182-35-1
700 pages, $49.99
Fall 2010

Seam in Action
by Dan Allen
  Foreword by Norman Richards

ISBN: 978-1-933988-40-5
624 pages, $44.99
September 2008

Test Driven
Practical TDD and Acceptance TDD for Java Developers
by Lasse Koskela

ISBN: 978-1-932394-85-6
544 pages, $44.99
October 2007

The Quick Python Book
by Vernon L. Ceder

ISBN: 978-1-935182-20-7
360 pages, $39.99
January 2010

For ordering information go to www.manning.com

YOU MAY ALSO BE INTERESTED IN ...

The Art of Unit Testing
with Examples in .NET
by Roy Osherove

> ISBN: 978-1-933988-27-6
> 320 pages, $39.99
> May 2009

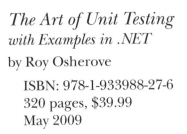

JBoss in Action
Configuring the JBoss Application Server
by Javid Jamae and Peter Johnson

> ISBN: 978-1-933988-02-3
> 496 pages, $49.99
> January 2009

Ant in Action
Second Edition of Java Development with Ant
by Steve Loughran and Erik Hatcher

> ISBN: 978-1-932394-80-1
> 600 pages, $49.99
> July 2007

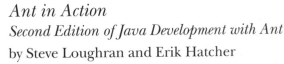

Java Persistence with Hibernate
Second Edition of Hibernate in Action
by Christian Bauer and Gavin King

> ISBN: 978-1-932394-88-7
> 880 pages, $59.99
> November 2006

YOU MAY ALSO BE INTERESTED IN ...

Stuts 2 in Action

by Donald Brown, Chad Michael Davis,
  and Scott Stanlick

   ISBN: 978-1-933988-07-8
   424 pages, $44.99
   May 2008

EJB 3 in Action

by Debu Panda, Reza Rahman, and Derek Lane

   ISBN: 978-1-933988-34-4
   712 pages, $44.99
   April 2007

Ruby in Practice

by Jeremy McAnally and Assaf Arkin

   ISBN: 978-1-933988-47-4
   360 pages, $39.99
   March 2009

Hello World!
Computer Programming for Kids and Other Beginners
by Warren D. Sande and Carter Sande

   ISBN: 978-1-933988-49-8
   432 pages, $34.99
   March 2009

For ordering information go to www.manning.com